Companions of the Sun

History and Mystery in
Iranian Dance, Music & Ritual

Companions of the Sun

History and Mystery in Iranian Dance, Music & Ritual

Farima Berenji, PhD

HOHM PRESS
Chino Valley, AZ

Cover design: Farima Berenji

Interior design and layout by Becky Fulker, Kubera Book Design

Photo Credits: see page ix

Print ISBN: 978-1-963433-08-1
E-Book ISBN: 978-1-963443-09-8

Library of Congress Control Number: 2025939539

Printed and bound in the United States of America

First printing October 2025

Hohm Press
P.O. Box 4410
Chino Valley, AZ 86323
(800) 381-2700
hohmpress.com

For my late father, Morteza Berenji, my uncle Abby Sardari,

and my friend and mentor Dr. Lloyd Miller.

Table of Contents

Figure Citations

Acknowledgments

The completion of this book stands as a testament to the unwavering guidance, inspiration, and support of my remarkable mentors: Dr. Lloyd Miller, Katherine St. John, and Pir Salman Hosseini. They have dedicated their lives to the noble mission of preserving and sharing the rich tapestry of music, dance, culture, and mysticism of the Iranic land—a mission often overlooked but profoundly impactful.

I extend profound gratitude to the Yadegar family and Pir Mohammad *Zolnuri* of the Ali Qalandar family in Kermanshah, Iran. Their invaluable guidance, boundless generosity, kindness, and blessings have significantly enriched the chapters dedicated to the Yarsan people, encompassing their music, legends, and beliefs. Their willingness to openly share their traditions and customs is a rare gift, deeply appreciated. These masters graciously introduced me to the sacred ways of their community, revealing the craftsmanship and artistry of the tanbur and sama. Through their introductions, I had the privilege of connecting with numerous mystics, masters, healers, and community members, gaining invaluable insight and knowledge.

A debt of gratitude is owed to Robert Taylor, Paula Barbari, Ibrahim Yavuz Akyunus, Gulhis Akyunus, Dr. Nirvana Anoosheh, Laaya Khamsi, Gita Franklin, Mindy Chang, Jeffrey Paul, Paria Parvizi, Bill Cope, Michael Saei, the Allied Arts Foundation, as well as numerous associates and family members who generously supported this project and all my endeavors. Special thanks are extended to cherished friends Kevin Greek, Bani Khalsa, Kristy Chapman, Travis Martin, Dawn Imada, Sara Kazemi, and Prof. Farhad Kazemi, whose dedicated research and editing significantly contributed to the creation of this book. Mitra Banejad's exceptional cover art, Varol Ozkaner's digital media expertise, Ahmad Odeh's cover photo, and Valerie Wolf's artistic contributions and illustrations have been instrumental in this endeavor.

Above all, I wish to express my deepest gratitude to my mother, Farkhondeh Sadari. From the inception of my dance journey, she has been my unwavering source of guidance, mentorship, inspiration, and love. As my first dance and mystic teacher, she laid the foundation for my career and supported me throughout my journey.

Foreword

Dr. Lloyd C. Miller of Eastern Arts

For centuries, astronomers have scrutinized the celestial dance, seeking meaning and purpose in the orchestrated movement of planets. Likewise, humanity has spun and turned with its own distinct intentions since ancient times. Dr. Farima Berenji, a distinguished scholar and artist, has delved into the annals of Iranian culture, studying the tapestry of myth, literature, archaeology, mysticism, dance, and traditional Persian music. As a devoted mystic and Yarsan adherent, she has shared her extensive research through TED talks, classes, lectures, performances, and now, in the pages of this book. Ms. Berenji stands among the select few intellectuals who bring newfound knowledge to the field and for that we are profoundly grateful.

Eastern Arts has had the privilege of being associated with Dr. Berenji for many years. Beyond her physical beauty, she brings a depth of scholarly and artistic knowledge to the presentation of these arts. The revelations in this text are both valuable and seldom known. A multilingual world traveler, Dr. Berenji's collaborations with scholars, artists, mystics, and practitioners have fortified the conclusions she presents. Readers will be treated to a treasure trove of ancient history, theories, and practices. This work is firmly grounded in rigorous academic research, harmoniously coupled with the highest caliber of artistic expression, offering extraordinary insights into the realm of Iranic mysticism and art.

Companions of the Sun is a much anticipated book that explains the evolution of Persian dance and music into the role they claim today within their traditions of spiritual belief, healing, and struggle. It describes the path to take to honor Persian and Silk Road sacred dance forms and culture today. In ancient times, the Persians considered music and dance a spiritual art that could introduce changes to the soul. In the millennia following, music, dance, and poetry were perfected in illusion, illustration, and meaning. According to Dr. Dariush Safvat and certain other music masters, it is necessary to follow a path of spiritual development to be able to truly absorb and perform Persian traditional music in its highest form. This is also true for Persian sacred dance forms. This reasoning stems from the ancient spiritual origins of both music and dance in Iran and its surroundings.

Practices of present-day Sufi orders in Iran and neighboring areas seem to reflect pre-Islamic as well as Islamic concepts. The ancient rituals and mystic practices of Iran such as Mithraism, Zoroastrianism, Yarsanism, as well as Hinduism, Buddhism, and even Christian overtones are detectable. One reason is that Iran and Afghanistan were always quick to adopt new ideas while finding a means to retain the old heritage within the new. Another explanation for the common resemblance of certain modern Sufi practices to those of former religions and religious paths is that God always reveals the same basic truths to those who seek Him.

In this book, the foundations of sacred dance in Iran are characterized by meditative practices and mystic philosophy. Profound meditations, zikrs, and sama are discussed, unveiling the unique history and form of Iranian mysticism based on local sacred beliefs and legends. The fabric of Yarsan culture and mysticism is particularly intriguing since its beliefs are intimately interwoven with sacred music on the tanbur. Sama, a mystical form of moving meditation, is explored in detail, along with the basic mystic practices, traditions, and art of sacred whirling dance. Whirling, one of the earliest known forms of Iranian sacred dance, connects the body and soul—a means of meditation and healing. Sama, born from the desire to elevate consciousness to a higher realm and find union with the Divine, reflects humanity's innate belief in a connection beyond the self.

Dance brings healing as it builds self-confidence, concentration, and unity in the community. Dance and music were applied in life traditions and transitions such as births, weddings, and funerals. It was also used for healing the sick of body and mind. Sacred traditions based on a manner of living, belief, work, struggle, and battle led to ritual warrior and martial arts dances or practices. Music and dance cannot be disassociated from Iranian culture.

Once it presents the foundations of Persian history, sacred art, and spiritual beliefs, this book follows with details of best practices for practitioners of this art. The book emphasizes the importance of feeling, styling, and expression of Iranian music and dance over technique. Music and poetry, art and dance synergistically combine. Basic Iranian music history, modes, and styling are presented to help the reader understand, interpret, and present dance appropriately. Details of many folkloric, ritual, or sacred dances are presented in this work.

It is with great pleasure that I endorse this text as an almost encyclopedic compendium of the genesis of sacred movement, music, and philosophy in the ancient Iranic world—practices that endure to this day. Dr. Berenji is a valuable living resource and proponent of Persian and Silk Road dance, an integrated healing practitioner, and an initiated master in the Iranian Sufi and mystic order. I cannot think of anyone more qualified to represent this art better, either on stage or at the lecture podium.

Dr. Lloyd Miller received his PhD in Persian Language and Literature from the University of Utah after spending seven years living in Iran where he had a weekly prime time television program titled "Kurosh Ali Khan va dastan" featuring musicians and other artists from around the world. Though planning to stay in Iran, he was urged to leave during the revolution in the late 70s. An expert in world music, including American jazz, Miller has made numerous recordings, the most popular being "Oriental Jazz," first released in 1968 and recently re-released by Vinyl Me Please, selling thousands of copies worldwide. A film about his extraordinary life includes six years in Europe as a jazzman and university student where he played with some of the most well-known musicians of the time. It was in Paris that he met his lifelong mentor, Dr. Daryush Safvat, who taught him the significance of Persian classical music. As founder of Eastern Arts, with the blessing of Dr. Safvat, Miller taught music, philosophy, history, dance, and culture to thousands of students at various universities for over forty years. Read more at https://en.wikipedia.org/wiki/Lloyd_Miller_(musician).

Preface

Once again a new beginning! Take all the veils of the past and make a new garment.

– Rumi

Modern day Iranian dance is rooted in an ancient spiritual culture. Exploring the history and diversity of Iranian dance inevitably reveals the sacred culture at it source. This book, therefore, is a resource for anyone interested in sacred dance, ancient mysticism, and/or Iranian spiritual traditions. My passion and love for sacred Iranian music and dance was instilled in me by my Iranian lineage and has allowed me to see that through dance, we as a world community can find connection, peace, and unification. This book seeks to transmit the same joy and inspiration people have experienced while participating in the many teachings and performances I have shared over the years.

A brief yet essential history of Iran and the Silk Road lays the foundation for understanding the origins of dance from different regions. Iranian culture, spanning twenty-five centuries, draws from the mythical origins of the land, which influence its art, literature, music, dance, and folklore. The significance of Iranian gods and goddesses and the types of rituals and spiritual observances practiced by its people cannot be separated from Iranian dance and music, which trace their origins back to the ancient religions of Mithraism and Zoroastrianism. Similarly, many folk dances today evolved from portraying epic battles that facilitated rigorous training for warriors. Music, dance, and other rituals created and sustained a civilization that survived millennia and the rise and fall of empires, a fact that highlights humanity's innate need and desire for ritual. The use of dance for magic and ancient healing practices continues to resonate today as well.

Spiritual observances are the foundation of Eastern and Iranian mysticism, dance, mythology, and folklore. Specific meditation techniques often accompany mystical dances, infusing them with spiritual power, and dance itself is often referred to as "prayer." The sacred rituals of music and moving meditation are discussed herein, including the practice of whirling, the original Iranian sama, and the customs of the Turkish Mevlevi order.

One of many ancient influences on Iranian dance and mysticism today is Yarsanism, an esoteric and syncretic order originating in Western Iran. Sacred Yarsan hymns contain narratives that preserve history and beliefs, and are accompanied by the tanbur, a heavenly instrument said to bring enlightenment to those weary of material sufferings. Details of the Yarsan tradition and music are presented as well as a study of traditional Iranian musical modes, which express universal laws within nature, the planets, stars, flowers, trees, animals, birds, all representing elements within the cosmic order.

Another major influence is that of Persian classical dance and poetry. Persian (Farsi) is a poetic language, developed and polished over hundreds of years in which poetry itself was considered the cornerstone of all aspects of culture. Persian dance and music are often structured according to poetic and narrative meaning, and dances are stylized to emphasize gesture, expression, and sacred geometry.

I have included practical guidelines for applying these ancient teachings in practice. Specific principles can be applied based on the time, space, and people involved in the performance. Words alone cannot fully describe the experience of music, movement, and emotion. The reader must immerse themself in practice to gain deeper insight and understanding. What is presented in this book seeks not only to preserve, honor, and share mystical traditions but also to enrich and enhance the enjoyment of this form of prayer.

Let the beauty you love be what you do.

– Rumi

CHAPTER 1

Embarking on a Mystical Path

Your body is the canvas, your movement is the brush, your soul is the artist, your dance becomes an art.

Sitting in a café, I casually gazed upon a Monet poster hanging on the wall. Some college students came over and began discussing the poster, uncertain of the symbolism and use of color. Politely interrupting them, I offered my interpretation of the work. One of them then said, "Are you a dancer? The way you used your hands to explain the brush strokes so passionately brings this art to life!" At that moment, I realized that dancers bring stories to life just as painters do. Da Vinci's Last Supper is a great example. Although Da Vinci was not present at that moment in history, his masterpiece draws us into it as if we were there. An artist becomes the medium that connects the past to the present.

As observers, we feel what Da Vinci felt when he painted the artwork and what the disciples might have felt at that last supper. A dancer, whether representing a warrior, a village girl, or an entity in nature such as a bird or plant, takes people on a journey, their movements like brushstrokes that bring the past back to life in a vibrant, living expression of human passion. Dance is one of the oldest human activities that still connects us with our ancestors.

Dance throughout history has been used to entertain, inspire, expose vulnerabilities, encourage, spiritually uplift, and heal. Dance evokes a range of human emotions and experiences for both the dancer and observers. Simultaneously a physical motion of the body, an artistic expression, and a narrative, dance invokes empathy, and stimulates the intellect. Dance is visually appealing, provokes the senses, and sparks inspiration. Every person has a dance within that can be discovered. When you find the dance inside you, you will find indescribable joy.

The Path to Iranian Sacred Dance

There are many ways to the Divine. I have chosen the ways of song, dance, and laughter.

– Rumi

I have always loved dance. As a child, I remember dancing to any music, anywhere. My family was highly involved in Persian and Iranian-Azerbaijani culture, arts, literature, mysticism, music, and dance. My mother and grandmother, both dancers, musicians, and poets, were my primary dance instructors and mentors. When our extended family came together it was a sacred gathering with whirling, praying, singing, and chanting. My mother came to the United States from Iran when I was just three years old. Although I grew up immersed in the Western way of life, she pushed me to preserve my heritage and encouraged me to study the history of my home country. As a child, I would return every summer with her to Iran to learn to read and write Farsi and be immersed in Iranian culture. I fell in love with the beauty of Iranian culture. These travels enabled me to meet exceptional people who profoundly influenced my life and shaped who I am today.

In the early 1980s, traveling in Iran was unsafe. The country had gone through a revolution and was in the midst of a bloody war. The smell of death and destruction filled the air, and the sound of the air raid warnings became a familiar melody to the ear. It was a time no child should experience. But for me, it was an adventure, not chaos. While people fled Iran or escaped the war-torn cities for safer refuge in nearby villages, I yearned to visit my grandmother in her city home with its poetry, music, and dancing. When the lights would black out, my grandmother would gather us together, telling folk tales and legends, her stories illuminating the room. When she sang or read poetry, the magic of a mystical world would emerge. It was as if I was no longer from this world but from the past. My grandmother asked me to remember the stories and poems and include them in my dance narratives to preserve age-old themes and legends. These moments sparked my love and fascination for ancient mystical dance and movement.

Figure 1.1: A dance inherited. Three generations of artists: grandmother (left), mother (center), and author (right).
Photo by author.

Growing up, I often wondered about a dance's history and how its performance style and costuming developed. I became an explorer and archaeologist, discovering all I could about dance and its mystical origins. The ancient rituals of Iran, its goddesses, and the brave acts of its warriors fascinated me. Classical Persian poetry and the folk tales of legendary figures inspired me to become a dance artist. In time, my interests led to professional studies in dance and archaeology. Traveling alone during my youth, with the guidance and permission of my mother, was a beautiful experience, taking me to remote villages in Iran, where I discovered dances still practiced for healing, community, and prayer. Along the way, I was blessed to meet beautiful mystic masters, musicians, and scholars who guided me and encouraged me in my journey.

The first encounter with spirituality in dance came as a child as I whirled, imitating my mother's movement, spinning and spiraling, and sometimes falling to the ground. During my teenage years, I began teaching mysticism and dance to my peers and other youth. That was when I met my first Sufi master and discovered the unique bond between instructor and student. Later, as a young adult, my master initiated me as a darvish[1] and mystic. When he congratulated me on my achievement I felt as if my spiritual journey had finally begun. "Now what?" I asked. He answered that my life would take a new path and I should develop a new perspective.

1 A darvish is a mystic who has studied mysticism and is granted that title by a master of the path. In the Turkish or Western world, it is spelled dervish; in Farsi it is darvish.

Across Iran and Central Asia I sought out original teachers who taught dances founded on mythology and symbolism. Throughout my life, I've returned to my homeland again and again, reclaiming my birthright among mystics, poets, and artists, doing archaeological research, and studying dance, music, poetry, art, history, and Iran's mythology and spiritual traditions. The nomads of the north taught me their tribal dances, the darvishes of the mountains shared secrets of their sacred movements, the masked women of the desert revealed their rituals, and the dancers of the land of the sun shared their devotional rites. I lived amidst people for whom sacred and folk dance traditions are still an essential part of life. In these villages, dance is not just entertainment but a golden thread woven into the fabric of life. Dance is a part of the Iranian people and always will be, wherever our souls' journey takes us in the world.

A Remarkable Discovery

When a sincere woman begins to dance, the seven heavens, the earth, and all creatures begin to dance.

– Shams-i Tabriz

Iranian Azerbaijan boasts a rich history dating back nine thousand years. With more than twelve hundred ancient sites, West Azerbaijan is a prominent province for archaeological excavations. There have been archaeological discoveries in the hills of Haftvan, Ahranjan, Kol Tepe Selmas, Hasanlovi Naghdeh, Rabat Sardasht, Gok Tepe, Digale Urmia, Takht Suleiman Takab, Qalaichi Bukan, Bastam Chaipareh, Pirahmad Kandi Mako, Barde Kante Mahabad, Piranshahr, and numerous other sites. Ahranjan Hill, also known as Kul Tepe Si, or "Gray Hill," has a nine-thousand-year-old history that has shaped the collective life in the region. One of the first villages to develop in the area, the archaeological

---

2 Urartu was an Iron Age kingdom centered around the Armenian highlands between Lake Van, Lake Urmia, and Lake Sevan.

3 Mannaea was an ancient kingdom around the 10th to 7th centuries BCE located in northwestern Iran south of Lake Urmia neighboring Assyria and Urartu.

findings reveal a vibrant and cultured civilization. Evidence attests to the influence of the Urartu,[2] Mannaea,[3] Assyrian,[4] Mitanni,[5] Median,[6] and Persian civilizations.

Figure 1.2: Archaeological find by the author revealing a tablet with a female figure at Tepe Lavin, West Azerbaijan, Iran. Photo by author.

One hot sunny day, while working as an archaeologist in the area, my team headed to a dig in the mountains of Piranshahr, to an ancient city once buried and forgotten, only recently re-discovered. The city had been destroyed and abandoned, possibly due to an invasion. Known as Tepe Lavin ("Lavin Hill") by locals, the site belonged to the Median warriors who ruled Iran from 678 to 549 BCE. As I dug in the ruins, I stumbled upon a trench. Excavating deeper, I soon discovered a fantastic ancient relief carving. Wiping away the dust revealed the figure of a female warrior and an inscription (Figure 1.2). My grandmother's stories of women warriors in ancient Iran had come to life. This discovery awakened in me the realization that mysticism in Iranian dance, like the legends of warriors, is still alive—powerful truths that have been buried in the sands of time are only waiting to be uncovered again. I showed the artifact to one of the village elders, who exclaimed, "This woman was not lost but sleeping and waiting for you to find her. She wants you to tell her story."

This serendipitous event was impossible to ignore. The more I studied, the more the universe guided me toward this lost history when women were warriors and commanders alongside men, ruled armies

4 Assyria was an ancient Mesopotamian civilization and empire that existed from the 21st century BCE to the 7th century BCE.

5 Mitanni (1550-1260 BCE) was a Hurrian-speaking state in northern Syria and southeast Anatolia.

6 Media was an ancient Iranian dynasty situated between Western and Northern Iran.

and nations, and were considered embodiments of the Divine. During this time I discovered that many of the beautiful, lyrical movements in traditional Iranian dance and whirling are derived from the sacred rites of ancient Iranian tribes, particularly the Elamite and Median peoples. Visiting these villages, I discovered they had many stories to share. They took me to sites where no outsider had been, and shared dances and rituals not performed for the public. The elders described what they saw in childhood, showing me secret journals as well as recounting rituals that have otherwise been forgotten. When one is willing to take a leap of faith and trust, roads open. To learn truths hidden in far reaches of human culture, you must have the spirit of an adventurer. It has taken me years to become an ethnologist and master in dance and mysticism. It has not always been easy, but I'm glad to have devoted my life to this path. I deeply believe, in this world full of overstimulation and distraction, a deep study of art and spirituality provides not only a respite, but an opportunity to live at our highest potential.

Dance as a Cultural Identifier

In your light, I learn how to love. In your beauty, how to make poems. You dance inside my chest, where no one sees you, but sometimes I do. And that sight becomes this art.

– Rumi

An understanding of dance begins with the context within which the dance originated. As a cultural anthropologist and dance ethnologist, I have discovered dance is a great cultural identifier. Like many other cultural identifiers, such as clothing, language, and music, dance is a means for people to define and express themselves and to differentiate their culture from others. The story of our lives and history, and who we are as people, are ingrained in movements passed down from generation to generation. During years of extensive research, I discovered traditional dances inspired people of all ages. Children in Iran learn to dance from an early age and every village has formed its own dance tradition. People remember dances from when they were young, such as dances used for ceremonies, festivals, celebrations, and even funerals that took place in their local villages. Over the millennia, dance, poetry, and music kept the spirit of the people alive during times of chaos, giving them strength.

Dance is a signature of the time and life of a people across ages—where, why, and how it is performed tells a story of their values, beliefs, interactions with the environment and other peoples, their harvests and relationship with nature, their triumphs and tragedies. Preserving these customs for future generations connects us to our ancestors and our descendants, linking us across time, from the past into the future. Anthropologists have found visible connections between the art of vanished cultures and those still in existence. Although early dance forms may have largely disappeared, their influence can be seen in current village dances. Dance is a timeless connection to the universe's creative force. The continuous thread of cultural evolution is the spirit of our ancestors and we are the warriors who are obliged to keep it alive.

Attunement and Empathy

I looked in temples, churches, and mosques.
But I found the Divine within my heart.

– Rumi

In Farsi, empathy is called *taghayyun, jazb-e makhsoos, yakdali* or *yaksimt tasavvur* (Sumit 2019). Empathy, the human capacity for compassion, is the foundation of dance's profound and invaluable power to communicate across all languages. Studies have shown that simply witnessing another person performing a movement or expressing an emotion or behavior can fire an identical set of neurons in both the actor and the observer. Just as hearing a story about injustice invokes indignation in most people, watching a dance performance will do the same. When a dancer expresses pain, loss, fear, or joy, one cannot help but identify with the message being danced. So even without actually engaging in dance, those who observe dance share the delight or sorrow, fear or confidence, through the dance narrative.

Empathy is a sublime sense of interconnectivity, an emotional merging. Studies on creating music and dance show how during cooperation, two people's brains attune to the same frequency. This kind of attunement is a key element of empathy. Do you realize that when you dance before flowers they bloom? If you cry and act depressed around flowers, they quickly die. But if you play music for the rose and dance and speak to it, look how beautifully it blooms. Flowers feel us as we feel each other.

Sacred dance is part of an ancient tradition and part of the current moment. The healing power of dance is recognized worldwide and transcends differences of faith and culture. Something as simple as walking methodically in a circle can unlock the natural flow of energy in the body to clear away old emotional blockages, memories, and beliefs that no longer have a purpose. Observers may participate in dance by drumming, singing, swaying, or simply paying attention. Whether one actively dances, observes, choreographs, or combines it with meditation, sacred dance can generate both mental and physical healing, enhance spiritual practice, and lead to a sense of well-being and wholeness. Full of meaning, the delicate, mystical, and beautiful movements can invoke deep emotion and spiritual yearning, personal devotion to a higher power, faith in oneself, empathy with others, passionate release, ecstatic expression, community connection, and love.

Various elements, both internal and external, help channel energy and attention in sacred dance. The external part may include props, accessories, and costumes from the period the dance was developed. Music portrays the dance ritual's essence and transfers the audience into a different, subtle dimension. By sustaining the participant's attention over extended periods, music facilitates the ritual's encounter between the Divine and terrestrial.

Dance is a universal language that explores the reality of the human condition as experienced across cultural variation. It mimics nature and the natural patterns that mathematics and science are developed from. It promotes understanding, tolerance, and friendship among national, racial, or religious groups, and helps nurture peace. Dance can teach us about our past so we may find a path to conduct ourselves in the present. Dance is a colorful mosaic of costume, music, and movement that can easily take away pain and put a smile on any face. Witnessing the beauty in dance, one rediscovers oneself and returns to simplicity, even amidst the complications of modern civilization. Dance embodies heritage, communal and personal healing, and a path to mystical union. It has been a lifetime journey of discovery for me.

Dancing for the Beloved

Today all dance, all, all dance!
Divine is dance! Divine, divine is dance!
Some dance in their stockings, some only in their shoes, some naked!
High! High, you naked dancers, high!
You beautiful and bold ones!
Today all dance, all, all dance!
Divine is dance! Divine is dance!

– Hafez

Throughout my life, I have sought challenges and faced obstacles, always pushing forward with courage and hope. I long for the time when dance celebrated the grace and joy of life, when people lived in harmony with each other and nature. Artistic expression still promises a way for the soul to find peace. In *Sufi: Expressions of the Mystic Quest*, Laleh Bakhtiar observes that through artistic expressions such as dance or poetry, "the resistance of the restless is gradually worn down" (Bakhtiar 1976, 24). One way communities can strive toward peace is by encouraging a creative life that loosens the toxic knots within the psyche. We are always learning. My students inspire me and are sometimes my best teachers by pushing me toward new goals.

Some of the greatest masters I have known are those who have faced many challenges which inspired them to keep searching and learning every day. Authentic dance takes passion, longing, love, and courage. It is more than technique; it is about feeling and moving through life itself as a dance. But it must be experienced. One can judge a book by its size and cover, but only by opening and reading it can one appreciate it. So too, one may speak about dance but words alone cannot fully describe it. One must therefore immerse oneself in dance.

In the tapestry of time, ancient Iran shines as a beacon of civilization, weaving a legacy of culture, wisdom, and enduring heritage.

CHAPTER 2

History of the Iranian Land

In the midst of ancient ruins, a profound stillness envelops the atmosphere, carrying a deep quiet that transcends the present to embrace all places and times. If one can welcome this silence into the soul, it becomes a portal to eternity.

From the dawn of history, Iran has been a distinct and important cultural entity, a cradle of art, wisdom, and mysticism for much of the world. Its position within a vast natural fortress of mountain ranges has enabled the Iranians to preserve their uniqueness, despite frequent conquests by invading armies over the centuries. The influence of Iran on many world developments is often overlooked. Iran was a thriving center of scientific achievement and cultural progress, as well as the meeting point between China and India in the East and Greece and Rome in the West. It was home to some of the earliest universities and libraries of the ancient world. Throughout history, the Persian culture dramatically influenced the fields of mathematics, engineering, astronomy, chemistry, anatomy, biology, botany, cosmology, and architecture. Today, Iran remains a country that is rich in traditions and culture and is known for its art, architecture, music, science, and literature.

Evidence of the earliest human presence in Iran is found at the Kashafrud and Ganj Par archaeological sites. Stone tools associated with early hominids like *homo erectus* have been discovered there, estimated to be around 800,000 to one million years old. Geology, meteorology, and DNA studies confirm humankind emerged at the end of the third Ice Age, as temperatures gradually warmed. Central Asia became suitable for civilization after the melting and receding of the Arctic ice cap. The Martian Mountains in Sistan and Baluchistan provinces date back four to five million years and contain fossils of fish and oysters scattered throughout, evidence of teeming life and plenty of food for the earliest inhabitants. These provinces were home to some of humankind's earliest civilizations. In the northern part are found the five thousand year old remains of the city of Shahr-e Sukteh, or "Burnt City," which was destroyed by fire three times. The site contains many of the earliest painted potteries and artifacts, including board games and an artificial eyeball. In the southeast lies the Valley of Saravan with beautiful and well-preserved ancient rock art—paintings, inscriptions, and carvings over forty thousand years old, illustrating human figures and wild animals.

The land of ancient Persia, at its height under Darius the Great (550-486 BCE), stretched from parts of the Balkan Peninsula bordering what is present-day Bulgaria, Romania, and Ukraine to the Indus River Valley in northwest India and south to Egypt. Human civilization existed in this region as early as 7,000 BCE, its earliest inhabitants first identified by their stone artifacts and, later, by their pottery. Paleolithic and Neolithic sites have been discovered in various parts of the Iranian plateau. In about 3,000 BCE, in the Chalcolithic Period, distinctive painted pottery appeared. At sites such as Tepe Sialk, Tepe Hesar, and Tepe Giyan, early painted pottery designs indicate similarities among the inhabitants.

Iran's first vigorous expansion began in the Neolithic era and by the third millennium BCE, it had become a civilization of great sophistication. Later, this ancient civilization was invaded by dynasties belonging to the Greeks, the Arabs, the Turks, and the notorious Mongols. Over time, these invaders both influenced and adopted Iran's rich culture, including diverse philosophical, artistic, scientific, and religious ideas. During the second millennia BCE, successive Indo-European invaders broke into the plateau of Tepe Sialk. On this mountain, the remains of their most ancient dwellings have been discovered (Figure 2.1).

Figure 2.1: Archaeological excavations with author at Tepe Sialk. Kashan, Iran.
Photo by author.

Those who settled in Iran were divided into

tribes—the Kayanians, Medes, and Elamites—distinguished by their different dialects. The Kayanians are a legendary dynasty in Iranian folklore, their kings the heroes recorded in the Avesta (the sacred text of Zoroastrianism) and the *Shahnameh*[7] (Iran's national epic tale). King Kay Khosrow, one such hero, became a central figure in Iranian epic poetry and mythology. He is considered a symbol of wisdom, justice, and valor in Persian literature.

The Medes inhabited an area known as Media, situated between Western and Northern Iran. They had the strongest warrior culture among the three tribes and are credited with establishing Iran as an empire. The ancient Greek historian Herodotus in the fifth century BCE wrote that Median women were fierce warriors, skilled archers, and powerful equestrians. Ancient artwork from the region confirms this and depicts women in roles associated with combat or hunting. Media became a major province in the first Iranian Empire, the largest of its day during the seventh to sixth century BCE, and prized by the empires that successively dominated it.

Susa, the capital of Elam and the home of the Elamites is located on the Mesopotamian plain, modern-day Khuzestan province.[8] The Elamite language has not been fully deciphered, as it was unlike any of the later languages of the region. To the northwest in the mountains of Elam lived the Kassites,[9] who also descended onto the plains of Mesopotamia. In the borders of Iran's present-day Azerbaijan province lived people named the Manneans.[10] Many of them also inhabited the regions around the Caspian Sea. Iranians from the west and Chinese

---

7 *Shahnameh,* The Book of Kings, is an epic poem written by Persian poet Ferdowsi between 977 and 1010 CE. It depicts the historical past of the Persian Empire from the creation of the world until the Muslim conquest in the seventh century.

8 Khuzestan province is in the southwest corner of Iran bordering Iraq and the Persian Gulf. It comprises much of ancient Elam.

9 The Kassites were a people from outside Mesopotamia, believed to originate from the Zagros Mountains, northwest of Iran, and were the predecessors of the Kurds.

10 The historic kingdom of Mannaea was situated east and south of Lake Urmia, amongst the border of today's West and East Azerbaijan.

from the east later migrated to meet in Central Asia, forming the Turks. Indians are a hybrid of early Dravidians[11] and Iranians. The region's cultures began to develop into two diverse geographic powers, India and Iran. On the Iranian plateau, two mighty civilizations emerged: the Medes and the tribes of Iran. The Medes settled in Ecbatana,[12] now Iran's modern-day Hamadan and Kurdistan provinces. The Medes were one of the ancestors of the modern-day Kurds who inhabit areas of Northwestern Iran, Eastern Iraq, Turkey, Syria, and Russia.

Finding ancient art illustrating the mythology of Persia is rare. The Greek historian Herodotus, the first scholar to give an outsider's view of Iran, remarked that Persian mythology is devoid of sculpted or painted imagery: its myths preserved in oral traditions, dance, culture, and written texts instead. Due to political and religious changes, most ancient texts are fragmentary, and the most recent are from after Iran had already been integrated into Islam. Nevertheless, the texts indicate that over the centuries, Persian culture and traditions developed very differently from its sister nations (Grimal 1965, 189).

The Rise and Reign of Early Iranian Dynasties

> *O man whoever you are and wherever you come from for I know you will come I am Cyrus who won the Persians their empire. Do not therefore begrudge me this bit of earth that covers my bones.*
>
> – Cyrus the Great

In Indo-Iranian mythology, the Iranian plateau housed two distinct lands. To the east (roughly corresponding to Central Asia to the east of Iran today) was Turan, the land of the Scythians,[13] Sogdians,[14] Massagetaes,[15] Saka,[16] Alans,[17] Sarmatians,[18] and Roxalans.[19] To the

---

11 The Dravidians are a linguistic and cultural group living primarily in Southern Asia.

12 Ecbatana or Hegmataneh was the capital of the Medes (around 700 BCE) and was founded by Deioces, the first king of the Medes. Ecbatana is now the site of the modern city of Hamadan, Iran.

13 The Scythians were an ancient Eastern Iranic equestrian nomadic tribe that migrated during the ninth to eighth centuries BCE from Central Asia to

west was the land of Iran (also known as Eran) where the Persians, Medes, and Parthians[20] settled. The Pishdadian ("predecessor") dynasty, with beginnings in the seventh century BCE, is the first legendary Iranian dynasty described in written form in the *Shahnameh* (collected and written by classical Persian poet Ferdowsi[21] around 1010 CE).

The *Shahnameh* is an epic tale of patriotism, justice, forgiveness, love of the Divine, chivalry, bravery, and battles against evil forces. One hero of the Pishdadian dynasty is Traetaona who battled Azhi Dahaka, a three-headed demon controlled by Ahriman, the lord of darkness. When Traetaona stabbed the demon in the chest, snakes and lizards poured out from the wound. To prevent the demon from poisoning the world, Traetaona trapped him inside a mountain where he would remain until the world ended, at which time, Azhi Dahaka would break free again until another hero, Keresaspa killed him.

---

the Pontic Steppe in modern-day Ukraine and Southern Russia, where they remained from the seventh to third century BCE.

14 The Sogdians were an Iranian people living between 700-800 CE in the region now recognized as Uzbekistan and Tajikistan.

15 The Massagetaes were an ancient Eastern Iranian Saka people who inhabited the steppes of Central Asia and were part of the wider Scythian cultures.

16 The Saka were a group of nomadic Eastern Iranian peoples who historically inhabited the northern and eastern Eurasian Steppe and the Tarim Basin.

17 The Alans were an ancient and medieval Iranic nomadic pastoral people who migrated to what is today North Caucasus while some continued on to Europe and later North-Africa.

18 The Sarmatians were a large confederation of ancient Eastern Iranian equestrian nomadic tribes who dominated the Pontic steppe from about the third century BCE to the fourth century CE. The Amazonian women who were very courageous fighters were from one such Samatian tribe.

19 The Roxolani were a Samatian people believed to be an offshoot of the Alans.

20 The Parthians were originally a nomadic tribe of Eastern Iranians known as the Parni who later conquered the region of Northeastern Persia known as Parthia in 247 BCE.

21 Abul-Qâsem Ferdowsi Tusi, or Ferdowsi (940-1019/1025) was a Persian poet and author of the epic *Shahnameh* (The Book of Kings). Ferdowsi is celebrated as one of the most influential figures of Persian literature and one of the greatest in the history of literature.

Timeline	Dynasty
3200-2700 BCE	Proto-Elamite Civilization
3000-5th c. BCE	Jiroft Civilization
2700-539 BCE	Elamite Dynasties
10th-7th c. BCE	Kingdom of Mannaea
728-550 BCE	Median Empire
7th-6th c. BCE?	Pishdadian Dynasty (mythical)
?	Kayanian Dynasty (mythical)
648-330 BCE	Achaemenid Empire
330-150 BCE	Seleucid Empire
250 BCE-226 CE	Parthian Empire
226-650	Sasanid Dynasty
637-651	Patriarchal Caliphate
640-829	Arab invasion and the advent of Islam
661-750	Umayyad Caliphate
750-1258	Abbasid Caliphate
821-873	Tahirid Dynasty
864-928	Alavid Dynasty
861-1003	Saffarid Dynasty
875-999	Samanid Dynasty
928-1043	Ziyarid Dynasty
934-1055	Buwayhid Dynasty
963-1187	Ghaznavid Empire
1149-1212	Ghauri Dynasty
1037-1194	Seljuk Empire
1077-1231	Khwarazmian Dynasty
1256-1353	Ilkhanate
1314-1393	Muzaffarid Dynasty
1337-1357	Chubanid Dynasty
1335-1432	Jalayirid Sultanate
1370-1506	Timurid Empire
1407-1468	Qara Qoyunlu Turkomans
1378-1508	Aq Qoyunlu Turkomans
1501-1722/1736	Safavid Empire
1709-1738	Hotak Dynasty
1736-1802	Afsharid Dynasty
1750-1794	Zand Dynasty
1781-1925	Qajar Dynasty
1925-1979	Pahlavi Dynasty
1979	Iranian Revolution
1979-1980	Provisional Government
1980-Present	Islamic Republic of Iran

Figure 2.2: Timeline of Iranian Dynasties

Figure 2.3: Rustam and the White Demon, Malek National Library and Museum, Tehran, Iran. *Shahnameh* exhibition, Malek Museum, Tehran.

Photo by author.

Good battles evil in these stories, man's end being either hell, purgatory, or heaven. Ferdowsi's ultimate advice in the *Shahnameh* is that wisdom is the greatest gift of life, and the way to become wise is to read and learn. The greatest hero of the *Shahnameh* was the legendary warrior Rustam[22] who, accompanied by his brave and faithful steed Rakhsh, was known for his exceptional combat skills, physical strength, courage, prowess, and noble character. Performing numerous heroic deeds, he encountered mythical creatures and defeated formidable foes, including a famous battle with the *Div-e Sepid* (White Demon) (Figure 2.3). Pledged to serve the Divine and defend Iran, the mighty Rustam is often compared to the Greek hero Hercules. He is celebrated as a national hero, and as a symbol of Persian identity he has inspired numerous works of dance, literature, art, and folklore.

According to the *Shahnameh*, King Jamshid, the founder of the Pishdadian Empire, was the mythical fourth king of the world and in the Avesta, he is said to be the legendary first human being. He commanded all the world's angels and demons and was both king and

[22] Rustam is also spelled Rostam.

Figure 2.4: Map of Achaemenid Empire 500 BCE.
Uirauna, Wikimedia Commons.

high priest. As a wise, just, and powerful king, he was responsible for a reign of unrivaled prosperity, credited with the invention of armor and weapons, the weaving and dyeing of linen, silk, and wool, the construction of brick houses, the mining of precious metals and gems, and world navigation. He created the first throne—the Throne of Jamshid—and sat on it to defeat a terrible winter, declaring that day Nowruz (the vernal equinox, beginning the month of Farvardin/March),[23] the first day of the Iranian New Year. King Jamshid ruled righteously for three hundred years, but his later years were marred by arrogance and a decline from grace, leading to his eventual downfall. As a central figure in Persian mythology, King Jamshid is a symbol of leadership, wisdom, and greatness, as well as potential for corruption and decline.

Iran was the melting pot of cultures and under Cyrus the Great (600-530 BCE) became the center of the world's first and largest empire (Figure 2.4). Conquering the Median Empire, Cyrus embraced and united the various civilized states and commanded the Achaemenid Empire to rule over the Balkans, North Africa, and Central Asia. He overthrew the Lydian[24] and neo-Babylonian Empires.[25] He brought

---

23 Nowruz is also spelled Nawrouz, Novruz, Nowrouz, Nowrouz, Nawrouz, Nauryz, Nooruz, Navruz, Nevruz, and Navruz.

24 Lydia was an Iron Age kingdom of western Asia Minor located in the modern western Turkish provinces of Uşak, Manisa, and inland Izmir.

25 The Neo-Babylonian Empire, or the Chaldean Empire, was a political entity centered in the city of Babylon.

Figure 2.5: Hall of Mirrors, Persepolis, Iran.
Ali Zifan, Wikimedia Commons.

nobles and civilian officials, Medes, Parthians, and Iranians into the government of his kingdom. Various ethnic and religious groups were given the right to be represented in the House of Parliament. He constructed city-states and appointed governors to represent him in each province. Libraries were built, and some old temples became universities. Cyrus established a unified army and implemented taxation to build infrastructure, towns, and a social care system for the people. This became the Achaemenid Empire,[26] the first ruling dynasty of Persia.

The accomplishments of the Achaemenid dynasty are exemplified in the grand palaces of Persepolis,[27] the ceremonial capital and jewel of the Achaemenid dynasty. Built in the sixth century BCE under the reign of Darius the Great, Persepolis served as a grand center for royal festivals and ceremonies (Figure 2.5). The Greeks called it "The Great City." The elaborate remains of its monuments attest to the absolute power of the Achaemenian Empire. Wealthy and multicultural, the city had the highest standard of living and modern technology of its time. Intricate

---

26 The Achaemenid Empire was named after an ancestor (possibly mythical) of Cyrus the Great, Achamaenes.

27 The word Persepolis is derived from the Greek meaning "the city of the Persians." To the ancient Persians the city was also known as Parsa, which is also the word for the region of Persia.

carvings and inscriptions appear around the city in various languages, including Old Persian, Elamite, and Akkadian. Persepolis demonstrates the use of complex geometric structures and a knowledge of astronomy. It is impossible to walk through these ruins without noticing the symbolism of the three deities Ahura Mazda, Mitra, and Anahita who represented the power of nature as well as the nation (Bashiri 2003).

Cyrus built the empire on a model of tolerance and respect for different cultures and religions, establishing a universal human rights charter, universal health care, the right to go to court, and the right of the people to have a lawyer represent them. People had the right to practice any religion and food was provided to the needy. Women had the right to own property, to divorce, and to gain child custody. Cyrus is regarded as one of the most outstanding figures in history. The Old Testament regards him as the savior of the Jewish people from Babylonian captivity, who decreed that the temple of Jerusalem be rebuilt. The Greek historian Xenophon called him a man of wisdom, resilient spirit, and guilelessness. The Persians called him the "Great Father." Cyrus's charter, documented on a clay cylinder, has been hailed as the first true charter of human rights, and in 1971, the United Nations published a translation of it. Despite its majesty, in just one night the great city was razed to the ground by Alexander the Great, who conquered Persia in 331 BCE, ushering in the Hellenistic period and the Seleucid Empire.

Alexander the Great was fascinated by the Persians and their civilization. Some say he was jealous of its progress, others say he hated that women possessed power, which to Greeks and Romans was forbidden. In fact, both Greeks and Romans spoke of Persian women as prostitutes who manipulated the weak Persian men. For this reason, among others, Alexander justified burning down Persepolis, destroying the great library and the ancient written history of the Persians.

The Hellenistic Seleucid Empire was followed by the Parthian and the Sasanian Empires. When the people of Greater Iran were invaded by Islamic forces in the seventh and eighth centuries, they joined an empire larger than anything previous under Iranian rule. Persianate culture, now blending Iranian and Islamic influences, flourished for nearly fourteen centuries, eventually becoming the dominant culture of the ruling and elite classes of Greater Iran, Asia Minor, and South Asia. Persianate culture refers to the impact and diffusion of Persian art, literature, language, and customs beyond the borders of Iran and includes the modes of consciousness, ethos, artistic and religious practices that persist in the Iranian world. Persianate culture, especially among the elite classes, dispersed throughout the world, spread by poets, artists, architects, artisans, jurists, and scholars traveling from Anatolia to India, to Central and South Asia, intermingling with people of varying sectarian, tribal, and ethnic allegiances and speaking a multiplicity of languages. It remains a rich and diverse cultural heritage that transcends national boundaries.

Unlike the surrounding former Byzantine territories, where the Islamic conquest led to the Arabization of language and culture, Iran retained its distinct identity. The new culture was primarily a blend of classical Iranian traditions and the Islamic customs introduced. Note that Arab speakers changed many Farsi words in Iran's vocabulary to facilitate their pronunciation, resulting in dual spelling. Farsi is the *arabicized* form of Parsi due to the lack of a "p" phenome in standard Arabic. For example, the letter P was changed to F in words such as dap to daf,[28] and others.

Cultural Insights

Iran, in its former incarnation as Persia, created the world's first empire, produced titanic figures like Cyrus, Darius, and Xerxes, and is one of the great fonts of world culture.

– Stephen Kinzer

The location of Iran and the difference between Iranians and Persians is often misunderstood in Western culture. The Middle East is often imagined as a single culture by a Western society unaware of the vast differences in religions, languages, ethnicities, and cultures in the region.

28 The daf is an Iranian frame drum used in sacred and classical music of South and Central Asia.

Modern Iran is bordered by the Persian Gulf to the south; the countries of Iraq, Turkey, Armenia, and Azerbaijan to the west; the Caspian Sea and Turkmenistan to the north; and Afghanistan and Pakistan to the east. Except for narrow coastal and frontier areas, Iran is a series of plateaus with an average height of between four and five thousand feet, covered in broad, arid plains bounded by jagged mountains, some of which are the highest in the world and are covered in snow five or six months a year. In sharp contrast are the green and well-watered valleys found in the folds of Iran's mountains.

The greater Persian world encompassed the vast territory between the Balkans in the west and Bengal (India) in the east, spanning West, Central, South Asia, and the Caucasus, where for a thousand years there was a sense of integrated moral, social, political, and aesthetic order. The legacy of the Persian language, literature, philosophy, art, and science was conveyed freely along the Silk Road.[29]

Iran and Persia refer to the same geographical area but have different historical and cultural connotations. The people of Iran are Indo-Iranians who once called themselves "Aryānām," an Old Persian term meaning "free, noble people," over time transforming from Aryan to Iran, meaning the "Land of the Aryans" or the "Land of the Noble Ones." Those that came to Iran were not a single people; they were Turk, Fars (Persians), Baluch, Turkmens, Arabs, Kurds, and others. For centuries this same land was referred to as Persia (Pars) due to the writings of Greek historians. They described Persia as the entire land occupied by the Iranian tribes from whom the Achaemenid dynasty arose. A Greek folk belief associates the Persian people, whom the Greeks call the *Persai,* with the children of the Greek hero Perseus. However, the native pronunciation, *Pārsa*, has always been pronounced with a long "a" not a short "e."

Until 1920, most of the Central Asian countries we know of today, such as Azerbaijan, Uzbekistan, Tajikistan, Afghanistan, Turkmenistan, Oman, Bahrain, and parts of Saudi Arabia, were part of Iran. During

---

29 The Silk Road was a network of Eurasian trade routes active from the second century BCE until the mid-15th century.

World War II, the Russians invaded Greater Iran, splitting it up, and incorporating most of the Central Asian countries into the USSR. In 1935, Iran's government, by order of Reza Shah,[30] officially named the country Iran, but the various people retained their ethnic nomenclature. By 1949, the UN declared that the Iranian people should be recognized by their broader cultural identity. Today, "Persia" is a historical and cultural term associated with ancient civilizations and the Persian Empire, and "Persian" is often used to refer to aspects of traditional Iranian culture, such as art, literature, language, cuisine, and dance. In comparison, "Iran" is the modern name of the country encompassing a wider range of ethnicities and cultures than just the Persian people.

Language, like dance, is a cultural identifier. In Iran today, there has been political, legal, and academic disagreement about whether the country's language should be named Persian or Farsi. Farsi is the endonym (what the people call themselves) while Persian is the exonym (a term used by others). In 1993 an institution established by the government of Iran, called The Academy of Persian Language and Literature (APLL), released a statement declaring "Persian" to be the "English translation" of "Farsi" (Nikoghosyan 2020). Academically, linguists use the term "Standard Persian" to refer to all variations of the language found regionally (with slight lexical, phonetic, and grammatical differences). At the beginning of the 20th century, all speakers of the Persian language in Iran, Afghanistan, and Central Asia called their language Farsi. In the 1920s, the Tajik SSR began to call their language, alphabet, and literature "Tajiki" and the term was widely used for the language of the Persian-speaking population of Central Asia. Today, Persian is the official spoken language in Iran, Afghanistan, and Tajikistan, though under different names—Farsi in Iran, Dari in Afghanistan, and Tajiki in Tajikistan—and all three are mutually intelligible.

Iran continues to be a land of migration with diverse beliefs and practices: Zoroastrianism, Judaism, Christianity, Baha'i, Sufism,

[30] Reza Shah Pahlavi (1878-1944) was an Iranian military officer and the founder of the Pahlavi dynasty. He reigned as Shah of Iran from 1925 until he was forced to abdicate after the Anglo-Soviet invasion of Iran in 1941.

Yarsanism, and Islam, both Shi'ite and Sunni. While the faiths of the Iranian people have always been diverse, by 650 BCE, the Zoroastrian faith had become the primary religion of ancient Persia. Later, Judaism and Christianity entered Persia via Mesopotamia, developing vibrant faith communities there. To the east in what is now Afghanistan and Central Asia, the regional kingdoms adopted Buddhism from India in the third century, adapting it to Zoroastrianism and Greek traditions. Sufism also predated both Islam and Christianity. With the spread of Islam in the mid-seventh century, the Persian-speaking world became predominantly Muslim, yet traces of the earlier pre-Islamic religious and philosophical traditions remained.

With the introduction of Islam into Persia, the traditional practices, beliefs, and rituals combined with Islamic teachings, including the concept of enlightenment through spiritual knowledge of the previous traditions. Codified Sufism evolved in the region in the 10th century. The Ismaili Shi'ite doctrine became prominent by the 11th century. Later, during the Safavid dynasty (1501-1722), much of Iran and Azerbaijan converted to the Twelver Shi'ite sect of Islam. The Baha'i faith developed in the 19th century, expanding to the Near East and beyond (Dinavari 2014).

With a civilization dating back to 4,000 BCE, Iran has ruled over numerous nations, from Egypt to India, has endured invasions and immigrations by foreign armies and nomadic tribes, yet has continually reasserted its national identity. Although the people of Iran are known as Iranians, a mixture of cultural and ethnic groups with different languages, religions, and cultures continue to exist there. Each group and historical epoch has developed specific languages, traditions, and dance styles associated with it. Understanding the arts requires recognition of the region's multifaceted geography, history, and culture.

Colors of the Soul.

Guided by the footsteps of the ancient ones, we tread the path of wisdom, tracing echoes of heritage, and whispers of eternity.

CHAPTER 3

Iranian Dance through Time and Tradition

Dancing amidst ancient ruins, I sense the echoes of ages past. My feet gracefully trace the steps of those who danced before me, uniting our spirits in a timeless celebration of human expression.

Dance has been an integral part of Iranian culture since at least the sixth millennium BCE, and became a well-developed and protected art form during the Persian Empire, threaded through every social and religious ritual (Kiann 2014). The central role of dance is evident from innumerable archaeological findings among the ancient hills of Iran such as Shahdad, Susa, and all over the Iranic lands.[31]

Figure 3.1: Dancers on a pottery fragment from Cheshmeh-Ali (Shahr-e Rey), Iran, 5,000 BCE.

Z9897, Wikimedia Commons.

Pottery fragments from the Fars Province show figures in dynamic postures, arms or legs raised, holding hands, uniform, facing the same direction, equally spaced—all details indicating dancers in rhythmic movement (Figures 3.1 to 3.3). Circle dances around the diameter of pottery vessels or cylinder seals are most common, but line, couple, and solo dance scenes have also been identified (Garfinkel 1998, 209). At a site named Tepe Musian, pottery from 3,600 BCE was found showing a silk scarf dance, still practiced today in Iran and the Near East.

Figure 3.2: Circle of dancers on pottery fragment from Khazineh, late eighth to early seventh millennium BCE.

Fragment from Khazineh, illustrated by Gautier & Lampre, 1905 (Garfinkel 214)

Tepe Musian is an archaeological site located in Elam province of western Iran known for its

---

[31] Iranic refers to the culturally diverse grouping of Indo-European peoples.

Figure 3.3: Bowl painted with three standing or dancing figures, c. 4,000 BCE. British Museum, London.

Osama Shukir Muhammed Amin FRCP (Glasg).

ancient artifacts that provide valuable insights into ancient civilizations in the region. Pottery fragments from 5,000 to 3,000 BCE, the Chalcolithic Period, depict dancers with a ladder below them signifying an ascent into the sky, the place of the gods. Parallel lines under their feet and above their heads mark the earth and sky. Similar pottery fragments found at Khazineh and Tepe Giyan, portray dancers either alone or linked by hands and arms with others, looking in the same direction, with straight or slightly flexed knees, evenly spaced, suggesting synchronized movement (*British Museum* n.d.). A similar example from 5,000 BCE was found on a clay vessel obtained from the Tal Jari hill, about twelve km south of Persepolis.

A Kassite group dance is depicted on a third millennium BCE bronze piece; the dancers' arms pass behind each other's necks to rest on each other's shoulders. A fragment from Lorestan[32] in the first millennium BCE illustrates the ancient people believed that just as their dancers danced on earth their gods danced in heaven.

A piece of pottery obtained from Tepe Sialk in Kashan, where a community settled in approximately 4,500 BCE, illustrates four women doing a group dance. The position of their arms and bodies, and the way they look to one side indicate that they are engaged in a sacred religious circle dance. We can still see such circle or line dances in Kurdistan today. Other examples from 4000 to 3000 BCE include a fragment of pottery from Tepe Hesar of Damghan showing a war dance with five men. In Kerman, pottery fragments from 1000 to 2000 BCE illustrate bird-masked dancers wearing long feathers from their arms—a dance known as a *samacheh* (masked dance). The wearing of feathers suggests these dances had spiritual significance. It was common among people of West Asia at this time to celebrate and observe the spirits of nature. With

32 Lorestan is a province in western Iran and is home to various ethnic groups including the Lurs. Also spelled Loristan, Luristan, and Lurestan.

this joyful dance, they sought to embody the god of the mountains and the Tree of Life.

While it is difficult to reconstruct the exact dances originally performed in prehistoric Iran, these images do provide details about the importance of dance in Iranian society, including religious rituals, royal court settings, and festivals (Figures 3.4 and 3.5). They provide glimpses into the lives of the ancient Iranian people and the beauty of the past. Vision and curiosity are needed to complete the stories from artifacts that have no words. Dances illustrated in rock, pottery, and frescoes clearly show that rituals were a primary means of worship, healing, and unification, and even suggest that many contemporary dance movements today are rooted in these ancient rituals.

Figure 3.4: Persian dancer wearing a soft cap and tunic over a sleeved and trousered dress. His hands are clasped over his head. Scaraboid engraving. Achaemenid era, circa 400 BCE.

Getty.edu, Wikimedia Commons.

Scholars divide the history of Iranian art and culture into four distinct eras—Old Iranian, Middle Iranian, Classical Iranian, and Modern Iranian—embodying distinct differences in language, art, literature, architecture, and dance styles. Because Iran's written history was destroyed by invasion and history has always been written by the occupying invaders, most Iranian history has survived mainly as an oral

Figure 3.5: Dancers and musicians depicted on a Sasanian silver hemispherical bowl, fifth to seventh century CE.

Rye-96, Wikimedia Commons.

tradition, with only sparse written records by Greek historians or others that survive today. What was lost included the history and culture of the Babylonians, the Elamites, and the Medes.

The Old Iranian era includes the Achaemenid dynasty, the founding of the Persian Empire in Pasargadae,[33] the Sasanian and Parthian Dynasties, and the Hellenistic period of the Greeks and Romans. Several emperors in the Achaemenid dynasty encouraged the advancement of different art forms enjoyed by the Iranian royal court. The Greek historian Ketzias writes about the popular and talented female dancer Zenon from Crete, the favorite court dancer of Ardeshir Shah II.[34] Another Greek historian, Polukleitos, reports that musicians, singers, and dancers of the Persian royal court were engaged to entertain at the marriage of Alexander the Great with Princess Roxana in Susa. Greek texts offer detailed descriptions of dances involving fire, swords, and horses.

During the reign of the Achaemenids through the Sasanians, ritual dance was adapted to the royal courts, much of which is captured in vibrant wall paintings, relief sculptures, and craft works that survive today, portraying the royal court, New Year celebrations, deities, and daily life scenes. The Parthian kings, like their Achaemenid predecessors, often danced in festivals wearing masks. During the Sasanian period, dance gradually lost its spiritual aspect, and was used as a means of amusement and entertainment, incorporating high aesthetic and cultural values. A collection of Sasanian era silver dishes shows scenes of battles or hunting, and four very distinct dishes show scenes of the emperor and his courtiers gracefully engaged in dancing and music. During the Hellenistic period (323-31 BCE), Greek theater and dance were adapted to Persian taste and traditions, especially by the Parthians. Sasanian kings, in particular Bahram Gur[35] and Khosrow Parviz,[36] favored music, and musicians gained a privileged position in

---

33 Pasargadae is in modern-day Shiraz, where Persepolis is located. Pasargadae means "protector of the land of Pars."

34 Ardeshir Shah II was the Iranian Sasanian king from 379 to 383 CE.

35 Bahram Gur or Bahram V was the Sasanian Emperor from 420 to 438 CE.

36 Khosrow Parviz is considered to be the last great Sasanian king of Iran (590 to 628 CE).

court. Sasanian kings used to invite dancers from India during special ceremonies, creating a link between the cultures.

The Middle Iranian era, from the seventh to the 15th century CE, saw changes in language and culture that emerged following the Islamic conquest, including the development of Middle Persian (Pahlavi) and Sogdian, and the beginning of the Silk Road trade routes. The dance traditions, particularly royal court dances, of this time came to influence the dance movement vocabularies of peoples from the Caucasus throughout Central Asia and India.

The Classical Iranian era corresponds to the flourishing of literature, art, and education starting from the ninth century when Persian language and culture played a central role in the Golden Age. After the arrival of Islam in Iran, dance became more romanticized and was accompanied by mystical poetry and music. Even though Islam prohibited music, an exception was its use in sacred circles and ceremonies. Muslim instruments included the oud,[37] harp, tanbur,[38] and flute, backed up with tambourines, cymbals, and drums. During the Umayyad and Abbasid Caliphates, wealthy families showed great interest in musical instruments, singing, and dancing, and an envoy traveled to Iran and Damascus to invite male and female dancers to Arabia. Foreign musicians renewed the customs of the Sasanian era and the Caliphate court assigned ranks and degrees to the artists. Games and dances were performed wearing masks during Nowruz. After the formation of local governments in Iran, the art of music and singing became accessible to average people.

Between the eighth and 14th centuries, dance was the essential form of entertainment for the Abbasid court in Baghdad. Master composers and musicians such as Ibrahim al-Mawşili (d. 804) and his son Ishaq al-Mawşili (d. 850) were renowned for selecting promising slave girls, training them in dance, music, and poetry, then selling them to noblemen and princes for a profit (Pourjavady 2023, 49). The more lovely,

---

[37] The *oud* is a Middle Eastern short-neck lute. Fretless and pear-shaped, it usually has 11 strings grouped in six courses.

[38] The tanbur is an ancient long-necked string instrument played in the traditional music of Southern or Central Asia.

intelligent, and talented these women were, the more valuable they would be. From the Safavid to Qajar period, female court performers largely fell into two groups: concubines and courtesans. Concubines were mostly slave women owned by the ruling class. Courtesans were upper class women who entertained within their own homes and were occasionally invited to perform at governing courts. They had a role in society, but because of their inferior social status and the stigma of being entertainers, their lives were never recorded except on occasion by European travelers in their travelogues.

We know that sacred dance was integral to Iranian culture from the beginning, but as Islam gained influence, dance became forbidden. In fact, there are no words for "dancing" in Iranian languages, including Sasanian Pahlavi. Dancing was preserved by relabeling it as "gaming." In Khorasan, especially in Nishapur,[39] dance is still called "playing." Some Armenians also identify dancing as a game. Words used in place of "dance" are *bazi* "game," c*hobazi* "stick game," and *paibazi* "foot game." Dances using ropes, chains, sticks, and swords were recognized as games, and are still performed today.

In addition to the words based on *bazi,* there are the variations *paikobi*, *vachik*, and *vasht*. *Paikobi* (a combination of *pa* and *kobi* meaning "foot" and "beating" or "striking") is a traditional style of foot dance with stylistic steps and stamps. The Arabic word *raghs* (or *raqs*) has been used in Persian literature and poetry to mean "dance," as well as *raghghas* (male dancer) and *raghghaseh* (female dancer); today professional dancers call themselves *raghsandeh*, which is gender neutral. Due to its Arabic origin, Ferdowsi avoided the word *raghs* in his work insisting on using the Old Persian word for dance *vashtan* or *vasht*, and *vashtghar (*dancer), which survives in the Gilaki (*voshtan*), Mazani (*voshtan*), and Talysh (*veshtan*) languages as the verb "to jump" or "to play." The Pahlavi term for dance is *vachik* but this has been supplanted by the word *bazi* in New Persian. The word *sama* also is used to denote Iranian ritual dance or folk dance.

---

39 Nishapur, officially romanized as Neyshabur, means "new Shapur" or "the new city of Shapur."

Post-Islamic period dances can be divided into sama,[40] epic narrative, and folkloric dances. With the integration of Sufism into Islamic culture and philosophy, a meditative dance known as sama emerged as a means to connect people with the Divine. Sama was considered a supreme level of worship and an intensely personal experience.

Epic narrative dance accompanies the ancient folk legends of Ferdowsi in the *Shahnameh.* These martial dances symbolize the triumph of good over evil. Folkloric dances originated among villages and tribes all over Iran, traveling and spreading or cross-breeding with those of other cultures. These dances embodied ethnic pride and served various social functions.

During the Safavid period, dancing was almost exclusively practiced by women, while men mostly played music and sang (Figure 3.6). Boys sometimes dressed as women and danced in tea houses to attract customers. During the 15th century male dancers began to be more sought after. By the 16th and 17th centuries, groups of male dancers (called *mukhannath* or "dancing boys") performed in public and private settings (Pourjavady 2023, 74). *Mukhannath* referred to those who performed dance, music, or acrobatics in public, and later to cross-dressers and passive homosexuals. Dancing boys were young professional dancers recruited and trained to perform at all-male gatherings.

Figure 3.6: Fresco of Safavid dancer, late 16th century, Aali Qapu Imperial Palace, Isfahan, Iran.

Photo by author.

40 Săma (sema, in Turkish) is a ritual dance of whirling and prayer in the Sufi tradition. Some Iranian folk dances are named sama.

Figure 3.7: Royal banquet with dancers, 17th century, Hasht Behesht Palace, Isfahan, Iran.

Public domain.

The era of Modern Iran began with the Qajar dynasty (Figure 3.7). During the Qajar era (1789-1925), there were male and female ensembles of musicians and dancers. Male ensembles consisted of several string and percussion musicians, a vocalist, one or two dancers, and some actors. A popular dance was the *Shateri*, based on the stages of wheat cultivation, harvesting, kneading dough, putting it in the oven and removing it to be eaten. The 19th century saw changes in the role and representation of women. Female dancers portrayed an ideal beloved, a lover, a mother, or some combination of all three.

During the period of Qajar prince Muzaffar al-Din Shah (1896-1907), nomadic and ethnic dances were adopted and performed by the wider community, including the bell dance, the cherry dance, the candlestick dance, the tulip dance, and the swinging dance. During the constitutionalism of Iran and the expansion of cultural and artistic relations with Western countries, European dances were brought in, which were rapidly developed and refined by Iranians themselves.

Iranian dances today include the folkloric, sacred, classical, and contemporary. Each is an entity unto itself, requiring immense practice and dexterity. Many dances originate from ancient rituals passed down through generations, or reflect the lifestyle of everyday people from ancient times to the modern day. They illustrate ways of living, values, work, play, struggles, battles fought, celebration, and faith. Movements portray ordinary activities such as combing hair, sewing, gathering silk, picking cotton or fruit, washing clothes, drawing water, or serving tea. In ancient times, people would dance with the tools used in their daily work and articles found in their everyday life. Specialized dances facilitated wedding ceremonies, worship, mourning, and martial practice. Although minor movements, props, and attire may have changed over time, the stories and the meanings remain the same. Dance is a joyful manifestation of the bonds and life cycle of a community.

Every tribe and era developed unique dances for emotional expression and communication with others, different ways to portray their identity, strengths, customs, and philosophical and spiritual development. In essence, dance reflects the diversity of people's climate, history, culture, beliefs, and music. Artists from all over the world came to the Persian Empire to enter the cultural exchange that has been described as one of Iran's most distinctive characteristics, fostering connection, integration, and cross-pollination of ideas between disparate peoples.

In the celestial dance of day, the Sun Goddess reigns supreme,
her golden rays weaving magic across the sky.

CHAPTER 4

Mithraism and the Origin of Sacred Dance

Mitra–the Goddess of vast green pastures–we do praise;
To "First Celestial Goddess" our voices raise.
Before the sun shines from hilltops, indeed,
The everlasting sun, Mitra will proceed.
It is the first being with ornaments of gold
That from mountaintops the earth does behold.
And from there, the powerful Mitra will
Watch the abode of the Magi calm and still.

– Unknown

Figure 4.1: Divine emblem of the sun goddess upon the rock facade of the tombs of Qizqapan, Sulaymaniyah, Iraqi Kurdistan. Achaemenid era, sixth-fifth century BCE.

Dr. Osama Shukir Muhammed Amin, Wikimedia Commons.

At the dawn of Iranian civilization, the sun illuminated the region's mountains, steppes, and valleys. As the source of life, the sun was considered preeminent, Divine, and the people worshiped it daily from dawn to dusk. Kneeling down at sunrise, the faithful recited prayers and sang hymns to please the Divine Light, creating many rituals to honor it (Figure 4.1). Associated with all aspects of culture, worship of the sun held a central position in ancient Iranian life, developing into rituals to celebrate important events with singing and dancing. Early Iranian dances reenacted the beginning of creation to honor this sacred relationship with light. The sun was embodied in the goddess, Mitra, the leading figure in Mithraism, a mystery religion that eventually spread over the entire Roman Empire. The evolution of Iranian dance as an independent and distinctive art form began with the birth of Mithraism and spread with its acceptance.

Also known as Mehr worship, the rituals of Mithraism included the singing of hymns. The Greek historian Xenophon noted the importance of hymns in the Achaemenid court (553-330 BCE). Until the collapse of the Sasanian Empire (224-651 CE), group celebrations with the singing of hymns were an integral part of Iranian culture. One of the oldest Iranian hymns is performed as a group ritual reflecting inner mystical states.

The emergence of Zoroastrianism in the 6th century BCE, which reduced the number of acknowledged deities, caused a change in primitive beliefs among most of the tribes living on the Iranian plateau, diminishing their repertoire to only those rituals and dances related to the new primary deities.

Ahura Mazda (meaning Lord of Wisdom), also known as Ohrmazd or Hormazd, is the supreme deity in Zoroastrianism, representing divine authority, wisdom, reason, and truth. Spenta Mainyu is the Holy Spirit, the benevolent and creative aspect of Ahura Mazda. According to Zoroastrianism, Ahura Mazda created both Anahita, the goddess of water, fertility, and healing, and Mitra, the sun goddess. These three are Iran's sacred triad of gods. Ahura Mazda also created the Amesha Spenta (the seven divine spirits)[41] and Ahriman (the destructive spirit of darkness). According to ancient Zoroastrian beliefs, the perpetual conflict between positive and negative energies was a fundamental aspect of the universe in which human beings participated. Our connection to the Creator (Ahura Mazda), however, would enable us to ultimately prevail. Through sacred dance and celebration people presented gifts freely and joyfully to the supreme deity and the community on earth as an expression of

---

41 In Zoroastrianism, the Amesha Spenta is a class of seven archangels or divine entities created by Ahura Mazda to assist him in promoting truth, power, immortality, devotion, wholeness, and other qualities.

gratitude to Ahura Mazda and the ultimate triumph of positive energy.

Figure 4.2: Sasanian relief in Tagh-e Bostan depicting the investiture of Ardashir II (right) (379-383 CE), who is bestowed the 'Farr' (Divine Glory) by Ahura Mazda (center) and the sun-rayed Mithra wielding a ceremonial sword (left). Kermanshah, Iran.
Philippe Chavin, Wikimedia Commons.

As the sun goddess, Mitra symbolized power, strength, light, resurrection, liberty, and order (Figure 4.2). Often known as the daughter of Anahita, she was born on the first day of autumn known as Mehr Rooz. In early Zoroastrianism, Mitra and Anahita were separate deities. In late Zoroastrianism, the influence of other monotheistic religions led to efforts to reform Zoroastrianism as a monotheist religion, blending Mitra and Anahita into one. Many ancient Persian books and even parts of the Avesta describe Mitra as the one true goddess and the Lady of Justice. The common noun *mitra* means "contract, covenant, treaty;" thus Mitra is the Iranian deity of covenants and she was a protector of tribal society, the celestial deity who oversaw all solemn commitments between individuals or sociopolitical entities. Breaking such agreements was severely punished. Mitra is traditionally symbolized by the astrological sign for the sun, as well as the lion and horse which are her animal nature. Earth represents Mitra's domain, the palm tree, lotus blossom, and sunflower represent her plant nature, and gold is her metal. She is associated with red, yellow, orange, gold, and purple; ruby is her favorite jewel (Bashiri 2003).

Mitra, predating Zoroastrianism itself, stands out as the sole Iranian deity assimilated by the West. Brought by migrating Iranian tribes to India and Rome, she eventually evolved into a male version known as Mithras (Mitra is a female name and Mithras is a male name), central to the religion of the Roman legions. To the Romans, Mithras was known as *Deus Sol Invictus,* "The Unconquered Sun God." Over

Figure 4.3: Ancient wall carving of Iranian Sun god/goddess Mithra compared to the Statue of Liberty.
Public domain (left), Nataraj Munoli, via Pexels (right).

different historical periods and cultures, the deity's gender became ambiguous, with both male and female identities. In response to the Roman Empire's confusing interpretation of Mitra the goddess as the male god Mithras, the Iranian Sasanian dynasty (224–651) renamed the deity Mithra, which could be interpreted as a man or a woman. Statues of Mithra were built in the Persian Empire as half man and half woman. Mitra is often portrayed as a female who holds the fire, or a cow with a golden horn, representing the goddess of justice. She is also portrayed as a man holding a spear. The French derived the concept of Lady Liberty from Mitra. It was believed that in ancient Iran, the emperors or empresses would erect a statue of Mitra on any land they conquered or saved, as a sign of "Liberty." The statue of Mitra was often placed in royal courts or town squares as a sign of "Liberty and Justice for All." The rays of light emanating from the head of the Statue of Liberty monument in New York distinctly echo the symbology of Mitra (Figure 4.3). Depictions of the legendary Mithra have been excavated in Iran, Asia, Africa, and Europe.

Mithraism profoundly influenced the formation, symbology, and theology of Christianity. When the Romans converted to Christianity, Mithraism and its elements remained. The holy trinity was derived from the ancient triad of Iranian gods Ahura Mazda, Mithra, and Anahita. In the Threefold Path of Asha (the core teaching of Zoroastrianism—good thoughts, good words, good deeds), Ahura Mazda came to represent the Father, Mithra the Son, and Anahita the Holy Spirit. Many religious ceremonies performed by Christians today originate from ancient rituals honoring Mithra, such as the customs of baptism, the ringing of church bells, and the ritual consumption of wine and bread. Mithraic rituals including the presence of candles in a sanctuary and the singing of hymns and psalms appear to have carried over into Christian customs. According to a Christian text by St. Jerome, there were seven degrees of initiation a Mithraic convert must undergo. At each stage, he or she assumed a different name: Raven, Occult, Soldier, Lion, Persian, Runner of the Sun, and Father. These seven stages can be compared to the seven sacraments in Christianity, as well as the crossing of the seven valleys to reach the Divine in Sufi philosophy.

Mithraism considered Sunday, the day of the sun, as a sacred day. After Emperor Constantine's conversion to Christianity, Sunday became the designated day of worship for Christians, perhaps carrying on the Mithraic custom. Likewise, many of the ancient Iranian holidays came to be associated with Western religious holidays—Yalda, the winter solstice, became Christmas; Sepandārmazgān, a celebration of the feminine, became Valentine's Day; Nowruz, celebrating the arrival of Spring and the triumph of good over evil, became Easter, and so on. In Mithraism, the cypress, an evergreen tree, was an emblem of immortality, freedom, and perseverance against deadly forces. In the evening, on the anniversary of the birth of Mitra, a "Cypress of Mehr" would be decorated and offerings would be placed at its feet.

In his work *Histories*, Greek historian Herodotus of Halikarnassos describes the cultural and social habits of Persians, including the worship of Mithra. The earliest record of Persian dance was a sacrificial bull dance performed in honor of Mitra. In Book VII of *Histories*, Herodotus wrote that when he traveled to Persia, he saw people chanting, clapping, and dancing in whirling patterns around a great bull. Amazed, he asked what was going on and was told it was a celebration honoring the new year. In Book IX, he wrote that the ritual dance was to promote vigor through baptism in the blood of a bull, followed by a beautiful ritual dance performed by priestesses. This ceremonial act "is a connection between humanity and the Divine Light; as they dance, the priestesses become one with Mitra." A priestess was one of the most prestigious positions, and whirling was very much a woman's practice in this ancient tradition. Following the conquest of Persia by Alexander, the power and prestige of women was diminished, and gender separation became more pronounced. The theology and customs of the occupying Greeks and then the Islamic invaders spelled the end of women's honored role in the culture.

Many ancient prayers and ceremonies persist in Iran, manifesting in various forms of dance, the lighting of candles, and the placement of lamps over graves at sacred sites. In *Cyropaedia*, a book on Cyrus the Great written by Xenophon, a student of Socrates, he wrote "Cyrus offered sacrifice according to the law, and led the sacred dance of his Persians after the manner of his forefathers" (Xenophon 2011). During the Achaemenid Empire, the Greek historian and geographer Strabo recorded that while visiting Persia to celebrate Mehregan, the Persian festival of Mitra, and the autumn equinox, he observed the Magi[42] perform a ritual around a bull. During Mehregan, dancers gathered to pray and worship Mehr,[43] the sun god. Kings, whether Parthian or Achaemenid, danced in the Mehregan festival, often wearing masks. An example of these masks can be seen on the wall of the ruined palace of al-Hadra (Hatra) in the west of Mosul, Iraq, the only remnant of a large Parthian city. Evidence also shows group dances were performed for religious ceremonies in the halls of Persepolis.

The Avesta divides the Persian year into two equal parts or seasons: summer and winter. The beginning of the former would be celebrated with Nowruz and the beginning of the latter with Mehregan, a harvest festival celebrated during Mehr, the seventh month of the Persian Solar calendar. Dating back more than fourteen centuries, the Mehregan festival would be celebrated for six days as a reminder for the Zoroastrians to pursue good words, good deeds, and good thoughts. Mehregan once

---

42 The Magi are Zoroastrian priests highly trained in fields such as science, medicine, history, philosophy, and astronomy.

43 Mehr is a modern term for Mithra.

took place in ancient Persepolis, when people from across the Persian Empire brought gifts to mark their prosperity, contribute to the celebration, and give homage to Mitra. It became a Mehregan custom to send or give gifts to their king and each other. Pottery specimens from 3,600 BCE show that Mehregan was celebrated with a harvesting and threshing dance from the hill of Moses, "Mosian Hill." Grasping silk handkerchiefs, the dancers would hold each other's hands or little fingers against their shoulders. This type of dance gesture is still common among the Armenian and Assyrian Iranians.

Figure 4.4: The element of fire is represented by the candle dance, presented by the Simorgh Dance Collective and Dr. Farima Berenji.
Kevin Greek

Many dances were performed in ancient times to pray for abundance during planting and harvest. These dances may have included movements reproducing the labor of sowing, tending, or harvesting crops. One such dance is the Baluchi Sohbat, known as the Wheat Dance, which is performed for festivals of thanksgiving and harvest even today as an expression of community, culture, and celebration.

Innumerable temples were dedicated to Mitra around the ancient world, and depictions of Mitra/Mithra have been excavated in Iran, Asia, Europe, Africa, and even as far as London in 1954, when a Roman Mithraeum was discovered at a building site. Sacred dance was an integral part of worshiping the goddess in these temples. Priestesses would perform fire dances, evidence of which is still visible in the temple of Mitra in western Iran near Kurdistan Province. Fresco paintings show women dressed in plain clothing holding trays of light, engaged in different movements. With this sacred dance, the sun goddess would be honored as the flames illuminated the "Presence of the Divine" within, purifying any darkness and beautifying the inner self.

Certain movements of the dance would direct the energy of the candle and light to the four compass directions, and then to the fifth, which is to the center of oneself. The candle or ray of light symbolizes mystic inspiration or creative illumination. This practice brought us the tradition of lighting candles for Yalda, the Iranian winter solstice festival (and later, Christmas). The act of lighting candles has long been seen as a symbol of sanctification, often marking the commencement of various sacred rites. Illumination by candlelight provides a symbolic experience of spiritual light. The candlestick motifs found on Mevlevi tombstones are another example related to the ubiquity of this symbolism (Gündüzöz 2018, 44).

Archaeological discoveries in various regions of Iran, including Shahdad and Sush, suggest the prevalence of dance as a social ritual to honor Mitra at least as far back as the sixth millennium BCE. Ancient paintings on rocks, cave walls, as well as ancient pottery, show the existence of *paikobi*, a celebration dance throughout the Iranian plateau. Abu Rayhan al-Biruni, an Iranian scholar and polymath (973-1050 CE), observed dancers stomping, clapping, and turning about a large bonfire at Sadeh,[44] Nowruz, and Abrizgan[45] ritual celebrations. The ancient sacred dances to Mitra are thought to be the origin and inspiration for many of today's zikrs,[46] samas, and folk dances. *Lampa sama*, the dance of light, is one such dance in the ancient tradition of Mitra. In this dance, dancers wore oil lamps on their heads to illuminate and chase away the dark. Today, this beautiful lamp dance continues to be celebrated for weddings and other festivals in the Mazandaran province, the Caspian Sea region. Other dances are thought to originate from the rituals that summoned strength from the power of the sun.

---

44 Sadeh is an ancient Iranian tradition that celebrates 50 days before Nowruz.

45 Abrizgan is an ancient ritual celebration wherein participants sprinkled water on each other among other enjoyments.

46 Zikr is a spiritual practice, ritual, or prayer that includes ritualistic and rhythmic focused recitations, movement, and breath control. Sama is also considered a sacred circle dance of ancient origin in Iran.

Today the rituals of Mitra/Mithra continue to celebrate the redemptive and regenerative life force and are typically performed for festivals and ceremonies of thanksgiving, harvest, community, and culture. They live on in Iran in new forms such as the practice of placing lamps over graves or in holy places, dances of light with candles, or dances honouring harvest. As we will see, the rituals performed for other deities of nature, such as those of water or wind, also influenced sacred and folk dances seen in Iran today.

The dance of the priestess, unlike the dance of a stage performer, does not depend on physical fitness and youth. Her dance was the dance of the soul, and no physical frailty could obscure its radiance.

– Jalaja Bonheim

CHAPTER 5

On the Path of the Ancient Ones

Dance will take us on the path of the ancients—a journey of discovery through space and time.

Dance marks the beat of human life, from beginning to end: birth, coming of age, the various stages of adult life, elderhood, death, and the world beyond. Harmony and rhythm originate in natural processes, from the creation of the world, galaxies, planets, and stars to the cycles of night and day, the changing seasons, and precipitation in its various forms. Anthropologists consider many of the rhythmic movements of primitive tribes to be analogous, evidence that the impulse to dance has always been with us, even before the development of the written language. Before the earliest civilization, before written history, dance was born, conveying stories, myth, prayers, spiritual aspiration, and inspiration. Dance was the first form of worship and spiritual expression. Many art forms began as ritual communication with or about spiritual forces or realms.

From its most ancient origins, Iranian dance has primarily been a means of invoking blessings from and offering supplications to nature and the spirits. Dance was performed for the gods and goddesses, for the elements, or cosmic entities such as the Sun or Moon, to honor the sacred or empower the dancer. Dance became one of the most prestigious professions in ancient Iran. Priestesses engaged in dance as an integral part of sacred rituals, channeling energies to and from the Divine, calling for prosperity, healing, beneficial circumstances, and protection.

Anahita, Goddess of All Waters

Mighty Anahita with splendor will shine,
Incarnated as a youthful divine.
Full of charm her beauty she will display…
Straight-figured, she is a noble bride…
Her cloak is all decorated with gold…
Anahita, the eternal flame will always burn within your shrine.

– An invocation to Anahita from the Avesta

A sacred element among many civilizations, water played an important part in the mythology of ancient cultures. In Iranian mythology, water was created from the sky and wind. It was a messenger of light and purity. It was believed that a single drop created all the oceans, rivers, rain, and snow. Anahita was the goddess of all waters and the cosmic ocean (Figure 5.1). Apam Napat, an ancient Vedic Hindu deity, was one of the children of Anahita and served as a guardian to ensure water stayed clean and healthy. This guardian is depicted in many ancient Iranian statues.

Figure 5.1: Bust of goddess Anahita, Temple of Anahita, Kangavar, Kermanshah, Iran.
Photo by author.

Water purifies and is the symbol of freshness, life, brightness, cleanliness, prosperity, love, and innocence. The ocean is said to cleanse, refresh, invigorate, and release. Women and maternity were associated with water and water-bearing was an essential part of ancient cultures.

The seven sacred waters in Zoroastrianism (Qulī́zādah Khusraw 2009), also known as the "Haurvatat Waters," are: *Gush-i Ab-i Hayyat*, the Water of Life, which represents immortality and spiritual rejuvenation; *Gush-i Ab-i Salamat*, the Water of Health, commands physical vitality and healing; *Gush-i Ab-i Nihad*, the Water of Strength, both physical and spiritual, provides power to overcome adversity; *Gush-i Ab-i Frashgard*, the Water of Prosperity, promotes abundance, growth, and the flourishing of life; *Gush-i Ab-i Ardawahisht*, the Water of Purity, represents spiritual and moral purity, and cleanses the soul; *Gush-i Ab-i Khurdad*, the Water of Virtue, symbolizes righteousness, goodness, and moral uprightness; *Gush-i Ab-i Ameretat*, the Water of Wisdom, casts enlightenment, knowledge, and spiritual insight (Qulī́zādah Khusraw 2009).

Figure 5.2: Statue of Anahita in carriage drawn by white horses in Fuman, Iran.
Photo by author.

As she was the creator of all waters, Anahita was considered the essence of water, and water was her temple, whether in the form of snow, rain, hail, or a drop of dew. She was the mother goddess, the source of all life, the patroness of women, eligible girls, and childbirth. Anahita means "the immaculate one." Her full title was Aredvi Sura Anahita, meaning "moist, mighty, and immaculate." As a celestial being, she was also sometimes referred to as the "Imperial Stars." She was often portrayed as a very tall and beautiful young woman, dressed in a golden cloak and wearing a diamond tiara. Her favorite color was white, the pearl was her jewel, her astronomical sign the moon, and the lotus blossom her plant (Bashiri 2003).

As a warrior maiden, she was accompanied by mighty lions, carrying a water pitcher, or holding a *baresman*.[47] She rode a chariot carried by four white horses, representing wind, rain, clouds, and hail (Figure 5.2). Bulls, rams, and other horned animals also accompanied

47 *Baresman* is a sacred and ceremonial bundle of twigs of select medicinal plants.

Figure 5.3: Inscription of King Naresh of Sasanian Empire at Naqsh-i Rustam, Persepolis. Investiture of King Narseh (center) by goddess Anahita (right). Late third or early fourth century CE.

Photo by author.

her. In the Avesta, Ahura Mazda appeared before Zoroaster,[48] describing Anahita as "the life-increasing and holy, the herd-increasing and holy, the fold-increasing and holy, the wealth-increasing and holy, the country-increasing and holy."[49] Ancient kings would be crowned by their queens in Anahita's temples (Figure 5.3) to gain her support and protection. Anahita is sometimes depicted as the consort of Mithra, representing the union of fire and water. Because of Anahita's connection with life, warriors in battle prayed to her for survival and victory. The historian Herodotus referred to Anahita as equivalent to the Greek goddess Aphrodite. Later, she was known as the Iranian Artemis. Numerous statuettes of Anahita have been found near the ancient city of Susa, in the Zagros Mountains, from the early fourth millennium BCE. The tradition of worshiping the mother goddess

48 Zoroaster was an Iranian religious reformer who challenged the tenets of the contemporary Ancient Iranian religion, becoming the spiritual founder of Zoroastrianism.

49 The Avesta 2:10.

spread to other cultures such as Mesopotamia and Africa, and Anahita was one of the forms of the "Great Goddess" in Egypt. The temples of Anahita at Ecbatana in Media were considered the most glorious sanctuaries of the time with gilded columns, silver tiles, and gold bricks. The palace was later stripped by Alexander and by the Seleucid kings. Among Anahita's many titles was "Lady of Heaven and Mistress of the Gods," "Lady of the Mountain," "Mother of the Gods," "Mistress of the Sky," and the "Virgin Anat." The shrine of Bibi Shahrbanu[50] was likely once dedicated to Anahita. This is one of the "most beloved mountain shrines of the Zoroastrians of Yazd,[51] set beside a living spring and a great confluence of water courses" (Boyce 1967, 38).

There is a legend of 1,001 rivers whose base was the river Alwand, associated with Anahita. The Alwand River headwaters flow from the mountain of Dalahu in the Zagros mountain range in Kermanshah. Part of the river was thought to flow to the *sarab* (oasis) of Bisotun[52] in Kermanshah and another part was thought to flow to the oasis of Kangavar;[53] both locations honor the sacred waters of Anahita.

Reverence for water is deeply ingrained in Iranian culture today and in many traditional communities offerings are regularly made to the household well or nearby stream. Derived from an ancient Iranian ritual, *Suz Hotin* (Call for Rain) in Uzbekistan involves a procession of women who climb a hill nearest to the village and appeal to the goddess Suz Hotin with incantations. According to local belief, the performance of these songs brings forth clouds and heavy rain (Sultanova 2014, 183). Among the people of Lorestan, the ritual dance of *Arvotalo*

---

50 Bibi Shahrbanu ("Lady of the Land" in Farsi) or Banu-Pars was a legendary Sassanid princess who was captured during the Muslim conquest of Persia. Revered today as a saint among Shia denominations and Persians (Iranians), her shrine is a pilgrimage site in the city of Ray, near Tehran.

51 Yazd is the capital of Yazd province, Iran. It is recognized as a World Heritage site by UNESCO.

52 Bisotun (from the Old Persian word *Bagastana* meaning the "Palace of Gods") is a city at the foot of Bisotun Mountain upon which is an important historical inscription left by Darius I.

53 Kangavar is an ancient city in the province of Kermanshah, Iran.

or *Baruvotalo* requires a young lady with a beautiful face to climb a high hill to ask for rain with heart-caressing gestures and clapping. On the final day of Nowruz, a “Celebration of the Holy Water” (later adapted by Roman Catholicism) takes place outdoors, calling for rain, purification, light, and celebrating nature. Indoor rituals are performed to bring health, prosperity, and love into the community. Another celebration known as *Jashn-e Nilufar* (Lotus Festival) is a ceremony that is held on the first weekend of July when lotus flowers are in bloom.

Jashan-e Abanegan is an ancient Iranian festival that pays homage to Anahita and even today commemorates water as nature’s most precious resource. Celebrated on the day of *Aban*, which occurs around October 26th according to the Zoroastrian calendar, the faithful praise Ahura Mazda for abundant life-giving waters, visiting shrines and temples dedicated to Anahita and the *apans*.[54] Anahita is revered for her wisdom and knowledge, her role in healing, fertility, balance, nature, and harmony, and the nourishment that water provides. While dances directly linked to worship or veneration of Anahita may not be extensively documented, it is possible to imagine dances inspired by her attributes including water dances, fertility celebrations, healing rituals, dances of wisdom and harmony, honoring nature, and ceremonies associated with the worship of Anahita.

Anahita is of great importance in the Caspian Sea region of Iran, where she is known as the goddess of the sea. As the world’s largest inland sea, the Caspian divides Asia and Europe, with miles of coastline in the Gilan province of northern Iran. The Caspian people have lived in Iran since 300 BCE as fishermen or farmers of grains, tobacco, and tea. In ancient Iran, people would dance and chant around the waters to thank Anahita for giving them food and prosperity. People of the Caspian Sea region, famous for its rice, celebrate with *binji sama*, a rice-harvesting dance sometimes known as the basket dance. The dance originates from the worship of Anahita and reenacts the movements of women picking and preparing rice (Figure 5.4). Flat trays or baskets are held in front of the body or on the head and the movements symbolize

[54] *Apans* is the Avestan term for “the waters.”

Figure 5.4: Women working in the rice fields, Gilan province, Iran.

Photo by author

cooking, winnowing chaff, and checking for and removing stones. The baskets they hold symbolize food, and their dance is a form of thanksgiving for harvest, abundance, and the tribe's preservation. A traditional dress design of bright colors (called *tour desmal* in the local dialect) has been worn by women of the Gilan province for thousands of years and is considered sacred. It includes a skirt made of colorful ribbons, a shirt in the color of one of the skirt ribbons, a short black vest, and a scarf. The colors chosen for their garments are inspired by the beauty and color of nature.

The *Lak Sari Sama* or *Cheke Sama* dances of the Mazandaran province were once sacred rituals honoring the water goddess, and are performed today at weddings, harvest festivals, births, or other special gatherings. *Lak Sari Sama* is a lively, lyrical dance performed for women's celebrations by women. A pan, pot, or basin is beaten with the hands to make music. *Cheke Sama* ("dance of clapping" in Mazandarani) is a ritual of happiness and romantic wishes performed with strong body movements and trembling of the limbs accompanied by clapping. This dance is mostly performed alone or in the presence of two people, but sometimes it is done among groups.

Goddesses of Earth and Nature

In the gentle sway of the trees and the song of the rivers, the goddess reveals her grace in a timeless melody that harmonizes with the earth's eternal rhythms.

The goddess Armaiti (whose name means "beneficent devotion") is the Zoroastrian goddess of earth, akin to Mother Nature, and shepherds the dead buried in the earth back to nature. Gentle, kind, humble, patient, and nurturing, she embodies devotion to righteousness, order, and moral integrity; she is considered a protector of the earth and all living beings; she is the provider of bountiful harvests and is invoked for blessings of agricultural bounty. Devotees seek her blessings for a harmonious and balanced life as she guides and nurtures their spiritual and ethical journey; she encourages them to act with kindness, fairness, and empathy, and lead a life of righteousness, truth, and moral integrity.

Ameretat, meaning "immortality," is an ancient Iranian goddess who rules the physical and spiritual aspects of eternal life and protects nature, especially in relation to plants. In Zoroastrianism, she is one of the seven Amesha Spenta, divine entities representing aspects of divine harmony and order. In ancient Iran, some of the greatest celebrations honoured Ameretat, especially the festival of spring, falling on the spring equinox and the thirteen days following. People from all walks of life would pay tribute to her and the earth for providing abundance and renewal. On this day, all regions of the empire would come together to show their unity, exchange gifts, and dance in honor of Ameretat.

The scarf dance known as *astmal sama* (handkerchief dance) was a sacred circle dance (*sama*) originally associated with Ameretat, earth, and unity. Several scarf dances are still popular in the Fars region of southwest Iran today, one of them a thousand years old. Dressed in colorful clothing and holding scarves, dancers gather in a circle, moving in unison. One such dance is celebrated by the Qashqai people, a conglomeration of Turkic clans living in Fars and other provinces in southern Iran. The Qashqai are nomadic shepherds who move their flocks from the highlands north of Shiraz in the summer to warmer pastures southwest of Shiraz near the Gulf of Iran in the winter.

Figure 5.5: Qashqai scarf dance with the author during a research trip to Shiraz, Iran.
Photo by author.

The nomadic Qashqai live in *siah chador* (black tents) with roofs woven from goat hair and side walls (*chiq* or *chit*) made of a combination of straw and goat hair. They are renowned for their carpets and other woven wool products. The wool produced in the mountains and valleys near Shiraz is exceptionally beautiful and soft, dying to a deeper color than wool from other parts of the country, and thus their carpets are the most famous in all of Iran.

The Qashqai scarf dance (Figure 5.5) also originated from Ameretat worship. Traditionally it begins by making a small fire around which the women begin to dance, holding a scarf in each hand. The fire honors moonlight, and the women are like stars circling the moon; when they raise their scarves in the air they collect heaven's blessings from the wind. When the fire strikes their feet, they rid themselves of their ego and selfishness. As the dance slowly progresses, each dancer follows another, choosing movements that depict their daily activities or creating movements as they please.

Cheerful, vibrant, and festive, the dance celebrates the coming of spring and joy, honoring the deities and Mother Earth. The colorful scarves signify different concepts such as purity, light, nature, fire, water, wind, love, happiness, and prosperity. As the dancers move toward the circle's center, they join the scarves together, symbolizing unification.

Their hand and arm movements mimic the motions of weaving and their traditional garments portray the designs found in their carpets. The dances are of two kinds: the *aqor halay*, slow and heavy, with heavy, falling steps and downward movements of the arms—conveying a solemn, weighty mood; and the *lakke halay,* which is faster, involving dynamic arm gestures, an upward emphasis, and a repeating musical pattern in which the dancers pause in place for a few measures (turning in place, dropping to their knees, and coming up slowly while shaking their shoulders). The Baluchis have a similar traditional dance known as *dahaan chap* in which dancers make graceful arm movements while holding scarves or pieces of cloth.

God and Goddess of Air

Celestial whispers grace the breeze, for in the heart of the wind the goddess of air dances, her ethereal presence a gentle caress upon the world's longing.

The Persians worshiped a dual-natured Zoroastrian deity of the wind: Vata-Vayu. Vata was god of all winds that blow and bring rain clouds, while Vayu influenced weather patterns and maintained a balance in the natural world. In the Rigveda,[55] Vayu is called "the soul of gods" and was regarded as the breath of life (Rajabzadeh 1987, 80). Vata-Vayu could be considered a *yazata* (spirit worthy of worship) or *daeva* (evil spirit), depending, literally, on which way the wind blew. Also

55 The Rigveda is the oldest known Vedic Sanskrit text, a collection of hymns, estimated to be composed some time between 2000 and 1000 BCE, prior to the Indian-Iranian separation.

known as Vy in Iranian mythology, he inhabited both dark and light, the realms between Ahura Mazda and Ahriman. Vata-Vayu could nurture or kill; if he brought rain it would bring life, but if the rain came in a violent storm, it would bring death. In times of danger, ancient Persians often sought divine assistance from Vata-Vayu, but his turbulent nature was unpredictable. Vayu was depicted as a fierce warrior armed with golden weapons who fought and scattered the forces of darkness to maintain order and protect God's creations, yet he could suddenly wheel about and become a formidable opponent of the forces of light.

Haurvatat ("wholeness" or "perfection") was the Persian goddess of health, prosperity, wholeness, oneness, the afterlife, and was the patron of air and whirling. In Zoroastrian cosmology, Haurvatat played a crucial role in maintaining harmony and balance in the universe along with her assistants: Vata-Vayu of the wind and atmosphere, Manthra Spenta of "bountiful spells," and the Fravashis, or guardian spirits. Holding a veil against the wind was thought to enable communication with the deities. Venturing into the mountains to honor them, people would hold small pieces of fabric against the wind to send a message to the other side; letting them go into the air represented an offering. This ancient ritual was often used to calm a coming storm, and has carried forward today as the vibrant *Raghs-e Parcheh* (scarf or veil dance) traditionally performed at weddings, Nowruz, and other festive events, its distinctive feature the use of a large, flowing veil.

The Eternal Fire

In the heart of sacred flames, The Eternal Fire flickers, a beacon of devotion, igniting souls with timeless reverence and eternal light.

Atar was the Persian god of light, the personification of the element of fire, and the son of Ahura Mazda. Wherever a fire was lit, it was considered the presence of Atar, and after the rise of Zoroastrianism, fire represented the presence of Ahura Mazda. Atar was closely associated with Mithra and was depicted as the flame behind Mithra's chariot in battle. Together they succeeded in rescuing the Divine Glory from

The Discovery of Fire

According to Iranian mythology, before history was written, during the time of the Pishdadian era, a mythical king named Hushang ruled the world. One day, he and his hunting retinue saw a huge, black, slithering, dragon-like creature with red shiny eyes—an *Azdah*. On seeing them, the creature fled. King Hushang and a few of his soldiers followed, hunting it down. In those days, their weapons were huge stones, which they hurled at it. Some stones missed their mark and hit other stones, causing sparks to fly and igniting the dry branches of a *Sadeh* tree nearby, resulting in a fire.

On seeing this gigantic blaze, the terrified soldiers started running away. However, King Hushang recognized the majesty of God in the blazing fire so he bowed down before it and offered praises to its Creator. He stopped the fleeing soldiers and exclaimed, "Don't fear this majestic Fire. It is the radiance of God. He who is wise shall revere it."

Relieved by their king's assurance, the soldiers returned, bowed down before the fire, and fed it with wood. That night the King and his subjects performed a thanksgiving ritual called Jashan around this fire with great zest and festivity. Exactly fifty days before the New Year, they celebrated this day as the festival of *Sadeh*.

the demon Azhi Dahaka. Atar's presence was believed to guard against dark forces, empower divine justice, and provide spiritual guidance to followers of the faith.

Fire has always played a vital role in Zoroastrian beliefs, rituals, and worship, with its transformative and purifying properties. The most holy element in Zoroastrianism, it is a symbol of purity, truth, and enlightenment, permeating the entire creation. Not only does it help prepare food, create warmth, and promote health, it is the force that fights and repels darkness and negativity. In folk tradition, the spirit of Ahriman cannot enter a house when a fire is lit. Fire was known to be the seventh and final creation of Ahura Mazda. The faithful offered meat as a sacrifice to Atar, at the same time holding a bundle of sacred twigs (*baresman*) in their hand and every house would have a hearth for making sacrifices and prayers:

> *O Atar, son of Ahura Mazda! Thou art worthy of sacrifice and invocation; mayest thou receive the sacrifice and the invocation in the houses of men.*[56]

Zoroastrian cosmology holds that seven sacred fires (*atash*) represent the cosmic forces that shape the world: *Atash Bahram*, the fire of victory, righteousness, strength, and triumph over darkness; *Atash Adaran*, the fire of home and hearth; *Atash Vohu-Fryana*, the fire of good leadership, justice, and fair governance; *Atash Atur-Fryana*, the fire of courage, valor, strength, and bravery in battle; *Atash Adur-Jansp*, the fire of generosity and hospitality; *Atash Azi Dahaka* (Fire of Fiendishness), the fire of evil, darkness, and malevolence that must be overcome; and *Atash Vanant*, the fire of vigor, vitality, and the drive for productivity and growth.

The element of fire, along with the sun itself, forms the basis for Zoroastrianism. The first religion to have a prophet, Zoroastrianism originated with the historical figure of Zoroaster,[57] whose lifetime is traditionally assumed to be around 628-551 BCE. Born in northern Persia, he was the son of a priest and early in life exhibited an interest in religion. At age thirty, he experienced a revelation in which he encountered Ahura Mazda and the existence of a singular, intelligent, unseen energy: the god of light. He began preaching against polytheism and emphasizing the importance of ethical living. Though his ideas initially met opposition he eventually converted King Hystaspes.[58] After Zoroaster's death, his religion continued to be influential until the Muslim conquest of the Persian Empire in 651 CE when Zoroastrianism largely disappeared.

---

56 The Avesta, Atash Niyayesh (Litany to the Fire).

57 Zoroaster is also known as Zarathushtra.

58 King Hystaspes, father of Darius I, was a member of the Persian Achaemenid royal house and an early patron of Zoroaster. Originally named Vishtaspa (Old Persian or Avestan), Hystaspes is his Hellenized name.

Zoroaster proclaimed that one God was the omnipotent creator of the universe, the human soul was created in God's image, and two forces governed the world: Ahura Mazda, the force of goodness, truth, and light, and Ahriman, an evil force of darkness, lies, and destruction. This dark force was not an independent entity, however, but lay solely within the human mind, and therefore the path to happiness required purifying one's thoughts so the seeds of good thoughts, words, and deeds could bloom (*Mystic Iran* 2008, 18:21). These became the three Zoroastrian tenets, also known as the Threefold Path of Asha: *humata* (good thoughts), cultivating a positive, constructive mindset free from harmful or negative thoughts; *hukhta* (good words), speaking truthfully, kindly, meaningfully, and with integrity; and *huvarshta (*good deeds), performing actions that are charitable, beneficial, and morally upright. Found in the book of Avesta (meaning "foundation" and "knowledge") and central to Zoroastrian ethics, these teachings guide adherents in leading a life of righteousness, goodness, and promoting the betterment of the world. Compiled over centuries and completed during the Sasanian period, the Avesta was written by Zoroaster in the old Iranian language[59] and includes a collection of sacred chants called *Gathas* that address cosmology, spiritual law, and the teachings of light, as well as purification instructions, prayers, hymns, and spells against dark forces.

Zoroastrians believe that God is the source of all good but also permits evil, giving rise to a spiritual and moral dualism in which human beings are responsible for advancing the good. The central theme of Iranian mythology is therefore the battle between good (Ahura Mazda) and evil (Ahriman) in the world. Although equally matched, Ahura Mazda is destined to win over darkness.

Zoroaster diminished the role of the old gods and spirits, who were viewed as agents of Ahriman, the lord of darkness, and emphasized Ahura Mazda as the supreme God—the first step toward monotheism. To help him promote truth and righteousness, however, Ahura Mazda created seven archangels, called the Amesha Spenta, who derived their features and powers from the pre-Zoroastrian gods. Hosts of angels

---

59 Avestan, now extinct.

(*yazatas*) and good spirits (*ashavans*) also fought on Ahura Mazda's side. Ahriman commanded an army of dark spirits (*dregvants*) and demons (*devas*). Plants and animals could be good or evil, depending on whether Ahura Mazda or Ahriman created and controlled them.

From the Zoroastrian perspective, humans have been created for the noble purpose of working together to repulse the Evil Spirit and human nature is held to be essentially good. With free will to follow the truth or not, individuals determine their own destinies based on their ethical choices. On a final judgment day, people go to heaven or hell depending on the moral quality of their lives. According to Zoroaster, although Ahura Mazda is the only God, the evil force of Ahriman is engaged in a struggle to capture human souls.

In addition to the physical body (*tanū*), an individual is believed to have several spiritual bodies. These are: the animating force (*ahu*), the breath of life (*vyāna*), the mind or spirit (*manah*), and the soul (*ruvan*). Additionally, each individual has a guardian angel (*fravarti*), and a spiritual double (*dainā*). It is the ruvan that is held accountable for a person's actions during their life, and will meet its future reward or suffering. At the time of judgment, the ruvan encounters its spiritual double, the dainā, the embodiment of all of its deeds during life, appearing as a beautiful maiden or an ugly hag. Depending on how these deeds are weighed, the soul either crosses the *Chinvat Bridge*[60] safely to the other world or falls into the abyss. Each individual has an ancestral protective spirit (fravarti),[61] and all the fravartis together form a warrior band of guardian angels.

By absorbing multiple gods into aspects of one god Zoroastrianism began a monotheistic trend. Zoroastrian beliefs about dark forces at work in the world, a battle between good and evil, judgment upon death, heaven and hell, and a final judgment day, influenced the Abrahamic faiths of Judaism, Christianity, and Islam. Unlike some ancient belief systems, Iranian mythology remains alive outside the covers

60 The Bridge of the Requiter or "siftng bridge," which divides the world of the living from the world of the dead.

61 *Fravarti* is Old Persian, whereas the Avestan language form is *fravaṣi*.

of old books. It has survived without a pause for thousands of years. Zoroastrian communities still exist in India, where the descendants of immigrants from Iran are known as Parsis, a reference to their Persian origin. By the mid-fifth century BCE, Zoroastrian rituals dominated sacred dance. People worshiped under the open sky with fire always present. Fire rituals involved music and dancing that lasted for days. The sacred fire, as an embodiment of the light of god, Ahura Mazda, and the illuminated mind, was so important that no ritual or ceremony occurred without it, and it was never extinguished but kept burning continuously.

Early Zoroastrian rites were conducted in dedicated structures or natural settings. Some open-air temples in the high foothills of the Zagros and Bakhtiyari mountains date to a few hundred years before Herodotus.[62] Staircases led up terraces to a podium on which continuous sacred fires burned in special urns. By medieval times, most services had moved to indoor temples. The Zoroastrian fire temple is known as an *atash gahs*. Some atash gahs came to serve as courts of common law (*dadgah*), and their ritual fires were known as *atash dadgah*, while their temples were called *dar-e mehr*. The atash dadgah came to represent Asha, the law of God—honesty, truth, justice, righteousness, and wisdom—and the dar-e mehr became a place wherein only truth could be spoken. Said to have been created by immortal beings, Zoroastrian fire temples have stood since ancient times on three Iranic sacred sites: in Fars province (now in Shiraz), in Azerbaijan, and in Khorasan. The sacred fire in the Zoroastrian Fire temple of Yazd (Figure 5.6), kindled more than fifteen hundred years ago, still burns today as a reminder of divine illumination within the human soul.[63]

Iranian mystic customs include fasting and a cleansing of the seven body parts called the "fast of the seven limbs." The seven "limbs" are: the eyes, which should see good; the hands, which should give and receive

---

62 The Bakhtiari are the western mountains of Iran, adjacent to the present Iran-Iraq border.

63 Known as Atash Behram, meaning "Victorious Fire," dated to around 470 BCE, located in Yazd province, Iran.

Figure 5.6: Exterior (left) and interior (right) of Atash Behram (Victorious Fire) Zoroastrian fire temple, Yazd, Iran.
Zenith210, Wikimedia Commons (left), and photo by author (right).

good; the feet, which should stand on the good; and the tongue, which should speak clean and wholesome words. The mind must also be kept pure, wholesome, and disciplined through prayer, meditation, and controlling the ego. Nyberg claims Zoroastrian worship implements communication with the spirits in dance, silent meditation, trance, and by drinking substances made from the haoma plant (Nyberg 2005).[64] This sacred ritual is said to have evolved into the Sufi ceremonies of *sama* and *dhikr*.

Visiting Persia in 430 BCE, Herodotus described the worship and customs he encountered. He noted that the Magi were one of six Median tribes, whose lineage assumed the specialized priestly duties of the *athravan* or fire-keepers who tended to the sacred fire. The Magi, who predated Zoroastrianism, accurately recorded the positions of the stars and documented the sun's passage through the twelve constellations; charting, interpreting, and forecasting their movements. They held sacred rites and ceremonies for the community, including dance rituals, at significant moments. The Magi were unsurpassed in their knowledge of philosophy, history, geography, nature, medicine, and the celestial world. The people sought the advice of the Magi to help them make important life decisions or to heal the sick. Sources from pre-Islamic Iran assert that the Magi were also involved in administration,

64 The haoma is a sacred medicinal plant used to create a ritual drink.

education, politics, and legal affairs. Deeply revered, they were legendary beyond the borders of Iran and throughout the ancient world.

The Magi were responsible for performing sacred rites, offering sacrifices, and interpreting omens. Burning incense and lighting candles to purify their spirits, they performed the central devotional ceremony or *yasna*.[65] The *yasna* is also the central liturgical text of Zoroastrianism, and the *yashts*[66] are hymns dedicated to various deities. Both include recitations and ritualistic chants. Among other rites, the haoma plant is pounded and mixed with water and milk as a liquid offering presented by the priest to Ahura Mazda and other divine spirits. Jashan, a sacred thanksgiving ceremony, may also be performed on days such as Nowruz and Mehragan, and ceremonies related to healing and well-being may also performed. *Ashem vohu*, equivalent to the Western phrase "amen," is recited during prayer five times a day, from sunrise to sunset. *Ashem vohu* is the beginning and the end, the truth, the beauty, the goodness, and everything combined. It is believed the Islamic prayer, *Namaz,* originates from this ritual.

For Iranians, cleanliness is indeed close to godliness. Keeping clean through ritualized bathing and washing is practiced many times a day. When any kind of contamination is present, an additional process of purification is prescribed. The cleansing and purification ceremonies (both physical and spiritual) prepare a person, space, or article for a religious ceremony. As a sign of cleanliness, respect, and modesty, mystics and dancers wear white clothing and often cover their hair. Among some villages in Iran, where people still awake to the rooster's call at sunrise, mothers or grandmothers quickly open the windows, signifying the awakening of the Divine as people go outside, pour water by the street, and start cleaning, to welcome the Sun.

---

65 Derived from old Avestan, meaning "worship" or "offering."

66 The *Yashts* are a collection of twenty-one hymns in the Younger Avestan language. Each of these hymns invokes a specific Zoroastrian divinity or concept.

Devotional Fire Rituals

Unfold Yourself within me, O Lord. Grant me strength of character through Right-Mindedness. Through the holiest spirit, O Lord, grant me goodness as a reward for prayer. Grant me a life full of vigor through Truth, and may the pure Mind look after me.

– The Avesta

Ancient Iranian society viewed fire as a transformative and cleansing agent. Since fire is the manifestation of the sun, and transforms all it consumes into the likeness of itself, it was one of the most sacred elements. Iranian festivals have deep roots in the praise of sun and fire. Zoroastrians celebrate Sadeh, a festival that dates to the Achaemenid Empire. It is a mid-winter festival honoring the discovery of fire, its archangel Azarizad (Azar "fire" and Izad "goddess"), and its triumph over the forces of darkness, frost, and cold. Sadeh means "hundred" referring to one hundred days and nights since the end of summer and is celebrated a hundred days after summer and fifty days before Nowruz, which marks the beginning of spring. Today, this seasonal festival is not religious but a national secular event celebrated all over Iran. The chief preparation involves gathering wood, and everyone in the community is expected to contribute. The festival bonfire burns until sunrise as people dance and chant around it.

Chaharshanbeh Suri,[67] also known as Red Wednesday, is a festival observed on the last Tuesday night preceding Nowruz. The term *suri* means "red," or sometimes "festive," and signifies the sun, as well as a solar deity reminiscent of Surya (the sun god in Vedic India). This festival traces its origins to ancient rites honoring both the sun and departed souls. Celebrants commemorate ancestors and departed loved ones. In ancient Iran, families would light fires or torches on their doorsteps or rooftops, believing that it would aid the souls of deceased relatives in

---

67 Chaharshanbeh, the Persian word for Wednesday, is also spelled čahāršanbe.

finding their way home and deter evil forces. This tradition is similar to the later Jewish celebration of Passover.

A single fire represents the seven purifying fires, and its temporal flames are viewed as emblematic of a spiritual fire, the source of enlightenment, vitality, and virtue. People build bonfires, joyfully dance around them, and jump over them. This ensures unlucky nights will pass and good luck and happiness will come with the arrival of spring. As they jump, they make a wish that the yellowness from their body, representing illness, unhappiness, and animosity, is replaced by the redness of the fire, representing good health, happiness, harmony, and friendship. Because Ahriman fears fire, it cleanses the soul and removes negativity, allowing one to be pure for the New Year.

Another activity involves wearing masks or painting the face to confuse Ahriman. Children wear costumes and knock at the doors of houses, asking the occupants for treats as blessings to keep Ahriman from haunting them. In another tradition, women disguise themselves, visit homes, and bang on pots with a spoon. At each home, they are treated with sweets or nuts. These practices are similar to the customs celebrated in the West around Halloween.

People of the world have always danced for their deities—whether in times of celebration, great change, or even despair—seeking blessings for fertility, family, abundance, and healing. Our ancestors were in awe of the power and mystery of nature and the cosmos, and believed divine beings observed and appreciated their rituals. They used dance to honor and connect to the Divine and to commune with nature and her mysteries. The origins of dance are strongly associated with gods, goddesses, spirits of nature, and the elements. When dance appealed to a higher power, it became a means of elevating everyday human experience.

Inner Transformation.

We are warriors of light, and with the strength of our love and of our will, we can change our destiny and that of many other people.

– Paulo Coelho

CHAPTER 6

Warriors of Light: Epic and Battle Dances

In the tapestry of ancient tales, Iranian warriors emerge as fierce and noble defenders, their courage echoing through the ages, their strength a testament to the resilience of the human spirit.

Figure 6.1: Iranian vessel with warrior illustration. Ninth-seventh century BCE.

J.H. Payne and E.A. Payne Fund. MFA Boston. Photo by author.

Iranian dances reflect a manner of living—working, celebrating, struggling, and battling—that spans thousands of years. Because Iran has been repeatedly attacked and invaded, many dances arose among warriors as a form of physical training or simulating battle, their movements originating from stylized martial practices expressing power, perseverance, national solidarity, and narratives of heroism. They invoke spiritual devotion and valor to fight weakness and destroy darkness. The ancient Iranian warrior god Verethragna acts as an aggressive, victorious force against the forces of darkness. In the *Bahram Yasht*, a hymn dedicated to him, he takes ten different forms: a strong wind, a bull with golden horns, a white horse, a burden-bearing camel, a male boar, a youth at the ideal age of fifteen, a swift bird, a wild ram, a fighting deer, and a man holding a sword with a golden blade. Through ritual dance, Iranian warriors attempted to manifest the force of Verethragna as they sought to conquer evil.

Various movements and styles in Iranian dance, especially folk or epic dances, come from these martial practices, such as the sword dance,

Figure 6.2: Stick dance by Qashqai nomads during a research expedition by the author.
Photo by author.

the acrobatic horse dance, and various types of stick dances from the Khorasan region, the Bakhtiari, and Qashqai tribes (Figure 6.2). The Turkmen dagger dance and dances from Azerbaijan such as Kazakh or Lezginka demonstrate these qualities as well. One of the primary distinctive features of these dances is their display of heroic skill and agility.

Some funeral dances performed by mountain people commemorate a deed of valor by great warriors. In one such dance, *chapi*, a group of men form a circle, each holding onto another's belt (Knapp 1979, 20). The dancers strike the earth with their feet, then raise one foot, pointing it upward. The leader of the group then dances and waves his scarf while singing passionately. Another circle dance called *chovaki*, performed by the Sistani, involves striking special sticks (*cho* or *chub* in Farsi) to the front and back while alternately turning in the circle (Hojjati 2023, 263). The term *Jangi* means "military" or "warlike" and refers to dances which involve mimicry of combat movements, swordplay, archery, and other maneuvers. Various props representing swords or daggers may be used.

Sword dances are performed as part of cultural celebrations or historical reenactments with traditional music and costumes. The performers are usually skilled in the art of swordsmanship and are known for their agility, precision, and control. In the Sistan and Baluchistan provinces, a sword dance or "wood dance" called *shamshir-bazi,* is a martial performance accompanied by drums. While not a dance in the conventional sense, it incorporates choreographed movements with a sword. Among the Sistani, dancers hold a sword in both hands and enact a battle with a partner, one dancer circling the other (Hojjati 2023, 263). *Souri*, from the ethnic Kurdish regions of Iran, is a traditional dance characterized by intense, powerful movements associated with bravery and the valor of warriors. The word *souri* means to battle against darkness. *Raghs-e Parsi* is a traditional Persian martial arts dance using symbolic weapons similar to swords or daggers to mimic combat techniques with dynamic movements such as blocks, strikes, and evasive maneuvers. The Iranian folk dance *golriz* involves spins, high jumps, and dynamic footwork, reflecting the strength and agility of warriors.

Figure 6.3: Nomads of Lorestan with the author during a research expedition. Photo by author.

The handkerchief sometimes takes the place of a weapon. A white handkerchief is symbolic of peace whereas a red one represents readiness for war and defense. Often the dancer leading a line carries the handkerchief. For the people of Zagros, a military captain would lead his squad with a handkerchief instead of a weapon when weapons were not permitted in the royal palace.

Dance is a major part of people's lives in Lorestan for almost every major event in life—weddings, funerals, mourning, etc. (Figure 6.3). For the Lurs as well as the Kurds, stomping one's feet on the ground shows patriotism and commitment to their homeland. This stomping ritual is called *paikobi* and it develops strength and rhythm while communicating unity and equality in love and friendship. Other Iranian martial dances honor the bravery of warriors by depicting battle scenes. *Raghs-e Parcheh*, also known as the "flag dance," is one such stylized performance. Dancers carry colorful flags and move in coordinated patterns like the movement of armies on the battlefield. *Shateri* is a martial dance involving large, energetic movements inspired by horse-mounted warriors in combat. The *khaleghi* is named after a heroic figure in Persian folklore. Characterized by vigorous movements, *Khaleghi* dancers often carry symbolic weapons like spears or swords to evoke the spirit of battle.

Baluchi *pahluan* singers are told that *pahlu* is derived from the Pahlavi language and means brave and strong. In *Lorestan*, the *chobazi* (stick dance) or *tarka-bazi* (twig dance) is a martial dance performed by two men performing choreographed combat sequences using wooden sticks. A similar stick dance among the Khorasani is *Razm-e Chob* (Battle of the Stick) whose movements portray the military march of the Parthian army. Some martial dances are for mystic warriors of light who battle the dark inner realms. The Gonabadi Sufi order has a form of battle dance named *Raghs-e Kharabati* or the "Dance of Destruction." This highly energetic and vigorous dance signifies the spiritual struggle against ego.

To acquaint their horses with the turbulent scenes of war, the Persians used to execute a "military dance." They choreographed military scenes, clashed weapons together rhythmically, and danced with their horses (Kiann 2014). The Iranian warriors had different specializations according to region. The Ardalans[68] were known to be excellent fighters on horseback, the Sarmatians were known for fighting with spears, and the best female archers were the Scythians. Many Scythian rituals have been compared to those of Sufi whirling and sama, and the ritual of *zurkhaneh*[69] in practice today (Nyberg 2005). The Hazarabam[70] fighting units were famous for their excellent sword skills and were known as the "Immortal Army."

The word Amazon is likely derived from the ancient Iranian word *Ha-mazan,* meaning "woman warriors." These were female fighters of the early fifth century in the Caspian region and Azerbaijan, Iran's northwestern province. They were known for their marksmanship in archery and spear craft, for their horseback riding skills in battle, and as commanders and empresses. The Iranian tribes that formed the Amazons were connected with the Parthian and Saka tribes, nomadic groups legendary for their warriorship. Recent archaeological findings

---

68 Ardalan is a Farsi word meaning "the mighty fighter." The Ardalans had a reputation for producing skilled warriors.

69 A system of athletics and martial arts to train warriors in Iran.

70 A unit of 1,000 Persian soldiers.

in the steppes of western Russia and in ancient Persian regions align with the legends that the Amazons held significant roles as strategists, leaders, and warriors among the ancient Iranian tribes. It is believed that they are the founders of the Pahlavani traditions of the zurkhaneh today. When encountering these fierce female warriors during their expeditions in the East, the Greeks heard the term *Ha-mazan*, turning it into *Amazones*.

Another form of epic warrior dance is the *Raghs-e Khanjar* (dagger dance) by the Turkmen of the Sahara. The history of this dance dates to about three centuries before the advent of Islam. It began as a ritual dance with an epic narrative performed by Turkmen tribes before hunting to promote morale. Later, it became a complete preparation for battle, including fighters putting their swords in order before leaving for the battlefield. Today, dancers wear traditional clothing with a decorative dagger at the waist symbolizing bravery and valor. Typically performed in groups of ten or more people showcasing the skill and dexterity of the performers, the dancers hold hands, gather, spin, and thrust in rhythmic movements. Shouting, they prepare themselves for the battlefield.

The Turkmen and Yamuts[71] use the dagger dance as a healing treatment for psychotic imbalance, to remove wounds and illness from the body and mind. The affected person is placed on the ground while believers stand around in a circle. A leader begins to recite verses while others circle the patient and perform warrior-like movements. There is no instrumental accompaniment. This is repeated for hours until the patient gradually becomes ecstatic. When the healer feels the time is right, he breaks the circle of participants and shocks the patient by inserting the sharp tip of his dagger into the patient's body to release any illness.

The epic narrative poems of the pre-Islamic era were connected to the bravery of the tribal warriors. But after the advent of Islam, these poems were adapted to praise God and the divine saints, taking on

71 The Yamuts are a Turkman tribe mainly engaged in agriculture.

more spiritual significance. Thus, the dagger dance came to signify battling one's ego or anything preventing one from reaching the Divine.

He Lepe Reki (derived from the word *he leper,* which means to move fast and attack) is another warrior dance often performed for battles, with ancient roots in Zoroastrianism. In the dance line, the first and last person each hold a handkerchief as a sign of the equality of all group members, including both women and men. Stomping the ground symbolizes the dancers' strength and readiness to awaken the earth to protect their homeland. Shouting while dancing is meant to intimidate and scare the enemy. If the group kneels down or sits during the ritual, it symbolizes that they are bowing to the enemy. Raising a hand above the head means that they have regained strength for fighting. Yelling "*Yazdan Pak*" (Divine Spirit) is an appeal to the Divine for strength.

The dancers join in a circle showing their unity in protection and defense. There is a stone inscription in the Hae Pir fortress of the first millennium BCE that shows musicians playing *zurna*[72] and a line of people holding hands who appear to be moving. The Kurdish people were historically engaged in tribal wars, so in order to have a strong body and will, they practiced *Hae Pir* in the interval between wars. Omar Khayyam[73] in his *Nowruznameh* states that, according to the *Shahnameh*, when Fereydun saved the Iranian people from Zahhak[74] the people celebrated by performing He Lepe Reki. Today this dance is performed for celebrations, weddings, and at times of mourning and grief. Also called Hae Pir, it is considered one of the oldest of dances.

---

72 The *zurna* is a double reed wind instrument played in Central and West Asia, the Caucasus, Southeast Europe and parts of North Africa. The name is derived from the Persian *surney*, meaning "banquet, feast" (*sur*) and "reed, pipe" for *ney*.

73 Ibrahim al-Khayyam Nishapuri or Omar Khayyam (1048-1131), was a polymath, known for his contributions to mathematics, astronomy, philosophy, and poetry.

74 Fereydun is an Iranian mythical king and hero from the Pishdadian dynasty. In the *Shahnameh*, Fereydun helped defeat the tyrant Zahhak to become king.

In the Heart of Khorasan: Land of the Rising Sun

I was raised in Khorasan… The land of the Rising Sun.
Attar was the spirit, Sanai its two eyes, I follow their shadow…
Attar has toured the Seven Cities of Love, I am at the turn of an alley.

– Rumi

In the age before Zoroaster, important rituals to worship the sun deity took place in the land known as Khorasan, which in Persian means "where the sun arrives from." When Alexander conquered Persia, the old Mithraic ceremonies took on new life and spread throughout the Hellenistic world. The region of Khorasan became culturally important in Iran and across Central Asia as a major center of religious and mystical thought. The land that became known as Khorasan was part of Greater Iran and the region where Zoroastrianism would become the predominant religion.

During Sasanian times, Iran was divided into four geographic sections, with Khorasan in the east. Khorasan was further separated into four smaller provinces: Nishapur, Marv, Herat, and Balkh. The fertile intellectual soil of Khorasan nurtured many spiritual traditions. Before the region was Islamized, its inhabitants had generally practiced Zoroastrianism, but in different eras, the traditions of Manichaeism, Mithraism, Nestorianism, paganism, Buddhism, and Judaism had also taken root. Khorasan is also one of two birthplaces of Sufism (the second being Mesopotamia).

The popularity and awareness of Sufism in the world today is largely attributed to Jalal al-Din Muhammad Balkhi (Rumi), who was born and raised in Khorasan. Khorasan is also one of the wealthiest and most beautiful mystical music cultures.

Ritual dances from the time of Mitra continue in the Khorasan region today in the form of folk dances, martial arts, and sacred dances. *Torbat-e Jam*[75] (Figure 6.4) is a ritual dance honoring the sun. Men traditionally danced with weapons and a warrior spirit. The dance recalls a time when

75 Torbat-e Jam is also the name of a city and the capital of Khorasan province.

Figure 6.4: Torbat-e Jam folk dancer in Razavi, Khorasan, Iran.
Simin Shakeri, Wikimedia Commons.

harvest tools were used as weapons of defense. Sticks are now used instead of daggers, swords, or harvesting tools in these dances. Still one of the most popular types of traditional dance in the Khorasan region, *Torbat-e Jam* is derived from the Khorasan sama, a dance to worship the sun and earth. Using warrior movements to display honour and convey protection, it is a beautiful celebratory dance performed in a large circle.

Like Torbat-e Jam, *chobazi* originated as a sacred ritual dance but today is danced as a martial arts dance. Two chobazi dancers face off with sticks in a competition of male strength and prowess. The dance begins with the sticks on the ground, intersecting at right angles. The dancers move and step in opposite clockwise and counterclockwise circular patterns (Mürer 2023, 226). The dancer with the shorter stick attacks the other who holds the longer stick on the defensive. Following the attack, the dancers trade sticks and roles and the dance repeats. Among the Kurds in Khorasan, the dance is defined by the movements of the dancers, the manner and rhythm of striking sticks, and the footwork.

Another sacred Khorasani ritual is the Dance of the Wood, or *Rahsatu*, which has two variations. In the first variation, participants dance in a circle with wooden sticks in hand, portraying nature and the connection to the soul. The other variation has two dancers holding sticks in each hand as if they're in battle. This dance illustrates stories of the *Shahnameh*, primarily the battles faced by Rustam.

Attan

Because traditional dances have come to us from peoples who have had their share of difficulties, the dances reflect this, and teach us valuable skills to help us through times of challenge and change.

– Laura Shannon

The *attan*[76] is a traditional Eastern Iranian dance that originated in the Khorasan among the Pashtun tribes who migrated to and settled in what is now Eastern Afghanistan. Historians believe this dance existed as far back as 2,000 BCE with Mithraic roots. In ancient times the Pashtu word *attan* meant "sun," evolving over time to mean "dance."Attan became a warrior dance performed before battle, the soldiers wielding weapons, to gain divine strength. In Iranian folklore, King Yama instructed his army to do the attan before battle to give them confidence and victory. He also celebrated Nowruz by performing an attan with his warriors.

Attan is now enjoyed as a folk-dance during weddings and other festivities. Of the many regional and tribal variations of attan, the most famous are Khattak, Kochyano, Wardaki, Logari, Paktia, Khosti, Kandahari, and Herati. Closely related circle dances can be found in Iran's Khorasan, Sistan, and Baluchestan provinces. The Afghan attan is also originally a battle dance performed in an open circle; the dance gradually increases in speed until members break from the line and begin spinning quickly.

Tribes developed variations of attan, including both men and women who might dance separately, as a soloist, or in a group. The dancers start with singing and small, slow steps; once the pace quickens the singing stops. Various steps are punctuated with singing, shouting,

---

76 *Attan* is also spelled *atan.*

hand clapping, or finger snapping. Props such as handkerchiefs, flutes, knives, or rifles are used and sometimes the dancers will swing swords or shoot their guns in the air. The dance features quick spinning and whirling movements. In wilder versions, men sport long flying hair. During student exhibitions, children may dance in their own lines. Attan is performed to the accompaniment of a *dhol* (a double-headed barrel drum) or separate combinations of the rebab, tanbur, dilruba, harmonium, and dhol (Miller and St. John 2011a, 349). The dance can go on for hours, sometimes all night, slowing as it ends.

Khaf is a village in Iranian Khorasan bordering Afghanistan. Although geographically it is in Iran, many of its inhabitants are culturally Afghani. The attan from Khaf is essentially a men's dance. The dancers travel in a circle, alternately facing the center, spinning to the outside, and then stepping back in the circle. The dance begins with hand-clapping and a simple stepping sequence marking the 7/8 rhythm. As the dance advances the movements become more complicated with a combination of spins, push-ups, squats, leaps, drops, claps, and spins. When women dance it, they omit any acrobatic patterns and spin more gently.

In Herat, versions of attan include urban, village, or *kuchi* (nomadic). The urban style begins with a greeting called Mauzun Qadam (elegant rhythmic step), which is also referred to as Rasm-o Gozasht (tradition and passage), and starts with dancers in a row, the leader standing on one foot.

The Baluchis are a nomadic Indo-Iranian tribe living in southwest Afghanistan, southeast Iran, and western Pakistan, and speak a Persian dialect. Much like the attan, Baluchi dance is characterized by the dancer stepping and turning in and out of a circle. Between the turns, the men often perform squatting steps with their feet fairly far apart. Men and women may dance separately or together. The women's style is more demure, adding graceful leaning movements and abrupt hand gestures causing bracelets to make a sound. They wear long-sleeves that drape below the hand, allowing the fabric to flow beautifully while turning. Golbang is a similar circle dance of the Baluchis that makes use of anklet bells which add a rhythmic ring to the dance.

Zurkhaneh: The House of Strength

Make thy own self pure, O righteous man! Anyone in the world here below can win purity for his own self, namely, when he cleanses his own self with good thoughts, words, and deeds.

– The Avesta

Iran has always fostered deep veneration for spiritual and physical cultivation, a search for ideal embodiment of courage, strength, nobility, and godliness, exemplified among athletes training at the *zurkhaneh*, or "house of strength," a traditional Iranian-style gymnasium and system of athletics originally developed to train warriors (Figure 6.5). Today many of these traditions have been carried forward for wrestler training, weight training, and aerobic exercise.

During the time of Mithraism, a zurkhaneh was a house of healing which can be seen in the traditional design that closely resembles ancient Mithraic temples. Ancient Roman Mithraic rituals were similar to those performed today by the *pahlevans*,[77] the wrestler athletes of the zurkhaneh. This ancient instruction of martial arts was preparation for military operations, calvary, archery, hand-to-hand combat, acrobatics, and wrestling. Iranian society still attaches special value to these athletes today. The physical discipline is intended to free the mind and the soul, to develop spiritual courage along with physical strength.

Figure 6.5: Pahlevan Namjoo Zurkhaneh, Tehran, Iran.
Reza Dehshiri, Tasnim News Agency.

The zurkhaneh was predominantly built in the back alleys of cities. Its traditional main room is often sunken slightly below street

[77] *Pahlevan* means "noble," "wrestler," "hero," or "champion."

level to help control temperature and restrict drafts that might harm the perspiring athletes. The dome-shaped roof contains windows to bring in light. Access to the main room is only possible by passing through a low door leading down a narrow corridor with a low roof, requiring everyone to bow in respect as they enter the main hall. In the center of the room is the *gowd*, an octagonal or hexagonal sunken arena surrounded by stands for spectators and booths for sports equipment as well as for athletes to change. Surrounding the court is a gallery for the *ostad* (master) or *murshid* (spiritual leader) and the musicians. The circular shape of the gowd and dome symbolizes unity and equality among all participants.

Central to zurkhaneh training is the use of a variety of traditional equipment which evolved from ancient weaponry such as *meels* (wooden clubs), *gada* (mace), *sang* (a large shield), *zir* (a set of chain mail), and *kabbadeh* (a bow-shaped iron bar). Additionally, the zurkhaneh stone is the same as a shield, and the zurkhaneh drum is reminiscent of a battle drum.

The *sardam*, an elevated and decorated seat, was reserved for the man who directed the exercises with rhythmic drumming and chanting of poetry, including that of Rumi, Ferdowsi, Saadi,[78] Hafez,[79] and other great classic poets, as well as a type of *masnavi*[80] specific to the zurkhaneh called the *gol-e koshti* (flower of wrestling) (Chehabi 2006). Since the early 20th century, the drummer has been called a *murshid*, a title previously reserved for the group's most senior member. Specific rhythms became associated with distinct movements for displays of strength in manipulating heavy objects (e.g., weights and chains), acrobatics, archery, shield-wielding practice, and more. Ritualized wrestling

---

78 Sheikh Muslihud-Din Saadi (Saadi-e-Shirazi), or Saadi (1210-1291/1292), was a Persian poet and prose author widely recognized as one of the greatest poets of the classical literary tradition.

79 Khaja Shamsu Din Muhammad Hafez (Hafez-e-Shirazi), or Hafez (1325-1390), was a Persian lyric poet and mystic whose collected works are regarded by many Iranians as the apex of Persian literature. Hafez is also spelled as Hafiz.

80 A *masnavi* is a poetic collection of spiritual anecdotes and stories derived from mysticism and everyday tales. It also means the book of mysteries.

movements known as *Raghs-e Pa,* are a kind of foot dance for training in martial arts and sports, though it should be noted that participants do not call their activity "dance."

Figure 6.6: Pahlavan of Hossein Golzar-e Kermanshahi Zurkhaneh, Kermanshah, Iran. Photo by author.

Because the zurkhaneh is a place to cultivate the body and soul, the traditional music and poetry inspire bravery and vision as well as strength. The poetry offers meaningful advice for overcoming limiting beliefs. Zurkhaneh sessions start with a set of ritualistic movements and gestures that serve to create a spiritual and focused atmosphere. Following a master-student tradition, the practices are passed down from master pahlevans to younger generations, so respect for elders and masters is core to the institution. Cultivating a sense of community and brotherhood among its members, the zurkhaneh is also a social and cultural gathering place. In addition, it is considered a spiritual and sacred place where physical activity is practiced in the context of spiritual values. Xenophon observed the connection between physical education and self-cultivation among the Persians, writing that by going through many levels of physical training, Persians not only learned physical skill and strength (as well as looking youthful), they also became heroic in mind and character.

During one of my visits to the four hundred year old zurkhaneh of Hossein Golzar-e Kermanshahi (also known as Sangh Tarash meaning "stone cutter") in Kermanshah,[81] I had the honor of training with a legendary pahlavan.[82] To enter the gowd in the center of the zurkhaneh hall one must be pure and humble like a darvish.[83] Regardless of

81 Kermanshah province is in Western Iran and borders Iraq.

82 A *pahlevan* is a wrestler or athlete trained in the practice of the *zurkhaneh*.

83 A spiritual mendicant.

physical strength, he explained, a pahlavan's power comes from inside. Wearing his traditional embroidered trousers (Figure 6.6), he explained that zurkhaneh is a lifestyle that brings us closer to the Divine:

> *This path of Haqq (the truth) is not for everyone. A warrior of light must embody purity, faith, and love. Strength is nothing without a good heart. When a warrior enters battle, he knows the path will be challenging. The fight might take him to his death but it is all because of love. In battle, when the enemy surrounds you and there is no place to go, you hold your sword and spin, creating a vortex and destroying the enemy. Become a Warrior of Light, receive the light from the Divine, spin, and destroy the darkness around you. The greatest warriors of our time were known to be the best whirlers!*

As a pahlavan, physical training alone doesn't make the warrior; devotion is necessary—devotion to community, self, and the Divine. The warrior sama of the zurkhaneh evolved into sacred whirling dances—one kind of warrior fighting the enemies of the country, the other, the warrior of light fighting the enemies of the soul, their whirling aimed at awakening. In these sacred whirling ceremonies, as the murshid drummed and sang, participants would enter a state of ecstasy, test the ego, release dark energy, and become one with the Divine. Today these dances are often performed more as sport, but they are traditional Iranian institutions, appearing either in the zurkhaneh or in village folk tradition, carrying the honor and tradition of the Iranian people throughout history.

The Path of Light.

Dance is a sacred journey of the soul.

CHAPTER 7

Before Medicine There Was Dance

Just as the ancients danced to call upon the spirits in nature,
we too can dance to find the spirits within ourselves
that have been long buried and forgotten.

– Anna Halprin

Since antiquity, dance has been used to promote physical and emotional well-being. Traditionally, people used dance to summon the assistance of potent spirits and the forces of nature needed for healing rituals. The practitioner's mystical communion in dance and music enabled them to channel these powers. In many parts of Iran, with its nomadic culture, dances are still performed to relieve those afflicted with illness or despair. As the afflicted person goes into a trance, they can more easily throw off unwanted energies or illness. The healer helps the patient enter the trance during which the occupying spirit of the ailment is drawn out and dispelled.

The Persian language makes a distinction between the meanings of curing and healing. *Darman*, in Farsi, means "cure" and is about eliminating the effects of disease quickly. *Shafa*, on the other hand, means "healing," and is concerned with integrating body, mind, and soul into a balanced, healthy sense of being. Only when both physical and spiritual dimensions have been treated can it be said that an individual is healed. However, even without a physical cure, healing may be experienced. The satisfaction and peace gained from belonging to a community and achieving spiritual welfare can constitute the most valuable form of healing.

Before the earliest civilization, before written history, dance was born in myths, in ritual, and provided spiritual expression, healing, prayer, and inspiration. Dance is seeking closeness to the Divine and remembrance of its beauty and spirit. Rituals attempt to bridge the relationship between the human and the supernatural. While on a research trip to Iran, I visited and interviewed many nomadic people. They often get up before sunrise, go about harvesting, and live a very difficult life. In the evening, they return to their village or tent, pick up their instruments, sit in a circle, play music, and dance. One of the elderly gentlemen I met told me, "No matter what we go through each day, we know that tomorrow is another day, a reason to celebrate. We celebrate being alive through dance." When the people gather around the evening fire, their music, song, and dance provide connection, solace, and wisdom.

Accounts abound of spontaneous healing during ritual circles—a mute whose speech was restored or someone healed of cancer. In Iran, the details of the healers or healed are not revealed lest they be used as leverage for material gain or status, which deprives it of its spiritual connection to divinity. Mystic orders believe that healing is the power of the Divine and that the healer only conducts this power to those in need. A healer is a sort of tradesman who helps relate the consumer's request to the Divine manufacturer and then delivers the healing power to the patient. To qualify for this position, healers should be physically and spiritually pure and have a deep, regular connection with the Divine.

Magic dance is one means whereby a practitioner may direct healing universal forces to protect, treat illness, and dispel unwanted spirits. Whereas sacred dance seeks to honor supernatural forces, magic dance attempts to conduct them. Magic dance has a communally crucial function. This is apparent in the Iranian ritual of *zar*, in which guides oversee the healing of patients through trance. The ecstatic practice of these rituals shares the same foundations as zikr and sama.

Magic has been practiced by humankind since the earliest times. The mysterious art of magic enables its practitioner to come into direct contact with the supernatural or metaphysical. The word "magic" derives from the ancient Persian word *magu*, the name for the priests or magi. It is the magician's goal, as it is that of the spiritually devout, to penetrate and understand the functioning of the universe. Initiation rituals and religious practices such as prayer, incantation, and dance allow the participant to appeal directly to a higher power, surpassing the mortal and rational condition.

As the intermediaries between the physical and spiritual worlds, magi utilize methods including dance, music, meditation, repetition of mystical formulae, magic amulets, and others we often associate with witchcraft and sorcery. But Iranian healers are messengers who use their intimate relationship with the forces of creativity, harmony, sexuality, life, health, and death to awaken feelings of awe and wonder which nurture the soul, restoring the balance between the inner forces of man and the external spiritual forces surrounding him. It is believed that the unnurtured human soul may become weak, leaving it vulnerable to invasion by unwanted spirits or demons who can take control of the body's feelings, senses, and functions. When this happens, intervention is needed to expel the spirits and demons by activation of inner forces to achieve balance with cosmic forces.

In the domain of childbirth, midwives were the first healers and guardians of life, with knowledge of the healing properties of plants and herbs, animal allies, and earth elements. Female healers, like men, completed a process of initiation whereby the spirits granted them the right to perform. Male and female healers have different helping spirits and different healing and divination practices.

Music and movement are crucial ingredients of traditional magic still used today among Iranic tribes. Drums and other instruments, sometimes a belt, sieve, wooden serving spoon, staff, mirror, or cup with water may be used as ritual objects. Magic robes, mimicking beasts and wild animals, accessories, and wild solo dances, enabled the magic healer to communicate with spirits and direct them to restore balance or dispel unwanted energies. Even today, some aspects of Iranian folkloric dances resemble the movements of these rituals.

One example of magic dance is the *lazghi* from the Khorezm region of northwest Uzbekistan. The people there are descendants of Iranians. Legend has it that the soul did not want to enter the body because it was so dark and frightening. The creator therefore sent sounds to attract the soul so it would enter the body where it would begin shaking the fingers, hands, arms, shoulders, neck, and head. Khorezm lies right beside the Amu Darya River, an extremely cold region. The Khorezm people would dance around the fire sometimes imitating the fire itself, or animals or each other as a way to get a little warmer during the winter. These movements were collected over time into a lively dance with characteristic fluttery hand movements, postures, and gestures resembling the movements of birds and animals. It features a lot of trembling, shaking hands from a loose wrist, clapping, snapping fingers, *beshkan,*[84] and knocking sticks together to make noise. Shouting or hissing sounds chase away bad spirits or expel them if they've entered the body.

The Iranian *guati* and *zar* are two rituals that collect a group of dancers, chanters, and musicians to call upon the spirits to heal the ailing. Similarly, traditional rituals of lament facilitate communal grieving. Both forms of magic dance may be found in Baluchistan in southeastern Iran and use the power of trance to help cure the afflicted of oppressive forces and bring them calm and resolution. The Baluchis are descendants of Iranians who moved to the region in the early 10th century CE. Their lifestyle is famous for special celebrations and feasts. Originally nomadic sheep or goat herders as well as camel breeders in the greater Iranian region, the Baluchis speak Rakhshani Baluchi, an Iranian language. They still live in rural areas, although some now live in cities and towns.

Guati

Love sometimes gets tired of speaking sweetly and wants to rip to shreds all your erroneous notions of the truth that make you fight within yourself, dear one, and with others, causing the world to weep on too many fine days... The Beloved sometimes wants to do us a great favor: Hold us upside down and shake all the nonsense out.

– Hafez

The *guati* ritual is an exorcism performed by the Baluchi tribe of southern coastal Iran. *Guat* means "wind" in the Baluchi language, referring to a mysterious ill spirit, a "wind" that can invade the body. Someone possessed with guat has their spiritual, psychological, or physical

84 *Beshkan* is a traditional finger snap using the index fingers of both hands clasped together.

balance disturbed, affecting their soul. The privilege of leading a guati is passed down within the tribe and a tribal leader must permit or grant the right to perform the ritual as it requires a trained healer, musicians, and watcher at all times.

Before starting the guati, the spirit healer leads the group in imitating the movements of animals and planets, shaking their heads and performing other difficult movements. Men and women gather around the bonfire in the middle of the circle, drumming, chanting, playing music, singing, clapping, dancing. Music is played until the guat that possesses the afflicted person manifests. Spiritual poetry is recited including verses in praise of their ancestral lineage.

The women, who remain on their knees for much of the performance, are veiled in fine fabric beneath which they are heavily adorned with henna, jewels, and headpieces; believing gold and silver to be effective in treating some diseases, they shake their jeweled hands and forearms to help energize the treatment; they unfurl their long hair, toss it with their heads, and enter a trance. The women can continue for hours and the ceremony can last all night.

The ritual entails several stages, depending on the severity of the afflicted. As participants toss their heads, clap, and chant around the fire, they call the afflicted by name. Either the continuous repetition of the music or the healer's movement leads the guati patient into a trance or state of ecstasy; they may fall, shake, dance, shout, and cry. Eventually the afflicted person's soul compels the body to release the negative energy. The patient either recovers or collapses in convulsions to be later revived. In the former case, the session is considered finished and disbands. Otherwise, the gathering is repeated the following nights.

Ecstasy itself is the boundary between life and death. All ritual practices can push participants into a state of trance whereby they may experience the descent and return of consciousness. The person who reaches a trance stage succeeds in accessing supernatural powers. In this realm, music and dance are practiced as medicine. The term "guati" can refer to "psychological" patients who have recovered through music, as well as to a form of heatstroke for which the cure is dancing and music. Despite dissimilarities in culture and distance between continents, ritual practices around the world use chanting or rhythmic music and cadenced movement of the head, with a leader controlling the tempo of these movements, guiding their participants' minds to flow in and out.

At one time, every village and district in Baluchestan had a local spiritual healer who specialized in curing anyone in need. It has been claimed that the absence of therapeutic music and dance invites an invasion by the guat spirit (St. John and Miller 1987, 191).

Zar

You provide the motion, God provides the blessing.

– Persian proverb

The *zar* ritual may have been introduced by African trade brought to Iran during the Indian Ocean slave trade and is said to be influenced by the African voodoo tradition. Zar has been practiced in North Africa, Iran, Iraq, Oman, Zanzibar, Ethiopia, East Africa, Egypt, and Sudan. Today it is usually performed in the southern part of Iran near the Persian Gulf.

The word zar is thought to be derived from the Arabic verb *zara*, or *zabar*, which means "becoming visible" or "perceptible." In Farsi, zar is also the word for the afflicted who is lost, in ecstasy, or completely drunken. Zar also refers to any type of spiritual possession that harms health. In the Amharic language, zar means "evil," and it is believed there is a genie named Zar who entered the Islamic world from Abyssinia. The word *munzara* is used to describe a participant in the zar ritual.

The afflicted for whom the zar ritual is convened typically request the ceremony because of a troubling illness caused by an occupying spirit that is felt to be causing an illness, physical handicap, chronic pain, mental illness, or even social unluckiness, which is also considered an illness. It is believed that when someone is possessed with negative energy their spirit is *havaiee* (lost and confused). The purpose of the ritual is to reconcile the afflicted with the visiting or "possessing" spirit through supplication and placation.

Each zar has its special character and music and may last from one to several days. Participants gather around a fire pit while a ritual leader lights a fire and pours a special substance into it. Men and women sit together in the assembly chanting and beating drums or bells; special music is played and people dance around the fire repeating healing words, invocations, prayers, and incantations, to achieve communication with the afflicting spirit. Offerings are made to the spirit, including incense, food, drink, and symbolic items to satisfy its demands and seek its departure. All those who are tired sleep in the circle during the day. The ritual typically resumes at nightfall.

The person who facilitates the ritual is called Baba Zar (father zar) or Mama Zar (mother zar). They may also be addressed as sheikh (male chief) or sheikha (female chief). The sheikh or sheikha leads the one to be healed in repetitive movements to repetitive music to induce a hypnotic effect on both the dancer and the spectators. When the afflicted can identify the spirit, the spirit is drawn into dialogue. Arcs and contractions of the rib cage and abdomen are the signature moves of this ritual. The dancer's moves synchronize with the drumbeats and steadily increase in intensity. Once the dancer moves more intensely, or as a spectator reacts to a song, the sheikha and their assistants stand directly over that person, drumming and singing, encouraging maximum strength and participation in the dance. This intensification of the charged atmosphere assures the success of the zar.

Eventually, the dancer collapses into a trance but is later revived. As the dancer's hands emerge from beneath the veil, they salute the four compass points, North, East, South, and West followed by obeisances to the four elements: fire, water, air, and earth. She touches her abdomen, heart, and head, quickly flicking her fingers toward all who are present to spread good energy, peace, and spiritual love. Throughout the zar, individuals may experience a sense of relief, catharsis, or even a feeling of being cleansed from the affliction. It is believed that the spirit departs once its demands have been met.

Laments

I felt in need of a great pilgrimage, so I sat still for three days.
– Hafez

Throughout Iran's history, different beliefs, religions, and cultures have existed, bringing with them many diverse practices. Regardless of origins, funerary practices called upon the power of lamentation to enable the community to collectively grieve, heal, and rekindle its energy. Iran had two very different periods of funerary practices and beliefs. The first, marked by fairly standard practices of burial and entombment, started sometime in the third millennium BCE among those who would, over many generations, eventually divide themselves into Indian and Iranian cultural groups. These practices were similar in some respects to those of many surrounding ancient cultures.

The second period was marked by Zoroastrian culture and belief (Sipper n.d.). After the person died, it was believed their soul would walk the earth for three days while the deceased's family offered prayers and animal sacrifices to help the soul find its way. After the soul descended into the underworld, the only way he or she could be cared for was through regular offerings given by the descendants or heirs of the deceased. Most of the offerings were made during the first year after death but could continue for up to thirty years after the person died. On the final days of each year, known as Hamaspathmaedaya[85] or All Souls, the family of the deceased would make offerings to sustain their ancestors (Sipper n.d.).

Today in Lorestan and parts of Kurdistan, *Khaskam Rara* or *Khankam Rara* ("Dance of Death") is held at the passing of khans (community leaders), nobility, and important people. In this processional ceremony, a person holding a container of flowers greets mourners, who rub flowers on their head, shoulders, or clothes upon entering the mourning place.

---

85 Hamaspathmaedaya is the Zoroastrian name for the festival celebrated upon the final five days of the Iranian year at the time of the vernal equinox. It is now being celebrated as the Farvardinegan festival.

After the procession, participants form a circle holding hands and dance around the deceased making counterclockwise movements while bending up and down as a musician plays the *davul*.[86] The dance is accompanied by traditional music made by drums, flutes, and sometimes stringed instruments. Meanwhile, a chorus of men chant the phrase *khankam rara* as a facilitator recites verses describing the good deeds of the deceased. The dance is deeply emotional, with participants expressing their sorrow through movements, facial expressions, and sometimes vocalizations. The ceremony is a communal expression of grief and support during the mourning process. The ritual reflects the close bonds within the community and the reverence for departed loved ones.

In the south of Iran, a processional dance is performed whenever there is a death in the community. Since the sea is important and much of the population survives by fishing, a special dance ritual named the *Dammam Zani* (Call of the Sea) is performed. Instead of mourning, it is a celebration, as community members believe that the soul reunites with the Divine upon the night of *oruj* (ascension). The *sanj* (hand cymbal) and *dammam* (drum) are played in a peaceful rhythm. The sanj is played with pure intentions and because dark forces are afraid of metal, as they accompany the dammam musicians they are freed from negative energies. The beginning and end of the Dammam Zani ceremony is announced with a trumpet call.

Collective mourning and crying is also a custom in Iran, performed mainly by women. The ancient sacred chant *mur khani*, a deeply significant and somber observance, is offered as prayers and longing for the dead. The simple vocals, derived from sounds of nature, evoke profound sobbing. In many parts of Iran, women cut their hair to show sympathy and grief for someone who has passed. Hair is a sign of power and strength, and in mystic culture, hair symbolizes being one with the Divine. As a symbol of longing, protest, or entreaty, cutting the hair is a great sacrifice. The *Shahnameh* mentions women cutting their hair as a way of releasing anger and sadness.

---

86 The davul, dhol, or tapan is a large double-headed drum that is played with mallets.

Sama ceremonies are also part of the funerary tradition of Iran, especially the Kurdistan region. *Chap sama* (left whirling) has been practiced as a means to guide the soul of the deceased to the Divine and embark on rebirth. Whirling to the left allows inner mourning and longing, while also communicating joy that the soul has reached the angels. The Mevlevi[87] ceremony called *Sheb-i Arus* ("wedding night," honoring Rumi's death, also known as the "night of ascension") is derived from the older Iranian chap sama, which honors the reunion of a soul with the Beloved. The original ceremony was known as *Shab-é Oruj*.

Dance as a Pathway to Inner Healing

Dance, when you're broken open. Dance, if you've torn the bandage off. Dance in the middle of the fighting. Dance in your blood. Dance when you're perfectly free.

– Rumi

When one dances freely, a magical process occurs in the body. A huge amount of energy is set in motion that sweeps away blockages, old memories, and unexpressed frustrations, restoring balance and a sense of well-being. Dance can make people euphoric and help them process the struggles of life, to feel more joy and happiness and shake off stress and anxiety. Today, studies show dance is a mood enhancer and can help in the treatment of depression, lowering the activation of the amygdala (which generates fear and aggression), reducing levels of stress hormones while releasing hormones that boost positive emotional processes in the brain (Poikonen 2017).

Regardless of the style of dance or music, the main instrument is the body. Regular dancing supports individuals in showing appreciation for their bodies and themselves, improving physical and mental health and vitality. It strengthens the body's organs, including the joints, muscles, and bones, and improves heart rate, blood pressure, and the electrical

87 The Mevlevi (or Mawlawiyah in Farsi) Sufi order originated in Konya, Turkey, founded by the followers of Jalal al-Din Muhammad Balkhi Rumi.

potential of the muscles. By exercising both sides of the body at once it helps develop and maintain balance. Researchers have noted that dance and movement therapy has been associated with greatly improved self-esteem (Lidicker 2018).

Dance gives one the power and energy to progress. It helps enlighten the mind, allowing for creative thinking, problem-solving, and healing. Because dance requires substantial physical and cognitive engagement, it improves muscle tone, strength, balance, coordination, memory, and attention. Harmony with the rhythm of music is effective in creating mental balance. Dance builds self-confidence, concentration, and communication inside and out.

Dancing with a group fosters empathy and strengthens connection among people. As a social experience, it is a wholesome recreational activity, making it easy to develop new friends with common interests. Dancing is a means of healing and connection across cultural and language barriers, enhancing cultural awareness, unity, and peace. Our common humanity is revealed when we dance, create, and perform together, thereby enhancing the health and integration of the individual, family, and greater community.

Neuroscience researchers have found that empathy has cognitive, affective, and kinesthetic dimensions, creating mental, emotional, and physiological experience. Studies have shown that simply witnessing another person performing a movement or expressing an emotion or behavior can fire an identical set of neurons in both the performer and the observer (Behrends 2012, 107). Just as hearing a story about injustice evokes strong emotions in most people, watching a dance performance about that injustice will also move them. An audience feels the emotions expressed through the motions of a dancer—whether it is pain, loss, fear, joy, or love. So even without actually engaging in dance, those who observe dance share in the experience of the dance narrative and its positive benefits.

To encounter the sacred is to be alive
at the deepest center of human existence.

– N. Scott Momaday

CHAPTER 8

The Sacred Seven

Arise oh day! The atoms are dancing!
For him the spheres and wind are dancing
Souls ecstatic with joy are dancing
I'll whisper in your ear where they are dancing
Each atom in the wind or desert
Is good-natured, like this, we are enchanted
Each atom, whether happy or sad
Is bewildered by the sun, happy without reason.

– Rumi

Most world cultures hold certain numbers to be especially significant, and these numbers are reflected in their religions and spirituality. For the Iranians, the number seven symbolizes spiritual and material perfection and is a number of great importance within their culture, mythology, and spirituality. In Iranian mysticism, the number seven relates to spiritual awakening, introspection, and the development of wisdom.

In Zoroastrian cosmology, there were seven creations, which included the sky, water, earth, plants, animals, humans, and fire. When Ahura Mazda cast a beam of his pure light into the empty void, life began in the form of a lotus blossoming forth from the archaic waters. Once the lotus blossomed, it opened the way for Anahita, the goddess of the cosmic ocean. Riding on her chariot pulled by four horses, Anahita traveled the seven seas to wake the creative deities. Homa, goddess of the sky, awoke and created a round empty shell of rock crystal, passing beneath as well as above the earth. The crystals were the stars of the universe. Ufratu, the Epirus River, goddess of rivers and streams, was awakened, connecting the rivers of the seven major kingdoms, which flowed through the land, creating mountains and valleys.

The Wind gave the news to Verethragna, the Persian god of victory, courage, and martial prowess, who with his strength created soil on the land. From the depths of the land rose Ameretat, goddess of plants and animals, who introduced flora and fauna and planted the Tree of Knowledge. The butterflies and nightingale carried the news to Vayu, the goddess of air and breath, who created humanity, connecting breath and soul to the body. The human was the sixth creation.

The number six is considered an unfavorable number as it is not complete. For humanity to become complete, they needed to receive light. In ancient Iranian mythology (since before Zoroastrianism) the seventh creation was fire, representing the birth of Light, allowing humanity to perceive the difference between dark and light. This started the cycle of life and the Earth began to spin and orbit around the sun, creating day and night.

All these creations were seen as interconnected and part of the divine plan. Rain flooded the low-lying regions and water divided the land into seven regions called *Haft Keshvar*, the seven kingdoms. Each region was associated with a specific geographical area and had its own unique characteristics. The central region, the Khvanirath, as large as the other six put together, was inhabited by humans. The world would endure for fourteen thousand years, starting from the creation, with seven thousand years spent in the act of creation and seven thousand years in maintaining it.

When Cyrus the Great freed the Jewish people to return to Judea, they took with them many concepts from the Persians, including the importance of the number seven. The Jewish Bible, as well as the Quran and ancient Egyptian mythology, all commonly mention that the earth was created in seven days. The seven days of creation are sometimes metaphorically interpreted to represent stages in the soul's evolution.

Like many ancient civilizations, the Persians divided time into a seven-day week. Each day of the week was associated with a celestial body or planet, a deity with special attributes, as a focus of prayer and ritual. Sunday was named Mehr Shid in honor of Mithra, the Sun deity. On this day, representing covenants, life, unity, and friendship among all, people would gather to honor Mithra, give thanks, and ask for forgiveness. Monday was dedicated to the bright and luminous moon, Mah Shid. Tuesday was dedicated to Bahram Shid or Verethragna, the god of victory who fought for light over the forces of darkness. Wednesday is associated with the god of rain and arrows, Tyr Shid, who prevented drought when Ahura Mazda asked him to shoot an arrow into the clouds to bring rain. Thursday is for Ormuzd Shid (another name for divine light), the god of invocation, granting power and strength. Friday is the day of Anahita, the goddess of water, symbolizing prosperity. Saturday is the day of Kewan Shid, whose name means "big planet," and is another bringer of light and illumination.

Figure 8.1: Tomb of Cyrus the Great is built upon the seven sacred steps to heaven, Pasegadae, Iran.
Photo by author.

The number seven appears repeatedly throughout Iranian history, culture, mythology, and architecture. There are seven walls surrounding the city of Hamadan, seven steps of the tomb of Cyrus (Figure 8.1), and six noblemen along with Darius the Great (known as the seven warriors) who took the kingdom from Bardiya.[88] There were seven aristocratic classes during Sasanian rule and seven original Iranian tribes. In Zoroastrian burial customs, the deceased were placed on elevated structures known as Towers of Silence of which there were usually seven. Iranian mystics honor the *Haft Tan*,[89] the seven souls who manifested from angels to help guide the affairs of man.

According to ancient Iranian mysticism, the soul is composed of seven parts, as is the physical body: matter and sensation, the body frame,

88 Bardiya was a false king of Persia who was slain by Darius and six noblemen. Darius subsequently ascended the throne as king.

89 *Haft Tan*, meaning seven people, is also spelled as Haftan.

nervous system, skeleton, muscles, astral body, ethereal substance, and the spiritual essence. During life, the seven elements work together in the physical dimension. After death, the parts of our physical body pass, leaving only the spirit, which through the persistence of good deeds, unites with the Creator. This concept later became the core of Sufism and "the seven levels of being." Since dance and music are closely associated with mysticism, it is unsurprising that the number seven has special meaning in the realm of sacred dance.

The ancient Persians, like many cultures, recognized seven primary colors: red, orange, yellow, green, blue, indigo, and violet, which are in turn associated with different energies of sacred objects, elements of nature, and emotions. The rainbow is sometimes used as a metaphor in Iranian mysticism, each color corresponding to a particular stage of the spiritual journey or a different aspect of the Divine. All colors united represent the Divine.

Seven appears prominently in Iranian festivals and is essential for both Nowruz and Mehregan. Both holidays involve getting the *Haft Seen*[90] tables ready with the "seven articles" symbolizing the triumph of light over darkness. The seven branches of the sacred trees, the seven branches of Nowruz, and the seeds of the seven chains of the seven fruits of Nowruz all demonstrate the sacred significance of the number seven.

The Persian epic, the *Shahnameh,* tells the story of *Haftkhān-e Rustam* (The Seven Thrones of Rustam),[91] in which he overcomes seven obstacles as a part of his heroic deeds. A similar tale in the *Shahnameh* is the Seven Labors or Seven Battles of Esfandiyar. In this legend, the Kayanian Prince of Iran and hero of the Zoroastrian holy wars must

---

90 The *Haft Seen* (seven S's) is a traditional Iranian New Year custom of decorating a table with seven symbolic objects whose names start with S. These elements are *Sabzeh* (wheatgrass grown in a dish), *Samanu* (sweet pudding made from wheat germ), *Senjed* (sweet dry fruit of the lotus tree), *Serkeh* (vinegar), *Seeb* (apple), *Seer* (garlic) and *Somaq* (sumac). In addition to these elements, Iranians tend to put other items such as a mirror, candle, colored eggs, a bowl of water with an orange floating in it, goldfish, coins, hyacinth, and traditional sweets and pastries.

91 The Seven Thrones of Rustam is also known as the Seven Labors of Rustam.

conquer seven obstacles as he suppresses a rebellion and rescues his two sisters, who are held captive by the King of Turan.

Beyond the seven entities of creation that the deities shepherded together to start the cycle of life, a supernatural and infinite eighth entity is believed to exist beyond our perception. Like many spiritual traditions, Iranian mysticism often describes multiple realms or planes of reality. The term "Seven Heavens" describes a progression of spiritual states, levels of existence, attainment, ascension, or transformation. Each signifies a higher "ladder rung" of awareness or realization. The concepts of *Haft Keshvar*, *Haft Wâdi* (Seven Valleys), or *Haft Šahr* (Seven Cities) are similar. According to Attar,[92] mystics define the *Haft Wâdi* or *Haft Šahr* as the pathway a seeker must travel to receive enlightenment. Additionally, a seeker must manifest and unite the Seven Creations of Life to be one with the Divine.

The Yarsanis[93] believe there are seven sacred mountains in Iran and India associated with seven mystic saints who are believed to reside within them. According to Yarsani and other Iranian mystic traditions, prior to Adam, seven angels (*yazatas*) were created to guard the holy creations of the universe. These angels appear in human incarnations during different epochs, and in the Fourth Epoch they appeared as the following seven saints or *Haft Tan* (Seven Souls) responsible for the affairs of the inner world: Benyamin (Benjamin), Davud (David), Pir Musi, Pir Mustafa, Khatun-e Ramzbar, Pir Baba Yadegar, and Shah Ibrahim. Each of the Seven Souls is associated with a different day of the week, color, taste, feeling, flower, or animal.[94]

Upon the creation of the world, Jupiter formed seven *Sepehrs* (heavens), guarded by the *Haftorang*, seven stars also known as the seven

---

92 Abu Ḥamid bin Abu Bakr Ibrahim (1145–1221), more commonly known as Farid ud-Din or Attar of Nishapur, was a Persian poet and Sufi philosopher who had an immense and lasting influence on Persian poetry and Sufism.

93 The Yarsan mystics practice Yarsanism, an esoteric tradition founded in 14th century Iran.

94 For more about the Yarsani see Chapter 14: *Companions of the Sun.*

companions. These stars played a protective role, shielding the Sepehr from potential destruction. The domain of the Sepehr was composed of seven parts. The first Sepehr was the home of clouds. The second Sepehr was the home of the stars.

Within the second Sepehr were: the star *Tishtar* (Aldebaran), the commander of the east; *Haftorang* (Fomalhaut), the guardian of the south; *Satevis* (Antares); the guardian of the west; and *Vanant* (Regulus), the guardian of the north. The polar star was the commander of all stars.

The third Sepehr was the position of the especially bright stars, followed by the fourth Sepehr as the position of the Moon. The fifth Sepehr was the home of the Sun, followed by the sixth Sepehr as the place of *Emshaspandan.*[95] The seventh Sepehr was the throne of Ahura Mazda.

In Persian metallurgy, seven primary metals were recognized: gold, silver, copper, iron, tin, lead, and quicksilver (mercury). These immutable elements held not only practical but symbolic significance in their culture, including in mystical alchemy. In Iranian-Islamic alchemy, the work of physical and chemical transmutation was paired with psychic and spiritual processes. The alchemist was tasked with climbing a ladder of spiritual transformation, its steps symbolized by each metal and its hue. The darkest, heaviest metal (lead) indicated ignorance, which must be transformed at each stage, the color becoming more luminous until it reaches the brightest white or the perfect radiance of gold (associated with the sun).

In Iran, there are seven sacred rivers or water sources: Tashar, located in the city of Nowsud; Hanita (or Anahita), located in the Dalahu Mountains in Kermanshah province; Zamzam, Kosar, and Tahour, are all mythical or extinct and have no known location; the sacred water of Ghaslan (Figure 8.2), known as the holy water of Anahita, also in the Dalahu Mountains near the tomb of Baba Yadegar (it is said that Baba Yadegar dug this spring himself); and the river Vazghel may be found in the village of Havar. There is an eighth sacred river, the Alwand, now located within the borders of Iran and Iraq.

---

95 *Emshaspandan* is a mythical place of manifestation, a place where newly created creatures appear.

Figure 8.2: Sacred water from the Ghaslan river, Dalahu, Kermanshah, Iran. Pictured: Seyed Salman (left) and author (right).
Photo by author.

In Persian folklore, the mirror is said to project seven reflections, even though we can only see one. The magic mirror that belongs to the evil queen in the fairy tale Sleeping Beauty was likely based on this belief that mirrors portray more than we see. In Iranian mysticism the mirror has multiple meanings and as a symbol reveals deep truth:

> *Have you ever tried to see your own heart in the mirror? Have you tried to put aside the seven reflections and only see the nothingness in the mirror? Have you ever tried to understand the mirror? The mirror never speaks. It is always silent… The Blessed ones are those who have mirror-like hearts… Try to see the heart itself.*
>
> – Shams i-Tabriz[96]

It is believed that humans have seven personalities, based on seven heartbeats and seven feelings. According to Sufi spiritual psychology,

96 Author's translation of Rumi's *Mathnawî-yé Ma`nawî* IV: 2460-2486.

there are seven special psychospiritual energy centers known as the *Lataif-e-sitta.* They are imagined to be spinning disks of energy corresponding to bundles of nerves, major organs, and areas of the body that affect our emotional and physical well-being. Within each disk are seven levels of consciousness. These concepts are applied to whirling and sacred dance, especially in the Dance of the Seven Senses. In Iranian sacred dance, the hands are said to be an extension of the heart center, so naturally, there is much focus on hand movements.

Ancient Iranian mystics and the Magi believed that humans are born with seven souls, influenced by the power of the seven planets: the Sun, Moon, Venus, Jupiter, Mars, Mercury, and Saturn. These souls manifest through the seven senses of vision, smell, taste, hearing, and touch, plus the vestibular and proprioception systems. The vestibular system located in the inner ear, refers to our perception of our movement, speed, balance, and coordination. Proprioception is the body's sense of its position in space, with receptors in the muscles, tendons, and joints.

Yarsanis name seven sacred sounds to be used in music, prayers, and healing. In ancient Iran, there were seven initiatory stages of behavior needed for one to understand the mysteries. There were seven doors to enter the shrine, there were seven altars, seven prayers, and seven ladders for one to ascend from the world to reach perfection. In the Iranian mystic tradition, the human body is said to have seven levels of being and is composed of seven sacred elements, including flowers, animals, birds, colors, and stars. Each bird, animal, or flower serves as our guardian and protector. The soul must connect to and find all its sacred elements to be complete, thus uniting with the Divine.

Echoes of the Infinite.

. . . Hear us, O Mazda! Thou livest
in truth and in heavenly gladness;
Cleanse us from falsehood, and keep us
from evil and bondage to badness;
Pour out the light and the joy of Thy life
on our darkness and sadness . . .

– Excerpts from *Zoroastrian Magi*

CHAPTER 9

Traces of Mysticism

God bears in mind all prayers made to Him, past, present, and future; those made by ordinary people as well as the believers in many Gods.

– The Avesta

It is hard to define mysticism precisely, however mysticism would not exist without spirituality. Spirituality is the belief that there is something greater than oneself, something more to being human than a sensory experience, and that the greater whole of which we are part is spiritual or divine in nature. Mysticism is a form of spiritual reasoning and is the path and practice a mystic follows to be closer to the Divine. Mysticism "is a belief that personal communication or union with the Divine may be achieved through intuition, faith, introspective religious practice, or sudden insight as opposed to more traditional forms of public worship" (Emerick 2008, 12). In practice, mysticism leads to the dissolution of one's personal will into that of an ultimate reality, Truth, or God. One can reach this ultimate reality through different means, such as art, music, dance, religious ceremonies, and worship.

A mystic is guided by the Divine speaking through the heart, which also receives messages from nature. Omar Khayyam, Hafez, and Rumi all wrote their poetry with the influence of nature, spiritual energy, and the elements. When we open our hearts and listen, we realize that everything in nature speaks, everything in nature has a soul, and everything in nature has a face. When you truly believe everything in this world is there for a reason and you respect that, then you are a mystic. Mystics welcome their sorrows, walk among difficulties, and accept their circumstances. Whatever their circumstances, a mystic helps create smiles in others. A natural mystic is enthusiastic about educating themselves and others about real life, and their training can never be complete; they are always learning.

In early civilizations, when science and knowledge were limited, people trusted their intuition and imagination more than reason or logic. People resorted to instinctive perceptions to make sense of the world's mysteries. As long as civilization has existed, mystical thinking has also existed alongside other forms of thought. Mysticism predates any religious or philosophical knowledge. Iranians believed that the soul guided the mind and body and gave it consciousness. They also believed the universe was guided by a spirit world, comprised of a collective consciousness. This belief in a higher order is the first principle of religion. A Muslim, Christian, and Jew may have religious differences, but they can still appreciate the same common mystical experience. One can be a highly knowledgeable scientist and also a mystic thinker.

A darvish is someone who has studied the mystic world and is granted that title by a master of the path. The Farsi word *dar* means "door" and *vish* is said to mean "the Divine." Some also say that *vish* also means "awakened" or "begs for the Divine." On the other hand, Iranian mythology explains the darvishes as those who built a wall (metaphorically) to protect us against *divs* (demons), thus protecting people from darkness and evil.

Superficially, a darvish may also refer to a wandering mystic, a beggar who goes from door to door, a mendicant. Darvishes believe in two worlds: the physical and the spiritual, the seen and the unseen. Darvishes bridge these two worlds, and may cross the threshold into the spiritual world to travel and work there. They believe it is necessary to reach the state of enlightenment, whereupon the chosen ones will meet the Divine (*Mystic Iran* 2008, 23:22). As a believer in two worlds, the darvish embodies two aspects of being simultaneously, which creates a constant longing for, reaching out to, and awareness of the Presence of the Divine Beloved (Reinhertz 2001, 1).

The essence of a darvish is not limited to one sect or one path. At the moment when Jesus knocked over the tables of the moneylenders in the temple, he was a darvish. Shams-i Tabriz acted in the role of a darvish when he threw the books of Rumi's father, Baha'uddin, down the well and pulled them out dry. Buddha, after abstaining for so long, ate the sweets offered by the women and stepped onto the path of the darvish. In most mystic orders, a darvish focuses on the universal values of love and service, deserting the illusions of ego to reach God. As a mystic, the darvish has a pure heart. In folklore, darvishes are often credited with the ability to perform magic or miracles and may be described as sorcerers.

Ancient Wisdom

Every age of the world has seen awakened souls, and as it is impossible to limit wisdom to any one period or place, so it is impossible to date the origin of Sufism. Not only have there been illuminated souls at all times, but there have been times when a wave of illumination has passed over humanity as a whole.

– Hazrat Inayat Khan

Mysticism is untraceable and mysterious, and that is what makes it beautiful. We cannot apply a date to the emergence of mysticism because it has existed in every age. Similarly, there is no single explanation for where the word *sufi* comes from. Some suggest it is derived from *suf*, which means "wool" in Farsi, and might have referred to mendicants wearing simple, rough, woolen robes. Others speculate that it came from *saaf*, meaning purity. The word *suf* also implies the "other-worldliness" of the spirit in contrast to the body's physical domain. Another explanation is a link with the Greek word for wisdom, *sophia*, or from St. Sophia, a Christian saint who converted to Islam. Other scholars claim the word *sufi* comes from the Safavid dynasty. Some claim that the word Sufi is derived from the Arabic word *suffa*, meaning veranda or porch, the place where those close to Muhammad fervently prayed (Gowin 2010, ix). For Sufis themselves, such debates are of only mild interest. It is being a Sufi that captures their attention.

What we call Sufism today arose within Christian sects residing in and around Baghdad during the Sasanian Empire. Some of these sects had denounced worldly goods and were leading lives of abstinence, prayer, and devotion. They lived a simple lifestyle and were shunned. Nothing in the material world mattered, only the soul. In Iran, Sufism had its roots in the ancient traditions of Mithraism, Zoroastrianism,

Figure 9.1: Sheikh Safi al-Din dances in ecstasy. Ismā'il bin Bazzāz, 1590, Shiraz, Iran. Wikimedia Commons.

and Yarsanism, and later combined Islamic teachings with esoteric Gnosticism (emphasizing personal experience). It embraced the idea of enlightenment through spiritual knowledge and individual effort. Sufism was never limited to Islam; it has existed through all of time. It is a name for the urge in humans to experience reality beyond the senses, beyond the material, beyond belief and form. The Sufi orders that originated in Iran preserved the truths and wisdom of ancient Iranian mystical teachings and the inspiration of the mystic poets.

Persian mysticism and poetry have always co-existed and evolved together. Magis, mystics, and darvishes traveled to foreign lands to study at centers abroad. They carried along their own beliefs and knowledge and brought back new ideas. Mystical concepts encoded in poetry, art, dance, and music spread these mystical concepts among a wide variety of groups and cultures.

In Sufism, love guides and paves the seeker's path to union with the Divine. Through the intoxication of love, mystics learn to let go of their ego and open their heart to the truth that binds all creation. A thankful heart connected to the mind is the ultimate way to unify the mind, body, and spirit. If we have a heart full of love and faith, but a head full of doubt, we're lost. When the heart and mind are connected, decisions and choices are made based on compassion.

Every true religion has both an exoteric and an esoteric side (Miller 1977c, 3). The esoteric side involves secret knowledge only to be shared within a small circle of people with specialized knowledge or interest. The exoteric side is more accessible to a wider range of people. Sometimes when minority religious groups or mystic orders were suppressed or persecuted, they practiced their beliefs secretly to escape detection, developing an esoteric side that remained even after the oppression ended because they believed that their existence would cease if their secrets were revealed. Many traditions, both East and West, still have a hidden, esoteric side.

Sufi communities have existed worldwide, and their practices have been greatly varied. Some Sufis focus on solitary practice and retreat, others on community service. Some stress commitment to one or another interpretation of Islamic law (*sharia*) and others subscribe to a more hidden, inner observance. Some utilize specific methods to cultivate "annihilation in God," and others are more oriented toward a devotional approach. Some practice with a tranquil, somber demeanor and others express themselves in a passionate, "drunken" manner (Seidel n.d.).

Only some Sufi orders practice whirling; all others practice various zikrs or prayers. I have visited some Sufi orders to teach whirling because their order does not. One should not assume that every mystic practices the same rituals. Masters may open their own practices, initiate members, teach and lead students in a unique way. A *pir* is one who leads the masters, community, or order. They have the authority to set guidelines for the path and its members. The pir is believed to be the force connecting the sacred and material. The Sufi lodge (*jamkhaneh,*[97] *khanqah,* or *tekke*) is the center for the communal life of a darvish; it includes the kitchen, sleeping quarters, study, meditation room, and *samakhaneh* (ritual house). In Turkey, Iran, and formerly Ottoman areas like Albania, Bosnia, and Herzegovina, tekke is the preferred term, whereas in Iran, khanqah and jamkhaneh are more common. Often there is a shrine of a Sufi saint (*dargah*) adjacent to a khanqah or tekke.

> *Mysticism is so congenial to the Iranian race, and its influence has been so great in almost every department of their life and thought, that some knowledge of the history and doctrines of the Sufis, as the*

---

[97] *Jamkhaneh* means "house of unity." Some *jamkhaneh* have small inner chambers known as *malas*, where individuals enter a forty-day secluded retreat known as the *khalvat* or *chelle-neshastan* to purify their souls and acquire spiritual knowledge.

> *Muhammadan mystics call themselves, is absolutely indispensable to the student of Persian literature.* (Nicholson 1905, 5)

Since its origins, Iranian culture and art have been strongly influenced by mysticism. Persian music, painting, poetry, and dance all developed with a mystical context saturating everyday life. The roots of this mystical thinking are found among Persian myths and legends, such as the *Shahnameh* by Ferdowsi, as well as among the beliefs and travails of its heroes, kings, and deities. The *Shahnameh* expresses that the Divine is in everything, that ego is closely associated with abuse of power, and that the forces of good and evil are held in balance only with our help.

The deeply rooted spiritual and philosophical wisdom of Persian culture and history is called *irfan*.[98] Irfan traveled continuously throughout the ancient civilizations from Mithraism to Zoroastrianism to Gnosticism, an ancient Greek school of esoteric mysticism. During the Islamic period, irfan was skillfully integrated into the new forms—the ancient beliefs took cover under the guise of Islam while retaining their former essence and were distributed throughout the Islamic world by way of Sufi orders.

Welcoming by its very nature the absorption of other cultures, Iranian mysticism is based not on a single source but on many. For example, Christian overtones have been traced to Ibn Arabi, whose Spanish heritage exposed him to Christian concepts. Hindu ideas that became common in the subcontinental Sufi orders are said to have been brought to Iran and Afghanistan by the Shah Ni'matullah Vali[99] of Kerman. Buddhist beliefs in Afghanistan seeped into the Sufism of that region (Miller 1978, 1). The ancient Iranian prophet Mani (216-276 CE), founder of Manichaeism, traveled far and wide studying Christianity, Buddhism, Zoroastrianism, Hinduism, Rabbinic Judaism, Gnostic movements, Babylonian cults and other mystery cults, to form his own syncretic teaching. Whether one believes concepts diffuse

---

98 *Irfan* may also be spelled *erfan*.

99 Shah Ni'matullahis Vali was a Persian Sufi Master and poet from the 14th and 15th centuries.

from man to man or from God to man, the fact is that Sufism carries traces of many ideologies within a mystic framework.

Iranian mysticism teaches us that all people are equal and that one reaches higher, more refined levels of existence with the Divine only through devotion. Empathy, too, is a recurrent theme in Persian mysticism and its poetry. Leonard Lewisohn writes that "Empathy is the cornerstone of Persian mysticism" (Sumit 2019). The Persian mystics and poets Attar, Rumi, Hafez, Sanai,[100] Khaqani,[101] Ganjavi,[102] 'Orfi Shirazi,[103] Anvar,[104] Jami,[105] and Amir Khosrau[106] all advocated that one spirit of universal connection abounds through all creatures, living or not.

Hafez said, "Love appeared and the whole world was set on fire!" This was uncommon amongst the Sufis in either Baghdad or Cairo and was specific to the Iranian Sufis. Our empathy provides universal vision and profound insights into mind and matter. Coleman Barks writes that Rumi wouldn't even kick a stone because he believed that even a stone had a form of consciousness and it, too, deserved respect! In truth, Rumi wrote that he felt the same degree of love for a stone as he would if it belonged to him (Sumit 2019). In this age of differences and worldwide turmoil, a good measure of empathy and universal acceptance can save us all.

---

100 Hakim Sanai (1080-1131?) was a poet from Ghazni who wrote in Persian.

101 Afzal al-Dīn Badīl ibn 'Alī ibn 'Othmān, otherwise known as Khaqani (1120-1199), was a Persian poet and prose-writer.

102 Nizami Ganjavi (1141-1209) was a 12th century poet considered the greatest romantic epic poet in Persian literature. He is celebrated for his five major narrative poems, including *Layla and Majnun* and *Shirin and Farhad.*

103 'Orfi Shirazi (1555-1591) was a Persian poet born in Shiraz.

104 Qasim-i Anvar (1356-433) was a Sufi mystic, poet, and leading da'i (preacher) of the Safavid order.

105 Nūr ad-Dīn 'Abd ar-Rahmān Jāmī, otherwise known as Jami, (1414-1492) was a Sunni Sufi poet known as a prolific scholar and author of mystical Sufi literature.

106 Amir Khosrau (1253-1325) was an Indo-Persian Sufi singer, musician, poet, and scholar who lived during the period of the Delhi Sultanate.

Today, Iranian mysticism is recognized for its distinctive practices and philosophy, setting it apart from Western mysticism and other traditions. Iranian mystics are known for their sama whirling, daf, and tanbur, their belief in love as the means to reach the Divine, their faith in beauty, and their preservation of ancient mystical traditions. The khanqah or jamkhaneh, the spiritual center of the community, is a place for religious practice, meetings of the faithful, devotional studies, and communal prayers. Mystic leaders have always encouraged the importance of fellowship, brotherhood, and self-sacrifice as well as opposing oppression and supporting the community. As practiced by the Khorasani and Yarsan mystics today, the spiritual centers are headed by a community master or pir, who institutes a code of conduct and identifies the special fellowship of the center's residents, patrons, and followers (Lewisohn 1999 Vol. I, 111-112).

A common cultural thread in Iranian mysticism is seeking and nourishing beauty. Living in the ancient land of Iran was as beautiful as it was challenging. The wide variety of climates and ethnic diversity resulted in a multiplicity of traditions, customs, and rituals, yet profound connections have existed among the people of this land for seven thousand years. Regardless of their ethnicity, Iranians have spared no effort in creating beauty and reaching for perfection. The long history of monotheism in Iran comes from this impulse.

Due to geographic isolation and other factors, compared to other cultures the Iranian mystic traditions have been less adulterated by invaders and alternate theocracies. While some ancient roots of music and dance were lost, in Kurdistan, Lorestan, Baluchistan, and other regions, one can still see the origins of the ancient traditions. They have kept the ancient music and movements alive. This is why Iranian mysticism such as the Yarsan culture is so essential because they have preserved their traditions from Mithraism until now. Their beliefs were held secret and they refused to allow foreign invasions or cultural influences to alter it. This is a culture frozen in time, unlike other mystic orders with many outside influences.

In the Footsteps of Mystics

The Darvish who gives away
the secret teachings, and all he owns,
as freely as his own breath...
That Darvish lives by the grace
of someone else's hand.

– Rumi

Mysticism involves two types of knowledge: the knowledge of the heart and the knowledge of the mind. For those pursuing the darvish path, the most important knowledge can't be found in a book. Those who carry knowledge through oral history are known as the people of the heart. Mystics believe the first and most important knowledge is that which comes from the heart by inspiration and by the Divine. There are also two types of knowledge to study: written ("black ink") and oral ("white ink"). Iranian spiritual knowledge has primarily been passed on by oral tradition. Those who study written knowledge are known as the people of the mind and reason.

Under the guidance of a leader or pir, mystics will gather regularly for study, discussion, reflection, or to sing and move together. These practices deepen both intellectual understanding and the bonds of love and companionship. All Sufi or mystic organizations engage in zikr, a devotional practice in which phrases, prayers, or names of the Divine are repeated. *Sohbet*, a spiritual lecture and discussion, is the means of collective study. Retreat is encouraged for a specified period of reflection in isolation and quiet prayer. The room that serves as a place for retreat (*khalwat*), is a sacred space where one invokes, silently or aloud, the name of God.

In mysticism, one strives to become fully human in a multidimensional sense. One strives to find the Divine and be an emissary of the compassion and mercy of the Beloved. Three types of union with the Divine occur in every religious tradition, and all three are present in mysticism: ecstatic union, intellectual union, and the union of love.

Ecstatic union is a special state in which awareness of one's own body is greatly reduced as the soul is transported to a higher level of spiritual awareness. Intoxicated with the Divine, ecstatics are dissociated from the ordinary world. Mystics honor their ecstatics and affectionately refer to them as "drunken." Many Persian poems use the word *mast* (drunken state) to describe the ecstatic, trance-like state. But such ecstatic experience is rare—only the few are called to it.

All mystics expect to see the Divine after death but they are impatient; they want to experience the ecstatic state integrated into ordinary life. Intellectual union is reminiscent of how Zen Buddhism, Gnosticism, or intellectual mysticism find the Divine by combining intuitive knowing with faith. The object of this union is not an altered state but an altered character.

The class of mystics who wish to know union by Love is the largest because it taps into the strongest emotion of the human heart. The wisdom of the heart is far different from the wisdom of the mind. Appearances can mislead the head; but the heart sees the inner reality. The Sufi relates to the Divine as lover to Beloved. For centuries, Sufis have journeyed deep within themselves, into the secret chamber of the heart where the lover and the Beloved share the ecstasy of union.

Nearly every religion has a version of what is known as the Golden Rule: do unto others as you would have them do unto you. This fundamental ethical concept is intuitive to all people, it appears within the very nature of things. At the core of the Golden Rule are two principles. The first is unity—we are not separate from each other or the earth's community of life. The second is kindness, the compassion and love of this relative world, which is united within the ultimate reality.

The Law, Path, Knowledge, and Awakening

Dedication to purity from birth onwards is best for mankind.
For Mother Earth should we toil, leading all men to the realms of light.

– The Avesta

There are four stages of practice and understanding in mystic orders: shariat (the law), tariqat (the path), marifat (the divine knowledge), and haqiqat (the awakening). The underlying wish of a mystic is to follow and fulfill each of these stages. These stages are also followed by the mystic dancer. Some orders deviate on which of these concepts should be fulfilled first, but it is important to understand these stages.

The first concept is to follow shariat, to follow the rules of the path. Shariat makes the external life clean, orderly, and attractive.

Tariqat is the path in the desert that the mystic would take to travel from one oasis to another. The path is not plainly mapped or marked, nor is it clearly visible. To navigate one must know the area intimately or have a guide. It is a journey that doesn't have a clear end. The guide that helps you navigate is a master instructor, the pir. The tariqat intends to make the inner life clean and pure. Tariqat is the phase during which a seeker also becomes increasingly aware of and responsive to inner guidance.

Marifat represents mystical, intuitive knowledge of spiritual truth, unveiled through experience rather than acquired through rational study. It refers to an ongoing state of harmony with the Divine and with truth. It is the knowledge of the heart, attained by very few; only the prophets, sages, and saints.

Haqiqat is the truth, the real meaning of the practice of shariat and tariqat. It is the learned experience of mysticism and God within. Without such experience, seekers follow blindly, attempting to imitate those who know, those who have attained the rank of haqiqat. Until reaching the deep understanding that comes from experience, one follows the teachings and practices of others mechanically. Haqiqat is less a stage in itself and more the marker of a higher level of consciousness.

Among the four stages, there is a manner for showing respect that comes through graciousness, consideration, and love (Reinhertz 2001, 90). Doing the appropriate thing, at the appropriate time, in the most efficient way possible is known as *adab*. Adab simply means respect with common sense. The expression of adab is shown in courtesy, politeness, and a pleasant social demeanor. The aim of adab is to act and speak in a way that pleases the Divine and the people around you. In Farsi, adab means etiquette, manners, morals, and respect.

To attain the awakening state, sacred dancers and mystics must cultivate eight virtues. These virtues are purity, gratitude, humility, compassion, generosity, patience, knowledge, and discipline. Purity is foremost about our thoughts, words, and actions rather than purity in the body. A person is said to be holy only if their thoughts are pure since thoughts are a reflection of who we are. If we possess pure thoughts, then what we say will be right. Gratitude and humility are the virtues of a minimalist ego. Compassion and generosity are the most essential virtues to have. True knowledge is the source of all virtues. Discipline in daily life means self-control.

There is no certification standard or measure for when one completes a stage; the master will acknowledge the level attained. Ultimately, it is a personal challenge for the seeker to be aware of the level they are working on, the development of their own character, and act appropriately. There are three central ideas in mystic psychology, the *nafs*, the *qalb*, and the *ruh*.

The ruh is the spirit and is directly connected with the Divine, even if one is unaware of that connection.

Nafs is an Arabic term generally translated as "ego" or "self." It carries the sense of "that which incites wrongdoing." The ego is a part of our psyche that consistently leads us off the spiritual path, a part of the self that commands us to do wrong. This includes egotism, selfishness, greed, unending desire for possessions, conceit, and arrogance. The self at its lowest level consists of these negative tendencies, controlled by emotions.

The qalb is the spiritual heart, the center of spiritual knowledge. The qalb mediates between the nafs and ruh. Its task is to control the ego and promote connection with the spirit. In mysticism, the goal is to develop a sincere, loving, and compassionate heart, which has a more grounded intelligence than the rational, abstract intellect of the mind. Just as the physical heart supplies blood to the body, the spiritual heart seeks to nourish the soul with wisdom and spiritual light and to purify the base personality traits.

The term e*shqh*[107] (Divine Love) is used extensively in Sufi poetry and literature to describe spiritual, selfless, and passionate love, as it is considered key to the connection between man and God. There are

---

107 *Eshqh* in Farsi is equivalent to *ishq* in Arabic and *aşk* in Turkish.

three types: *Eshqh-e Majāzi,* natural love, *Eshqh-e Rasūl,* love of mankind, and *Eshqh-e Haqeeqi,* love of God. Natural love is love for another person based on attraction; it is considered a small part of the greater love between the soul and divinity. Love of mankind is that experienced by those who live together as a family, or as a married couple. It is also the love experienced between a master and an apprentice. The love of God is a Divine Love, not based on any constraints or conditions. Other philosophers have similarly described different types of love. British author and theologian C. S. Lewis postulated there were four types of love: affection, friendship, erotic love, and charity (Lewis 1960).

Fanaa is the annihilation or "passing away" of the self through a complete denial of self and realization of the Divine. It may be attained by continual meditation and contemplation on the attributes of the Divine, coupled with renunciation of base human attributes. Some mystics hold that upon fanaa, the self becomes an instrument of the Divine's plan for the world. Those who enter this enlightened state obtain awareness of the intrinsic unity between God and all that exists. The highest state of fanaa occurs when even the memory of having attained fanaa is lost. Persian mystic poets frequently use metaphors and allegories to convey the experience of union with the Divine. Rumi wrote that achieving fanaa is like entering a place where everything is nothing and nothing is everything. Fanaa is like a thumbprint—each one's experience is unique. Many Persian fables and allegories contain Sufi thought with its mystic and moral principles, and classic poets wove such concepts and ideals into stories and myths that were disseminated, popularized, and retold in oral history, literature, and poetry. Three of the most popularly cited fables in Persian literature and thought are The Seven Valleys, The Candle and the Moth, and The Rose and the Nightingale.

Through the language of movement, we connect to the Divine rhythm of existence in dance.

CHAPTER 10

Seven Valleys of Spiritual Wisdom

It was in China, late one moonless night, the Simurgh first appeared to mortal sight. He let a feather float down through the air, and rumors of its fame spread everywhere.

– Attar of Nishapur

The seven valleys of spiritual wisdom are explained in the *Conference of the Birds*, the best-known work of Attar, a 12th century Persian poet who was born in Nishapur, in northeast Iran (Figure 10.1). He was probably influenced to write his epic poem after the short treatise, *The Bird*, by Ibn Sina (Avicenna),[108] in which the human journey is depicted by a bird who is freed from a cage by other birds, and flies off with his new companions on a journey to the "Great King." The group flies over seven high mountain peaks before reaching the king's court.

Figure 10.1: Tomb of Attar, Nishapur, Iran. Photo by author.

In Attar's allegorical masterpiece, The *Conference of the Birds*, all the world's birds meet to decide who should be their king. The Hoopoe, the wisest of them all, proposes that they should find the legendary

108 Ibn Sina (Avicenna) (980-1037) was a preeminent philosopher and physician in the Islamic Golden Age in Iran, considered the father of modern medicine.

Figure 10.2: Monument of Simurgh, Nishapur, Iran.
Photo by author.

Simurgh[109] who lives behind the far-away mountains of Kaf. The birds, searching for hope and wisdom, decide to follow his advice. The Hoopoe leads them across seven valleys, each one representing a stage on the mystic path in the search for the Divine: Quest, Love, Understanding or knowledge of the path, Detachment, Unity or becoming one with the Beloved, Emptiness and Bewilderment, and Poverty and Awakening.

Each valley depicts a human desire, the main challenge of that stage, as well as the ambition and determination necessary to cross further. Overcoming faults and weaknesses brings the seeker closer to the goal. Many birds drop out during the journey, unable to endure it. Those who leave possess a human fault that prevents them from attaining enlightenment. Of the many birds that begin the epic journey, only thirty birds survive and reach the dwelling of the Simurgh. There, the birds fly over the final ocean to the Simurgh's throne where the reflection upon the mirror-like surface of the water shows them the visage of the Simurgh; seeing this, they realize they are the Simurgh (Figure 10.2). Each bird in this fable portrays a common human behavior or trait. The dove represents unity, the swan represents weakness, the peacock represents ego, the falcon represents strength, and so on. By combining their qualities synergistically, they access a greater power that enables them to finally make it to their destination. As we confront darkness, we tend to look for a leader or some external light source to

---

109 Simurgh (SEE-murg) may also be spelled Simorgh. In Farsi it can be read as Si (thirty) Murgh (birds), "thirty birds."

follow, but in the end, it is all of our combined strengths and weaknesses that create the light.

Each of the Seven Valleys teaches us something about life and ourselves. Mysticism was never simply a doctrine to which one intellectually assented; it is a discipline for life, and its followers accept challenges such as the Seven Valleys as a means to learn the true nature of the Divine. Sacred dance is one way to enter this path: one can go on a quest, reach love, gain knowledge and understanding, surrender, create unity, find astonishment, and be awakened. Like Sufism, it follows various stages on a journey to face one's faults to find the Divine. Each stage contains its challenges, its valley one must cross.

In the **Valley of the Quest**, a hundred difficulties will assail you; you will endure great challenges and re-invent yourself for several years. You will need to abandon all that once seemed precious to you until you possess nothing. Even then, you still will have to detach yourself from all that exists. Those who enter here will be filled with such longing they will want to give up completely on the quest. Patience and passion are necessary. In this valley, everything within the seven elements is very sacred to us. The seven spirits enter the souls of seven animals, colors, poets, planets, birds, and flowers. The wandering souls of the seven saints are here to guide us, because as humans we are lost. As seekers, we need to be able to see with our third eye, to feel with our hearts, and to understand with our intuition.

After one has been tested in the Valley of the Quest, one learns in the **Valley of Love** that love has nothing to do with reason. To enter the valley, one must be a flaming fire. True love knows no after-thoughts; with love, good and ego cease to exist. To understand love, one must be willing to burn in its fire. Here, one needs to enter into solitude, to absorb, study, and come to understand life. When we are young, we think that material love will make us happy, but in the Valley of Love we learn about Divine Love and nothing else will make us happy until we find Divine Love within our hearts.

Once during sama I became brokenhearted and started crying bitterly. The pir explained to me it was no ordinary cry. Two kinds of tears are very difficult for humans: losing a loved one and heartbreak.

"A piece of your heart has broken," he explained. It is not like ordinary tears, when we see a movie or break or lose something. As mystics, we give our hearts away, like a moth throws itself into a flame, we throw ourselves into this love, for people, the Divine, things that are important to us. When something tragic happens, a piece of our heart dies. In the end, when it is all gone, and our entire heart is burnt to ashes, our soul is free. This is the outcome of the Valley of Love. This valley can be so beautiful, it will open the heart; but we must risk something to achieve that beauty.

> *In my love, in my valley, the Valley of Love, Love is represented by many things. Love is represented by light, fire, disappearance, disappointment, and discouragement. But love can appear as a friend, sadness, companion, or reason. If you possess inner sight, all the atoms in you will be visible and they will guide you. Only a man who understands the Valley of Quest and is willing to take the risk will understand the Valley of Love. He who undertakes this journey should have a thousand hearts prepared because each heart will be sacrificed for something. At each moment a piece of your heart will break. At each moment a piece of you will burn. At each moment you will long, you will cry, you will suffer. So, I ask you, are you loyal to take this path?* (Attar 1984).

The **Valley of Understanding and Knowledge** has neither beginning nor end and the distance to cross it is beyond reckoning. It teaches that knowledge is temporary, but understanding endures. The soul, like the body, is in a state of progress or decline; the Spiritual Way only reveals itself to the degree that the traveler has overcome his faults and weaknesses. All birds do not fly alike; understanding can be attained through various methods. In the Valley of Understanding, it is important to use one's own methods based on one's own qualifications. Whether an individual is aware or not, there are many realities, and one must understand one's qualifications in relation to these realities. Sometimes too many skills and too much knowledge can make one a failure. Sometimes failure or the inability to get what one wants can unexpectedly bring a person back to success. If a person is aware of their unique set of qualities and skills (including their faults), they know which path to follow. Thus, one discovers one's true value and essence. One learns not to hold onto the grief of yesterday, or carry the sorrow of things that haven't come. Crossing the Valley of Understanding is impossible if one seeks pleasantness or gets caught up in futile affairs. Those who find understanding will no longer be preoccupied with themselves (Attar 1984).

In the **Valley of Detachment**, one has no desire to possess nor any wish to discover. The seeker at this stage has developed an indifference to material things, has become inwardly happy, and has no desire to change. To cross this difficult valley one must be roused from apathy to renounce inner and outer attachments so that one can become self-sufficient. This valley teaches us that we must separate ourselves from past behaviors to discover new things in the world. Those who find the determination to endure difficult situations for the sake of the greater good may cross. At this stage, the seeker has lost all ego, and praises the Divine for all creations in the world. The seeker finds the Beloved in whatever is seen, even in the enemy. The world is a place of beauty regardless of what life offers (Das 2019). We need the solitude and despair of the Valley of Detachment to understand why the Valley of Unity is important. When we lose everything and become empty and alone, we might think of changing for the better so we can receive better.

From the Valley of Detachment, we enter the **Valley of Unity** to meet the people we are supposed to be with for our spiritual development. Typically, no matter how many people surround us, we are still alone. We may not find happiness with a thousand superficial friends, but we are happy with five people who understand us. Material gratifications make one happy for a short time, but from emptiness one is filled with joy. We make our heaven and hell here on earth in this life. Upon entering the Valley of Unity, the Hoopoe declares that although one may perceive numerous beings, in reality there is only one. As long as one thinks one is separate, good and evil will arise; but when one loses the sense of separateness in the divine essence, the self/ego will be transcended by love. In this valley, everything is shattered and then unified. Although you seem to see many beings, in reality, there is only one, complete in its unity (Attar 1984).

The sixth valley is the **Valley of Emptiness and Bewilderment** where one loses all passion and fire. There is sorrow and lamentation within, and a burning eagerness. After unification, one forgets again and becomes lost in the Valley of Bewilderment to fall prey to sadness and dejection. In this valley, there is neither the desire to possess or discover. In this valley nothing old or new has value; what you have makes no difference. How can one continue? One has lost the path.

In the Valley of Bewilderment, there are another seven journeys to take, seven walks, seven ecstasies, seven spirals, and seven circles. We have seven voices. We have seven *maqams*[110] (place, location, or melody) and seven stages of departure and arrival. We have *oj*, the level of reaching the heavens, and *moj*, connections with our roots. There are seven ways to enter the soul. When you learn the stages of *fanaa* (annihilation of the self) that is when you enter the Valley of Bewilderment, the vast valley. Until then you are not able to reach it. Until then you are not ready, or the Master might not consider you to be ready.

There are various stages of fanaa. One stage involves becoming one with the master—one learns to fall in love with people irrespective of their age or gender, and so you become devoted to your master. Another stage is to become one with the breath through exercises and listening— the senses of smell, sight, and touch become heightened. Another stage is the fanaa of the path, whereby the goal is to become one with the sacred text of the path through study. To become one with the light is the fanaa of nothingness. Once you learn and absorb this you may proceed to the next valley.

In this Valley of Bewilderment, sometimes our love and longing become so strong that we are unable to continue the path, so we languish in the Valley. That is why we need to enter the state of fanaa, a place beyond the limits of our physical body where our soul may enter. We seek to train our soul so it may travel without our body. Your physical body will never leave the Valley of Bewilderment. To leave one must learn to transcend the Valley by connecting to one's soul and spirit.

---

110 In Yarsanism, *maqam* literally means "station," "rank," or "spiritual level." It also refers to a spiritual musical mode.

In the **Valley of Poverty and Awakening**, the Hoopoe declares this last valley of deprivation and death nearly impossible to describe. This last stage is referred to as the state of annihilation in the Divine. Now the seeker becomes completely empty of all ego and concepts of a separate self. In the sheer magnitude of the divine ocean, the present and the future world dissolve in obscurity. Realizing the individual self does not really exist, one drop becomes part of the vast sea forever in peace.

We tend to think too much and use our minds more than our hearts. We are obsessed with following directions, rules, or timing. Often we should skip the rules and follow our intuition, be kind to ourselves and have faith. If one needs to stay in a certain valley for a while, then stay and enjoy that valley. Don't worry about the time or the space. The path through the Seven Valleys is not easy; it requires determination and patience as well as a willingness to get back up when life knocks you down. Take the lead of a master or guide, someone who specializes in spiritual knowledge, and learn from that instructor earnestly. Following the path of the Seven Valleys is a way to the Divine, which requires determination, patience, and humility. It is a sacred odyssey, a lifelong commitment marked by dedication, discipline, and profound respect for the spiritual journey.

The Candle and the Moth

A candle has been lit
inside me,
for which
the sun
is a moth.

– Bahauddin Walad

One night a group of moths gathered together, tormented by the desire to unite with the candle. They all said: "We must find one who can give us some news of that we seek so earnestly." One moth flew to a palace door a little distance from the candle and gazed at its light. He returned and told the others what he had seen, describing the candle as intelligently as possible. But the wise moth, chief of their assembly,

Figure 10.3: The moth or butterfly symbolizes man's venture for the Divine light in Persian mysticism.
Valerie Runningwolf.

observed: "He has no real information to give us of the candle." Another moth approached the candle, soaring close enough to the light to touch the flame with his wings, but the candle's heat drove him back. He returned and explained a little of what the union with the candle meant, but the wise moth said to him: "Thine explanation is of no more worth than that of thy comrade." A third moth rose, intoxicated with love, flew forward and hurled himself violently into the candle's flame. As he entered its embrace, he became red like the flame itself. When the wise moth saw from afar that the moth had unified with the candle's light, he said: "This moth has accomplished his desire, but he alone comprehends that which he has attained. No other knows it, and that is all."

The sincere seeker of the Divine is drawn to the light, approaching closer and closer until willingly abandoning all and diving into the flame, where all traits of ego are consumed. The allegory of the moth tells us there is no way of knowing God except by becoming one with him. God cannot be known from the outside. God cannot be experienced so long as "you" are there. Only when "you" cease to be, when you lose yourself in God—then and then alone will you know.

The moth's willingness to face the pain of burning in the flame is a metaphor for the seeker's acceptance of the challenges and difficulties encountered along the spiritual path. The moth's annihilation by the flame is fanaa. When we reach fanaa, we are the moth in the flame. Before then, we prize beauty and belongings, thinking they will make us happy, or we hope to achieve love by charming others. But ultimate love involves risk, relinquishing personal desires, and throwing ourselves into the fire of love, sacrificing ourselves to understand love's true meaning.

The Rose and the Nightingale
Love, Longing, and the Beloved

The rose offers to me thy message of love.
I offer to thee my Devotion in Rose.

– Unknown

In Iranian mysticism, as in many other religions, the rose is a sacred symbol appearing throughout mystical writings. It symbolizes love, passion, innocence, sacrifice for the beloved, longing, the unfolding of higher consciousness, realization, and the mystery of union with the Divine. There are many mystic references to the rose symbolizing the Beloved to whom the earthly lover might channel Divine Love. The rose symbolizes Divine Love indirectly because the rose is the symbol of the heart which is the seat of the soul.

Figure 10.4: The rose is a symbol of the heart.
Valerie Runningwolf.

While the rose (*Gol-e Sorkh*) is a metaphor for beauty and perfection, the nightingale (*bolbol*) symbolizes the devoted lover of beauty. Humans are always seeking, longing. When we seek Divine Love we become the nightingale seeking the rose. Longing for its beloved, the nightingale sings to the rose unceasingly, inspired by its beauty, and singing even more vividly on the days the rose blooms. In Sufi thought, the nightingale's song and the rose's beauty are not separate entities. They are manifestations of a deeper, unified reality, representing the union of the lover (seeker) and the Beloved (the Divine).

Love, it should be remembered, includes pain and anguish which is symbolized by the rose's thorns. In order to reach the Beloved there are seven thorns the mystic has to pass. The more difficult the beloved is to reach, the greater the lover suffers. The goal of love is union, but just as love demands union, so also it demands separation, without which it cannot exist. True love proves itself by becoming more intense when the beloved is far away. The nightingale's longing is the test of her love.

The Mevlevi Sufis use the Persian phrase *gülbang* as the name for a ceremonial prayer that usually concludes a gathering. "Gül" means rose and "bang" means voice, so gülbang refers to the voice or sound of a rose and is a metaphor for the song of the nightingale. The *Ruh-i Gulab* (Soul of the Rose) is a phrase for the Divine essence of the rose. It is thought the absolute perfected essence of the rose exists within the flower itself, just as the perfected essence of the soul exists within the human body (Chishti 1985, 112). The moth and the nightingale are both victims of longing for the Divine. In their art, the poet, dancer, and artist convey the mystic beauty of the candle or the rose we seek.

Seeking a Spiritual Guide

Unless you really want to keep stumbling on this path alone,
then sharpen your sight on the dust of a spiritual master's foot.

– Rumi

To take the path of a mystic or sacred dancer, one must search for the truth rather than entertainment or material profit. Spiritual practice begins in the form of study, meditation, and zikr. As the practice moves forward and becomes challenging, the student requires the help of a spiritual guide. One of the main principles of nearly all mystic orders is the importance of a spiritual master. Mystics believe that a master, when recognized and accepted, can guide students along the right path to enlightenment. The journey forward under a true teacher's guidance is a challenge, but the greater challenge is preparing oneself for such a journey. The student must look inside and ask what they are looking for, if it is really necessary to understand and learn about the Divine, how resolved they are to meet the goal, and what can help guide them through this path. No goal that comes easy has value.

Some instructors claim that one can choose whatever approach one likes and adapt it freely. Unfortunately, many students take this too far. Rules and struggles are necessary to achieve true freedom, which is not freedom of the ego but freedom of the soul. When one chooses this path, one must use common sense, be responsible, and follow the rules to guide oneself and be aligned with others. When one is a darvish or mystic, one needs the discipline to follow the process, the path, and to understand what the soul (not the ego) needs.

Putting one's trust in the wrong guide carries the risk of complications, despair, and loss. One should choose a guide who has integrity and expertise. Just like an engineer or mechanic must be highly qualified to install highly complicated equipment that our safety relies on, a spiritual guide must be competent and qualified. Be aware of who you learn from and trust for guidance. One cannot call oneself a master or guide without legitimate training.

Today, students undertaking the mystic journey often seem more immediately interested in the outer credentials of their instructors, or new-age trends, rather than in their own inner being and qualities. The presence of a teacher who knows the way is one of the essential elements in both a spiritual path and sacred dance, but the student must also be qualified in order to receive the instructions of the teacher. There is a close correspondence between the student and the instructor. The practice of meditation and concentration given by the teacher helps a qualified student open the gates to understanding the Divine.

It is important to understand that only some musicians may be mystics, and not every whirler one sees is a darvish. Some can be great dancers, yet have no idea what sacredness is. One can find a qualified teacher in dance and music, but it isn't as easy to know if that instructor is spiritual. To uncover the difference, you need to ask good questions. An instructor should prioritize the principles and truth of their profession over their ego. Do they understand the laws of the mystics, the rules, the way, the path, and the truth? Pay close attention to the way the teacher is using words because many false people can be quite intelligent and manipulative with their words. Anyone may call themselves a darvish or a Sufi, yet not be a good example of one.

Discussions of Iranian mystic thought fill volumes of books today, including those of many different orders. An understanding of Iranian mysticism is absolutely indispensable to the student of Persian literature, music, art, and dance. Explore many sources, both online and in print, to discover more details and different perspectives. There is no final level of understanding; it is an ongoing venture as one seeks mystic knowledge and awakening. The path of a mystic or darvish is not a destination but a journey that encompasses years of dedication and profound respect. It is a lifelong commitment to cultivate spiritual depth. It means embracing humility and denial of ego to surrender to divine will. The mystic path rests upon sincerity and authenticity. Honoring the wisdom of the predecessors and the spiritual traditions, the darvish seeks the profound inner transformation of a purified heart, expanded consciousness, and heightened awareness, all a process that unfolds over many years. A mystic is truth-seeking, is receptive to making a first-hand connection to a higher power, and values faith more than ego. In order for an emerging mystic to be best prepared to enter a sacred ritual they should have a knowledge of basic mysticism and poetry, have received training in contemplative breathing, meditation, and meditative movement, have been working with a spiritual guide, and be willing to open their heart.

The Wheel of Stillness.

The gift of learning to meditate is the greatest gift you can give yourself in this lifetime.

– Sogyal Rinpoche

CHAPTER 11

Awaken the Soul

Make everything in you an ear, each atom of your being, and you will hear at every moment what the Source is whispering to you, just to you and for you, without any need for my words or anyone else's.

– Rumi

Effective breathing and meditation practices have been performed and perfected among all world cultures. These methods help focus the practitioner on deeper transformation and spiritual development by reducing distraction and opening insight. Meditation increases one's capacity for compassion, awareness, confidence, and benevolence and helps one find a sense of purpose. One of the simplest ways to reduce stress is to simply focus attention on the breath. Breath awareness is a form of "entry-level" meditation that anyone can do for an immediate sense of relaxation. It helps the mind focus on the present and can serve as a foundation for deeper meditative states. If you enjoy it, breath meditation can be a gateway to the broader practice of mindfulness, whereby one learns to stop battling with one's own stressful thoughts and feelings to accept and appreciate life ("Breath meditation," 2014). Combined practices of breathing and meditation help one control and enhance the experience of the mind and body.

The earliest known description of breathing meditation in Persia is found in the writings of 14th century authors (Ernst 2012, 133), including a voluminous encyclopedia compiled by a noted Shi'i scholar and physician, Shams Amuli, describing the Sufi five-element breathing technique. A more detailed Persian text acquired in 1622, written by a Persian intellectual in India who became interested in yogic practices of breath control, also described a breath control method dividing the breath types corresponding to the classical physical elements. These methods have been adopted as the Sufi five-element breath technique.

Connecting with the Elements

May the flames of Fire inspire and transform you.
May the gentle breeze of Air purify you and set you free.
May the solid ground of Earth uphold and sustain you.
And may the blessings of flowing Water make you wise.

Breath brings life and sustains and heals our bodies and minds, connecting us with all of life. For thousands of years, seekers of mystical traditions have engaged breathing practices to enhance their spiritual growth. Rumi, one of the most well-known Sufis, spoke highly of the practice of conscious breathing. Effective breathing and awareness of one's breath is universally practiced in mindfulness. It is also one of the first, most fundamental basics of dance. A sacred dancer is always aware of the breath. Initially, dancers can be so focused on learning movements and choreography that they overlook effective breathing, but the more integrated one's breathing, the more relaxed and present one is able to be, providing greater fluidity of movement and rhythm. Appearing stiff in dance could be a result of ineffective breathing. Although we think of breathing as a natural skill, life experiences can stifle our ability to breathe effectively.

Nafas (breathing) is the cause and result of every movement in life and of life itself. The regularity and quality of one's respiration significantly impacts a person's well-being. Focused and mindful breathing can help purify and balance our emotional disposition, invigorate and heal the body, and reduce attention on the ego. The mystics believe that ineffective breathing leads to the accumulation of nafs, the ego. When we breathe effectively with intention, we are in tune with life-giving nafas; if not, we struggle with nafs.

Proper purificatory breathing is the result of practice. Conscious breathing is much more than simply exchanging air in and out of the body; it is founded on an assumption that different energies and vibrations exist that man needs to feed his inner life. Breathing exercises are sometimes disguised as prayers or physical activities; sometimes they are produced involuntarily in people; sometimes they are labeled with a definite religious or philosophical meaning, like "invocation of the name of God."

Our breath connects us with all living things through the four physical elements of earth, water, fire, and air. In mystic meditation and breathing practices, the physical elements correspond to ancient alchemical concepts, including a fifth philosophical element known as ether, a celestial energy that fills all spaces, which the alchemists called quintessence. Ether does not have a physical presence but heat, light, and sound are believed to be transmitted through it. It connects all living things to some degree, including those beings that exist outside our normal perception. Together, the five elements sustain and purify the body.

Iranians believe each breath is associated with an angel and/or an element: Jabra'il (Gabriel, earth), Mika'il (Michael, water), Izrail (Azrael, fire), Israfil (Rafael, air), and the soul is associated with ether, but not with any angel. Purifying breathing exercises begin by taking deep, slow breaths and imagining that you are sending that breath to different parts of your body. This visualization can help you imagine breathing as an activity that involves the whole body, not just the chest and lungs.

Eliminate distractions, clear your mind, close your eyes, and concentrate on your breath. Visualize the purification of your being on all levels: physical, mental, heart, soul, and spirit. An excellent practice is to combine breathing with walking. To start, try walking three steps on your inhale and three on your exhale; after a while, you can walk five or six steps on each inhale and exhale. This exercise is an excellent way to bring mindfulness to breathing and encourage the coordination of breath and movement. These element or purification breaths may be done each morning, preferably near an open window if that is convenient and if the temperature permits. Practice for ten minutes breathing naturally. Sometimes this technique also involves long breath retention either after inhalation or exhalation. Experience the purification of your being on all levels: physical, mental, heart, soul, and spirit. The following passages offer recitations to practice breathing the five elements: earth, water, air, fire, and ether.

Figure 11.1: The Earth keeps us grounded. It offers a sense of stability and security.

Valerie Runningwolf.

Earth:

The breath of earth connects us to the denseness of earth, its minerals, lush deep soil, and the dust we originate from. Breathing techniques related to Earth may focus on deep, slow breaths that help establish a sense of rootedness and stability. This can help calm the mind and reduce anxiety. Practice the earth breath for patience, endurance, humility, and gratitude.

Inhale through the nose, exhale through the nose. The breath of earth, associated with the angel Gabriel, is deep and grounding. Imagine earth's energy is drawn up through the ground to circulate, replenish, and renew. Slower breathing brings clarity. Relax the body imagining it is part of our great earth, a grain of earth kneaded for generations, inextricably connected with the clay, mud, and soil of the Earth. The sacred earth forms the clay of our flesh and the stone of our bones. As we exhale, golden yellow and ochre flow in all directions across a landscape of never-ending plains. Focus on this scene and try not to think of anything else.

Figure 11.2: Water is the symbol of purification and renewal.

Valerie Runningwolf.

Water:

The breath of water, associated with the angel Michael, brings generosity, repentance, renewal, agility, and release. Water washes away negative desire, acquisitiveness, fickleness in love, and lust, transforming them into benevolence and generosity. Breathing exercises inspired by water emphasize smooth, continuous breaths to promote a sense of ease, emotional balance, and flexibility in the mental and physical state.

Inhale through the nose, exhale through the mouth. Visualize ancient stream beds, and deep pools of sea green water. Imagine a soft rain shower with drops dancing on green leaves and petals. Envision a waterfall of clear energy pouring into you from the heavens above, flowing through your body and purifying anything within you that might block the flow of life energy.

Air:

The breath of air dissipates vanity, vicious wit, and cynicism, transforming them into joy and exultation, releasing self-consciousness. Air is linked to intellect and communication. Breathing techniques related to air may involve mindful, controlled breaths that focus on mental clarity and concentration. This can be particularly useful for stress reduction and meditation.

Figure 11.3: Air is the symbol of mind, thought, and intellect.
Valerie Runningwolf.

Inhale through the mouth and exhale through the mouth. Air flows freely throughout the body, controls breathing, nourishes the cells with oxygen, and helps to give movement to biological functions. Air relates to the sense of touch and the rhythm of change. Air is mobile, dynamic, light, cold, and dry. Hear the wind in the trees, a whispering chorus of rustling leaves, telling secrets. Visualize the color blue, a robin soaring high in the blue sky, her blue eggs waiting in the nest. Imagine the wind blowing through you like a mist purifying you, dissipating conceit and doubt. Listen to the rhythm of your heartbeat. Imagine the Angel Rafael is before you surrounded by clouds.

Fire:

The breath of fire brings a blaze that burns away rage, anger, and spite, transforming these emotions into light, affection, the passion for life, creation, and truth. Practice the fire breath for passion, affection, conviction, hopefulness, supplication, and selflessness. Breathing practices inspired by fire may involve vigorous or energizing breaths to help increase focus, alertness, and vitality.

Figure 11.4: Fire is the symbol of rebirth and transformation.
Valerie Runningwolf.

Inhale through the mouth, exhale through the nose. Fire lights our way for cleansing and transformation. Visualize the color red of a flame or sunset. Angel Azrael is before you surrounded by light. Let the breath flow, concentrate on your solar plexus as you inhale, and then radiate the light from your heart center. Shine this light between your shoulder blades like a fountain of light, up through the crown of your head. Inhaling fire, exhaling light, imagine a purifying fire gathering any remaining impurities or congestion within and burning them into radiance and light.

Ether:
The breath of ether is subtle and refined. Rather than actively breathing, let the Divine breath flow through you. Let the subtle breath of ether dissolve any sense of solidity or density. Let the heart and mind open to be clear and vast like the great sky. Practice the ether breath to address sadness, humility, peace, and acceptance.

Breathe less perceptively in through the nose, out through the nose. You may barely feel this energy moving through your body. As the human being is surrounded by the four elements, we become the fifth. This breath brings in peace, a feeling of unity with others and nature. This is the breath of the soul. Use this breath to be united with yourself, to bring calmness and peace.

Gazing Meditations

There are two ways of spreading light:
to be the candle or the mirror that reflects it.

– Edith Wharton

Focused meditation helps suppress distracting thoughts by focusing one's attention on an object or sensation. While the left side of the brain is occupied with a visual, auditory, or tactile sensation, the right side, the center of creativity, psychic abilities, and magic is free to become a transmitter and receiver. Important messages from the deep inner self, which is connected with the Beloved, may emerge during focused meditation. One form of focused meditation is gazing meditation, which is an ancient Iranian ritual. It can be done between the master and student, with a candle or mirror, or done alone without using an external object. Gazing meditation is done first with the eyes open and then with the eyes closed to train both the concentration and visualization powers of the mind. After closing the eyes, one should keep the image of the object of focus in your "mind's eye." Gazing meditation may also be focused on the facets, colors, and energies of a crystal or gemstone, the vastness of the sky (particularly during sunset or sunrise), or another symbol or image that holds significance to the practitioner. The subject for gazing meditation may also be a flower, tree, mountain, or other entity in nature. It's important to note that while gazing meditation can be a powerful tool, it's not recommended for those with eye conditions or severe eye strain.

The ancient Iranian candle gazing ritual allows the mind to become calm and collected and lets the breath become serene, even, and regular. The eyes are open, the gaze gently fixed upon the flame of a candle placed at a distance of about two feet from the eyes. One continues to focus on the candle until the eyes water. When this occurs, one closes the eyes, makes a cup-like shape with the hands, and places them over the eyes. An afterimage of the candle flame will be seen, which the participant must keep in their mental vision as long as possible.

Rumi spoke highly of the practice of gazing at the Beloved. He practiced it by sitting down across from his master and looking into his eyes, as both held each other's gaze and surrendered to the transformation that ensued. This is Bond of Love gazing meditation. The objective is to dissolve any sense of separation between the student and master so the aspirant can see through the eyes of the master, and possess his virtues, wisdom, and purity.

In the first stage, the seeker imagines the face of his master in his heart and annihilates himself in it. As this annihilation takes place, the lover sees the face of the Beloved in their own face, and they form a bond that enables them to take on the very being of their master. The seeker's soul is illuminated and shines with the light of the master.

The second stage focuses on the seeker's attention. The seeker fixes attention lovingly upon the spirituality of the master which manifests itself within the seeker, raising the seeker above creation. Slowly, the seeker begins to acquire the state of the master.

The third and final stage focuses on the seeker's visualization. In their mind's eye, the seeker imagines the spirituality of their guide as a circle of light and pictures themself in the center of that light. As the master manifests in the light of the seeker's heart, he draws them toward perfection. At this point, ecstasy takes control of the seeker and they leave their being. The master's spirituality will never be separate from this image; whenever and wherever the seeker calls upon that image it will help him. If the seeker, coming into the presence of the master, annihilates and binds themself to that presence, the master can, in a single instant, raise him to the Beloved.

The core of Iranian mystic meditation is being conscious of the Divine at all times until nothing separates meditation, the Divine, and daily life. This core state is called oneness, the complete merging with the Beloved and the cessation of duality. Another meditation called the Contemplation of God is twofold: first, keep your attention focused on God, awakening love in your heart so that you can merge with the Beloved; second, constantly watch your mind so that no other thought except that of the Divine enters.

Mirrors reflect the essence of the soul. The Iranians believed that if one focuses one's gaze upon a mirror, blocking out all but one's own image, over time the reflection will begin to communicate and to ask questions. In answering the mirror, one starts to see divisions. Whatever lies in one's mind will come out and one will see it in the mirror.

Steps to the Sacred

Every step I take is a blessing.

– Rumi

The hands and feet are a communication channel between all that is sacred above and below. The feet stand upon the soil of our ancestors, receiving energy from the Earth. The feet should be on sacred ground when whirling or performing sacred dance and not upon a place of darkness. Do not consider performing sacred dance or whirling when the feet feel a dark energy from the ground. Your feet are a communication path to our ancestors who are buried below and the stance must be grounded close to the earth. Sacred dance is not intended for entertainment. For meditation, prayer, or zikr, feet are washed just as hands would be. To best connect to the energy of the earth a full, clean contact with the feet is needed. The feet are considered to be a connection between you and your angelic form.

The Sufi walking meditation known as *Nazar Bar Kadam* (watch your step) focuses on walking mindfully and consciously with the feet grounded. This is a slow-motion walk, sometimes called "earthing." During walking meditation, one avoids looking about aimlessly, as this distracts from the meditation. One's gaze may be directed, the body relaxed, posture erect but comfortable, and deep, patient breathing must be coordinated with each step. This ritual is often used to warm up before whirling or cool down afterward. There is a difference between a material walk and a spiritual walk. For a material walk our brain is used to walking quickly. The spiritual walk is slow and measured with a relaxed breath. The practice helps condition the brain for slow breathing while walking and fosters a connection with the oneness of Earth.

Zikr: Divine Remembrance

You become the zikr and the zikr becomes you.

– Unknown

In ancient Iran, people appealed to the deities for good fortune, for help in grief, and in praise and gratitude. These sacred chants were their messages to the gods. *Zikr*, meaning remembrance, originated in these ancient prayers and evolved to include rhythmic recitations, movement, and breath control, repetition of prayers and the names of God, either silently or aloud. Any form of meditation including chanting, playing music, whirling, listening to ambient sounds, clapping, silent visualization, prayer with or without fasting, and even thinking good thoughts, can be considered zikr. Zikr may be performed solo or jointly in groups while sitting, standing, lying down, or moving. The combination of sound, motion, intentional breathing, and rhythmic and repetitive processes are a way to focus the mind, achieve a state of mindfulness, and cultivate spiritual connection, eventually piercing into the consciousness and releasing a state of ecstasy. The rhythm of the breath is an essential aspect of the zikr practice. Zikr has innumerable variations throughout the world yet every zikr shares the common purpose of achieving a state of spiritual presence, mindfulness, and closeness to the Divine. It is believed that through this practice, individuals can attain a state of inner peace, transcendence, and spiritual insight.

Zikr requires dedication, time, effort, and self-discipline. Be patient with yourself for your first zikr; most of us drift off or lose concentration until we become more experienced. Unless one is experienced, one should not undertake zikr practice without an accomplished master's direct supervision and guidance.

To engage in a zikr session one must have some object on which to focus the mind—the Divine, an idea, image, or light. Whatever thoughts, ideas, or emotions arise, do not allow them to consume the zikr; let them play out. The natural wanderings of the mind are part of the meditation process. One should observe them with detachment when they arise. Anytime the mind strays, bring it back gently into whatever the zikr is focusing on.

These exercises bring about a transformation of energies, which both strengthen and liberate us from the physical body, even if we are not aware of this happening. The duration of the zikr is determined by the number of repetitions, time, the energy exhausted, or distance covered with the guidance of the meditation leader; it is their responsibility to instruct and carefully observe the participant, lest they be exposed to mental, physical, or psychic phenomena they are not prepared for. As always, one should be careful and thoroughly informed whenever choosing a guide to lead meditation. One should always finish a zikr feeling invigorated and fully refreshed. Never practice a zikr to the point of fatigue—it should end with an exhilaration of the spirit.

In one basic form of zikr, members stand shoulder to shoulder or sit in a circle, hands clasped. The rhythm of breath is essential. On the in-breath one says within one's heart "Aal," and on the out-breath one says "Laah." Among the Iranians, the main texts of most zikrs are Quranic verses or Zoroastrian chants, generally involving God's names or the names of angels, including Persian mystical poems and sacred lyrics. The Yarsanis use the sacred *kalam*, primarily the *Kalām-e Saranjam,*[111] as the main source for zikr. These sacred texts are an inseparable part of the practice. To Yarsanis, the sacred kalam is not meant to be understood by human logic; kept as a *serr* (secret), it carries an extraordinary power of sacred spirit, which can only be revealed to individuals who have the competence.

Reading and reflecting on mystic poetry (especially the works of Rumi, Hafez, and Omar Khayyam exploring deep philosophical and spiritual themes) can serve as a form of meditative practice. Iranians have used sacred words to heal illness and as a cure against spells and misfortunes. The Avesta describes three types of healers: those who heal with medications, those who heal through surgery, and those who heal by sacred incantations. In the Avesta, those physicians who heal by words hold a more privileged status. The belief that divine words can heal all ailments can still be found among Iran's many ethnic groups.

Inviting spirits to come to special gatherings by reciting sacred texts is common. The Yarsanis believe that reciting sacred kalam not only helps heal but influences all aspects of human life, as long as the secret truth embedded in the words is truly heard. Repeated recitations help individuals reach a higher spiritual awareness. Three levels of recitation are recognized: that of the tongue, that of the heart, and that of the secret zikr. In the first level, followers practice learning the words in preparation for the second level, in which followers internalize the kalams and begin to feel their spiritual power in their hearts. At the third

---

111 The *Kalam-e Saranjam,* or *kalam,* is the ancient Yarsan sacred text which is read privately among their privileged few.

and final level, one instinctively comprehends the meaning of divine truth from the words, and divine illumination is present. Individuals who reach the highest spiritual stage by repeating sacred poems gain an esoteric experience that they cannot divulge. This experience will differ from person to person, and each person must achieve the illumination by themselves.

Five different names of God—*Hu, Hai, Haqq, Ha*, and *Hey*—are chanted in prayers or to achieve spiritual upliftment, uttered whenever one takes and releases a deep breath, especially during zikr or whirling. They may be called during a zikr for rhythm, cue, or emphasis. Repeatedly uttering these five names helps one enter the trance of zikr. Hu is the name for "breath of God." In Arabic, Allah means God, and Allah Hu means "God himself." Haqq means "the truth" and is often exclaimed when attaining ecstasy during zikr or whirling. When the words Haqq or Hu are called it means that one's breath is equal to the Divine. Hey is used when asking the supreme being to listen to oneself. Hai and Ha are "invisible" names, expressing a letting go.

Reciting particular phrases or litanies from sacred texts is considered a kind of zikr. Which ones are used varies from order to order, but they are always taken under the guidance of a master. Zikr has two main categories: *khafi* and *jali*. Zikr khafi is a personal zikr that is exercised silently, internally, with elaborate breath control. Solitude in a comfortable place is important for this zikr; the remembrance occurs within the heart and mind. The final step of Zikr khafi is to enter one's own drunken state, the point of ecstasy with God.

Zikr jali is a group zikr recited as a chorus, with choreography, sama, clapping, and music. It is loud, boisterous, high energy, and powerful. These group rituals vary by sect and leader but generally follow a two-part format: seated and standing. Initially, participants sit in a circle and listen to readings or religious songs, chant prayers, and sway. Most vocal zikrs share two aspects: emphatic calling of God's name with controlled breathing through specialized vocalizations, and experiencing God's presence during trance. These two aspects clear the mind to focus on God. Once the sheikh feels that everyone is ready, he signals all to stand to begin the main zikr which involves an uninterrupted crescendo of sound and motion that induces a trance through hyperventilation, sound over-stimulation, spatial disorientation, and disturbed equilibrium. Both jali and khafi, if practiced long enough, can induce auditory and visual hallucinations.

Another type of zikr called *Zikr-e Sirr* (awareness of the heart) involves concentration on the rhythm and beat of one's heart. It is one of the two central practices of the Naqshbandi Sufi, a major school of Sunni Sufism descended from Ali and Abu Bakr. Zikr-e Sirr can be practiced seated or lying down for at least half an hour. One starts by collecting one's dispersed energies back into oneself. The mind and senses are stilled so one can focus on the inner reality of the heart. Next, attention is focused intensely on the place where the physical heart is located, forgetting all else, even oneself. By listening to the heartbeat as a form of mantra, one begins to hear the sound of the heartbeat even during daily life. The third step varies according to the mystic order and source, but in all of them one remains thinking of God, the angels, or one's spiritual master, and stays focused on the heart center while simultaneously cultivating feelings of love for God.

Standing and moving zikr helps seekers avoid the lethargy and torpor that long periods of seated zikr cause and helps invigorate and build strength and stamina. Sama is a wonderful form of moving zikr and can help the seeker get into the flow of their body and experience relief in times of great emotional anxiety or stress. The combination of sound and movement—drumming, dancing, and chanting—gives rise to specific breathing patterns, which may consciously intensify. In dance we go beyond thought, beyond mind, and beyond individuality to become one in ecstatic union with the cosmic spirit. This is the essence of entering prayer and zikr through dance. Zikrs may be accompanied by movements engaged in unison such as when sitting, holding hands and swaying, or nodding the head or moving it rhythmically from right to left, or when standing, the whole body moving from side to side. One's hands may be placed on the heart or chest, or extended right or left in time with the litany. Additional steps and arm movements may be added.

Self-study of the works of Persian poets and philosophers can offer insights into Persian contemplative traditions. For best results, practice the zikr and meditation methods in this chapter only with or as a competent master. The wisdom of an experienced leader is important because it is their responsibility to guide the student and see to their safety. Silent zikrs are for personal use and therefore are safe, but other zikrs are extremely powerful and may be harmful if you don't know what you are doing. Always defer to the master to select and lead a spiritual zikr. Zikrs done without a guide's permission may have an unexpected outcome. Take precautions and be thoroughly informed when choosing a guide to study from. In your search beware of schemes that focus more on a purchase or trade rather than legitimate openness and guidance. We all start as beginners with a limited understanding of the traditional ways. Many of us lack the cultural experience and training. We do not start with the experience needed to lead our own meditation, let alone that of others. We need to follow a guide who has extensive experience and understanding. It is recommended to find a comfortable environment with minimal distractions before starting a session. Resist the temptation to enter a trance as a means of intoxication. Being in a high state of consciousness should be your goal.

A Call to Love

Every child has known God.
Not the God of names.
Not the God of don'ts.
Not the God of whomever anything weird.
But the God who only knows four words
And keeps repeating them saying:
"Come dance with me, come dance."

- Hafez

Hands, particularly the palms, play a crucial role in whirling, zikr, and other rituals. During zikr or any sacred gathering, clapping opens the portal, wakes up the heart and soul, echoes the heartbeat, and is the call to love. By carrying sound through the air, it is also the primary means to dance with the element of air. We clap so the breath hears us while our chanting awakens the angels. Clapping hands has miraculous benefits—creating a burst of vibration that can cleanse negative energy and open up the secondary chakras (energy points) in the palms. But such clapping must be performed in the right way as it is different from clapping at a party or concert. This is a hidden, ancient spiritual practice.

In Iranian spiritual clapping, we receive energy from the right palm and give energy to the left. So it is important to hold the left hand still and clap with the right, which brings in good energy. While clapping, raise the hands to the sky, projecting them as a beacon of energy, signaling the divine realms. The rhythm of music channels the energy of the Divine. When the energy enters the gathering, clapping opens the heart, and the voices and words of the gathering become sacred. When speaking with sacred words, your posture should be pure and sacred—clapping, words, cleanliness, attitude, and praise all combine to create beauty and hope in the gathering. All this needs to combine in order to fall into a state of drunkenness.

Mystics wash their hands before a sacred ritual to ensure they give and receive positive energy. It is said a mystic must have a clean hand, but clean does not necessarily mean hands that are washed, it also means the hand of a caregiver, the one that receives and gives positive things. This is why when we conclude sacred dance or whirling, we kiss the hand of our masters or our fellow darvishes, or we may hold hands, because our hands have received the positive energy our master transmits.

As previously mentioned, various subtle breathing and meditation exercises help prepare one for sacred dance, to relax and enter the present without distraction, and to call on the ancients, nature, elements, and cosmos. And there is no question that awareness of breath sustains our body and is essential for dance. The position or movement of the body is the next factor, whether sitting, standing, walking, performing the motions of zikr, whirling, or dancing. Dancing blends moving meditation and breathing technique and is one of the most healing exercises. When mind and body are combined in focus, one is prepared to make the connection to what is both immediate and at the same time limitless, mysterious, and unfathomable.

Your dance just took me today and suddenly I began to whirl.
All the realms spun around me in endless celebration.
My soul lost its grip,
My body shed its fatigue.
Hearing your hands clap and your drum beat,
I floated up to the heavens!

– Rumi

CHAPTER 12

Dance of the Soul

Every breath we take makes a sound. Every sound forms a word, and every word defines who we are. To be present as a being is to listen to our soul. This, in essence, is our prayer. This is our sama.

Whirling is one of the oldest spiritual acts of the human being, used by the ancient Iranians to connect the body and soul. Encircling and surrounding a sacred object, or sometimes a person, can be a means to endow it with energy and power. Along with music, chanting, song, and poetry, whirling is a wonderful means of communicating with the Divine and creates a bridge between the material and spiritual world. When we whirl we are no longer ourselves; we become what the Divine wants us to be. Whirling is incredibly powerful because it is the physical expression of music and music is a representation of the universe. Whirling is an expression of a profound connection to the deepest levels of reality.

Figure 12.1: Dancing darvishes. Folio from Divan of Hafez by Biznad, ca 1480. Wikimedia Commons.

Whirling lets us break free from the ties that bind us to the material world and reconnects us to the "heart center," which is where love, music, faith, and poetry are found. Whirling is a dance of the soul. When I whirl I listen to my soul, summon legends of ancient times, and become one with the natural ways of existence. The music consumes and transforms me. Free, as if flying, I create expressions with my hands, arms, and face by invoking the energy and essence of elements, nature, and anything that surrounds me. In allowing these energies to take control

I am no longer myself. I am moving yet there is stillness. This is what makes whirling so beautiful.

In small villages, secret gatherings, receiving the teachings of wise men and pirs, I learned the truth about mysticism and whirling. I learned the authentic sacred dance and rituals of sama—unlike anything portrayed in popular culture—which involves whirling, zikr, moving meditations, and prayer ceremonies. In Farsi, sama means "hearing" or "listening," as in listening to poems, melodies, the breath, listening for the voice of the Beloved, or being absorbed in selflessness. Some scholars suggest the word sama comes from the Avestan word *asman* meaning "sky." But in practice, sama may be interpreted as "worship with joy."

According to legends in the *Shahnameh*, Kay Khosrow, the mythical king of Iran during the Kayanian dynasty, was the first person to perform sama. He whirled for five weeks, seeking meanings and secrets from the creator. Ancient Greek historians Xenophon and Herodotus reported that Persian women were whirling, chanting, and playing drums. In Iran, women played an important part in ancient ceremonies, as whirling priestesses. The beauty of whirling has been so enduring that Iranian mysticism and Sufism used dancing as a spiritual means to "become one with the Divine," which is the ultimate goal of this faith. Much later, the advent of Islam in Iran meant Sufism and mysticism became suppressed. For its preservation, the practice of whirling blended with Islamic themes and in time became popular again by distancing itself from previous religious forms, taking on a new appearance.

In the mystic tradition, the phrase *raghs-e ruh* or in ancient Zoroastrian *vasht mana* (both meaning "dance of the soul") is the old, original name for sama, especially in the Kurdistan region. This is because sama communicates directly with the soul. Mystics trained to participate in sama are known as *samazans*. It is said that the samazan is whirling even when they are not physically doing so (McClure 2018, 3), as through the practice of sama, their ego has been weakened, allowing universal prayer to be heard in their lives. Prayer in this sense is not a means of petitioning God for what one wants, but rather a step towards the Divine. Whirling is a spiritual flight ascending through intelligence and love

Figure 12.2: Persian Miniature by Nezami Ganjavi (1141-1209) from the book of Panj Ganj.
Public domain.

to perfection. Turning toward the heart, the samazan grows through love, transcends the ego, meets the truth, and arrives at perfection. The samazan returns from the journey able to love and serve all creatures. Unity, purification, and love are the spiritual essence of whirling.

The Zoroastrian tenets of human thriving form the triad of good words, good thoughts, and good deeds, the Threefold Path of Asha. The symbolism of a triangle in this case suggests that if the triangle points up toward heaven, it represents positive thoughts, words, and deeds, whereas if the triangle points down it represents negative thoughts, words, and deeds. During whirling, a triangle is formed by the two eyes plus the third eye in the forehead; it points up toward the third eye which is open. The ears should be listening to the positive (appropriate music, poetry, or silence). The mouth should speak good words (spiritual, intentional words). Energy released when whirling and during prayer should be kept within. The triangle must be pointing to the sky, to heaven, emphasizing the heart and the spiritual eye.

The third eye, sometimes called the Eye of the Soul, is an eye of intuition and perceives things beyond the reach of our two physical eyes. While the material eyes may be closed at times, the third eye is always open. Even with closed eyes, trust in the spiritual eye can serve as a guiding force for good. The spiritual eye sees things people cannot physically see or even imagine. The third eye reflects the soul or the inner vision, and is the eye used during sacred dance. When whirling, you mustn't use your material eyes because if you do, it becomes a regular dance.

In the vocabulary of a dancer, turns may be spotted or unspotted. Spotting is a technique where the head whips around for each turn, keeping one's eyes fixed on a chosen spot in the room. In whirling, by contrast, vision is defocused to avoid distraction. Whirling uses internal focus to maintain physical position and foster conditions for meditation, whereas spotted turns use external focus. With training, unspotted turns desensitize the vestibular system, which controls the sense of balance and vertigo (dizziness) (Kheradmand 2016).

The word "dance" should not be used to refer to sama, because the mystics themselves would not use that word for something which is a sacred activity. The ritual of sama honors cycles of birth, death, and regeneration. It is more respectful to describe the sacred ritual as a moving meditation or prayer of devotion.

During the ritual of sama, the darvish opens to the Divine. Sama allows the darvish to transcend their everyday self, transforming their state of awareness. It is a means to attain unity with the Divine by integrating body, mind, and emotion. Darvishes practice sama as a means to see outside the ordinary senses and go beyond the material world to reach a higher state of consciousness. Some have visions, others chase away bad spirits, but all experience the presence of the Divine within their heart (*Mystic Iran* 2008, 31:10).

Spinning is universal, having evolved from careful observation of natural laws. Whirling has been practiced in Mithraism, Zoroastrianism, Sufism, and other mystic traditions worldwide, including by the Tibetans, whose whirling style is significantly different. As the first rite of the Five Tibetan Rites of Rejuvenation, Tibetan Lamas believe that whirling casts out negative energy, strengthens the tie between the body's right and left hemispheres, awakens the chakras, and stimulates the energy system. Some practitioners and teachers of the Five Tibetan Rites have adopted movements from Sufi and Iranian mystic traditions. In the 1890s, a researcher, Fernand Grenard, observed that the whirling dance of mystics in Tibet resembled that of darvishes, except the Tibetan dancers covered their faces with masks (And 1976, 36).

In the earliest days of sama, a few devotees would gather together for poetry and song. Later, instruments were introduced. The beauty and sacredness of the music and song drew those quietly listening closer to the Divine; as the music filled them, they became enraptured, stood up, and began to move. Music can be compared to wine and sama compared to the *masti* (drunken, metaphorically speaking). The instruments as well as the melodies have been practiced for thousands of years. Originally, the most important musical instruments during sama were the *daf*[112] and *ney*;[113] the daf represents the human heartbeat and the ney is the breath or the cry of longing for the Divine. Music played on these instruments, in the sacred tradition, helps awaken ecstasy and surrender.

Later, the *tanbur*[114] was added, which is believed to represent the human body, angels, and the voice of God. As these gatherings spread through spiritual communities, more music, poetry, instruments, and movements were added. A leader of the spiritual community began to organize the event, a certain time was set aside, and the gatherings became larger. The devotees would prepare themselves by cleansing or sitting quietly in meditation to still the mind of worldly thoughts. In time, various mystic orders began to meet at their khanqah or jamkhaneh for sacred gatherings and sama.

Whirling brings healing as part of regular spiritual practice. As a mystic or sacred dancer, we deeply believe in the spiritual world which is central to healing and well-being—it is the source of healing energy. For mystics, faith in the Divine resides in the heart. Divine Energy enters the dancer like a radio wave to an antenna, induces the human heart to hold and intensify the sacred energy, then directs it outward to the earth and creation.

---

112 A flat hand drum, usually with metal plates or rings set around the edges of the frame or inside of it to add a jingling sound.

113 An end-blown flute made of cane or reed, which has been played for over 4500 years, making it one of the oldest musical instruments still in use.

114 A long-necked stringed instrument, like a lute.

The Wheel of Mitra: The Origin of Whirling

Whirling around the still point of ecstasy… I spun like the wheel of heaven.

- Rumi

Figure 12.3: The Wheel of Mitra, the Sun God/Goddess.

Valerie Runningwolf.

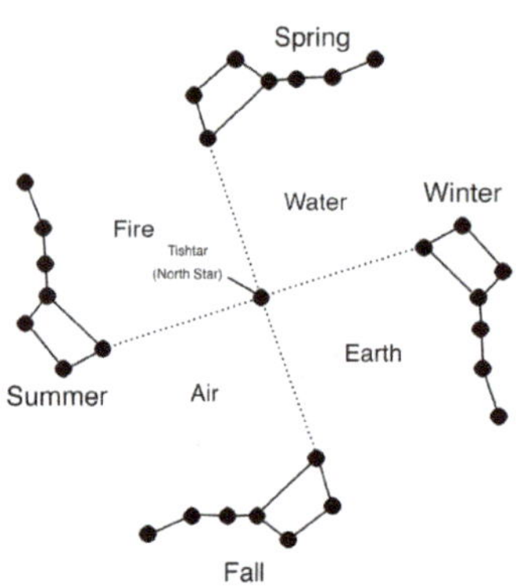

Figure 12.4: The seasonal rotation of the Big Dipper (Ursa Major) about the north star portrays the Wheel of Mitra in the four phases of time.

Aethelwolf Emsworth, Wikimedia Commons.

Thousands of years ago, whirling was a means of praise and reverence to the goddess Mithra.[115] Long before the Islamic age of Iran or the Turkish Sufi Mevlevi order, this primitive dance imitated the planetary motions observed by early astronomers. When a dancer whirled they became the Wheel of Mitra (*Gardune-ye Mehr*)—symbolic of the motion of the sun, the four seasons, the four directions, and the elements—also known as *Charkesh-e Mitra,*[116] *charkesh* meaning turning or spinning, and representing fire, infinity, or continuing creation. The sun was imagined as the center of the wheel; the seasons, directions, and elements its spokes that turned with time.

The Wheel of Mitra also symbolized the significant seasonal rotation of Ursa Major (the Big Dipper) around the north star (Figure 12.4), which for the Iranians was a clear expression of the perpetually revolving cosmos turning around a fixed center on the axis of time—from life's origin, creation, and birth, its rise and decline

115 Goddess Mitra would later be recognized as an androgynous deity, renamed as Mithra.

116 In Iranian mysticism, this symbol is also called *jam* and lends its meaning to *jamkhaneh*, the word for Unity House, a Yarsani place of worship.

to old age, death, and transformation, returning again to creation and birth. This depiction was called *Chlipa-ye Shekaste* (broken cross). The four legs of the cross represent the four elements of nature in our lives, the four seasons, the four sacred directions, the four archangels (Gabriel, Michael, Azrael, and Rafael), the four temperaments, humors, and states of matter and energy.[117] Divide the empty spaces within the cross into another four divisions and this creates an eight-pointed star known as the *shamsa*,[118] another important symbol of Iranian tradition and mysticism, also depicting the sun.

Numerous temples and depictions of the legendary Wheel of Mitra have been excavated in Iran, Asia, and Africa. It appears as a motif in many Iranian buildings, architecture, mosques, gardens, and classical Persian art. The repeated "S" motif is a common protective symbol and the basis for the Wheel of Mitra (Figure 12.5). Traditional Iranian dances often honor the four corners of the Wheel of Mitra.

12.5: Pottery fragment depicting Wheel of Mitra, National Museum of Iran, Tehran.
Photo by author.

In Iran, many warriors would tattoo this symbol on their arms to represent the power and equality of men and women, and their oneness with the sun deity and the elements. The ancient Iranian female fighters (Amazons) also had it tattooed on their left arm as a sign of strength. If one visits Kermanshah today, one will find this symbol everywhere, including in the Bedouin villages. Spiritual women and nomads will tattoo this symbol of power on their chin, hand, wrist,

117 Greek physician Hippocrates proposed the four temperaments as part of the ancient medical concept of humors, that four bodily fluids (blood, yellow bile, black bile, and phlegm) affect human personality traits and behaviors (sanguine, choleric, melancholic, and phlegmatic). The four ages of man are childhood, adolescence, youth, and old age. The four states of matter are solid, liquid, gas, and plasma. Modern physics recognizes 14 types of energy but the ancient four are kinetic, potential, magnetic, and radiant.

118 The term *shamsa* means "little sun," from the term *shams*, meaning "sun" in Arabic.

or arm. Kurdish and Luri nomads draw the Wheel of Mitra on their tent poles to honor that the sun is the symbolic guardian of their flocks. Considered a symbol of light, unity, and trust, it was unfortunately co-opted by the Nazis who used it to symbolize their Aryan Nation. It is, however, still a sacred symbol within Iran, among the Parsis of India, for Buddhists, Hindus, and many South Asian Indic religions.

Another interpretation of the broken cross is that the four elements or directions are spreading out from a fifth element, the soul, at the center. It has also been compared to a diagram for the relationship between the body, soul, and universal spirit, as seen from two perspectives. In both, the spokes of the wheel symbolize the human soul. From the view of one trying to reach the Divine, the center is the human body and the space outside the circumference is the Universal Spirit or Divine. But according to the hidden view of one who has found the Divine or is a prophet, the circumference represents the body which, through the soul, journeys to the center to commune with the Divine (Bakhtiar 1976, 8).

Faravahar: The Divine Messenger

To them, the Pure Mind, who is united in God, through his power replied: associate closely with Truth. Be good and unite with Right-Mindedness. Hold fast unto them.

– The Avesta

The *faravahar*, one of the best-known symbols of Zoroastrianism, is a winged disc bearing similarities to the shape of a falcon, upon which is seated a male figure. There is no record of what the faravahar originally meant when it was created. Scholars agree that ancient Iranian religion and history were disseminated by oral tradition until the Sasanians wrote it down, but once that empire fell to the Muslim Arabs in 651 CE, many of these texts were destroyed including any which might have shed light on the original meaning of the symbol. The Achaemenian Empire may have written and recorded their history extensively, but whatever was written was turned to ash when Alexander the Great burned Persepolis to the ground in 330 BCE.

Figure 12.6: The attributes of the Faravahar.
Wikimedia Commons.

Still, many interpretations of the faravahar exist. According to some, it represents the guardian spirit of light, knowledge, law, and order, as well as conquering ego and finding unity with the Divine. Another interpretation is that it represents the divine power of the king, as it appears prominently on the ancient palaces of Persepolis and Susa. It is believed that when Zoroaster died his soul transformed into a faravahar (the human falcon), who represents the god of the Sun, union, and the afterlife. It also represents Ahura Mazda, the supreme god, and the tenets of Zoroastrianism.

Figure 12.6 shows the different elements making up the faravahar. The human form in the center (1) is said to represent the individual soul, or the adherent, as well as the guidance and wisdom of age. The head of the figure faces forward, symbolizing a positive and progressive approach to life. The three sections in the wings (2) represent good thoughts, good words, and good deeds. Opened to the sky, these wings are capable of flying, full of energy, but require all three in union to support the soul's journey toward higher spiritual realms. The wings also symbolize divine protection. The tail with its three sections (3) represents unity and the Threefold Path of Asha which overcomes the three faults of the ego: Druj (falsehood and deceit), Aeshma (wrath), and Aka Manah (dark thoughts). The two descending "legs" with the loops (4) represent the opposites of Ahura Mazda and Ahriman, good and evil. The circle, from which the figure emerges (5) symbolizes the immortality of the soul, the cyclical nature of life, and the karmic law of reciprocity. The right hand of the figure gestures upwards (6) indicating that righteousness is the only path forward, while the other holds a ring that represents one's oath to Ahura Mazda, pledging to pursue good and forsake the ways of evil. It represents the free will and responsibility of an individual to choose their thoughts, words, and deeds. This ring also reflects the ring of power held by Mehr (Mitra). The tradition of wearing a gold wedding band on the left hand for marital loyalty and faithfulness is derived from the ancient use of a ring as a symbol of commitment.

The Faravahar perfectly symbolizes the whirler in sama and may have been the inspiration for whirling as an expression of prayer—opening one's wings to ascend beyond the earthly world, seeking unity with the Divine. Spinning movement is found everywhere in the universe from atoms to planets and galaxies. The circle at the center of the Faravahar represents this unending spinning movement of the universe. In sama, the whirler spins around the axis of their being, spreading the power of divine grace throughout this earthly existence. Like the Faravahar, the upraised hand of the whirler collects the power of righteousness, and their feet tread on the negative energy of the ego where the Faravahar tail resides.

Sogdian Whirling

A divine dance appears in the soul and the body at the time of peace and union. Anyone can learn this dance, just listen to the music.

– Rumi

During the seventh and eighth centuries CE, the Sogdians, an Iranian people situated in the region now recognized as Uzbekistan and Tajikistan, played a dominant role in the Silk Road trade in East Turkestan, with two major cities—Samarkand and Bukhara—centrally located along this trading route. Sogdian merchants were known for their cunning business sense and skill in serving the growing economic and cultural exchange, using their savvy and influence to open the way for nomads, traders, entertainers, religious teachers, and craftsmen to come together. Music, song, and dance were Silk Road commodities as well. The Sogdians practiced and combined dances from India, Burma, and Cambodia, performing at both the royal court and the public marketplace in every Silk Road town. The Sogdians were Zoroastrian, and after the fall of the Persian empire, many moved to Central and East Asia as well as China, spreading Zoroastrian influence along the way. Some believe Zoroastrianism was the foundation of Buddhism, suggesting the term Buddha comes from the name Ahura.

Very little record is left of the Iranic sacred traditions of the Sogdians, whose descendants are now a nomadic people living in China, but Chinese texts describe the Sogdians as performing several types of acrobatic or energetic dances. Considered the best among Sogdian dancers were those from Chach (present-day Tashkent, Uzbekistan), identified by the Tang poet Liu Yanshi as "Iranian." These young dancers accompanied other entertainers in the Silk Road caravans; some arrived as gifts to the Chinese court, some arrived as slaves from Central Asian rulers, and others came as itinerant free agents, entertaining both Chinese and foreigners living in China.

In particular, the Sogdians were known for performing a now forgotten whirling dance, known as the Sogdian Whirl, described as a "whirlwind with a swirling technique." In its time, it became a genuine dance craze, as the exchange of cultural concepts became a primary function of the Buddhist era of the Sogdian Empire (Houseal 2016). It had even become part of the Buddhist devotional practice, as well as a staple of the Tang dynasty court dance repertory. The Sogdian Whirl accompanied Buddhism as it moved along the Silk Road into China and became extremely popular during the Tang dynasty,[119] taking the Tang capital by storm, as shown in popular Buddhist art from that era.

[119] Tang dynasty (618-907), an imperial dynasty of China.

Figure 12.7: Pilgrim flask depicting Sogdian whirling, China, sixth century CE.

7th/9th century artist, public domain, via Wikimedia Commons.

Since very little record of the dance survives, scholars use artwork to infer how it was done. It was usually performed on a small, circular carpet as the dancers spun in impressive, high energy, full body turns (Figure 12.7).

Dance is lavishly illustrated in the Mogao Grottoes of Dunhuang, and other Buddhist caves in China and along the Silk Road, often filled with complex narrative paintings. This cave art served as historical records as well as spiritual narratives for illiterate people, transcending the many languages spoken. Many important activities took place in the caves, including offerings, teaching, music, and dance. In China today, the palaces display artwork depicting the Sogdian dances, performed to music played on Persian lutes and harps. One piece shows a female dancer wearing a long jacket with extended sleeves engaged in a dance known as the bird dance. Today, many dances of China use this style of quick turns and expressiveness in their dances.

Wall paintings in Cavern number 220 in the Magao Caves show a scene called "The Physician from the East Changes the Whole Earth," painted in 642 CE. Four women dance on small round mats, each in a different posture, encompassed by long streaming scarves which flow, undulating, all the way from above their heads to curl up near their feet. The flying streamer motif is common in Persian miniature paintings as well as Chinese paintings and Chinese and Korean traditional dance (St. John 2010, 26). The Sogdians also engaged in various dances popular during the Tang dynasty. The "Dance of the Barbarian Leap" is a well known work of art from the Tang dynasty that demonstrates the spinning, leaps, and backflips that characterized the dance.

Today, the quick turns popularized by the Sogdian Whirl still appear in many dances of Central Asia and China., and are also still practiced in the zurkhaneh to help athletes train for coordination and balance. Asian martial arts also use quick spins in defensive tactics. Spinning was once used in battle to force assailants away from a surrounded warrior. Spinning quickly, holding a blade in either hand, would make the warrior a "deadly whirlwind" to encounter in battle (Grey 2024, 61).

Devotional Path of Whirling

Dance darvish dance–
Bring the face of God before you.
Only love can lift the heart up so high
That its true color is restored by the sun!
See Him near and clapping,
That Perfect One who fathers Divine rhythm.
O dance darvish, darvish dance,
And know you bring your Master happiness
Whenever you smile.

- Hafez

Iranian mystical dance and whirling emphasize the movements of nature, the elements, and the cosmos, incorporating movements evocative of animals, birds, flowers, trees, fire, water, wind, Earth, and celestial motion. Ancient Iranians worshiped nature and believed that everything in nature had a soul. Their art and dance grew out of their relationship to the cosmic order; their architecture, miniature painting, musical composition, city planning, sacred spaces, and dance movements all comply with their understanding of space and time and the basic underlying patterns found in nature. Whirling is not only circular and cyclic but also spiral, growing and expanding in a way that radiates from the center out. It is also said that the ego can be compared to a circular loop repeating the same cycle over and over again, whereas a spiral indicates the intuited sense of ongoing evolution, development, and transcendence. Iranian sacred dance and whirling are in complete harmony with this understanding and cosmic movement.

There are many kinds of whirling styles with highly varied movements of arms, hands, head, and torso. In the Iranian tradition it is understood that everything has energy we can engage with and embody through the different movements. Whirling gestures capture the energy from the surroundings and release the energy when needed. The direction of the turn can be used for invoking different kinds of energy. Turning to the right, known as *rast* sama, connects to the sun's energy, and was once commonly used for celebrations or moments of joy. However, the ancient tradition of turning to the right has largely been forgotten, overshadowed by the left turn, or *chap* sama, traditionally danced to recognize or overcome bereavement and sadness. This left turn style is the tradition of the Mevlevi order of Turkey and is a celebration of passage for the dead. The Mevlevi and Islamic tradition of turning left for mourning or to honor our ancestors, and in remembrance of dead souls, is derived from a very ancient tradition even mentioned among the stories of the *Shahnameh*.

In Iranian whirling, the hair of the samazan is often uncovered as hair symbolizes the Divine Essence, and tossing one's head and hair is very important for exchanging energy and is connected to the state of *hal* (ecstasy). Hand movements and gestures also are an important part of this tradition. Every movement, finger, and gesture has a symbolism. For example, raised hands pointing above represent the longing for the Beloved, hands pressed over the heart are a sign of humbleness, and whirling with palms on the stomach represents embracing the soul.

During sama, the movements of whirling, singing, chanting, clapping hands, and stomping have significant meanings. Spinning symbolizes the movement of the world revolving, stomping signifies losing oneself and stepping on everything in the material world, and spreading out hands is a sign of overcoming oneself and reaching a state of perfection. Overall, there are seven emotive or sensual levels of spiritual elevation found in sama which are visible in its different elements: verbal greetings or calls, musical accompaniment, physical movements (e.g., head tossing, jumping, whirling), crying, entering trance, visions, and spiritual joy (Miller 1978, 53). The mystics believe the whirling activates the body through the seven levels, to become the tree of life. The feet lie at the first level, the roots of the tree, grounding the dancer. As one turns, the arms open up and become branches. The tree, your body, needs to be watered and nourished, which is done by the music and rhythm, water and "wine of the body." The wind generated by turning stimulates growth. Then the head enters the movement. Once the seventh position is reached, one may enter ecstasy and go into twilight. These are the seven levels embodying the Tree of Life.

Moj to Oj: Descending to Ascending

Man must rise above the Earth–to the top of the atmosphere and beyond–only thus will he fully understand the world in which he lives.

– Socrates

Persian mystical poetry, art, sacred music, and dance can be identified by four levels of mood, energy, or behavior. Dance is the physical embodiment of emotion. Emotions are not just an idea in your head. Whirling invites a state of exhilaration that the Mevlevi Sufi call *badrab*, or "the presence," each step moving us upward toward a new freedom of the spirit, toward ecstasy. As we pass through these four levels we find each has a distinct sensory threshold. These thresholds are stillness and grounding, the flow of the objective observer, the embodiment of the soul through fanaa, and the return to grounding. The levels generally appear in this sequence: *daramad, moj, oj,* and *faroud.*

Daramad[120] (entering) is an introduction, a greeting and preparing, a means to do all that is necessary to begin. In music, this is the point when tuning is finished, in poetry when the poet is about to start his verse, and in art when the artist is about to do his sketch. As a dancer, this may include a prayer giving thanks to the ground you tread on and to the forces that be. Both the musician and dancer respect the entrance or opening of the other. Never at any moment does the dancer enter and start dancing without regard to the opening of the musicians.

Following daramad there may be moj or oj. Moj is characterized by slow movements, a mood like gentle ocean waves. In music, it marks

[120] A daramad is also a genre of traditional Persian instrumental music meaning "prelude."

the period of a *taksim*[121] or a steady motif. The moj is thought of as "earth and waves," and is the point of lower pitch, tempo, or volume. Oj is a point where the music volume, tempo, or tone increases substantially and eventually peaks. The energy of the dance increases with the music, intensifying to a level of high excitement and ecstasy. With oj, dancers will use strong and energetic gestures, emphasizing the strength and vigor of their performance, projecting a sense of power and intensity through their movements. Oj portrays "up," "heaven," or "sky," and this is when you are in a state of drunkenness or ecstasy. Oj is well-suited for more upbeat and celebratory dance styles whereas moj is slower, softer, and less intense. From moj we receive and through oj we release.

The level of energy for oj cannot be sustained indefinitely. Following the oj comes a calming transition known as faroud and a return to moj. From moj, the piece may again cycle to oj and faroud, or the piece may end. As a dancer, one should recognize these major points accentuated in music. In Iranian sacred dance, dancers are adept at interpreting both oj and moj, transitioning seamlessly between the two as the music dictates. Together, oj and moj introduce a balance in dance, portraying powerful and dynamic movements along with graceful and flowing gestures. Dancers often integrate these qualities to express a wide range of emotions in their performances. The choice of oj to moj is influenced by the style of dance, the mood of the music, and the narrative or emotions the dancer wishes to convey.

Waves are omnipresent in our world in many forms such as light, sound, and water. Waves move through space from one point to another along a line, or in a spiral along different levels, according to different intensities, frequencies, mediums, or directions. During whirling, waves follow different directions, paths, rates, and amplitudes according to the body's movement. The pointed index finger is sometimes known as the longing finger and plays an important part in whirling; it is a communication channel between the soul and the Divine. When your

121 A taksim is a solo musical improvisation, a term commonly applied to Balkan or Middle Eastern music.

finger is pointed to oj (sky) and your arm is raised like an antenna, it symbolizes that you are receiving the energy from the heavens and are longing for the Divine.

Whirling in silence, solely to the rhythm of one's heart, enables one to focus on finding calm and peace. In silence, you hear the voices muffled by the busy world. Before there was music we listened to the heart—people started to dance and make music by listening to their own heartbeat. Although circumstances vary, those who practice silent whirling within a group are often more likely to experience and share a wide range of emotions. If you are sad, angry, or anxious, your heartbeat changes. In parts of Iran, healers asked their patients to clap their hands to the rhythm of their heart; as they listened, they could tell if someone was healthy or sick, and could diagnose the ailment. This clapping is a form of zikr in Iran. When we clap, we say it opens up the portal of the heart.

As an extension of the four levels of energy and mood of sama, there are four stages experienced by the participants. The first stage consists of giving respect to tradition and shariat. This is the time of ritual preparation and greetings to honor elders, masters, nature, and God. It marks the mystic's point of departure from the material world. In the second stage, the sacred movements and whirling begin. During the third stage, ecstasy takes control and movements become more dynamic, rising skyward. An awakening occurs, fanaa, the identification of the soul with the Divine and loss of the separate self is experienced. The fourth level is the faroud (landing), marking descent and completion.

Reaching Ecstasy

I breathe fragrance into your heart's essence, tearing away the veil
Of your sorrowful sigh; I am the flute which plays music to your ears,
I am nature's call, the echo of mountains, the wild dance of a swelling ocean.

– Jayita Bhattacharjee

Sama allows the mystic to transcend their limited, everyday self, transforming their state of awareness through the power of ritual. This experience is said to be like dying to this world (fanaa) to be revived in an eternal dance of the soul, eternal life in the Divine (*baqaa*).[122] This is the ecstasy of sama. Ecstasy may be found in the world of dreamers and artists, those who show us the value and sacredness of life and spirit. Every saint has seen a moment of ecstasy and peace, which, however profound, may only be a mile marker upon their journey to ultimate, universal union. Rumi, Buddha, and Christ crossed here. So did Moses, Rabia,[123] and Abraham. These saints crossed into the halls of union and brought back with them the guidelines of truth.

Capturing the senses, ecstasy is the opposite of what is rational and materialistic; it is the sensuous as distinct from the sensual. The word ecstasy comes from the Greek *ekstasis*, meaning "to stand outside oneself." To be in a state of ecstasy is to be filled with a sense of joy too powerful for the body to contain or the rational mind to understand. The state of ecstasy in sama is also known as *mast* or *hal*. Hal is an intense state of the soul, an interior fire, often provoking experiences of self-transcendence. The ego and individual identity may dissolve temporarily, producing a feeling of union with Universal Truth, a sense of "right feeling" with the Divine.

During whirling, the soul and body may be in separate places at the same time. When Rumi was whirling in Konya, people in other places said they saw him. Since he was in the state of fanaa, what they saw was his spirit. One night after whirling until midnight, I left the hall to sleep. The next morning, one of my friends greeted me and said, "I love the way you were whirling while the sun was rising." I was shocked! My friend was sincere but it couldn't have been me. While still in disbelief, another samazan approached me to remark that my sunrise whirling held their attention. Listening, our Baba explained to them that it was my spirit they saw. Even in sleep, one can be in a state of fanaa. I had to sleep because my body was so exhausted, but my heart and mind were left still whirling. There is a saying that when you are so attracted to

---

122 *Baqaa* is the state in which you become a permanent part of the Divine.

123 Rabia al-'Adawiyya (718-801 CE), sometimes known as Rabia al-Basri, was an Arab Muslim saint who is attributed with being the first Sufi mystic in history to advocate love and intimacy as the only true way to reach the Divine.

a place, you can leave a part of your heart there, and that is when you enter a state of fanaa.

Unlike traditional dance, which is aimed at entertainment of an audience through art, ecstatic dance is designed to induce altered states of consciousness, for the dancer to enter ecstasy and offer their body to the Divine. Since entrance into the ecstatic state appears to happen spontaneously, one is said to be seized or possessed by the ecstasy, sometimes regarded as an outside force.

Dance by its very nature is ecstatic. Ecstasy is a feeling of glory, joy, happiness, and satisfaction. The experience is associated with a feeling of timelessness or eternity, one may have a sensation of elevation or levitation, or of being filled by a rising spring or part of a flowing stream. There may also be sensations of heightened consciousness, awareness, or deep stillness and peace, as well as freedom from self, guilt, sorrow, and desire. When a whirler is filled with ecstasy, they feel they have reached an awareness and knowledge of a totally new kind. They are now capable of identifying with the universe, with all living things, and with the Divine. This ecstatic experience, however brief, comes when everyday consciousness is stripped away, leaving only the essential self. An ecstatic experience creates both catharsis and creative inspiration, making the body an empty vessel prepared for the Divine to enter. Once the Divine spirit takes possession of the whirler, it extinguishes their consciousness completely.

Whirling is the purest form of devotional dance. One becomes harmonized with the motion of the universe, a harmony as immense as the planets in our solar system and as small as the electron revolving about an atom's nucleus. Turning with outstretched arms, energy is collected from the environment and redirected through the body and back to the earth. I have had many ecstatic experiences performing sama to live music in a sacred gathering. While turning, I sensed that something had changed and was evolving. Uniting with the music and rhythm, I was suddenly no longer aware of my surroundings nor consciously following my body. As my outstretched arms relaxed, a cloud of energy surrounded and lifted me; as I was effortlessly floating upward toward the ceiling, entirely engrossed in the moment's wonder, I felt the purest joy!

At the same time, the dancer does not attempt to lose control but rather to change consciousness, remaining able to control their behavior and capable of awakening at any time from trance. This ecstatic state is not easy to enter, but with practice in meditation, zikr, breath work, chanting, movement, and prayer it becomes easier. Additionally, the state of ecstasy is not to be entered on a whim, as this can lead to habit, escapism, or dependency. Instead, one should visit the ecstatic realm to carry the experience into the balance and harmony of daily life. Mystics also believe one should abandon their nafs (i.e., ego or personal desires) before entry into sama. One who rejects their ego and ventures to reach spiritual maturity and unity with the Divine is not identified with their smaller self anymore. Sama operates according to karmic law. If one enters sama with good intentions, then good will be returned. If one enters sama with selfish intentions, then it works against them. In sama, we begin to listen to our soul; this is why whirling is known as the "dance of the soul."

Any religion or spirituality may seek nothingness through meditation and prayer. As a whirler, when I hit that point of ecstasy that is nothingness, I am in the state of mast, a completely interior state. In the mystic tradition, there are two states of our being: internal and external. When in the internal state, there are times that I do not remember what was said or done. It resembles the experience of drifting into sleep and entering the realm of dreams. However, when the body is ready to wake up, it wakes up.

As with any form of training, various environmental factors and physical or mental conditions greatly influence performance, creativity, and inspiration, which can differ from one day to the next. Aside from training, the amount of sleep, level of nutrition, and the use of stimulants can create highly variable effects in the outcome of the sama, altering how long or steadily each samazan may turn with minimal exhaustion, distraction, or discomfort. Imam Ahmad al-Ghazali[124] discussed the importance of the time, place, and people involved in the sama. With

124 Ahmad al-Ghazali (1061-1123 or 1126) was a Sunni Muslim, Persian Sufi mystic, writer, preacher, and the head of Al-Nizamiyya of Baghdad.

regard to time, he explained that sama is useless when the mind is busy or when the heart is not quiet and calm. As for the place, sama is unsuitable for any environment where the heart is distracted. He also explained that sama takes a person to the presence of the Divine and separates him from the physical world.

Until sama reveals its power it is essential not to force it, but once it gains momentum, we should not resist it. We must follow the "moment" accordingly. If it arouses, be aroused; if it makes you calm, be calm. To participate in a sama, one must possess enough discernment to receive the Divine Energy and recognize its true value. When that influence shows itself in the heart, it should be honored, and when its power dies down one must not try to hold on. Sometimes one becomes completely lost in the ecstasy and one needs to be revived or roused from trance. That is the moment when it is evident that the Divine Energy has entered you. This is one of the reasons why it is essential to learn sacred dance from the right masters. It is important to honor the spiritual power and respect the sacred traditions passed down through the lineage. Do not use sacred dance, sama, or zikr just to imitate the rituals, movement, and patterns. If you plan on performing, make sure it is done the right way with respect and honor to the traditions. Let the performance be a prayer.

There are many different Sufi orders and mystical teachings. Some involve whirling while others do not. Sufi orders such as the Mevlevi, Khaksar, Qadiriyya, Ni'matullahi, Naqshbandi, Qalandariyya, and Bektashi have their own approaches to sama and/or whirling within their religious community. They have different rules, teachings, rituals, and ceremonial garments. For example, Iranian sama is free-form, manifests earthly energies, spins around the axis of the Sun, and is often known as *shams* sama or *rast* sama for the right-directional turn. The Mevlevi sama is a more codified ritual originally created by Sultan Walad, Rumi's son, after his father's passing. The Qadiriyya sama does not involve whirling but standing and rocking the body back and forth.

We need to be living and thinking purely to be worthy of the Divine and to inspire those we share our art with. My own master achieved this, as have other trained mystics. Advanced technique is not needed in this art form. Often, a new movement is created from within the subconscious during whirling. When this would happen with my master he would smile at the divine revelation. When we practice sama we become one with the circular motions inside us at the level of the DNA, cells, molecules, and atoms that compose us. As Rumi says, we are all atoms and the atoms are dancing. As we enter an interior spiral, we find that inner circle. As we turn to the outside and leave the spiral we venture toward a better understanding of the world. As one brings these spirals and circles into life by whirling, one becomes more aware and better able to communicate with everything. The circle of whirling represents the circle of life.

Iranian dances were once entirely group activities of prayer or celebration. Later, especially after the sixth century, during the Iranian Renaissance, the practice developed a more introspective dimension. This was a time when people started to seek more self-understanding, often through contemplation in solitude, and individual sama began to be practiced in addition to the group forms.

Dancers can become capable of physical effort, prowess, and endurance far beyond their normal powers. Darvishes can whirl ecstatically for long durations without appearing tired or giddy. Some Indonesian dancers can strike daggers against their bare chests without obvious pain or injury (Mackrell 2020), and fire walking, or glass chewing with no apparent pain or bleeding have also been noted.

Most of us dance for the pleasure of experiencing the body and expressing and communicating our emotions. Strong emotional reactions can manifest from whirling. Sometimes the whirler cries when they come out of trance. Other times they feel happiness and joy. It really depends on the dancer and what they see and hear when they enter or emerge from a trance. It is difficult to explain. While in the state of ecstasy, it is as if one is in sleep mode, from which one can whirl endlessly. When one fully falls into sama, it takes control. One must train the brain to wake up under this trance.

Neurophysiological studies have shown that prolonged whirling rotations at a pace of twenty to thirty times per minute are observed to coincide with theta wave rhythms of the brain (Waterman n.d.). Theta brain waves are pronounced when one is in a very deeply relaxed, hypnotic, or meditative state of mind, as well as when sleeping or dreaming. Experts believe that theta waves are the dominant frequency in healing and highly creative states, and are important for processing information and memory. Studies also show that the hormone serotonin is released in the brain in a surprising way during whirling, prayers, or meditation to a higher power. Serotonin brings a sense of comfort and happiness and is often called the body's "feel good" chemical.

Rhythm of the Heart

Only from the heart can you touch the sky.

– Rumi

Sacred dance or whirling is only possible with a healthy, kind heart. When the heart is broken or defensive, the dancer cannot effectively participate in sacred dance. When the heart is sad, it affects the entire body. Mystics believe that undigested grief lets in disease, creating anxiety. Therefore in sacred dance we bow and put our right hand over our heart to show we will support and protect it. We cover the heart like a shield so that darkness doesn't penetrate. If you are sad or depressed and want to communicate with the Divine, put your hand on your heart. Feel the rhythm of your heartbeat. If you concentrate on that rhythm, it makes you want to dance. The heart is the voice of the soul, deep inside, which is always dancing. As Rumi said, "There is a dancer inside of you. You just have to find it."

We use drums (especially the daf) in zikr, sacred dance, or whirling because it represents the heart's rhythm. It is a form of communication with the Divine; sama enables us to dance to the "rhythm of the heart" and to communicate with it. In Iranian traditions, it is believed each beat of the drum is the beating of the heart. The faster the beat, the faster we turn. Rhythm is also inherent in poetry, and poetry is a foundation of mysticism and one of the pillars of hal. Rumi, the most venerated of the Sufi spiritual masters, made dancing a central element in Sufi doctrine. Sufi literary scholars draw parallels between Rumi's poetry and the rhythm found in the traditional music of sama. In sama, one might call the rhythm the axis, the pole about which the poem and the whirler turn. Rumi has several poems in which whirling is identified in the word rhythm itself, either by a noun like sama or by a verb like *gashtan*, "to turn," in various conjugated forms (Lewisohn 1999 Vol. II, 72).

In Iran, it was believed that there were two sources for the heart: one is the anatomical or physical heart, and the other the spiritual heart, the heart of feeling. The ancients believed that the spiritual heart was located in the abdomen. In Farsi, *del* has alternate meanings; it might mean the heart but also the center, the soul. It represents the area between the heart and the abdomen. That's where del or the center is. There is a Persian saying, *Del-be-Del,* meaning heart-to-soul, which honors the connection between the two. During sacred dance or whirling, the two hearts should be equal in importance and one's center should connect to the Divine.

Music is the most critical part of dance and sama. Music played for sacred dance is rhythmic and fundamentally originated with ritual. Music and song heighten the mystical beauty of the dance. Its powerful rhythm reminds us of the heartbeat and leads us to the mystical intoxication of the sama.

Principles of Whirling

Let yourself be silently drawn by the stronger pull of what you really love.

– Rumi

Sama is a sacred ritual that requires rules, known as the shariat, to keep it respectful. Although whirling in many mystic orders is a means of free-form expression, the samazan should be respectful of the shariat. For instance, the shariat does not allow a samazan to drink alcohol. One cannot enter a church and disturb the peace by smoking, screaming, and running around, and then claim they meant to complete prayers in church. In the same way, there is a way to conduct oneself during sama that respects and preserves the sanctity of the space, even when one is being freely expressive. Free expression whirling outside the customs of sama is called "personal turns." Personal turns occur when one opens up, allowing oneself to say, "Take me!" These expressive movements may come naturally in the rapture of the moment or by choice. Sama is an intimate experience, and personal turns serve as a mode of self-expression beyond choreographed ceremonial norms.

Imam al-Ghazali[125] outlines three fundamental tenets deemed essential for participation in sama. The first rule is *sam*, the act of listening. Listening is said to be the most important sense during sama. Ali al-Hujwiri[126] emphasizes that hearing is superior to sight. To listen means that one should be "empty," free of ego, and without frustration or anger. Once empty, one can hear the heart, nature, and the surrounding energies. The second rule is *dărk*, which is to feel the passion. Music played for sama has poetic, mystical themes associated with powerful feelings. Listening and understanding the meaning and themes of the music or rhythm inspires the dancer's emotions and movement.

Imam al-Ghazali adds that music is not only heard with the ears but tasted with the heart. Music helps a listener achieve "mystical intuition." When music possesses the heart, the body is prepared to receive spiritual energy and healing. Deep listening can be described as listening to learn and requires a beneath-the-surface analysis of all that is heard, not just whatever one's usual focus of listening might be. This depth of listening is essential to the process of unlocking the layers of meaning within mystical music, poetry, or the words of a sacred text.

It is said that mystics are divided into two categories: those that hear the sound and those that hear the meaning. Those who hear the sound become ecstatic and fall into a trance by listening to the music.

Those who hear the meaning become ecstatic by paying attention to the poetry and praises they hear. Both approaches have had their fans over time, and both are accompanied by deep, sophisticated philosophies. But it is said that people who hear meaning are more spiritually connected and are more affiliated to the Divine.

The third and final tenet is *harekat*, movement. When the heart is heard and understood, and the feelings are followed, the body starts to

---

125 Imam al-Ghazali (1058-1111 CE) was a Persian Shafi'i Sunni Muslim scholar, jurist, philosopher, and mystic.

126 Ali al-Hujwiri (1009-1072/77 CE) was a prominent Iranian Sufi, Sunni Muslim mystic, theologian, and preacher.

move. Sama involves a wide array of movements and feelings, including a time for rest from movement, a pause to pray and listen, which provides balance. In Iranian sama, these three tenets are followed and completed before the first movement. These rules help prepare and guide the samazan to find the inspiration and feeling to enter a sama with free-form expression.

Sama is an internal journey to another world where the truth can be found. The three tenets, deep listening, feeling, and movement, open the door to sama and help the soul leave the material world to find its home. Sama is the dance of truth, a journey from sam (listening) through dărk (feeling) to harekat (movement). Rumi never expected he was going to create or choreograph a sama. Instead, once there was the spark, feeling, and movement that inspired him, the sama followed.

Sacred dance and whirling have been accompanied by ritual since time immemorial: mystical poetry, music, gestures and movements, emotional outbursts, physical extremes, direction-specific turning, gender customs, and sacred garments. The hypnotic circular motion of whirlers, their skirt's rippling motion, and the music's inspiring rhythm and poetry all work together to raise the experience of sama to one of rapture and ecstasy. Sama is held in a circular space on the floor, which some believe is a symbol of its primordial and timeless nature, without beginning or end. The movement of the darvish's body in sama also has its own meaning. For example, one darvish's palm faces the sky while whirling and the other palm faces the ground. Both create a bridge between heaven and earth and establish a mystical relationship with the Divine conveyed by the samazan to earth.

In the mystic tradition, followers kiss all that is given to them as an expression of humility, respect, and gratefulness. They kneel to kiss the floor upon which they pray. The darvish kisses his tanbur or daf before or after its use. They may kiss a sacred garment as they set it down. This simple gesture is an act of sacred remembrance. The task of the mystic is to act from tranquility, love, and a continuous remembrance. The mystic knows there must be beauty both inside and outside. The whirling darvishes were known to dance the dance of angels, representing the spirit of angels and their angelic work. Darvish musicians who play sacred music on traditional instruments and vocalists who sing sacred songs represent the spirit of the angels and saints. These darvishes have a responsibility to act with good, to be humble and grateful.

In Iran, most sacred dances and rituals in the fire temple were performed in white garments. White represents emptiness, sanctity, unity (since white is all colors combined), and purification. Sometimes, one might see different colored garments in sama, seven colors representing the different planets and their representative qualities, or the seven sacred flowers, or the seven angels. Regardless, proper ceremonial garments and accessories are required and should faithfully be worn during a ceremony, based on the protocols of the given order with which one is dancing. One needs to be respectful when entering the sacred house with regard to dress, and not just enter the ceremony wearing any type of clothes. One may of course find the proper garments for sale, but the garments that a master awards you are the most sacred and symbolic. Wearing these indicate that one has reached a certain level of discipline, knowledge, and honor. When one receives a *hirke*[127] it is a mark of honor. It is disrespectful to wear such garments if they have not been given. It would be like wearing a military uniform with badges and metals that one did not earn. Interestingly, the cap and gown worn during graduation ceremonies originates from an ancient tradition of Mithraism and Zoroastrianism. Once an initiate completed their training to become a Magi, they would be hooded and awarded a hat to wear.

The whirling skirt is a crucial element of sama as it enhances the dancer's circular motion. The long flowing skirt of the samazan fans out in waves resembling wings, the energy of the wind, or the aura surrounding the sun. Sometimes the waves are so pronounced they appear stationary; at other times smaller ripples appear and disappear more rapidly (Figure 12.8). How these waves are formed and how they may be recreated has long been a mystery. Researchers in physics have even been fascinated enough by the phenomenon that they've created mathematical models to investigate how it occurs. They were surprised to find that they could not reproduce any of the patterns. It was not until

127 A hirke is a long black sama ceremonial cloak. Also known as kesve in Farsi.

Figure 12.8: Whirling skirt motion with three and four stationary crests by author.

Photo and retouchment by Varol Ozkaner.

they introduced an effect observed by meteorologists in the formation of cyclones that the harmonic motion of the skirts could be explained, having to do with the interplay of forces caused by the earth spinning on its axis.[128] While modern science attempts to understand how such forces work, ancient mystics have been observing and honoring them for millennia from the deep wisdom of the heart.

Respectful Presentation

In order to understand the dance one must be still. And in order to truly understand stillness one must dance.

– Rumi

Performing sama authentically for an audience is an opportunity to share these hypnotic and sacred rituals. Mystics believe in brotherhood with other religions and welcome all to experience sama and its sacred energy. Observers feel the beauty of the sama and fall into hal, giving

[128] In 1835, a paper by Gaspard-Gustave de Coriolis discussed the dynamics of a water wheel and supplemental forces in a rotating frame of reference. The forces he described have since been called the Coriolis force and the centrifugal force.

them the opportunity to be cleansed of worldly matters. Naturally, as ancient societies evolved, original mystical dances evolved into various styles and purposes across cultures and time, yet still, the initial impulse has been preserved. Unfortunately today, sacred dance is being practiced more for entertainment than as a means of connection to the sacred, and thereby loses its real purpose.

In the Mevlevi cultural center of Konya, for example, once the ritual was presented publicly, a demand arose for its performance at weddings, with tour groups, or even at shopping malls and restaurants. Increasingly, it was taken outside the dargah or sacred lodge. Focus shifted away from its sacred purpose to finding ways to maintain audience interest or improve ticket sales. In entertainment, the personal and sacred intention of the dancer is not needed; it has become only an external act to be observed. It is no longer a sacred act.

If a performance deviates significantly from its sacred purpose, it is disrespectful to refer to it as Sufi whirling, particularly if the dancer isn't a Sufi or a mystic. Those who just "whirl" or "dance" without any sacred connection to the mystic path, even if wearing traditional attire, are not necessarily Sufi whirlers, darvishes, or mystics. Whirling can be performed by any dancer, in any costume, with any music, outside the sacred house. It can be thrilling to watch a dancer whirling skillfully with unique props such as a sword, flaming skirt hem, baton, or with lights glowing from the skirt. But this has nothing to do with sama in the traditional sense.

During sama, the role of the audience is to share in the collective prayer, rather than just passively attend. Participants should be fully present and aware of the journey that is a sama. First-time audience members should be prompted that the program is a religious ceremony and they are kindly requested to refrain from applause. Audience members should understand there will be periods of restful meditation and repetitive movements in sama. A sama might range from a large ceremonial gathering with many live musicians playing and several samazans whirling all surrounded by seated participants, or it may be a small family or personal gathering. Joining a traditional sama gathering is the best way to understand the intimacy and power of it. Your sama, zikr, or sacred dance becomes a part of your life; you become the sama and the sama becomes you.

When hosting a sama, always get the permission of a spiritual leader of the order. As the host, ensure that the sama follows the order's guidelines and traditions and does not offend the elders. Keep an open mind and an open heart and be sensitive and respectful of the traditions. Ask for feedback from the spiritual leader of the order. Use appropriate terminology and language when describing sama and avoid misrepresenting or mislabeling the dance form. Provide context about the origins and significance of whirling and the practices associated with it. This can help an audience understand and appreciate its importance. Avoid using stereotypes in the ritual. Be authentic and represent the ritual in a way that respects the depth and complexity of the culture. Sama is a sacred gathering directed toward devotion and reverence to the Divine.

In a sacred dance ritual, there isn't a division between performer and spectator where the artist performs and the audience contemplates and feels the effect. Rather, the members of the assembled community all participate together in some way, supportively if not actively. The sacred ritual is prevented from degenerating into mere spectacle or entertainment. Observers help focus the energy of the dance and music to amplify their power. The participants are there to pray, encourage, energize, and take part in the experience. Keeping this in mind will help people to understand sacred dance in its various forms and social contexts.

Mysteries of the Heart.

Dancing is not rising to your feet painlessly like a whirl of dust blown about by the wind. Dancing is when you rise above both worlds, tearing your heart to pieces and giving up your soul.

– Rumi

CHAPTER 13

Mawlawiyah (Mevlevi)

The dance goes on, and in the joy of the sun is hiding a God who teaches us to whirl.

– Rumi

The Mevlevi Sufi order derived its whirling from ancient Iranian traditions, such as Mithraism, but has many of its own ceremonial customs. It originated in Konya, modern-day Turkey, where it was developed by the followers of Rumi, a 13th century Persian Sufi, mystic, poet, and Islamic theologian. In 2005, UNESCO proclaimed the Mevlevi sama ceremony to be one of the Masterpieces of the Oral and Intangible Heritage of Humanity. In 2008, it was added to the Representative List of the Intangible Cultural Heritage of Humanity.

The origins of the Mawlawiyah or Mevlevi Sufi order date to the beginning of the Turkish Ottoman period following the death of the

Figure 13.1: Mevlevi darvishes in Istanbul, c. 1900-1910.
Wikimedia Commons.

Persian poet and philosopher Jalal al-Din Muḥammad Balkhi (1207-1273 CE), otherwise known as Mawlana in Iran and as Mevlana in Turkey.[129] Jalal al-Din is a male Muslim name meaning "majesty of faith." In Iran and Greater Khorasan, he was called *Khodavandeghar*, "our Lord." He is popularly known as Rumi, meaning "from Rum."[130] He was born September 30th, 1207, in the Balkh province of historic Greater Khorasan, Iran.

At the time, Khorasan was an important regional center of Persian culture and had its own form of Sufism. Rumi's father was a renowned scholar and mystic, Baha ud-Din Walad, who fled from Balkh with his family during the Mongol invasions. After roaming for ten years, they settled in Konya in the province of Rum when Rumi was twenty-two years old. The Seljuk capital with its worldly population of Christians, Jews, Greeks, and Armenians afforded him the atmosphere to evolve and express his unique independent spirit and unorthodox ideas. There he achieved distinction as a young theologian and Sufi master. Among his primary works are his collections of poems the *Divan-i Kabir*, the *Rubaiyat*, and the *Divan-i Shams-i Tabrizi*. Rumi devoted the last decade of his life to composing the *Masnavi* or *Masnavi-ye-Ma'navi,* a six-volume epic poem that became one of the most influential works in Sufism. It has been compared to Dante's *Divine Comedy* and Shakespeare's plays. Rumi's poetry has the distinctive marks of Sufi symbolism and poetic allegory, especially his *Masnavi,* which is drawn from the mystic ideas of Neo-Platonism, Chinese thought, Indian, Persian, and Greek mythology, stories from Holy Books, and Arab and Persian legends and folk stories.

A year after Rumi's death, his followers, aided by his son Sultan Walad,[131] founded what is now known as the Mevlevi Sufi order. With religion at its core, the Mevlevi were scholars and artists with an important influence on the classical Turkish arts until the founding of the

---

129 Mawlana or Mevlana is an Arabic term for "our master."

130 "Rum" was a term coined for pre-Islamic Anatolia when it was part of the Eastern Roman Empire.

131 Sultan Walad is also spelled as Sultan Veled.

Turkish Republic in 1925. That year with the subsequent push toward secularism, the Turkish government decreed the dissolution of all Sufi fraternities. The order was banned, darvish lodges were converted into museums, and the practice was pushed underground. Later, in 1954, the Turkish government granted the order special permission to perform ritual whirling practices in public only as a display for tourists or to promote culture—a move to reinvigorate the tourism industry rather than a gesture of religious tolerance. Later, in the 1990s, the original restrictions were eased; although the law is still on the books in Turkey, it is rarely enforced today. Some private groups have begun re-establishing the ceremony's original spiritual character, though over the years, as the focus was more on music and songs and less on spiritual texts and teachings, its intimate spiritual character was lost. Consequently, some sama ceremonies in Turkey are not performed in an authentic way, the sacred traditions having been commercialized to the point that whirling darvishes are featured in advertisements and segments of sacred music can be heard in commercials and as background music in shopping malls.

The Mevlevi order is based on teaching forgiveness, tolerance, and enlightenment. Through dance and zikr, the followers use their bodies as an instrument of contemplation, striving towards knowledge of the Divine. The Mevlevi practice is inspired by mystical poets, especially Hafez, Saadi, and Rumi, the three Persian poets who extolled dance in their poems and used this art form as a means to become one with God.

The Turkish Mevlevi are more choreographed and rule-based in their sama customs than the Iranian mystic traditions. Over time, the role of women diminished in the Mevlevi order, the separation of men and women became more pronounced, and only men were allowed to participate in the sama ritual in public. However, that is beginning to change as the order recognizes that for its whirling to remain relevant, it must welcome women back into its ranks (Hathaway 2015).

There is a legend that Rumi came across a child who was spinning in circles, delighted and smiling, enjoying it so much he kept turning and turning, joyful and careless of the world. He watched the child, curiously. Then, while listening to the strokes of a blacksmith hammering metal nearby, Rumi started spinning as the child had done. He, too, kept turning and turning, until he realized that he was everywhere and nowhere all at once. He had discovered that although his body remained in one spot, his mind and soul could travel elsewhere. He imagined this to be how the earth could seem still even as it traveled its orbit. Some say he whirled for thirty-six hours, a crowd gathering around him in wonder, assuming he was mad. People would come and go as time progressed, the area about him would change, but he continued whirling. Finally, the body could not whirl any more, and he fell. People were laughing and told him he hadn't moved in a day and a half. Rumi, in turn, laughed. He exclaimed that one needs to pack and journey a day and a half in the desert to reach Mecca and seek God, yet he could reach God without ever stepping outside of where he turned. He told them they, too, could remain in one place and still find God, traveling great distances from where they stood.

Sama, according to Rumi, is a passionate ritual of spiritual love, fire, and drunkenness. Under the influence of poetry and music, Rumi and his companions, impatient to meet their Beloved, emptied themselves by clapping, jumping, and dancing, dropping the heavy burden of daily life from their shoulders. Ascending beyond the earthly world, opening their arms as a sign of eagerness to fly, or as a sign of surrender, they would spin around the axis of their being, sprinkling the dust of divine grace, spreading it over the aridity of our earthly existence as the state of sacred ecstasy was reached (Zarrinkoob n.d.).

Sama Ceremony: A Sacred Celebration through Whirling

The sama is the soul's adornment which helps it to discover love, to feel the shudder of the encounter, to take off the veils, and to be in the Presence of God.

– Rumi

Salah al-Din Zarkub, a goldsmith, became Rumi's beloved friend and teacher. When Zarkub knew he was dying, he requested before his death that his passing not be mourned but celebrated. Rumi honored that request, and on the day of Zarkub's funeral, there was music and turning. Indeed, Rumi himself wrote many poems about the nature of death and dying. Often, while returning from prayers on Friday night, he and his followers would begin spontaneously turning in the street (Reinhertz 2001, 11).

Shams-i Tabriz, a wandering darvish from Iran, would become Rumi's mentor, his teachings and presence profoundly impacting Rumi's life and work. Rumi was already an accomplished scholar and academic headmaster when they met. Shams was a mystic of great spiritual depth and insight, and he pushed Rumi to explore the deepest corners of his being. He emphasized the importance of experiencing Divine Love, instead of merely studying it intellectually. From the time they met in Konya in 1244, and for a little over a year, the two men became so inseparable that Rumi neglected his ordinary duties, much to the alarm of his family, friends, and students. Scholars say it was Shams who introduced Rumi to the practice of turning as a form of sacred prayer. Throughout the latter part of his life, Rumi would continue to practice whirling and music as a gateway to the Divine. Rumi's devotion to sama might be considered a principal reason for its perseverance today.

One night in December 1247, Shams simply disappeared. Rumor had it he was secretly murdered by Rumi's son or a jealous disciple, but this is doubtful since Shams is buried in Khoy, Iran.[132] Devastated at the loss, Rumi worked through his despair by composing epic works of poetry, the most famous being *Divan-i Shams-i Tabrizi*, written in Shams's honor. He also wrote the compilation, *Divan-i Kabir*, and the *Masnavi*, considered his greatest work. Rumi died on December 17, 1273, in Konya, Turkey, at the age of sixty-six. The year after Rumi's death, his wife Fatima and two of his granddaughters, Seref and Mutahhara, helped his close disciple, Husameddin Chelebi, and Rumi's son Sultan Walad, to establish the Mevlevi order. They were each teachers in their own right (Reinhertz 2001, xxi-xxii). While Rumi was alive,

---

132 Khoy lies about one hundred miles northwest of Tabriz, Iran.

Figure 13.2: Mevlevi sama (whirling), Galata Mevlevi House, Istanbul, Turkey. Public domain.

ritual sama was done at any time, any place, even without music. The Mevlevi ceremonial sama ritual was later created by Sultan Walad to honor his father.

Mevlevi style turns are slow and steady-paced, unlike the Iranian style, which is characterized by fast steps and arm work evoking the elements. In the Mevlevi style, the samazan starts by standing, arms crossing the chest, feet together in first position. This is known as the *alif* position because it resembles the first letter of the Arabic alphabet; it symbolizes oneness. The right arm crosses over the left and the right foot's large toe overlaps the left foot's large toe. Legend has it this is in honor of Rumi's chef, Ateşbaz-i Veli, who burned his left big toe in a kitchen fire and then later wished to conceal his injury. In the traditional Mevlevi sama custom, a full turn is completed in a single step to the left, closing with the feet together. As the turn speed increases, the samazan's arms gradually unfold with the right palm directed to the sky, representing readiness to receive the Beloved, or the power of the Divine. During the turn, the samazan gazes toward the heart and upon the left hand whose palm is turned to the earth. The samazan receives the Divine Energy from the right palm, conveys it through the heart, and returns it to the earth through the left palm. This position is meant to bring love from God down to earth and its people.

The Mevlevi's whirling sama is inspired by the ancient Iranian chap sama, as an expression of longing. It is believed that while turning counterclockwise, like the orbit of the earth around the sun, a samazan revolves around the heart. The samazan aims to abandon their ego and enter a state of drunken love. Whirling may be further transformed into a silent zikr by silently reciting the name of God with each footfall. In whirling, one is no longer part of the material world but a part of the world beyond.

The Mevlevi customs are strongly influenced by the symbolism of ancient Iranian deities. The white *tennure*, the whirling skirt, is like those of the Iranian priestesses of Mithra or Mehr—the sun diety. Standing in the *alif* position, symbolizing oneness, honors Ahura Mazda, the higher power, and the Source of Light. The arms opening like wings flying into the sky is reminiscent of the wings of Faravahar and of returning to God.

Since Rumi's poems and teachings are full of appreciation for music, the Mevlevis consider music to be high art. Traditional musical instruments accompanying the Mevlevi sama are commonly the *ney* (sacred reed flute), a *kudüm* (a small drum covered in camel or sheep skin played with two sticks), and a *bendir* (frame drum). In darvish lodges, the musicians, chanters, and choir comprise a band called the *mutrip*[133] which is assembled for a formal sama. Music in the Mevlevi Sufi order was believed to transport the human being from everyday life into another sphere. The ney specifically was thought to free the soul from its egoic desires and fill it instead with a spiritual passion to reunite with God.

Listen to the reed flute, how it tells a tale
Complaining of separation, it tells of love's travail
(Saying), "Ever since I was cut from the reed bed,
In my passionate grief, men and women shed tears in dread"
I wish to rend my breast, in agony and woe
To tell the pain of yearning, and the longing's throe.

– Rumi

133 *Mutrip*, in Turkish, or *mutrib*, in Old or Ottoman Farsi.

The Mevlevi *ayin* is a structured musical composition developed during the Ottoman Empire specifically to accompany the sama. Predominantly a vocal genre, the overall composition and main vocal parts were written by a single composer, while the instrumental pieces like the *pesrev* and *semai* (introductory and closing) were taken from other, often secular sources. Following the vocals, the ney was the primary instrument of the ayin due to its symbolic importance in Rumi's poetry. For the Mevlevi, the music and whirling relate to the creation of the universe. The four main movements of the ayin (the Four Salams) symbolize the four elements, the four seasons, the four compass directions, and the four stages of spiritual progression.

The Mevlevi sama is regulated by strict rules and the ceremony is precise. The sama floor is located in front of the *mutriphane*[134] (band stage). A special red sheepskin called the "post" is placed directly across from the entrance to the samakhaneh (the ceremonial space) and in front of the stage, to mark the most honored position where the *postneshin* (spiritual master/sheikh) stands or sits. If the master is not there, the red sheepskin represents the absent master. During the ceremony, the darvishes pass by the postneshin three times, each time exchanging greetings, until the whirling starts. An audience, if any, is seated on the periphery of the floor or, if there is one, in the mezzanine. The red color of the "post" represents the attainment of God since it is said that Rumi died, rejoining his creator, during sunset. Also, since the sky is red whenever the sun rises or sets, the red color of the post represents the sinking of the darvish from the material world and the spiritual birth of the darvish like the sun (Gündüzöz 2018, 46).

The sight line between the post and the entrance to the hall is called *hatt-i istiva* (Figure 13.3), dividing the ceremonial circle in half. This is the shortest path to unity, the path to truth. The sheikh is the only person who may tread this line during the ritual. The post is the highest spiritual point upon the sama floor. The arc of the circle starting from the pole opposite the post, traveling to the right and ending at the post, is known as the arc of ascent. This represents the path the samazan

---

134 In Old or Ottoman Farsi, *mutriphane* means the "house of the musicians."

walks to reach the station of the divine spirit. The opposite arc leaving the post and ending at the pole is known as the arc of descent, the path the samazan would take to leave the divine spirit and return to the human soul. During the ceremonial Sultan Walad Walk, a samazan at either the post or pole bows and steps over the *hatt-i istiva* sight line then turns to respectfully face and bow to the next samazan. If there is no one either in front of or behind the samazan approaching either post or pole then when they reach either point they still bow, cross, turn, and bow to the opposite side (Bakhtiar 1976, 6, 15).

The sama ceremony is often a weekly practice for each Mevlevi lodge (tekke) including everyone in the community—musicians, women, and non-resident mystics. Today, Mevlevi orders observe a formal sama ritual once yearly on December 17th, the date of Rumi's passing, in a special remembrance sama known as *Sheb-i Arus,* which means "wedding night" and is a celebration because that is the way Rumi would have wanted it; he believed the moment of death was not a time of mourning, but one of joy, since it also meant union with God, a state he could only temporarily achieve by whirling. The original ritual was known as *Shab-é Oruj*, where *Oruj* is a Farsi word meaning night of ascension.[135] In the ancient or mystic tradition of Iran, when a Magi (Zoroastrian priest), a saint, or a darvish died, people celebrated instead of mourning. The name was later adopted as *arus* by the Mevlevi.

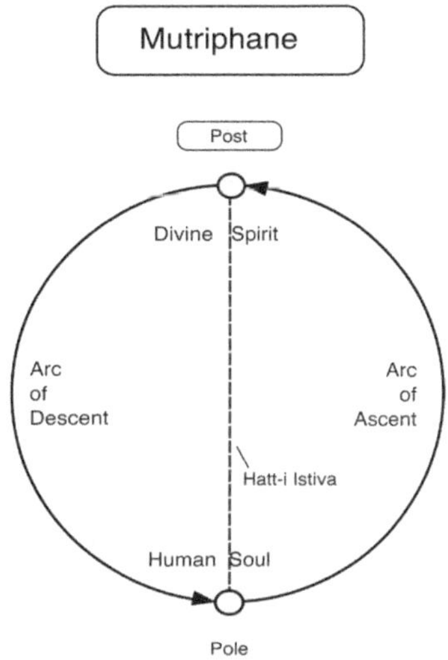

13.3: Traditional Mevlevi sama layout with Arcs of Ascent and Descent.
Kevin Greek, public domain.

There are seven stages to the Mevlevi sama, each stage sometimes called a *selam.*[136] The first stage starts with the line of samazans sitting on sheepskins dressed in their black cloaks called *hirke*. A eulogy

[135] *Shab-é Oruj* is also known as *Shab-é Miraj,* meaning "to rise."

[136] *Selam*, or *salam* in Farsi or Arabic, is a stage of sama or a greeting.

honoring the Prophet called the *Na't-i Shareef* ("Noble Praise of the Prophet") is sung to music. It is in the form of a Persian ode consisting of six lines and is believed to have been composed by Rumi himself. For the last three centuries, it has been sung according to the musical arrangement of Mustafa Itri. In this composition, praises of Rumi have been added to the original poem.

The second stage of the sama starts with a ney *taksim* (improvisation) evoking the opening lines of Rumi's masterpiece, the Masnavi. The ney represents the first breath that gives life to everything, the Divine Breath. It also represents the trumpet called the *sur*, which will be played by the Archangel Rafael on the Day of Reckoning to wake the dead and help them attain eternal life. At stage three, when the taksim ends, a drum strike signals all samazans to fall to the floor in prostration. This is the *debi celali*, the bow to glory, symbolizing the time of reckoning. Stage four is a ceremonial walk around the samakhaneh floor. With the permission of the master, the samazans stand and circle the floor three times in a slow measured step accompanied by music called *peshrev*. The samazans formally bow to each other to recognize the eternal soul at either post or pole. This is known as the Sultan Walad Walk, named for the son of Rumi who initiated the tradition. After completion of the final round, the samazans return to form a line shoulder to shoulder beside the post and the music stops.

The fifth stage of sama begins when the postneshin bows and all the samazans follow with a bow. Two samazanbashis (assistants to the postneshin) step forward, signaling the samazans to remove their hirke (the black cloak), kiss it, and carefully place it on the floor next to where they are standing with three folds: one in the name of Love, one in the name of Beauty, and one in the name of Unity. These motions are done in unison. Removal of the cloak is visually and spiritually moving, as it represents shedding the samazan's ego and reveals the white radiance of the tennure beneath. The postneshin never removes his hirke.

The samazanbashi next walks before the postneshin and bows in front of them to kiss their hand. When the postneshin bows, the samazans all bow in unison. The postneshin then kisses the samazanbashi's *sikke*.[137] This means the samazanbashi has permission to let his or her samazans turn in the samakhaneh. The samazans walk in line by slow measured steps to the post, whereupon, with the blessing of the postneshin, each samazan moves out whirling to find a place on the floor. A samazanbashi is in charge of keeping order and will intervene if it appears a samazan is wandering unknowingly outside their bounds or may collide with another. If a darvish should become too enraptured a samazanbashi will gently touch their frock to curb their movement.

The fifth stage of sama has four parts or musical movements of whirling, similar to acts within a drama. Each part ends when the music ends, the whirling stops, and the samazans slowly back out from the center, lining up shoulder-to-shoulder on either side of the hall. The first part, *çarh,* denotes birth and represents the period of up to twenty years of age, the spring of human life. It represents the darvish's acceptance of being created by God. The second part, *raghs*, representing the summer of human life between twenty and forty years of age, is dynamic, expressive, and full of motion with the happiness of witnessing the magnificence of creation. The third part, *muallak,* symbolizes the autumn of human life between forty and sixty years of age, "dissolving" into love and sacrificing oneself to love; it is giving in to total destruction by love. By dissolving into the rapture of love, the samazans annihilate themselves in the Beloved. At this point, the darvish enters a nearly trance-like state as he enters union with God.

The fourth and final part, *pertev*, represents the winter of life after sixty, and the darvish's descent back into his life after his spiritual journey. Throughout the ceremony the postneshin has stood at the post as witness to the ceremony. The postneshin now moves to the center of the circle of dancers; a ney improvisation begins while the postneshin turns in place slowly, arms folded. Upon completion, the postneshin returns to the post; the samazans stop whirling and slowly back out from the center as before. This is the completion of all four parts.

The sixth stage begins when a passage of the Holy Quran is recited. The samazans immediately stop turning, back up to either side of the

137 A *sikke* is the Sufi ceremonial camel hair hat; *kolah* in Farsi.

hall and sit down. Each samazan picks up their hirke, kisses it and drapes it about their shoulders. The ceremony concludes with a recitation of the Al-Fatiha (prayer). The samazans then prostrate themselves, touching the floor with their forehead, and stand. In the seventh and final stage of the sama, the postneshin offers a *gülbang* (a traditional prayer) and extends a final gesture of gratitude to the samazanbashis and the leader of the mutrip. This leads to the *selams*, a hand kissing ceremony. Each samazan bows to the postneshin, kisses their hand, then takes the first empty spot to stand beside and beyond them, receiving the same gesture from the next samazan. In silence, once the postneshin leaves the hall, the samazanbashis lead out the samazans. Everyone turns and bows to the post before exiting. Once the last samazan has left, the samazanbashi will return to the hall to retrieve the post in the same manner as for the sama opening.

Sacred Attire: Weaving Elegance into Spiritual Expression

In this hyper trance, turn, spin, whirl, up, down, left, right, let go and become, nameless, faceless, directionless.

–Broken Mystic

The various types of ceremonial hats, belts, and the black cloak of the Mevlevi Sufis have special meanings and are awarded based on achievement or status. Ceremonial garments are typically worn only for sacred rituals and are carefully maintained and stored. For samazans of the Mevlevi order, the traditional ceremonial garments include a sleeveless white whirling dress named *tennure* (a wide skirt), a *destegul* (short white jacket) worn over it, an *elifinemed* (black belt, *kamarband* in Farsi) to secure the skirt to the waist, and a *sikke*[138] on their head.

The tennure ("skin of light") worn by each samazan represents the ego's shroud. The hirke (black robe) represents the tomb and often symbolizes the hypocrisy of a religious pretender. In Farsi, the term is

[138] A tall, cylindrical felt hat, often made of camel hair.

kherqe-ye sālus, or "the hypocrite's robe." For traditional sama, samazans enter the samakhaneh wearing a hirke and by removing it, the samazan is spiritually reborn to the truth. This gesture with the hirke symbolically casts off the blackness of the grave to reveal the radiance of the tennure, the white shroud of resurrection.

The samazan's sikke represents the tombstone of the ego. The sikke is never removed while observing the traditional Mevlevi sama. Just as sultans have crowns, darvishes have sikke. Whereas the crown of a sultan represents material power, the sikke represents spiritual power. The status of a Mevlevi Sufi may be identified by the presence or type of *destar* (fabric band) around the sikke. The presence of a destar is a sign of maturity in the spiritual journey and different colors indicate their responsibility and seniority in their community. A samazan in training wears a sikke without a destar. A sikke with destar and a black robe indicates master status.

One might see different colored garments during sama honoring Rumi's "rose garden," with red for dusk, dawn, and love, green for tranquility, and yellow for unrequited love. Although the specific ceremonial attire may vary slightly depending on the lineage or branch of the Mevlevi Order, the white tennure is a consistent and central element. The attire is not just a traditional costume, but a visual representation of the spiritual journey and inner transformation sought by the samazans. Each aspect of the clothing carries deep symbolic meaning and serves to create a unified and sacred atmosphere during sama. In Iran, the traditional sacred costume resembles the Turkish Mevlevi garments and many items have the same purpose and meaning, however, unlike the Mevlevi tradition, Iranian mystics can wear a turban, hat, or even have uncovered loose hair.

There comes a point when one is fed up with the industrial world, fed up with the troubles of daily life in a metropolitan city, and fed up with the emotional burdens of living in a cage-like apartment. [The message of the sacred Yarsan maqam] is a reminder that this was never meant to be your true purpose in life and the fire within you is going to waste.

– Dr. Bahman Kazemi, Ethnomusicologist

CHAPTER 14

Yarsan: Companions of the Sun

In the unconscious mind of man, God is always high in the heavens, his eyes gazing upon the human who listens to Him (God). God is the only one who sees the samazan (whirler) as beautiful or understands their movements.

– Seyed Salman Hosseini

Over the years of my own mystic journey, I've heard stories of mystics and saints living in the rugged and distant Zagros mountains of Iran. Fascinated by their spiritual devotion and simple lifestyle, I was drawn to follow in their footsteps. The all-encompassing beauty of this sacred land has made lovers drunk with the wine of the Beloved. The mountain soil of Kermanshah, the land of Media, is where deities dueled, angels roamed, and saints were born. In this land, one can see the shadows of ancient souls and feel the presence of angels and the Haft Tan. Here we all become people of the sun. During my visits, I often accompanied Pir Seyed Salman Hosseini,[139] a prominent tanbur master, Yarsan leader and mystic, and a direct descendant from the lineage of Saint Baba Yadegar—one of the Seven Souls. With his guidance, I became acquainted with Yarsani culture and beliefs. There I learned of the real sama. There I learned rich details about the crafting of the sacred tanbur and its role in sacred music and dance. I learned of my own ancient past.

Traveling through the peaceful countryside of Kermanshah creates a sense of total separation from the modern world. Gentle breezes rustle the many mulberry and cypress trees blanketing the hills; flowing springs bubble and trickle; birds sing the songs of angels; the ancient

139 A pir is a Sufi master or guide.

carved stones tell stories of our ancestors. A countryside such as this is a place where the heart becomes full and the soul is understood. It has served as inspiration for artists, musicians, and mystics for eons. Here, one can experience the harmonious blend of tanbur music with nature.

Visiting the village of Sahneh, home to some of the greatest mystics, musicians, and darvishes (such as Seyed Khalil Alinezhad),[140] I immediately felt its energy and magnetism. The villagers welcomed me into their community with kindness, assisting me in every way. Men, women, and children gathered for sama and zikr, whirling as the tanbur and daf played. As the music quickened, I became captivated by the enormous range of emotions they expressed—happiness, curiosity, sadness, longing, ecstasy, and empathy—and was drawn, too, into ecstasy. Even when there was no music, they still moved with passion.

Visiting Yarsan sacred sites, recording their music, or attending their gatherings requires permission from the elders as their sacred music, prayer movements, rituals, sama, and zikr are extremely private. Only those who demonstrate respect and understanding are invited to observe and it is a tremendous gift to be among them, welcomed as part of their mystic family. The Yarsanis are very secretive and place trust only in those with a good heart. During my studies there, I received blessings and encouragement from the leaders of the community and many others. Near the city of Jayhunabad, where people visit the tombs of the great mystics to pay their respects, I visited the tomb of Shah Hayas. Each wall displayed a profile of one of the four archangels: Gabriel, Azrael, Michael, and Rafael. I felt immersed in and chilled by the soul-stirring energy of the angels, yet held in the warmth and calmness inside, sensing the angels seeing, hearing, feeling, and protecting.

Traveling alongside Pir Salman felt like crossing the seven valleys, reminiscent of Attar's quest for awakening, and I could feel my soul journeying the seven paths, a wandering darvish trying to find the Beloved. Pir Salman's home is in the remote village of Baktar. Situated upon one of the highest energy points of the Zagros mountain, it is

---

140 Seyed Khalil Alinezhad (1958-2001) was a great master of the spiritual tanbur, recognized as one of the best tanbur players ever known.

inhabited by farmers leading simple lives. Some of the greatest mystics, darvishes, and even mythical heroes of the *Shahnameh* are believed to have originated from this area. It is also home to one of the most ancient Zoroastrian fire temples.

Pir Salman's grandfather, Seyed Ghadamyar Hosseini (Figure 14.1), was a greatly respected master, healer, and national treasure of the tanbur and Yarsan maqams and songs. He was born and spent most of his life in Sahneh. Stories of him playing tanbur and healing people are well-known among the Yarsan people. Of the 120 years of his life, he spent at least 110 years singing those songs. With his careful research and memory, he helped to preserve the music and many of the songs of the Yarsan. He dedicated his life to teaching his students and others to carry on the traditions into the future. Known as a noble, wise, gentle, and kind person, Ghadamyar appeared to live in a separate reality, filled with an inner peace (*Song of God* 2018, 35:48).

Figure 14.1: Seyed Ghadamyar Hosseini, Sahneh, Kermanshah, Iran.

Seyed Salman Hosseini.

Born and raised in Kermanshah, Ghadamyar started playing the tanbur and reciting *kalam*[141] and maqam in his childhood with his father and uncle. Later he would study with Seyed Nasriddin Khamoushi to learn the tanbur professionally. One day Seyed Nasriddin called Ghadamyar in and awarded him a sacred tanbur created by Ostad Khodvardi, one of the most important master tanbur craftsmen. Ghadamyar would become one of the most gifted and lasting figures of Iranian music, receiving many honors. A group of Japanese researchers once visited Ghadamyar to determine his secret to long life. They analyzed his lifestyle, family history, and environment.

[141] Mystical theological texts.

During his 120 years alive he never took medication. When their analysis concluded, he explained to them, "You have correctly identified all the physical factors, but it is the soul that keeps harm away from the body, only if it is healthy, listens to good music, has healthy thoughts, is not jealous or mean-spirited, loves people, and doesn't allow negativity to enter. It is the soul that can bring harm and disease to the body."[142]

In the city of Kerend, the resting place of St. Benjamin, the incarnation of Angel Gabriel (Figure 14.2), we visited the house of Darvish Changiz (Figure 14.3). On the wall of his house hung a tanbur beside images of himself in his younger years. By way of welcome, he insisted on presenting me with a gift he made with his own hands. He began talking about his love—his love of light, love of God, love for his masters—and how it changed him. I asked him if he could still play the tanbur. "My hands are old now... I cannot create the sound of God," he explained, "but I will share some wisdom."

Figure 14.2: St. Benjamin shrine and tomb, Kerend, Kermanshah, Iran.

Photo by author.

Figure 14.3: Darvish Changiz (left) and Seyed Salman Hosseini (right), Kerend, Kermanshah, Iran.

Photo by author.

In his youth, Darvish Changiz left his work at a bank to seek a spiritual makeover. He found an old master named Baba Gholam to be his guide,

142 *Song of God* 2018, (33:35).

who insisted that he return to work. After trying farming, he decided he would eventually make a good blacksmith, and during his spare time, he found solace playing the tanbur. He worked as a blacksmith until his last days, much like the mythical Kaveh.[143] His smile convinced me that there are angels among us, and he seemed able to see into my soul. He compared mysticism—the source of art, culture, music, dance, beliefs—to a great river flowing through the East, spreading in many directions, connecting people, bringing water and life to diverse communities. He wholeheartedly welcomed me to come back whenever I had any questions. In parting, he encouraged me to continue my mystic path.

Our next destination was the small village of Qazvineh. We drove through a peaceful community of fruit trees and farms. Again, I could hear birds singing amidst a gentle early morning breeze and I could hear the subtle sound of a spring under an ancient mulberry tree. When we arrived in Qazvineh we were introduced to Pir Mohammad Zolnuri, a descendant of the Yarsan *khandan* (family)[144] of Saint *Zolnur Ali* Qalandar. Pir Zolnuri graciously accompanied us to the shrine of Seyed Farzi Khamoushi, a spiritual master of the 18th century during the reign of Nader Shah Afshar.[145] We visited the jamkhaneh, built in

Figure 14.4: Sheikh Amir Jamkhaneh, exterior (left) and interior (right), Qazvineh, Kermanshah, Iran. Shown from left: Seyed Salman, Seyed Basir Qazvineh, the author, and Pir Mohammad Zolnuri.
Photo by author.

---

143 Kaveh the Blacksmith is a mythical epic hero in Ferdowsi's *Shahnameh*.

144 A *khandan* is a Yarsan holy family and one of the 11 spiritual dynasties.

145 Nader Shah Afshar (1688-1747) was the founder of the Afsharid dynasty and one of the most powerful rulers in Iranian history.

1736 (Figure 14.4), and met local musicians playing the tanbur. Here mystics come from every walk of life—young and old, educated or simple. No matter their professional or family background, all share the belief that they are equal before God.

After having some fresh watermelon and fruit we gathered to discuss mysticism. Pir Zolnuri told us that when he was young there was a certain darvish who would rise to whirl whenever music was played, and each time, he would fall into such a deep trance that he would not feel fire or hot embers, as if an energy field protected him. He had never seen such an intense trance before. His grandfather told him that during sacred rituals in the jamkhaneh, when some people would fall into ecstasy, they could touch fire and no harm would come. Pir Zolnuri explained that this protective force surrounded the sacred space, generated by the power of the tanbur, the sama, and the people—such was the power of devotion to sama. He expressed that "new age" whirling has become worthless because it has lost its sacred connection to prayer, and is instead being used to entertain the public.

The jamkhaneh is elevated from the ground by only three steps. The exterior façade of the building is made of plain, featureless concrete with a dark green metal door in front, one of three entrances. Inside, light streams from four big windows. A small room within the structure was the original jamkhaneh where Seyed Farzi lived in solitude and prayed. The walls are adorned with sacred poetry by Seyed Farzi's student, Sheikh Amir, who wrote of his longing for the Divine and love for his beloved master. Later, a modern jamkhaneh was built over and around this room, preserving its foundations.

The story of Sheikh Amir and Seyed Farzi resembles that of Rumi and Shams so closely that some say they actually were Rumi and Shams, or embodied the souls of Rumi and Shams. It began one night when Sheikh Amir had a dream that he met Seyed Farzi. The next morning he was so impatient to find him that he immediately started the journey from Mosul, Iraq to the village of Qazvineh to find his Shams. Meanwhile, Seyed Farzi had foreseen Sheikh Amir coming, and at the moment Sheikh Amir took his first step, Seyed Farzi had already told the villagers they would soon have a special

Figure 14.5: Sama gathering at the house of Seyed Khalil Alinezhad, Sahneh, Kermanshah, Iran with author (left foreground).
Photo by author.

guest. On his journey, Sheikh Amir stopped to rest by the river and fell asleep. Discovering him along the path, Seyed Farzi removed his turban and gently covered Sheikh Amir's sleeping face to protect it from the sunlight so he could rest peacefully. When Sheikh Amir awakened, he was astonished and grateful. From then on they were inseparable. Today, Sheikh Amir lies buried next to the shrine of Seyed Farzi Khamoushi.

That evening, in the jamkhaneh, the musicians and darvishes gathered in a circle for a sama and zikr. Modestly dressed with green sashes and white darvish hats, the darvishes and musicians began to chant passages from the sacred text aloud and then silently. Participants began to move, bowing their heads and bodies with the chants. As the pace quickened they turned their heads right and left in time with the chanting and music. Soon the group was rapidly chanting, violently turning their heads, spinning, gesticulating, jumping, and sometimes screaming as the sama reached a crescendo in this beautiful sacred space. Pir Mohammad Zolnuri invited me to whirl as others joined in. As I was whirling, I suddenly heard an enchanting angelic voice rise above the room—it was Zolnuri, who had also entered a state of trance, singing an ancient zikr. I was told later that he never did this, but that at that moment something overcame him.

When I stopped whirling, everyone was silent with bowed heads. Pir Mohammad Zolnuri gazed at me with teary eyes and cried "You made us all cry, reminding us of our ancient rituals. Our sama has been awakened." We kissed hands the way mystics do and I thanked him, but he said "No, I should thank you! We have never before had a woman whirling nor leading a sama in this sacred sanctuary. We had waited for the right person to come at the right time. When I met you, I knew it was you. I saw a light and love in you that I have not seen in a long time. Our Holy House now belongs to you. God and the angels have seen your magnificent work." I will never forget the humbleness of this master and this special experience.

Culture and Beliefs

Oh lovers of the world
Oh pleasure seekers!
This world only lasts a breath
Just long enough to reap what you sow.

– Yarsan folk song

Within the beautiful Zagros mountains lie the secrets and legends of a fascinating culture of spiritual devotion. Mostly living in small towns and villages within a harsh terrain, the partial isolation of the Yarsan people has helped them preserve their traditions and culture. To survive demanding conditions and daily strains, they sought relief in music and poetry, which became an essential part of daily life and work, foundational to their religion and the preservation of their lifestyle.

Yar means "divine friend" or "beloved," and is one of the names of God itself. The Yarasani refer to themselves as the "companions of the sun," as the sun and Divine Light are central to their identity. They emphasize spiritual and ethical principles of equality, purity, righteousness, oneness, love, kindness, and compassion. Although Sufism's principles are apparent within the Yarsan beliefs, they do not see themselves as a branch of Sufism and do not follow the Islamic Sufi shariat but instead consider Sufism a branch of their own beliefs. The root of the

Yarsan mystic philosophy has foundations in Mithraism, Manism,[146] and Zoroastrianism.

The Yarsan people extend as far east as India and as far west as Greece, but mostly are found in Kurdistan.[147] Their history and home are in the Zagros mountains, the birthplace of their sacred culture. Most Yarsanis live in the Central-Western Iranian region of Kermanshah, but many also live in Lorestan, East Azerbaijan, Zanjan, Hamadan, Tehran and its suburbs, Khorasan, and other cities nearby (Sanjabi 2016). The Kurds are an Iranian ethnic group native to the northwestern Zagros mountains. They have a strong ethnic identity and, due to their isolation, they are practically the only Central Asian people that have remained unaffected by the influx of invading nations. The Mongols, the Arabs, the Persians, the Turks, and the Greeks all left their mark on the indigenous peoples of Asia. Secure in their mountainous homeland, the identity of the Kurds has survived these onslaughts.

The Yarsanis were originally a Mithraic people who lived on Mount Shahu, but when enemies attacked, they were forced to descend the mountains of Shahu in Ouraman and settle in the Dalahu Mountains near Kermanshah. It is said they brought only two things with them during this journey: a bottle of water from Tahar Spring as a symbol of vitality, and a tanbur as a symbol of their culture and music. Hafez mentioned in his poetry that the Yarsanis are from the City of Yaran, which means the city of companions. They preach the unity of all religions on the highest plane and strongly emphasize music as part of their spiritual path. The tanbur provides the Yarsanis with a unique manner of representing their beliefs and preserving their culture; through sacred songs they preserve and pass on their sacred texts and teachings, as well as narrate stories that have been retold for generations. One of these songs is the story of Kaveh the Blacksmith, a mythical epic hero in Ferdowsi's *Shahnameh*. Music is used in almost all their mystic

---

146 Manism or Manichaeism was a dualistic religion founded in Persia in the third century, founded by the Prophet Mani (216-276 CE). The belief was based on a supposed primeval conflict between light and darkness.

147 Kurdistan refers to a geo-cultural region covering parts of Turkey, Iraq, Iran, and Syria, in which the majority of people are Kurd.

practices; during their ritual gatherings called *jam*, their music conveys wisdom and arouses them spiritually, and the power of the sacred texts is said to be most effective.

The Yarsan tradition is one of the oldest still in existence with an identity and faith originating from over ten thousand years ago which had a strong influence on the development of Zoroastrianism and Sufism. It values tolerance and coexistence with people of different faiths. The basis of the tradition is to respect the four sacred elements, honor the truth, be pure, be a humble servant of the Divine, and surrender to destiny. The Yarsan people faithfully practice kindness towards each other and they have a saying, "*yekishān chehel bī, chelshān bī yak*" that translates as "one be forty and forty be one." For a Yarsani, this articulates their solidarity and unity. They say if one mystic is pierced with a needle, forty feel the pain. If one feels good, all feel good. In their well-being, one stands for all, and all stand for one.

Yarsanism is an esoteric mystic order that believes a single God created the earth and all beings in it. Occasionally God will come to earth in a physical form, an incarnation called a *mazhariyyat* (a saint or prophet), accompanied by seven angelic beings. In the beginning (the first epoch), the first incarnation called Khawandagar created the world, and the seven archangels were guardians of entities such as the sun, sky, moon, stars, water, earth, fire, and metal. In the second period or epoch, Alī and his seven saints succeeded the seven archangels. In the third, Shah Khoshin and his seven saints ascended to take their place. And in the fourth, Sultan Sahak[148] and his seven saints were the next incarnations. Since the 14th century CE, Sultan Sahak has been considered the founder of the Yarsani path after he received the eternal secrets from the Divine and shared them with his companions. His doctrine emphasized love, kindness, and compassion. As described in their sacred text, *Kalam-e Saranjam*, the secret teachings have been passed through these prophets, the details passed on to a few confidants during each mythical epoch. The Yarsani believe the text of the Kalam is sacred, immutable, and powerful.

---

[148] Sultan Sahak is also known as Sultan Izhak.

Yarsanism requires that each member follow a spiritual leader known as a pir, a descendent of a saint, for guidance. Since Sultan Sahak was unmarried and without children, he selected seven saints as guardians of the truth (known as the *Haftanan*, meaning "the Seven Companions"),[149] so new generations would always have pirs and guides. This guardianship was passed down through the families of the saints. It is generally agreed today that there are eleven khandans (families): the Shah Ibrahimi, Yadegari, Khamoushi, Qalandari, Mirsuri, Mostafayi, Hajji Babu Isa (one of the early followers of Sultan Sahak), Zolnuri, Atash Beygi (of Atesh Bey who lived in the 10th century), Baba Heidari, and Shah Hayasi (of Shah Ayaz who lived in the 10th century). Each khandan has a *seyed* (lord) or *pir* (elder), that has access to thc sacred text and is believed to be a direct descendant of one of the saints.

There are four hierarchies of being recognized by the Yarsanis, known as the Qultasiyan (the 28 souls): the Haft Tan (seven angels), Haftanan (seven people), the Haftvaneh (seven-wise), and the Haft Sardar (seven commanders). These 28 souls are believed to be the first that emanated from the divine essence and manifested in the form of human beings. Similarly, within each of the khandans, there are four categories of people. The first are those who have basic knowledge of the *Kalam-e Saranjam*, which amounts to anyone who is born a mystic Yarsani. The second are those who seek the truth, striving to fully understand the teachings of Sultan Sahak. The third are those go beyond "book learning" to seek the experiences of mysticism. The fourth is those who have reached the ultimate truth and can lead others along the way.

For many generations, the Kalam was only transmitted orally. Later, the teachings were recorded in the Gorani language. The Yarsanis insist on preserving this text exactly as it was written in the 15th century, as it has an inseparable bond with the tanbur, other sacred writings, and the Divine (Vatanpour 2017, 47). It is said the Kalam is not meant to be

---

149 The *Haftan* are the seven Angels, while the *Haftanan* are the seven human saints.

analyzed for its logic but for the power it reveals to the one reciting it (Vatanpour 2017, 49). It was not until the 19th century that the Kalam became more accessible when it was written in common language.

All Yarsan mystics are obliged to participate in two special events. The first is a pilgrimage to the sacred shrine of Sultan Sahak. The other is a three day fast known as *mar-e no* ("new cave") during the Iranian calendar month of Aban, which begins in October and ends in November. This fast is a remembrance of when the Sultan was under siege and the angels opened a cave in the mountain where the seven companions were able to take refuge, but they were without food and water for three days before they could escape.

The Yarsani believe the human being is divided into two opposing yet coexisting elements: the soul and the body, the negative and the positive, the good and the bad, the material and the spiritual. Every human being has these two parts. In order to become one with the Divine we must attempt to release our ego to be in union with the soul. Yarsan ethics is based on four central tenets proposed by Sultan Sahak: *paki* (purity), *rasti* (righteousness), *nisti* (inexistence or selflessness), and *rada* (generosity). The first tenet, paki, means cleanliness of body and clothes and purity of language, thoughts, and behaviors (this includes the "fast of the seven limbs" as mentioned on page 62). Rasti refers to taking the right path, honesty, integrity, and living according to divine will. The tenet of nisti means renunciation of one's pride, selfishness, desires, and lusts. The fourth tenet, rada, advocates generosity, serving others, sacrifice, and humbleness.

Another important concept is *Doon-a-Doon*,[150] the transmigration of the soul or reincarnation. Each soul must transmigrate 1,001 times in order to become perfect and made one with God. A soul may then choose to return to earth to teach those who have not yet reached perfection. Passing through each doon requires much suffering and sacrifice. Manifestation as a human being occurs in two forms: one is that of *zăate bashar* (human nature) where the qualities of God combine with

150 Meaning "cloth to cloth."

nature to manifest in a doon; and second, is that of *zăate mehman* (guest nature), which is the direct manifestation of God in physical matter.

People who have reached a high degree of purification in God's manifestation may embody zăate mehman, which is similar to the reality manifested in Sultan Sahak. Being mortal is a necessary step that happens when *zăte haqq* (the nature of God) leaves the body, but the soul of someone who manifests zăate mehman will link to *Haqq* (God, Truth) after death. When zăte mehman appears in a person's body, zăte bashar departs.

Yarsan tradition recognizes seven attributes of mystic wisdom. The first is *hyat dari*, the existence and spirit that occupies the body. *Bash dari*, the second, is the sense of love and appreciation for art and beauty. Third, *bou dari*, is the pervasive aura of beauty that a mystic exudes, like the perfume of the Divine. Fourth, *zare dari*, is the golden light within a mystic, received from the Divine. Fifth, *berah dari*, is a sense of fate and confidence in one's destiny. The sixth is *khalat dari*, the spiritual "dress" of knowledge and worth. The seventh and final attribute is *zăteaat dari*, which defines the angelic personality that the Divine wants you to be. When a person embodies all these attributes, they are considered to have attained the personality of Divine Nature. Achieving this level is a very long process.

Haft Tan: The Seven Holy Immortals

The man who has seen the rising moon break out of the clouds at midnight has been present like an archangel at the creation of light and of the world.

– Ralph Waldo Emerson

The Yarsanis believe there was absolute silence before creation. The Creation begins with a primordial sound, what the Yarsanis call the "Big Bang." Therefore, all creation is the sound or music of God (*Song of God* 2018, 8:18). Upon the creation of the universe, God formed the Seven Souls from His Essence, embodying them in seven angels: Gabriel, Rafael, Michael, Azrael, Hor, Yaqiq, and Aqiq. These angels are said to be present with God whenever He appears in this world, each assigned a special duty.

The angel Gabriel is the creator of souls and unites them to the human body; he is also the messenger of God, transmitting messages and revelations from the divine realm to humanity. He guides individuals on their spiritual journeys, and plays a role in revealing spiritual truths and teachings to enlightened individuals. To know Gabriel within one's being is to know God. Gabriel is credited with the creation of the original maqam symbolizing the essence of creation. When the time had come to bring humans into existence, the soul hesitated to enter the body, fearing the darkness within it. So God called upon Gabriel to play the tanbur. As Gabriel sat on the right shoulder of the human body he whispered, "I will now create you. I will put pieces of my soul into your body so that you may be human." With the sound of the tanbur, the soul was charmed into a trance and, drunken with joy, danced into the body, bringing it to life. However, once in the world, the soul suddenly found its blissful surroundings transformed into a harsh reality. Music became his only keepsake to remind him of his blessed origins (*Song of God* 2018, 12:00).

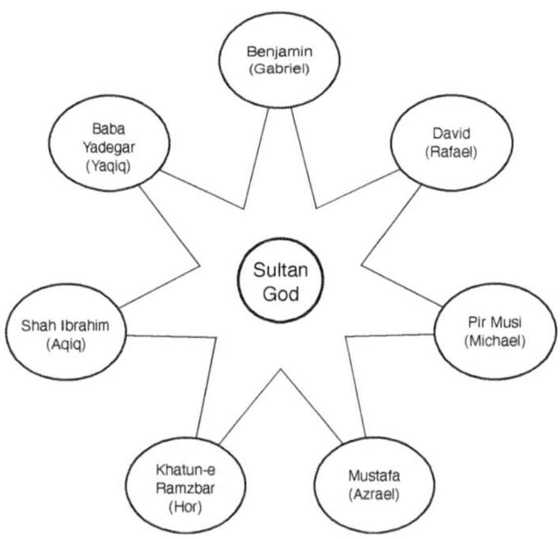

Figure 14.6: The sacred star of the seven saints and angels.
Kevin Greek, public domain.

God summoned the angel Rafael and told him to listen to people's longing and prayers, conveying them back to Him. When people are dancing, playing music, singing, painting, creating, and even bringing their hands together they are connecting with Rafael. In some traditions, Rafael is considered the angel of resurrection and judgment who is responsible for blowing the trumpet of awakening. In Yarsan belief, he holds a key role in the process of spiritual transformation and the ultimate reunion with the Divine, bestowing healing and showing mercy.

God gave the angel Michael the duty to impart knowledge and wisdom to humanity. He inspires poets, writers, and other mystics to read and write great works, and gives humanity the intelligence to make wise choices. In Yarsan belief, he is associated with providing sustenance and blessings to those who follow the path of righteousness.

To the angel Azrael God gave the task of bringing souls back to God at the time of death. Many perceive the Angel of Death as a fearsome figure, yet he serves as a compassionate guide for the departed soul. Azrael knows the longing and suffering of this world, and helps the soul return to its maker.

The angel Aqiq is linked to the unfolding of mystical truth. He is a mediator and guide between worlds. Yaqiq is associated with the heart, blood, love, and divine fire—the burning spiritual heat within. He also provides clarity and watchful presence.

Lastly, God summoned the angel Hor, the one female angel of the seven, as the representation of the female essence. Within Yarsan philosophy, the universe is evolving through different epochs. After the first epoch in which God manifested the Seven Souls or Angels, each epoch saw the reappearance of the Seven Souls or Haft Tan. In the First Epoch, they appeared in their true angelic form, while in subsequent Epochs they appeared in human incarnations. In the Fourth Epoch, these angels manifested in earthly form as saints, who were charged by Sultan Sahak with responsibility for the inner realms and to safeguard humanity. The names of each saint and their corresponding angel are: Benjamin (Gabriel), David (Rafael), Musi (Michael), Mustafa (Azrael), Khatun-e Ramzbar (Hor), Baba Yadegar (Yaqiq), and Shah Ibrahim (Aqiq) (Figure 14.6).

St. Benjamin, who is the Archangel Gabriel's incarnation, is the preceptor of all Yarsanis. St. Musi, the incarnation of the Archangel Michael, is the recording angel who keeps a record of all the acts of man, good and bad. Saint David, the incarnation of archangel Rafael, has the duty of evangelizing and blowing the trumpet upon the Day of Reckoning. St. Mustafa, the incarnation of Azrael, is the agent of souls and orders their affairs. The fifth is Shah Ibrahim, who is the embodiment of Aqiq, and Baba Yadegar is the embodiment of Yaqiq, both of whom are guides and messengers of faith.

The only female among them is Khatun Dairak Ramzbar, the incarnation of the angel Hor, and the mother of Sultan Sahak. She is known as the Divine Feminine and is similar to Mother Mary who is iconic in

Figure 14.7: Tomb of Sultan Sahak, Hawraman, Kurdistan. From left: Pir Dariush Hosseini, Seyed Salman, and author.
Photo by author.

Christianity. In Kurdish, the word *ramzbar* means "the one who tells the secrets" and *khatun* means "lady." Among the Yarsanis there is much respect paid to the Divine Feminine who also appears as a mysterious angel, Khatun-i Ramzbar (Lady of Secrets). The writer Frederic Macler claims that the name Ramzbar means "secret of the creator." When God was sitting on the waters and created Ramzbar, she gave birth to light. She brought out from the sea a round loaf of bread to symbolize the light and offered it to the World. By her order the angels formed a devotional assembly (jam), distributed the bread, offered prayers and exclaimed 'Hu!' Then the earth and the skies became one. The Creator then said, "I appoint that woman to be the Lady of the Resurrection who will one day be the helper and teacher of human beings." She was the final angel, completing the circle of the Seven Souls.

Sultan Sahak is not only the founder of the Yarsani faith but is considered to be God's incarnation. It is not known exactly when he lived, though it is likely to have been in the 14th century in the region of Sulaymaniyah in Kurdistan (Eastern Iraq today). Two narratives surround his birth. In the first, his mother Khatun-e Ramzbar was sleeping under a pomegranate tree when a bird was eating one of the fruits and dropped a seed into her open mouth. Miraculously, this seed grew into a baby, and thus Sultan Sahak was virgin born. The second narrative says he came to his mother as a falcon, and when he landed he turned into a baby boy (Kjellen n.d.).

The tomb of Sultan Sahak is a pilgrimage site for mystics, called Pardiwar. It lies in Shaykhan Gardens, near the Sirwan River in Kurdistan (Kermanshah Province, Western Iran) (Figure 14.7).

Herodotus mentions that it was in this river that the sacred white horse of King Cyrus the Great disappeared. Many claim the spirit of the white horse still appears from the river. It was also in this spot that the Battle of Diyala River took place in 693 BCE between the forces of the Assyrian empire and the Elamites of southern Iran.

Baba Yadegar, one of the great disciples of Sultan Sahak, traveled to India evangelizing the teachings of Yarsanism. One story recounts that he was killed there, his body carried in a coffin by a camel to be returned and buried. His tomb is located in "Ban Zardeh" village, Rijab City, Kermanshah, surrounded by a beautiful valley among old cypress and oak trees. In a corner of the space around the tomb is a spring that gives water used for blessing. Considered one of the seven sacred waters, this spring is renowned as the Fountain of Youth.

The seven days of the week are associated with the seven archangels and saints, and each day has special duties and rituals, including music, dance, and prayers honoring a given theme. Angel Gabriel and St. Benjamin are honored on Monday, the day of creation, healing, and prosperity. Monday is a day of blessings, for letting go, and observing healing. The battle against darkness was won on a Monday so dances might express gratitude for health and fortune, offer healing to others, relieve stress, and salute the power of light to banish dark. Tuesday is a day of strength, honoring Angel Michael, St. Musi, and all warriors; dances celebrate physical strength as well as strength of purpose and the power to fight against ego. Wednesday is a day to contemplate and turn within. The fourth Wednesday of the month is the day Ahriman pays a visit. It honors Angel Azreal and St. Mustafa who support remembrance of those lost, lovers separated, and the pain of longing. Thursday is the day of blessings and gratitude, a new beginning when darkness and sorrow pass. You are awakened and refreshed to start again, so it is a good day for a zikr during sunrise, celebrating rebirth. Thursday also honors Sultan Sahak, the divine being of the Yarsan people. Dances share blessings and offer gratitude.

Friday is a day of forgiveness, humility, and secrets. This is why it is the Islamic day of prayer, a time to share your secrets with God. Friday also honors St. Baba Yadegar; dances offer prayers for hope and protection in the great unknown. Saturday is considered the day of love, associated with the classic lovers, Laila and Majnun; lover and Beloved are finally together. It is also a day honoring the connection between master and disciple, pir (elder) and *murid* (student). Saturday is associated with Angel Hor and St. Khatun-e Ramzbar, the patron of all women. Dance on this day honors absent lovers rejoined and spreading good will. Sunday is dedicated to the Sun and the deity Mitra; the sun gives us energy and vitality so it is an active, productive day. It is also a day of friendship, togetherness, and unity. It honors Angel Rafael and St. David. Dances celebrate the life-giving energy of the sun.

Tanbur: The Instrument of Devotion

I cannot describe how I feel while playing tanbur. But I can tell you this much, spiritually I am elsewhere, in another time and space. It is the sound of "Khavankar," the sound of Truth. If I were to put it in one sentence, all I would say is that tanbur is not from this world, it is heavenly.

– Donya Kamali

The tanbur is deeply linked to the Yarsan culture and the region of *Kurdistan*, which is suffused with a unique devotion to their traditional music, sacred maqams, and the narrative songs and stories that have kept their culture alive for generations. The tanbur is the foremost symbol of their culture and music, considered a key component of prayer, sacred dance, and zikr. Darvish Ali Changi, a musician and poet from 16th century Transoxiana,[151] claimed the word "tanbur" comes from "tan" meaning heart or body, and "bur" meaning stroke, meaning an instrument that "plays the strings of the heart and touches your soul" (Vatanpour 2017, 39).

The tanbur is a long-necked wooden lute with a pear-shaped resonating bowl, measuring between seventy and eighty cm in length. It has fourteen frets and no quarter-frets. The frets are made of gut or metal

---

[151] Transoxania is the historic region of Turkistan in Central Asia east of the Amu Darya (Oxus River) and west of the Syr Darya (Jaxartes River).

Figure 14.8: Tanbur lesson with Pir Mohammad Zolnuri (left) and author (right), Kermanshah, Iran.
Seyed Salman Hosseini

strings wound around the neck two, three, or four times then tied with a special knot. When playing, musicians occasionally tap the instrument, creating a drum-like effect to add percussion to their piece. The earliest form of the tanbur was a two-string instrument (*dotar*), with the two strings representing Adam and Eve—the string that generates the melody symbolizes Eve and the string that harmonizes with it, as a drone, symbolizes Adam. The current version of the tanbur has three strings; the top two are tuned in unison and the bottom string is tuned to the fourth or fifth harmonic. Tanbur master Ostad Elahi, née Nur Ali (1895–1974) transformed the two-stringed tanbur by adding a third string detuned slightly from its twin then developed new playing techniques that used all ten fingers. The traditional masters favor the two and three-string tanburs, believing they are more true in sound and spirit.

One of the important spiritual aspects of the tanbur is the sacred numbers found within it. For example, the numbers seven, thirteen, and fourteen are all considered significant. The tanbur is the only instrument that has all these sacred numbers built into it. The first seven frets are likened to the Haft Tan, and the second seven to the Haftanan, the seven saints that emanate from the Haft Tan (Zavieh 2015, 510). It is also believed the tanbur symbolizes three saints and three angels:

the body is a symbol of Benjamin and Gabriel; the strings embody St. Musi and Michael; and the voice originates from St. David and Rafael, who is believed to play a trumpet on Judgment Day to awaken the dead. Playing the tanbur thus beckons the spirits of the Haft Tan to join the participants and bring positive energy for healing or strengthening their faith.

The tanbur is considered so sacred in this culture that masters kiss the instrument before playing it and whisper the phrase *aval o akhar yar* into it, which means "the first and the last is the divine friend." It is also a custom to display the instruments prominently from the highest point on their walls. The bond between a master and their tanbur is so deep that when a master dies their tanbur is buried along with them. The tanbur is their companion and part of their body, and the song which is played on it is the essence of their soul. The mystics say that when the tanbur is broken, the soul connected to that instrument is broken as well, and out of respect for the soul of the damaged instrument, it should be buried. Just as Rumi calls the sound of the tanbur and its stringed kin "the sound of the friend," Yarsanis also believe that the sound of tanbur is closely connected with the human soul. They call its voice "the sound of truth" and "the song of the Divine."

Figure 14.9: Terra-cotta figure of a tanbur player with Angel Gabriel on the right shoulder, early 10th century BCE, Elamite dynasty, Susa, Iran.

Photo by author.

The tanbur is one of the oldest stringed instruments still played today. Archaeological finds indicate that the Iranian tanbur dates back to at least 4,000 BCE, evidence of which was found during excavations near the tomb of Daniel the Prophet in Shush, Iran. Rock reliefs from three thousand years ago found in Bani Yunes Hills in Mousel, Iraq, show performers playing instruments similar to the tanbur. A figurine from the Median empire (700-550 BCE) in Kurdistan depicts an ancient tanbur player with a small man clutching his right shoulder (Figure 14.9). The tanbur has been mentioned in pre-Islamic books and manuscripts such as Asurig's poem *Derakht* (The Tree) and Ferdowsi's *Shahnameh*. The biography of King Ardashir-e Babkan also mentioned that he played tanbur. The post-Islamic poets, such as Rumi, Nezami Ganjavi, Hafez, Bidel Dehlavi, and Junayd of Baghdad, frequently mention the tanbur in their poems.

Iranian legends explain that before the Pishdadian age[152] there were seven darvish brothers within the Iranian lands who were so connected that if one darvish felt pain the others did as well. Then demons arrived bringing darkness and building walls cutting them off from nature and the Divine. Many heroes of the *Shahnameh* were only able to survive because of music, and it is believed that the tanbur was a gift from the angels to help protect us from evil. The tanbur has wandered the continents over the millennia, from the East to the shores of the Atlantic Ocean, from the North into Siberia, and from the South to India. The tanbur eventually made its way to China where it became known as tanbura. In Greece, they called it tanburas and the Byzantines named it Pandora. In local Kurdish regions, it is called Tamireh. Today, in one way or another, the tanbur is present in most lands—Africa, China, Egypt, Syria, the Balkans, Tajikistan, Georgia, Afghanistan, Bangladesh, Morocco, and Turkmenistan—and researchers believe that most stringed instruments today were derived from it.

The heavenly sound of the tanbur can take complete control of the soul, inducing incredible calmness and peace of mind, or inspiring ecstasy. When a master plays the tanbur, the musician and the instrument become one. Upon the music's climax, there comes an outpouring of all of humanity's secrets gathered since the manifestation of the first human. The tanbur has a noble soul that speaks to our inner emotions. It has been said that the maqam and the tanbur have a relationship like

---

152 In the *Shahnameh*, the Pishdadians were the first Iranian dynasty before the Achaemenids, who ruled for over two thousand years; their progenitor was Keyumars, the first human, like Adam of the Abrahamic faiths.

the soul has with the body. The soul is like the maqam which is enduring and indelible and the tanbur is like the body, the perishable container and actor of the spirit (Zavieh 2015, 510). Seyed Salman explains "The tanbur talks to me and plays my inner emotions." The Yarsanis regard the tanbur as a living entity that has the power to change human emotions and induce healing.

The divine-human relationship of tanbur has helped the Yarsan people carve a unique identity for themselves and their music. Generations of tanbur players have passed on their secrets so that the instrument can continue to be played and honored within their spiritual heritage. Those who play the tanbur in the Yarsan tradition are treated as spiritual masters and highly respected in the community. These masters are entrusted with the sacred heritage of the maqam.[153] Their duty is to pass on their skill and knowledge of maqams to the next generation, otherwise its history and significance in their culture will fade away. Each master tambur player learns to handcraft a tanbur in their own family tradition. If one wants a genuine mystical tanbur, it cannot be bought off the shelf at a shop—only a master craftsman and mystic can create sacred tanburs. The craft of constructing a tanbur is a valued family tradition passed from generation to generation and there is no separation between the tanbur craftsman and musician. It is believed the tree used to create a tanbur has a soul, so the tanbur craftsman treats the tree like a family member to be adopted, communicating with it to understand it, and only harvesting it during the right season. The preferred tree has experience and a history; it has seen love, loneliness, and struggles. It also has a gender, and only wood from a male tree of a certain age is used to create a tanbur.

There are two ways of creating the pear-shaped resonating bowl. One way is to glue several sections of wood together. Examples of this construction made by Ostad Khodavadi date back 120-130 years in the Sahneh region of Kermanshah. The other is to carve the body out of a single piece of wood. This construction is most prevalent among the

153 The sacred musical modes—melodies, scales, patterns, significant notes, modulation and development, etc.

Kurdish Gorani people of Kermanshah. The age of the wood is carefully chosen in either case. A mulberry tree is recommended as it is believed to have the best sound and is known as the tree of wisdom. Yarsani believe the mulberry tree has divine purpose and intelligence, as well as determination, wisdom, and patience. Since the mulberry tree bears sweet fruits, it also symbolizes abundance, fertility, and nourishment.

The instrument's wooden construction is considered to be its male aspect, while the strings and melody are considered its female aspect. And finally, there is the beauty of its voice, a voice that helps people let go of material concerns and connect to the spiritual world. Rumi describes the tanbur as an instrument whose singing invites those weary of material sufferings to commune in enlightenment and love.

The theory of Iranian music is difficult to learn. If the master presents too much too soon then it loses its spiritual essence; instead, the student must cultivate a loving relationship with it over time, learning to communicate with it; it is this communication that will produce the melody. This relationship must be developed before learning an excess of theory. Iranian music should originate from feeling and respect, not just technique.

Melodies of the Divine

Music is the language of the spirit. It opens the
secret of life bringing peace, abolishing strife.

- Kahlil Gibran

Iranian music is a spiritual art. Any spiritual music, regardless of its origin, can strengthen the good aspects of the soul. It can turn excitement into calmness and meditation. It can change sorrow into concentration and attention, anger into perseverance, fear into courage, passion into love, and hatred into empathy. Music helps to convey an audience into another dimension, sustaining their attention over extended periods, and aiding in the exchange between the Divine and the material realms.

A maqam is a system of music characterized by specific melodic intervals and development. Each maqam—performed according to specific rules and categorized by the time of day it is most effective—identifies a unique mood such as longing, strength, happiness, comfort, bravery, or power. Within Iranian music, there are two interpretations of a maqam: classical and spiritual. The classical type is performed for entertainment. The spiritual maqam accompanies and cultivates sacred ceremonies, prayer, meditation, healing, and dance. To play such a maqam for any other purpose or without traditional instruments is not done.

Some say the sacred maqam originated in primitive chants known as Hure Khani. Hure Khane mimic sounds of nature, such as the call of a partridge or song of a nightingale, vocalized from the throat, and may be similar to Native American or Shamanic chants. Our ancient ancestors acquired the art of singing from birds, which are believed to echo the voice of the Divine. The maqam played on the tanbur today is said to have been inspired by the sounds of birds and nature; in some, one may hear a resemblance to partridges singing, as this bird is believed to carry the souls of saints. From the south of Iran, there is an ancient chant known as *zahiruk*, which originates from the sound of a pigeon. These two tunes, from the west and south of Iran, are believed to be the oldest still surviving, developed during a time before speech by means of imitation of birds, a form of *avaz*.[154] One of the most famous types of avaz is from the nightingale. When played on the tanbur, the nightingale's song induces a state of ecstasy and beauty that is unparalleled by modern instruments.

The Hure Khani may also include prayers and recitations of sacred verses and hymns. There are two primary types of these: Ahura Khani and Mur Khani. Ahura Khani are prayers to Ahura (Lord or God in the Avestan language), whereas the Mur Khani are prayers for the departed so their soul can be returned to the Beloved. The Mur Khani is sung today at funerals or over the dead, resembling desperate sobbing or crying.

However the maqam originated, the sacred music came to be combined with mystic poetry. The beauty of sacred maqams combined with poetry originally helped disseminate the ideals of mysticism. In the

---

154 An avaz is an unmetered or free-rhythm portion of a Persian classical music mode, typical of vocal chants.

Iranian tradition, a sacred dancer understands the system of maqams as well. Anyone can play or dance to the musical notes of a maqam but for a spiritual maqam, one must understand its origin and purpose, and when, where, and how it may be danced or played. Those who play the tanbur in the Yarsan tradition are known to be wise; it is believed they have the light of God or the guidance of an angel. Regular musicians may claim to have the proper technique, but those who want to become masters and play spiritual maqams must be trained in the technique of the heart. When students understand this, they are ready to step onto the path.

A spiritual maqam is associated with the stages that a seeker must follow in order to become a mystic; its main objective is to connect to God. It transforms the feelings that a sacred dancer or darvish experiences in their daily life into their inherent longing for God. To be inspired by a maqam in sacred dance means to be internally transformed by it.

There are now only three schools in the world, all in Iran, where one is allowed to learn the spiritual maqam if one desires to be a mystic: in the cities of Guran and Sahneh, both in the Kurdistan region, and in the province of Lorestan. These three schools offer tanbur lessons according to the sacred maqam, each with its own manner of teaching. Those who want to learn the maqams must have an open heart and an open mind. This wisdom has been passed down from generation to generation, just as sacred dance and whirling have been passed down. Every movement of dance and note of maqam is sacred, so be certain to learn these from a master and be sure they are never altered, but followed and performed respectfully and faithfully.

The Transformative Power of Maqams and Sama

Some people hear the music while others feel it.

– Unknown

As previously mentioned, seven angels formed from Divine Energy descended to Earth and took on human form. Throughout the generations, the seven angels have continued to enter human form to teach for the good of humanity. These Seven Souls are believed to be constantly present among us. It is said that when all the seven timeless angels came together to unite their power into one being, that was when the tanbur was created.

All sacred maqams maintain a connection with the seven angels or the saints associated with them. They are summoned whenever the sacred maqams are played. Each of the angels is associated with a taste that correlates with a particular flavor of life. For example, Angel Michael is associated with salt, Angel Rafael is associated with sourness, Angel Azrael is associated with bitterness, and Angel Gabriel is associated with sweetness. Each maqam is therefore associated with a flavor, as well as a color, sense, element, and direction.

Understanding maqams means understanding the unique passion and emotion each maqam may offer for healing and inspiration. Different types of maqams are played for different situations, whether it is played for a public or sacred setting, or whether it applies to an ancient ceremony or a communal gathering, playing the appropriate maqam is important. Yarsan maqams can be categorized into three types: *majlisi* (ceremonial), *majazi* (contemporary), and *haqqani* (ancient).

The **majlisi** maqams are based on ancient stories, myths, and epics. These constitute the majority of known maqams and offer a language to express sorrow and happiness, separation, and epic narratives of legends for communal settings. They have lesser sanctity compared to the sacred maqams of the jamkhaneh.

The **majazi** maqams are created by master musicians for public settings. A musician may be allowed by their order to create a new maqam based on sacred poetry but not scripture or sacred text. These new maqams use the traditional elements and rules of ancient maqams, but are usually less than a hundred years old and typically are more technical, designed to demonstrate a musician's prowess. They are created for public concerts or recordings. Majazi maqams tend to jump around in loud bursts compared to the softer, confined music of its sacred cousin. They attempt to bring the attention of the listener outward whereas the sacred music of the darvish brings one inward. Vocals for majazi maqams are usually taken from mystical poetry with the words of Rumi, Hafez, or others.

The **haqqani** (the true) maqam has spiritual and holy significance and typically originates back to the 10th or 14th centuries. These maqams are based upon the sacred texts of the Yarsanis and are prohibited from being shared outside of the sacred jam ceremonies unless granted special exception by the master. There are 72 known haqqani maqams (Zavieh 2015, 510). They can be further subdivided into 1) *avazi*, 2) *sarband*, and 3) *sama* maqams.

1) The **avazi** maqams are typically played by pirs and masters to tell ancient tales of angels or saints with themes of longing and loneliness, love, patience, burdens, courage, and more. Some of the avazi maqams introduced below demonstrate the breadth of the themes.
   - The **Maqam of Tarz** is considered the "mother" of all spiritual maqams, the creation maqam. The word "tarz" means "the path." It is the first path a seeker chooses. Seven types of tarz maqams describe the story of the creation, the purpose of a given aspect of the soul, and the virtues of the Seven Valleys encountered upon the path to the Divine. The story of human creation starts at Mt. Sarandil. According to the legend, in the beginning, there was a kingdom of light, which had yellow soil, and a kingdom of dark, with black soil. Each human would be given a choice to follow the path to the light or the dark kingdom, as we each have both black mud (ego) and yellow mud (good) in ourselves. It is said that when Angel Gabriel began to play the Maqam of Tarz, the soul entered the body he created, and then began crying; it didn't want to be trapped in a body on earth. The angel told the soul not to worry, for some day the angel of death would come to take the soul back to heaven, but God placed it here in this world because it has a purpose. Angel Gabriel whispered into the ear of the soul, telling him to carry the feelings and voice of God for humanity. He explained that God had created this tanbur to give man the melody of the soul. This is why the tanbur is called the voice of God. Some say that when Gabriel played the Maqam of Tarz on the tanbur for the dismal soul, it began to dance in ecstasy and joy until it accepted its place and the body came to life. The Maqam of Tarz is not recorded in notebooks but has been passed down master to student for generations, and may only be played with

the approval of a master, with an understanding of its heritage, and with feeling. The color associated with Tarz is white.

- Similar to the upliftment a detached and longing soul feels after hearing the Maqam of Tarz, the **Maqam of Gharibi** is intended for the soul that feels despair, or lost, or alienated like a stranger. Gharibi means "lost soul." This maqam explains that everyone may feel isolated and unable to communicate with others. When we were created we had the sense we entered the world alone. This maqam reminds us that we are not alone and that the angels are there to protect us. It helps us feel as if we belong to something once more. It attempts to clear depression, loneliness, and anxiety. Gharibi is often played during twilight, between the time the sun has set and the moon rises, when we most need the hope and strength this maqam offers. The color associated with this maqam is light blue. When we whirl to the Maqam of Gharibi we release our despair and loneliness knowing that angels are with us, accompanying us to our awakening.
- The **Maqam of Majnuni** is meant to evoke feelings of love and compassion. Majnun means "the lover." This maqam represents our desperate search for Divine Love. Any form of love or longing can evoke this mood: the love between a mother and her child, the attraction of the moth to a flame, the longing to find God or one's own soul, the story of Shams and Rumi, an attraction between two lovers such as Romeo and Juliet. In Iranian folklore, this mood is exemplified by the story of Layla and Majnun. Composed in the seventh or eighth century, it is the story of a young man named Qays who falls in love with a girl named Layla. Her father steadfastly refuses to allow Qays to marry his daughter. But the young man's love is so strong he cannot let go and he gradually descends into a form of madness, as does Layla. Majnun is the lover searching for the lost beloved. This relationship between lover and Beloved is eternal and transcends sensual contact; it is a devotion that is free of self. This theme fills much of Sufi and mystic poetry and this is one of the most famous and important maqams in the mystic

tradition. When this maqam is played it explains that it is your nature to love and be loved, to experience joy and sorrow, and that one day the soul will be freed, but for now, while you are here, enjoy life. It is our destiny to always be longing for something we can never have. At times the longing carries us to the oj or the hal (state of ecstasy) and that is when we find the awakening.

- Following the Maqam of Majnuni is always the **Maqam of Sahari**. Sahari means the sunrise, the awakening. It represents the awakening state when the lover has found his beloved. This is the threshold where the Beloved is close and spiritual understanding is near. The whirlers reach ecstasy at this point. Maqam Sahari is dedicated to St. Benjamin, who represents Angel Gabriel. Once a Majnun finds what they are longing for, they finally see the light of sunrise, and they finally reach the awakened state. The Maqam of Sahari is played when the lover finds Divine Love and coincides with the whirler reaching the state of ecstasy. A sama begins with sunrise—a dance for the Divine. When the samazan falls in love, the sun rises, the light of the sun falls on the lover and they dance. The musicians may play the Maqam of Sahari but humans themselves may find themselves stuck in the role of Majnun for years. For seekers, this is the process of a lifetime.
- We are travelers in this world until we depart for another world entirely. The **Maqam of Barieh** portrays the nomad, the traveler, or a caravan. Barieh means "the traveler," or "to carry" something. This maqam is played for a soul lost in material life. It is played to encourage the lost soul who will eventually be reborn and free of ego. It may also be played if we feel a human being has lost connection to their soul, so the body can find the soul. Or it might be played for someone who is leaving on a journey of self-discovery, or departing on a treacherous trip, or leaving for war. This maqam has calming melodies that sound like sobbing or crying, yet it gives hope that life goes on. In dance, we perform the Maqam of Barieh when seeking

hope. *Bar* means burden; we carry our troubles on our backs and this maqam is played to alleviate that tension and pain. Our life feels long, but for God, it is only an hour. In that one hour, we waste our time not living fully, so our soul is lost. Why not enjoy life while you are here? Look how a child is living its life, careless and clueless, having fun. Live life like that and your soul will find you. This maqam is attributed to Barbad, a musician in the Sasanian court.

- Imagine riding overnight on a train that travels endlessly, one that never stops at your station. No conductor on this train can tell you its location nor does any station look different. Ghatar means "train." The **Maqam of Ghatar** expresses the sad monotony of a traveler whose every day is the same, never reaching his destination. It mimics the sound of a train in a sad, lonely way, using the half frets of the tambur. The pacing accelerates and slows down just as a train does between stops. The dance will vary between modes of oj and moj accordingly. This also symbolizes how the pace of life changes between fortune and poverty, delight and sorrow.
- **Tarz-e Rustam** is an epic maqam based on the national hero and warrior figure Rustam. Rustam fought the *divs* (demons) in order to save the Iranians. In the *Shahnameh*, the story called *Haftkhān-e Rustam* (Seven Thrones of Rustam) follows Rustam and his faithful steed Rakhsh as they undertake seven epic challenges. Each challenge presents a formidable opponent or obstacle that Rustam must conquer using his extraordinary abilities. The trials serve to highlight Rustam's unmatched prowess and establish him as a central figure in Persian heroic folklore. After completing his third challenge, however, Rustam becomes weary and sits down near a river to cry. His work conquering demons to save the people of this world seems unappreciated. A lovely woman suddenly appears from the woods promising to make him a great being, a king, and give him all he desires if he leaves his journey and accompanies her. Rustam regains hope upon listening to the

beautiful enchantress and promises to leave with her, but first he wants to play his tanbur in gratitude. Because the tanbur is the voice of God, the spell of the enchantress is broken and she is revealed as a gruesome demon, which he promptly slays with his sword. Because Rustam had been so sad and upset, his ego had opened an opportunity for the demon to trick him. An angel suddenly appears before Rustam from the tanbur; she explains that the gods had tested him to see if he would be trapped.

As a maqam, Tarz-e Rustam is important because it portrays the hardship we go through when we feel unappreciated and alone; it is then we are most vulnerable to the anger and ego within us. This warrior maqam helps us gain strength and direction and allows us to conquer our ego. If there's any darkness that wants to come inside of us, we stay strong and resolute. Whirling to the Maqam of Tarz-e Rustam inspires one to find the will and determination to defeat our "demons" in the quest for awakening.

- Every person has a duality of good and evil just as the rose possesses a beautiful color, fragrance, and bloom but it also has sharp thorns that can puncture and scratch. To compensate for its hurtful thorns, the rose must bloom at its largest and best. The **Maqam of Ghol-va Khakh** tells us that as humans we have a dark side, an ego, that we may never quite be rid of, but as we grow, showing our good and love to the world, our ego will diminish and be overshadowed. Ghol-va Khakh means "the rose and the mud." The rose represents our beauty and strength and the mud represents our dark, hidden side. Whirling to the Maqam of Ghol-va Khakh aids us in embracing both our light and dark sides, fostering personal growth and the discovery of inherent goodness. Whirlers may improvise devotional movements during this maqam. An alternative maqam known as **Ghol-va Khar** which means "the rose and the thorn" may be used in place of Ghol-va Khakh. It has a similar theme, reasoning that everything of beauty has an opposite side.

- The **Maqam of Ghele-va Dareh** is frequently played at funerals, guiding the soul on its journey home. Ghele-va Dareh means "the soul wants to return home." It is believed that upon death the soul leaves for a new home—either in a different human body, or joining nature. On other occasions, the Maqam of Ghele-va Dareh is used to reconnect the soul to the body when it is alienated or its sense of purpose has been lost due to depression, anger, trauma, or anxiety. This very melancholy maqam is played as a prayer to help the soul return home whether it is leaving its physical body in death or has lost direction and needs to return to its living body. It should be played any time one feels disconnected from the soul. When we whirl to Ghele-va Dareh we connect with a lost soul or someone we miss and attempt to send them a message and direct them home.
- Similar to the purpose of Maqam of Ghele-va Dareh, the **Maqam of Pa-va Muri** is performed at funerals, allowing the soul to ascend and reunite with the Beloved. Pa-va Muri means the "time has come" to sing a lament for the dead or to rise from the body. In comparison, Ghele-va Dareh is played or the *Mur* Khani is sung for the soul when it longs to return to human life, or seeks another form while its earthly body is still living. For this maqam, we use the chap (left) sama to prayerfully guide the soul to the Beloved.
- The **Maqam of Alvan** honors the Alwand River and the nearby mountain of Dalahu. The element of water is fundamental to this maqam, and is equated with the goddess Anahita. According to belief, the Alwand River served as the source for all rivers flowing towards temples dedicated to Anahita. The sacred water flowing down the river is said to be the tears of angels with the power to cleanse one's sense of ego and purify the soul. Thus, this maqam serves as a purifying ritual. For the Maqam of Alvan, our movements symbolize the motion of water such as waves, cascades, and rainfall. This maqam beautifully portrays the mountain as a source of hope and energy, flowing like water, pouring out wherever it is needed to nourish all corners of the world.

- The **Maqam of Abedini** is named after a saint who taught us to be humble and discard the ego. This maqam is intended for the curious, the ones who are always questioning. There is a legend of forty missionaries who fasted for forty days on the sacred mountain of Dalahu. Abedin was the one who always questioned the existence of God and was notorious for his denial of mysticism. When the missionaries came together in zikr, he was the one who noticed the moment they entered ecstasy and, in surprise, interrupted everyone to ask what was going on. A knowledgeable and scientific man, Abedin would often argue and question the beliefs of the mystics. He would deny angels existed and ask for proof. He was not intending to be unkind but he was curious; he sought the knowledge of the mind when others were using the knowledge of the heart. His ego made him appear as an iconoclast. In time, Abedin realized that he could never succeed in finding an explanation for everything in this world, nor discover the state of mind the others had reached. Desiring to feel the love the others were experiencing, he took a leap of faith and trusted the unknown. As he sat contemplating with his tanbur, he asked God to show him the way. In a vision, God told him "If you listen, I will play through you." He closed his eyes and found himself playing a maqam, the one that now bears his name. When dancing to the Maqam of Abedini, bring in movements that portray the ego.
- The **Maqam of Sheikh Amiri** combines a song narrative and zikr that tells the story of Sheikh Amir and Seyed Farzi Khamoush whose spiritual relationship echoed that of Rumi and Shams. The song is so sacred that only a great master, a pir, may be allowed to lead and sing it. This maqam has three mystical stories telling of Sheikh Amir's longing for his master. The essence of these stories and songs is for the listener to fall into prayer.
- The **Maqam of Sey Khamoushi** was crafted for those who dwell in silence and seclusion. The ancient word *sey* means secret, and the word *khamoush* means "silent." The Khamoushi

family of the village of Jeyhoun Abad is renowned for being reclusive, and their ancestors are believed to have hosted the soul of one of the seven sacred angels. They are very quiet hermits dwelling in the mountains and do everything they can without seeking the help of others. If you are in a cemetery of honored mystics and you see a tomb with no identification, it is likely a member of the Khamoushi family buried there. This is an ancient maqam created and dedicated to those who seek strength and humility within themselves in denial of ego. During this maqam, whirlers might choose movements that portray a sense of isolation that is overpowered by inner strength and courage.

2) **Sarband**, another subset of haqqani maqams, is meant to accompany a zikr, narrative, a prayer, or a story sung or chanted. An example of a zikr for a Sarband maqam is repetitive chanting of *Hu Hu Yar*, which means "the divine breath is my companion," with repetitive ritual movements. Sarband maqams are dedicated to the great masters and are connected to the seven feelings of the heart. There is one maqam each to treat sadness, anger, illness, stress, break ups, and more. When the master begins to chant and sing the ancient words, everyone in the gathering chants along. The Sarband acts as a calming conclusion for any superficial affliction we may experience during the day. Some sarband maqams are introduced here.
   - The **Maqam of Baba Heidar** is a healing zikr maqam. Baba Heidar was a mystic healer; the healing contact of his hands was so powerful that it was said he could heal anyone. The maqam is a zikr that summons his spirit to apply healing to those who need it. The zikr request repeats the words, "Baba Heidar please come to my aid, please come to my aid. I need your help. I need your help."
   - The **Maqam of Rezhyan Dalahu** means "Adorned Dalahu" (Zavieh 2015, 513). One of the beloved lands of the Yarsanis is the Mountain Dalahu and its surroundings. Many pilgrims travel there to be blessed by the places where several of the legendary angels and saints of Yarsan lore have appeared. Dalahu is considered an earthly Paradise adorned by divine presence.

When we play a maqam for these mountains we are giving thanks to nature and what God has provided us.

- The theme of **Maqam of Baba Naousi-Ghare Chupi** is death and rebirth. Named after Baba Naousi, a Yarsani master and saint known as "the dark shepherd," it is often played at funerals, and is sometimes called the "dance of death" or "dance of darkness." Mystics greet death as if the soul enters another realm, which is a cause for celebration. The sama of the left turn (chap sama) was created for the soul of the deceased who is now free to meet God. Baba Naousi is practiced as a solo zikr led by a pir but may become a sama maqam if played to a faster tempo.

  During this maqam the soul makes a journey of three parts, marking the transition between death and rebirth. The first indicates loss, the soul's departure from the deceased, and this part is played slowly with chap sama. The second part represents the transition to a new incarnation or a welcoming of the soul by God, and is played at a moderate tempo. The third and final stage is the rebirth, a homecoming of the soul celebrated by a fast tempo rast sama and is the exciting conclusion of the maqam. In the Lorestan and Kurdistan regions, a *saz* and *dhol*[155] are played during the funeral procession called a *chamari,* a very ancient ritual. The word chamari originates from two components: *cheh* asks "why?" and *mari* means "to take." So chamari asks "Why did you take this?" "Why did you take the soul? Why did you take it away?"
- The **Maqam of Chehel-Tan-Chelaneh** is the maqam of forty souls and forty missionaries (*chel-tan* means "forty souls"). This maqam tells the tale of forty villagers summoned by an angel to meet upon the sacred mountain of Dalahu. All forty came from different directions, climbing tirelessly and strenuously, until finally uniting upon the mountain to gather in a circle. Each villager thought that the other was a prophet sent by God,

155 Dhol is a double-sided barrel drum and a saz is a string instrument similar to the tanbur or dutar.

and they wondered what would come next. An angel appeared before them and explained that for their devotion and trust, each would become a missionary to help spread the word of God. Each missionary would receive a host soul, a part of the seven sacred angels. Today it is believed if a mystic completes forty days of isolation, prayer, and fasting they will unify with a soul from the forty missionaries.

- The **Zikr of Chehel-Tan-Chelaneh** is a rhythmic group zikr. Each of the forty missionaries who met on Mount Dalahu carried the essence of the soul of God and had their own valuable characteristic. For example, one was sweet, another was gentle, and another good. Once united, the forty missionaries performed a zikr together, clapping and chanting. Some say that in folklore their story was retold as Ali Baba and the Forty Thieves, one of the most famous tales collected in *One Thousand and One Nights*. Each of the forty missionaries later lent their name to a zikr and maqam. One of the most famous of these is the Maqam of Abedini.

3) **Sama** maqams are the third specialization of the haqqani maqams and they feature a higher tempo rhythm that invokes sacred dance and sama. When sama maqams are played they likely contain zikr and story elements of other haqqani forms. There are two ways to differentiate sama maqams. One is that the sama may be named for the particular movement or dance that characterizes it. For example, if a particular maqam makes one go crazy and toss their head, that maqam is called the "crazy head toss," or if the maqam is associated with a foot movement it will be named the "foot sama." The energy, rhythm, and meaning of the maqam help inspire the dancer and movements. As a whirler turns in a specific sama maqam, they often engage in the characteristic movements associated with that maqam. The second is that a sama maqam may be an adaption of an avazi maqam with a faster tempo or a different rhythm suitable for whirling.
   - In **Bal Vashan** sama maqam the whirler opens their arms like wings. *Bal* means wings and s*han* means shoulders. This sama is

like the Sahari Maqam in that it represents entering the awakened state. Sometimes this sama becomes a group circle dance or a zikr. When the group falls into a state of ecstasy, each dancer puts their arm on their neighbor's shoulder, linking hands to make a circle. As they turn together as a group it creates a circle of energy for all to unite and fly like angels.

- **Pisht-e Pah** and **Sejaran** are other sama maqams distinguished by their characteristic sama movements. When the Pisht-e Pah sama maqam is played it inspires the feet to dance faster. It means "in step" and is characterized by the use of the back of the foot. The Sejaran sama involves counts of three, the whirler making movements in sets of three, and with three slow steps forward it reminds one to be good, do good, and hear good. Sejaran is one of the most crucial sama maqams, encapsulating the three rules of Zoroaster. It is said that Sheikh Amir once told his apprentices that to understand sama one has to understand the Path of Asha.
- The **Maqam of Janghara,** a sama maqam, symbolizes the soul's battle against its own ego. Janghara means "path to war" and is played to inspire us with the courage to address the many battles we face in life, whether internal or external. There are many dark souls and demons one must face. A warrior dance or sama is usually performed to this maqam to improve strength. The maqam helps remind us that the four elements and the four angels they represent are within us to help win against the dark forces.
- The **Maqam of Jelo Shahi** serves as an introduction or prelude to another maqam. The Maqam of Jelo Shahi means "to bow before the king." Its purpose is to convey gratitude and respect to the master, creator, and Divine Nature for everything that sustains us in life. During this maqam you may hear undulating pitches, symbolizing a voice pleading for forgiveness or expressing humility in the presence of the Divine. The Maqam of Jelo Shahi allows for free-form devotional movement while whirling.

Whether the maqams are ancient, spiritual, or modern, it is important to study and understand them, their meaning, their purpose, and their unique elements.

The Jam Ritual: A Spiritual Gathering

Come out of the circle of time and into the circle of love.

– Rumi

The tanbur is instrumental in Yarsan sacred gatherings known as *jam* sessions that take place in the jamkhaneh. Jam in Farsi refers to a divine gathering, a circle of participants seeking spiritual empowerment. Jam means equality or "unity" and lends its meaning to jamkhaneh, the "house of unity." It is also derived from Jamshid, the emperor of the *Pishdadian* dynasty, and stands for "the presence of the Divine Sultan." The cross symbol and Wheel of Mitra are also known as jam. The jamkhaneh does not need to be built from the ground up as a specific place for jam rituals. Any place, even an open space outdoors, can be suitable for gatherings of jam as long as it is physically and spiritually clean. Wherever the jam takes place, it bestows blessings on the spot.

Figure 14.10: The Jam (unity).

Participants in a traditional jam don simple white gowns resembling a long-sleeved shirt that reaches the floor. A green sash, string, or belt is tied around the waist. Men wear woven hats known as a *sarband* to cover their head. This custom has been practiced since the time of Mithrasim and Zoroastrianism for both men and women. Although jam is united as one ritual, there are three separate rooms: one for men where the main ritual is held, one for elderly men, and one for women and children. Guests are allowed to watch and listen from around the outside of the circle; their focused attention on the service is a way to contribute and receive the blessings.

The Yarsanis only allow those who are gentle in heart to enter their jamkhaneh. It is important to purify the body and mind before entering the space. Negative energy and skepticism can affect the sacred ritual for everyone. Before entering, visitors remove their shoes, prostrate themselves, and kiss the doorstep as a gesture of honor. Once inside, the custom is to kiss each participant's right hand starting from the right side of the room and following the circle, kneeling down once they find an open space. They sit facing inside the circle, showing they are all equal, with the divine presence at the circle's heart.

A jam is composed of prayer or zikr, sama, dining, and offerings. The music and whirling of zikr and sama have great spiritual power, and the tanbur invites spiritual entities to join the circle to spread positive energy, mercy, and blessings. Spiritual arousal is the most important factor in the ritual—the passion and enthusiasm of the vocals may even drown out the tanbur as participants become intoxicated with the music and mood. Some may lose themselves, repeating only words such as *Haqq*, *Hu*, and *Ali*. The whole experience empties the heart of negative feelings and thoughts until a sense of love pervades. It is a potent space in which to pray to have one's problems—whether physical, mental, or financial—be resolved by the Divine. Pirs or a select few spiritual elders may facilitate healing rituals as the power of the music and Divine presence can transmit healing energy to the sick. The faith and love that are roused by music, prayer, and remembrance create receptivity to the spiritual energy delivered from God. The ceremony ends with prayers, vows, and a spiritual talk by the master.

Following the sama comes the dining and offerings service. The *seyed* ("lord" or elder) is always present to bless the food, and the *khadim* or "spiritual servant" assists, remaining standing throughout the jam. The khadim decides who can enter the sacred house and will ensure everything is in order. The third person who assists is the *khalifeh* or caliph, who sits next to the seyed at his right hand and is responsible for the service.

The khadim announces the start of a jam by entering the middle of the circle, standing to face the seyed, and exclaiming "*aval o akhar yar*," ("the first and the last is the divine friend"). This reminds the

Figure 14.11: Yarsan jam ceremony, Iran.
Seyed Salman Hosseini.

participants they all come from God and eventually will return to him, and seals the circle so it becomes a sacred space. Now that the jam is under way, no one can leave or shift from their seated position until the session is completed. The only exception is the khadim whose job is to distribute food among the followers. When he is not doing this, he may kneel on one knee and place his right hand on the ground to assist in the spiritual flow of energy. On cue, the khadim will bring a pitcher of water and basin to the seyed, pouring water on his hands for a ritual washing. It is essential to cleanse and purify the hands before touching the blessed food or instruments and it also symbolically represents cleansing all worldly thoughts from the mind for the ritual. The khadim repeats the offering of cleansing to each member in the circle in a counter-clockwise sequence.

The food offerings are blessed and divided into portions. The portions are called *bash* and each participant is given an equal portion before the remainder is distributed to those outside the gathering (generally women and young children). Often a food sacrifice is given to request something or as thanks (e.g., for a bountiful harvest or healing of a sick member) (Figure 14.11). The food sacrifices are of three types.

The first is a supplication offering, composed of anything edible but uncooked such as fruit, nuts, and raw vegetables. The second is given to fulfill a vow made in a time of distress—this may be a choice of pomegranate, fish, nutmeg, ceremonial bread, or grains roasted with sugar or red meat such as an unblemished rooster, ox, or goat less than a year old. Pomegranates are a sacred fruit for the mystic, thought of as the blood of angels, and are often featured in their ceremonies. The third sacrifice, served only on special occasions, is three kilos of rice prepared with ghee.

The men must prepare all the food for the meal except for specially baked bread usually prepared by the women. As the food is distributed, sacred songs resonate among the melodic tones of the tanbur. The first bash (portion) is allotted to Sultan Sahak who all Yarsanis believe is present during jam. The tanbur, which is considered a living entity, also symbolically receives a portion. The khadim receives the last portion and again announces "*aval o akhar yar!*" Following a prayer by the seyed over the food, the eating can begin.

After concluding the meal, as the remnants are cleared, the khadim again brings a pitcher and basin for hand-cleansing. Next, the khadim brings a pot of blessed water with healing powers from God for each participant to sip from. Following this, the khadim and every participant once again kiss each other's right hand, symbolizing honor, respect, and gratitude. To conclude, a final prayer is recited, marking the formal conclusion of the gathering. Sacred kalams (from the scriptures) are then sung accompanied by the spiritual music of the tanbur. The jam ritual may last between one to several hours depending on the number of offerings, and some participants enter ecstasy by listening to the kalams and music.

The four elements are your face.
Water, wind, fire and earth.
Each one is a blessing.

– Rumi

CHAPTER 15

Dance of the Elements

To be in harmony with the sacred elements, we must breathe, manifest, whirl, and dance with them. When we whirl, our ecstasy is fire, our turning embodies wind, water provides sustenance, and our connection to earth is profound.

Each object and being of the universe contains a varying degree of the four classical elements. According to mystics, our physical body and our existence depend on these elements: air to breathe, sun and fire for light and warmth, water to sustain and nurture, and earth as the source of our substance. The ancient philosopher Aristotle proposed a fifth conceptual element to these four elements: ether, the invisible and unknown space in which everything exists and acts. These five elements form the substance of the body and, at the same time, purify the body. These elements have both a material (outer and physical) aspect and a spiritual (inner and conceptual) sense. Ancient cultures in Greece, Egypt, Iran, Babylon, Japan, Tibet, and India all similarly conceived of five elements of nature, sometimes substituting "wind" for "air" and calling the fifth element "soul."

Figure 15.1: Wheel of Mitra, and the symbolism of the five elements. Sheikh Lotfollah Mosque, Isfahan, Iran.
Photo by author.

Ancient Iranians believed the Divine created the Universe by dividing the sky and earth and creating the elements as building blocks of nature. Healers, philosophers, and alchemists sought to explain, balance, and improve life by mystical or practical use of the five elements. Movements in Iranian and Babylonian sacred dance manifested the energy of wind, fire, and water. They saw the elements as the fundamentals of the mystic universe corresponding to the deities. Today, this relationship to the elements moves Iranians to conserve nature and the earth. The connection to the elements is so ingrained in the culture that their symbols are seen everywhere, whether in a mosque, a synagogue, a church, a Sufi lodge, a museum, or a garden.

Manifesting the qualities of the elements allows us to balance our energy and awaken our soul. Begin to notice them, connect yourself to their presence, and communicate with them. Each of the four elements is associated with a compass direction, and the fifth with the center. Learn the directions and qualities of each corresponding element and how to call upon them. To embody a specific element in dance, imagine yourself as the element. Our heartbeat is fire, our blood and body are water, we breathe the air, we walk on earth, and our soul is ether. According to Iranian mysticism, each of these elements is associated with an archangel, a host saint, a duty, a season, a taste, a musical instrument, and a color.

In our living environment, they are inseparable from each other and ourselves. They are the essential elements that represent all that was, is, and will be.

Flames of Devotion

She danced the dance of flames and fire; and the dance of swords and spears; she danced the dance of stars and the dance of space. And then she danced the dance of flowers in the wind.

– Khalil Gibran

In Iranian mystical tradition, fire has many mystical meanings: the fire of love, the fire of the soul, the fire of nature, the fire of victory, the fire of rebirth, the fire of wisdom, and the fire of physical healing. Fire represents the burning love and passion for the Divine and the intense longing for the Beloved. It represents the light of spiritual enlightenment. The transformative nature of fire is a powerful metaphor for the process of fanaa, the annihilation or consumption of self, and realization of the Divine.

The element of fire is associated with the Angel Azrael, who protects and carefully guides souls back to their creator. Azreal told humanity that he knew the longing and suffering they faced in this world, that he was there to help the confused souls upon their body's death return to heaven. The color black is associated with Azrael and the element of fire. Fire is central to ritual, representing the Sun, the greatest fire on this planet, upon which our lives depend. It is the element of ritual purity and a medium through which spiritual insight and wisdom are gained. Fire lights our way in the dark and is a transforming force. Fire is brilliant, super-charged, penetrating, warm, hot, sharp, and radiant in quality. The fire element powers creativity, energy, intensity, and passion. It is a manifestation of the heat and energy of the body and exists in all metabolic processes and chemical reactions in the body. It relates to physical, mental, and spiritual vision because of its light.

Figure 15.2: The sacred fire in Atash Behram (Victorious Fire) Fire Temple, Yazd, Iran.

Photo by author.

Fire is believed to be the essence of life and existence. Fire and light were the highest cosmic components for the ancients because they saw them emanating from lightning or the Sun and stars. Praised and venerated, fire is still worshiped in fire temples, and has remained prominent in Iranian traditions. Fire is a potent symbol of transformation and regeneration as it breaks things down to their essential components from which they can be renewed. In Iranian tradition, the first thing humanity saw upon creation was the sunlight.

As we whirl, fire energy emanates from the palms and fingers. Once the palms become warm during the sama of the Sun it signals the moment of ecstasy. Manifesting this energy of fire in dance or whirling can uplift our spirits, like basking in the life-giving Sun. The Sun's penetrating rays, the blinding light from which one cannot hide, and the all-consuming heat are powerful images to be mindful of as you dance. Fire is known to help one reach surrender and ecstasy easily. A fire dance may be either meditative and serene or dynamic and wild. Because fire is associated with energy, heat, and passion, fire dances evoke and reach a higher level of passion and energy than dances of all other elements. The dynamic and unpredictable nature of flames can be symbolized in movements of dramatic spins and expressive gestures. Wearing red flowing clothing allows one to personify the fire's dancing flames. Let yourself become the mythical firebird, the phoenix rising.

Divine Flow of Water

I have never seen a river that I could not love. Moving water... has a fascinating vitality. It has power and grace and associations. It has a thousand colors and a thousand shapes, yet it follows laws so definite that the tiniest streamlet is an exact replica of a great river.

– Roderick Haig-Brown

In Iranian mysticism, water symbolizes purity and cleansing the heart and soul from worldly attachments and negativity, preparing them for a deeper connection with the Divine. The fluid nature of water reminds the mystic to remain adaptable during their journey. Just as water flows and takes the shape of its container, the mystic learns to surrender and adapt to life circumstances. As water is essential for life, it can be viewed as the Divine source of spiritual sustenance, healing, and nourishment for the seeker. Water symbolizes intuition and emotions, and the still surface of water also represents the clarity and insight that come from inner stillness and contemplation.

There are two concepts of water in Iranian mysticism: *Aab-e Hyatt,* the water of life or spiritual water, and *Aab-e Madani,* the water of material. The water of life refers to liquids internal to us such as tears, sweat, blood, urine, and saliva. Material water is water that one may drink or see. Material water appears outside the body and may be seawater, rainwater, or water in a flowing stream. In Iranian mystic tradition, once a mystic is connected with the seven levels of water, the water becomes holy and confers holiness upon the soul. One may see a similar concept in Christianity in which holy water is believed to purify individuals through the act of baptism. Water is feminine energy and is highly connected with aspects of the goddess Anahita and associated with St. Musi, the Angel Michael, the direction south, the color grey, the taste of salt, and the fall season. The element of water is moving and magical, it is life's essence.

One may manifest the energy of water by being next to or in water, blessing the water, or even talking to water. Communicate with the elements and invite them to come into your body. Dance becomes sacred when unified with the elements. The basic movements used to manifest water may be visualized by imagining any kind of water and using that for whirling. Water is steady but also expresses fluidity, adaptability, and gracefulness. Water can be associated in dance with flowing and continuous movements that reflect its many characteristics, representing oceanic waves, streams, raindrops, etc. A dance of water can abruptly change speed and direction just as a river can change its course. A water dance may start as gently as a flowing spring and then swell to a raging, swirling river. When the flowing movements of water combine a whirlpool appears—which is when ecstasy happens. When you are in the water, your energy level is boundless; you may first rest upon a quiet wave and then rush over a waterfall. Water is reflective so movements that suggest reflection or mirroring may be incorporated. Water energy shows up as graceful swirls, spirals, ribbons, and long flowing patterns. The use of blue or green costumes communicate the theme of water and create a strong visual connection.

Celestial Breeze

The breeze at dawn has secrets to tell you. Don't go back to sleep.

– Rumi

Air is the breath and in Iranian mysticism it symbolizes the spiritual essence within, seen as a manifestation of the Divine Breath. By focusing

Figure 15.3: Air is transcendence. Veil dance, Dr. Farima Berenji.
Alizera Photography

on the breath, the mystic seeks to align with that essence. Air is also seen as the concept of transcendence and union with the Divine. Wind is associated with wings and flight so in Persian mysticism the liberated soul is imagined flying with wings above earthy attachments. Air may manifest as a gentle breeze, a violent tornado, or a cold wind. All of these are considered to be sacred.

According to Iranian mysticism, there are seven kinds of air: watery air, fiery air, the air we breathe, the air within, spiritual air, and material air. The physical gifts of air are the breath, wind, sound, scent, and memory. Air is symbolic of communication, embodied in the mind, thought, and intellect. Air sweeps our minds so that we can think clearly, write more powerfully, and act more efficiently. Air conveys and blends with other elements; it feeds fire, absorbs water, and stirs up the dust of the earth. Air is the invisible cloak that gives, enfolds, and transforms life. It is the unseen made visible by the motion of what is blown (e.g., veils or leaves). Answer the call to embrace air fully and allow it to work its magic in your life. Air is freedom, it enables us to release, to become one with the heavens, and it nurtures the soul.

To represent air, the dance should be light and use graceful, flowing movements that give the impression of being carried by the wind. The element of air gives lightness to movements such as jumps, leaps, and moments of suspension. Dancers use a veil to accentuate the element of air, to create flowing patterns and add elegance to their performance. Behind the veil, the dancer is offered protection, a shield that hides their identity and timidness. Dancers may wrap or drape themselves in the veil, creating intricate cascading patterns that add to the mystery of the dance. Working with a veil requires skill, balance, precision, and coordination.

The dancer can skillfully manipulate the veil to depict air with dynamic, flowing, circular, spinning, and sweeping movements. With their veils as an extension of their arms, dancers add an extra layer of depth to the performance and an ethereal dimension. The color of the veil can represent different entities; red might symbolize fire or passion whereas blue and green are often associated with water. Sacred dance or whirling with air should be completely relaxed and free. Imagine yourself as a bird flying with a sense of freedom, soaring, and gliding. The spirals and whirls of air currents may be represented with a sense of openness, interacting with and embracing the space around.

Embracing the Earth

The earth is not just our environment. We are the earth and the earth is us. We have always been one with the earth.

– Thich Nhat Hanh

The element of earth is the rhythm of life. Earth is protection, grounding, and stabilizing. Our posture and movement convey energy between our body, our heart center, and the earth beneath our feet. The element of earth is representative of our relationship with our mother, whose body was the source of our birth. It represents the solid state of matter. Earth is heavy, structured, stable, secure, compact, and rigid. Bones, teeth, muscles, fat, and the components of our different organs are derived from the earth element. Circle dances honor the earth and are an expression of prayer, gratitude, and healing. When we start to whirl and become one with the earth, it is through the connection of the soil that we can communicate with our past and future. Earth's rocks are considered sacred, carrying the secrets of humanity locked within. In Iran, rocks may be used to take away negative energy and pain. Palaces and castles were built with large stones not only for their strength but because it was believed they protected secrets and kept negative energy away.

Many traditional Iranian dances involve movements that are grounded and show a connection to earth. The movements in these dances can be strong, rhythmic, and have a sense of stability. In Iranian mysticism, the earth represents the physical body as well as the worldly attachments that tie individuals to material concerns. The mystic's path attempts to transcend these worldly attachments and obtain a deeper spiritual understanding while remaining connected to the earth as the foundation of our existence, grounding, fertility, growth, and the basis of spiritual development. Just like the earth represents stability when there are turbulent times, mystics emphasize the importance of patience in the face of challenges upon the spiritual journey.

In Iranian mysticism, the cultivation of virtues and spiritual qualities in the spiritual journey is analogous to the cultivation of crops. To illustrate cultivation of the earth, dancers may use movements that portray planting, crop tending, or gathering. Props such as baskets, pots, or other items associated with the earth may be used to enhance the narrative of the dance. Whole body turning can represent the Earth turning on its axis while orbiting the Sun. The dancer's movements keep a balance between the material and cosmic world. The purpose of manifesting the element of earth in dance or whirling is to clear all distracting thoughts and allow the spirit and body to become one with the Universe.

Ether: Transcendent Realm

I leap across the mountaintops,
Madly singing the song of all songs
I float through the ether, intoxicated, thrilled
I think only of your love, your calling to me
And I dance the thousand dances of love,
All returning to you.

– Rumi

Ether is the ancient concept of celestial energy that fills all spaces. Ether is the most subtle of all classical elements. The alchemists named it quintessence. Ether does not have a physical presence but light, sound, and heat are transmitted through it. It originates in consciousness itself, although less subtle than consciousness or spirit. According to some philosophies, ether acts as a bridge between the body and spirit. It is the element that all living things have to some degree that connects us and mostly exists outside our everyday awareness.

Ether represents the concept of a universal consciousness that pervades all of existence. It may also represent the spiritual space where seekers connect with the Divine or the unlimited potential of the spiritual journey. It is a realm of inner silence where the seeker transcends all noise and distractions of the external world to attain deeper spiritual insights. Ether might also be associated with the concept of wholeness in which all elements and aspects of existence are interconnected. Ether symbolizes the departure from the material world and the realization of spiritual truths. Incorporating all the surrounding elements, as one starts to whirl, one becomes ether, the final element, the center. A mystic can spend years with these elements in profound contemplation and experience.

Do not feel lonely, the entire universe is inside you.

– Rumi

CHAPTER 16

A Celestial Journey

Snakes coil, vines spiral, the Earth revolves, the planets orbit, and on our spinning planet, all the cells whirl, adding to the massive force of the universe.

The beauty and behavior of the planets in the night sky have sparked the Iranian people's imagination for ages. By observing celestial movements, and developing an immense body of scientific knowledge, the ancient Persians thought they could explain the mysteries of the universe. They paid close attention to the position of planets and stars for navigation and were able to see the relationship between the seasons to the celestial movements. They made predictions. When the positions of planets and stars resembled certain patterns, they were associated with good or bad omens. They interpreted the patterns as signs of the future and used their predictions to advise people, especially their king. The Farsi word *falak* has beautiful multi-layered meanings. It is used to describe heaven and the cosmos, the universe, as well as one's fate and destiny. It is said that the Persian astrologers sought to understand falak.

Each planet came to represent a deity who ruled a specific aspect of life. Divination sought answers and knowledge from these deities, who shaped the destiny of humans and controlled all events in life and the cosmos. This practice of predicting the future was an essential aspect of ancient Mesopotamian life. All phenomena were seen to be caused by supernatural forces whose future intentions could be revealed. Although we recognize nine planets today, in antiquity only five planets—Mercury, Venus, Mars, Jupiter, and Saturn—were known, because they were visible to the naked eye. In some interpretations the Sun and Moon were added to this list and appear in astrology charts and predictions (Panaino 2016). In Iran, seven colors were allocated, one to each planet and weekday. By allocating one color and feeling to each weekday, the Persians could draft predictions and correlations to the universe's behavior. In Iranian legend, each human is born with seven souls, and each soul is connected to one planet with its specific qualities, energies, and archetypal properties.

Sacred dance was thought of as the language of the cosmos, a means to communicate with the celestial world and deities. Through whirling, healing rituals, and sacred dance they attempted to align with the motions of the solar system as planets were observed to shift in the sky. According to Iranian cosmology, whirling and sacred rituals honor our sacred relationship with the universe. They represent our conscious mind and connect our hearts with the cosmic world. Persian dances incorporate movements and gestures that symbolize the qualities or energies associated with various celestial bodies. Costumes and visual elements in Persian dance may also incorporate colors and designs associated with celestial bodies in order to help evoke their energies and qualities. In Iranian mysticism, particularly in the traditions of Sufism and other esoteric philosophies, there is a profound symbolic and metaphysical connection between celestial bodies and the spiritual journey of individuals.

At first, the planets revealed the deities' will and their direct influence on human affairs. In later thinking, the pattern of planetary positions and configurations was believed to affect basic human impulses. To explain their interaction, some held that the physics of gravitation, motion, or possibly unknown forces directed the planets. Other astrologers believed the planets had no direct interaction among themselves but were the result of basic organizing principles of the universe. Regardless of the notion, astrology was continually developed to interpret the ebb and flow of human impulses according to the position and motion of the planets. Today there are different interpretations of astrology based on Western, Chinese, or Indian schools of thought in combination with both ancient and modern concepts.

Of course, our planetary system directly affects our nature and all nature—the phases of the Moon affect the Earth's tides, and the Earth's position in relation to the Sun governs the seasons. Planets combine forces as they come close or align in sympathetic motion. If your best friend is upset or crying you will feel empathy. The planets act the same; they can be closer to or farther from one another or the Earth. Astrology offers this as a reason why our impulses change. Understanding these planetary effects enables our whirling to be more meaningful. For example, celestial energies can be incorporated during whirling to honor a certain planet for more strength, healing, and love.

Dance of the Cosmos

The Universe spins, so we should spin in order to co-ordinate.

– Rumi

Figure 16.1: The Sun symbolizes the universe, life, and the spirit, the all-seeing eye of the self.
Valerie Runningwolf.

In the narrative of mystical philosophy, the Sun and Moon represent an ideal relationship between the mystic and the Divine. The Sun will always be a poetic symbol of love, the beloved, or the fire within. The Sun is a metaphor for the source of Divine Light, enlightenment, and spiritual illumination. It represents the ultimate truth and source of all existence. The rays of sunlight that illuminate the Moon represent Divine Intellect conveyed to the mystic. The moonlight, which is a reflection of the sun's light, represents spiritual intuition. Just as the mystic longs to meet the Divine it is said the Sun and Moon long for the moment they may meet each other. In that moment, the mystic achieves oneness with the Divine. Carried forward to astronomy, this relationship is most likely when the Sun and Moon align for a solar eclipse. In Iran, the solar eclipse announces the unification between the Sun and Moon. It represents the union of male and female energy. A solar eclipse is a sign of the oneness of the soul with the Divine Light. During the time of Cyrus the Great, it is said that the shadow of an eclipse once plunged the Iranian land into darkness but a glimpse of the Sun still shone upon the people. This sliver of light confirmed that celestial light exists even in darkness. Inspired, Cyrus the Great offered sacrifice and asked that the sacred dance of the Sun commence, and a beautiful ritual of the eclipse began. This important ritual is still relevant today and is held upon the occasion of an eclipse.

There is a beautiful tale about Yalda, the longest night of the year, regarding the love between the Moon and the Sun. Hoping to see the Sun, the Moon tried to stay awake all night but kept falling asleep just before the Sun arrived. On the night of Yalda, the Moon finally succeeded and stayed up late enough to see the Sun. Together at last, the Moon and Sun enjoyed each other's company and talked throughout the night. After the Moon departed, the Sun slept in late, and thus the night of Yalda lasts longer than any other day.

The Sun, represented by the deity Mithra, is considered to be one of the most sacred celestial bodies. We receive warmth and light through the Sun, and see beauty and soul. The Sun has warm and dry properties and exudes nobility, greatness, jubilation, and power. It heals, charges, warms, illuminates, and nourishes. Dancing for the Sun is a celebration of life. Those whirling to the Sun's energy are known as Sun turners. The Sun represents the initiated soul and the power of intuition. In Iran, turning to the right (rast sama) represents the Sun, light, life, energy, joy, and the divine spirit that illuminates this world and the next. Sun whirlers attempt to be close to the Sun and invoke the transformative energy of fire in their dance or whirling.

Figure 16.2: The Moon symbolizes intuition, dreams, and feelings.

Valerie Runningwolf.

The Moon represents beauty and the beloved. In the Persian Myth of Creation, the Moon kept the original seeds of the living world. The Moon is often used as a symbol of spiritual enlightenment and clarity, the light of divine knowledge that dispels the darkness of ignorance, and the Divine Light in the heart of the seeker. The heart is like a mirror that reflects the

Divine's beauty and illumination, just as the moon reflects the sun's light. In Persian literature, the face of a beautiful maiden is compared to the Moon; in Farsi, *mahru* or *mahrokh* means "Moon-faced," while *Mah* (Moon) itself often signifies the face. In Iranian tradition, the Moon deity is a bestower of radiance and fertility, giving the power of healing and medicine, wealth, and discernment, and is related to the goddess Anahita. The Moon gives mystical properties to manifest, rejuvenate, and enhance intuition.

In mystic poetry, the Moon takes on a myriad of meanings based on its phases and cyclical nature of existence. It waxes and wanes, representing the variation of worldly life. As it travels the night sky it symbolizes the spiritual journey through the darkness of worldly attachments towards the light of divine realization. At the same time, it also symbolizes eternity and the unchanging nature of the Divine. Particularly in the works of Sufi poets like Rumi, Hafez, and Attar, vivid metaphors of the Moon are used to convey deeper spiritual truths and experiences. The Moon cannot be seen unless the light of the Sun is upon it. The crescent Moon represents the bent shape of a darvish bowing to the source of light. The half-moon symbolizes the opposites existing in the psyche. The Moon is associated with Angel Azrael, the benevolent Angel of Death.

The whirling of the Moon is seen in the custom of the Mevlevi whirling tradition. By tradition they turn to the left (chap sama), which is also turning toward the heart, in solemn remembrance of Rumi. In particular, this is the practice during the *Sheb-i Arus* ceremony honoring the day of his death. As Islam became predominant in the Middle East, whirling to the right eventually faded away and left turning was taught as a rule. Moon turns and the dance of death became more popular than the dance of the Sun in celebration. In Turkey today, what remains is left turning. In contrast to the vitality and joy of the rast or Sun sama, chap or Moon sama is traditionally done for times of mourning, sadness, or longing. When we whirl to the left we are dancing for the Beloved. Dancers often release tears during chap sama because the left turn helps expose our longing.

Spheres of Eternity: The Celestial Dance

We are the children of the cosmos, born from celestial fire, our souls ignite by the spark of Divine Desire. With each whirl and spin, we paint the sky with grace, leaving traces of stardust in our celestial embrace.

– Unknown

In our solar system, the only planet that turns clockwise or to the right is Venus. **Venus** represents the duality of the soul, the ego, the nafs, and goodness. Known as the Evening Star or Morning Star, Venus is renowned for its radiant appearance in the night and morning sky. It is considered equal and opposite to the Earth. Venus is known as the imitative soul—it wants to imitate Earth, but instead mirrors the Earth. Earth turns to the left, whereas Venus turns to the right. If Earth looks into a mirror it sees Venus, likewise, if Venus looks into a mirror it becomes Earth. Associated with Satevis or Antares (the royal star of the west in Persia), Venus represents the energy of beauty, passion, kindness, love, and friendship, and has cool, moist qualities. In some interpretations, Venus may be associated with feminine qualities such as receptivity, nurturing, and intuition. This aligns with the concept of the Divine Feminine in mysticism. Its beauty and luminosity can be seen as a reflection of divine beauty and grace. In Iranian mythology, the goddess Anahita was believed to have lived among the stars, the brightest being the planet Venus (Noroozy 2013). Venus is also often associated with Daena, the goddess of love and friendship. Goddess Daena was correlated to the contemplative aspects of life, representing the need for self-reflection, discipline, and the pursuit of spiritual growth.

Mars and Earth are as equal as brothers but as opposite in demeanor as night and day. Mars is just like Venus in that it is a dual of Earth, but it is the dark twin rather than the mirror of Earth. The whirling of Mars is towards the left and is associated with energy, strength, and action. Mars fights against the forces of darkness, and its qualities are warm and dry. According to the *Shams al-Ma'arif*, an astrology spell book written by scholar Ahmad al-Buni (d. 1225 CE), Mars is believed to have magic powers. Legend says that Mars is associated with good and protective magic, just like the ancient Magis who were known to be "sorcerers" conducting their magic for good. Mars offers protection from illness, death, and dark forces. It was believed that by whirling and manifesting the energy of Mars, one could protect health and well-being. Mars embodies the powers of the eagle, lion, or lioness. The dancer empowered by the energy of Mars displays courage, strength, intensity, and enacts battle or warrior-like movements.

Saturn is associated with Venant or Regulus, the royal star of the north. Compared to the other planets, Saturn possesses cold, masculine energy and is associated with spiritual growth, introspection, discipline, responsibility, and control. Its color is mainly associated with black, it possesses a bitter taste, and represents the circle of internal organs. The mystic alchemists associated Saturn with the process of inner transformation and spiritual alchemy. In dance, Saturn might be represented by slow, deliberate movements of strength and a display of wisdom as achieved through experience and age, inner stability, and endurance. The sacred dance of Saturn combines two concentric circle dances—an inner circle of dancers with an outer circle of dancers serving as a ring around the planet.

Mercury is associated with Tishtar or Aldebaran, the royal star of the East, and is associated with extreme heat and cold as well as extreme emotions—one is very angry, very sad, or very happy. In Western astrology, when Mercury is moving retrograde, it signals tension or a mood change. In Mercury, there is no balance compared to other planets. Tīriya, the god associated with Mercury, was associated with intelligence, wisdom, agility, adaptability, and the power of communication. Dancers might use fluid, agile, creative, eloquent, and intellectual expressions to manifest Mercury. Whirling while manifesting the energy of Mercury, helps one ease sadness, be conscientious, and find balance. In mysticism, Mercury's association with intellect may be interpreted as an encouragement to seek deeper spiritual understanding through knowledge and insight. It can also be a reminder to be spontaneous and open-minded, to welcome new insights and experiences. Mercury's attributes might also encourage the seeker to find a balance between intellectual pursuits and matters of the heart, understanding that both are essential on a spiritual journey.

In Iranian tradition, the symbol of **Jupiter** typically appears upon the tombs of mystics or wise men. The planet Jupiter is the symbol of wisdom and higher knowledge in Sufism. It represents someone who has finished all his studies and has become a spiritual master. Jupiter is also associated with abundance, benevolence, expansion, and divine protection. Dominant among all other planets, Jupiter is a planet of greatness, yet according to the Shams al-Ma'arif, it is the least remembered—being hidden is a sign of spiritual maturity. To honor Jupiter, dancers might incorporate movements that convey a sense of openness, expansion, and outreach, in order to explore life using the generosity of the heart. In whirling, Jupiter's qualities are embodied through spirals and sparks. In mysticism, Jupiter's association with higher knowledge may be interpreted as encouragement to broaden one's perspective and expand consciousness in pursuit of spiritual growth. Characterized by abundance and benevolence, Jupiter might be seen as a symbol of the Divine's boundless generosity and provision for all beings.

Legends say that **Neptune** looked at the Moon one day and pleaded, "Oh, dear Moon, please tell the universe through your light, tell them about me, and tell them that even the king of the seas cries as well." In Iranian mythology, it is believed Neptune carries the secrets of our inner emotions, and contains the tears of humanity. When we cry, when we show longing, and when we hold a secret that burdens us, we can share it with Neptune, which carries our secrets and controls the release of our longing, distress, and tears. It is associated with dreams, illusions, the subconscious mind, and the mystical realm. Dancers might incorporate fluid movements and create a dreamlike, otherworldly atmosphere in their performance, inviting the audience to transcend the boundaries of the material world and journey into the realms of the soul and spirit, or convey a sense of inner peace, tranquility, and spiritual attunement. When whirling for Neptune, we release our longing, distress, and tears. Although Neptune possesses feminine energy, whirlers may turn right or left. In Persian poetry and mysticism, Neptune is often associated with the exploration of higher states of consciousness, and sometimes its power is associated with the dissolution of boundaries and the ego. It encourages the seeker to tap into their inner wisdom, transcend the restrictions of their ego and, like the great ocean, find the boundless expanse of love and compassion in the Divine; its mystery conveys the mysteries of the universe.

Dance of the Royal Stars

We came whirling out of nothingness, scattering stars like dust... The stars made a circle, and in the middle, we dance.

– Rumi

Figure 16.3: Iranians looked to the Royal Stars for predictions.

Like the planets, the four Royal Stars in the night sky have for ages been part of the imagination of the Iranian people. These are the brightest stars in their respective constellations, and were considered the four guardians of the universe due to their splendor and brightness. Each star guards one of the four directions and was valued for its navigational purposes. They announce the changes of the seasons and foretell the solstices and equinoxes. The Royal Stars were identified with the supreme deity Ahura Mazda, creator of the twin spirits, Ahriman (destruction) and Spenta Meynu (goodness). Each of these stars was believed to have a power that could be either positive or negative, and were thought to announce periods of prosperity or scarcity. They were seen as governing world events, causing major disasters, breakthroughs, or historical phenomena depending on their alignment in the sky during the event. When the stars were aligned appropriately, prosperity followed ("The Royal Stars," n.d.). Another star of great importance was the north star, which stayed constant in the heavens as the others pivoted around it each year with the seasons.

In Persian poetry and mysticism, the stars in the night sky represent celestial guides that provide direction and illuminate the spiritual path.

They symbolize Divine guidance that leads seekers toward union with the Beloved. The journey of the soul toward union with the Divine is often likened to a celestial voyage. The stars represent stops on this spiritual journey, guiding the seeker toward their ultimate destination, the vast expanse of stars representing the boundless nature of the Divine. The mystic held the belief that the light radiating from stars was the same as the divine spark or inner light, the source of spiritual illumination and connection with the Divine. In their regular orbits and positions, stars are evidence of the inherent order and harmony of the universe, the intelligence of the divine plan.

Aldebaran (Tishtar in New Persian, from the Zoroastrian deity Tishtrya[156]) is the alpha star of the Taurus constellation. Its name means "the creator of the universe," and it is the guardian of the eastern sky. At its brightest at the vernal equinox, it signals the coming of spring, Nowruz, and thus the Iranian New Year. Aldebaran is known as the creator of all water (moj), the first source of creation, and is connected with Anahita, the goddess of water, the ocean, and all water bodies. Also known as the "Eye of Taurus," Aldebaran is associated with the qualities of leadership, determination, and courage as well as themes of success and achievement.

In sacred dance or whirling, Aldebaran has the motions of waves and tides. The dance movements are expressed in the body areas where water is concentrated—in the eyes where we cry tears, in the mouth which has saliva, and especially the abdomen. Dancers use powerful gestures to convey qualities of leadership such as confidence, courage, strength, and determination. Aldebaran has its greatest power and connection in whirling when it is performed as a prayer or ritual during sunrise.

Regulus (Venant in Persian) is the Leo constellation's alpha star. As guardian of the northern sky, it marks the summer solstice. Regulus

---

156 Tishtrya (Tir in Middle or Modern Persian) is a benevolent Zoroastrian deity or *yazata* considered to have the power of life-bringing rainfall and fertility and is closely connected with agriculture and the well-being of nature. Tishtrya was part of an epic cosmic struggle against the drought-bringing demon Apaosha, his victory ensuring the release of imprisoned waters, leading to the rejuvenation of the world.

appears turquoise in the night sky, glistening with multiple rays. It is the companion of Spenta Armaiti, a female divinity of harmony and devotion and described in sacred literature as a Mother Nature figure. It is associated with all our senses and thriving health: touch, taste, sight, hearing, and smell. Also known as the "Heart of the Lion," Regulus is associated with qualities like power, authority, and strength and is often connected with royalty and leadership. Dancers might focus on portraying a regal and authoritative presence and gestures that convey a sense of strength and dominance. With its multiple bursting rays, whirling for Regulus is outward rather than inward, portraying devotion to the world and humanity outside. The star's energy is highest between midnight and 2:00 am, so whirling with Regulus is most effective at night.

Antares (Satevis in Persian), also known as thc "Heart of the Scorpion," is the alpha star of the Scorpio constellation. It is guardian of the western sky and marks the autumn equinox when the harvest festival of Mehregan is celebrated. Antares represents both male and female energy, fire, strength, warriorship, courage, protection, and transformation. It is often linked with themes of bravery and overcoming challenges. Antares is at its peak luminescence at sunset, appearing with a large spiral within, so whirling with Antares is best at twilight. In dance, movements that depict courage in the face of challenges are chosen and dancers might use flowing, transformative movements to represent change and growth. Whirling may be either to the right or left.

Fomalhaut, known as Haftorang (Seventh Star) in Persian, is the fourth and last royal star, the alpha of the constellation Pisces. In Persian mythology, Haftorang is the deity and ruler of the planet Mars, the light-giver, and the health restorer. As guardian of the southern sky, it marks the winter solstice. Known as the star of Oneness, it sometimes is referred to simply as "The Solitary One," as it stands out in what is otherwise an empty region of the sky. The star looks like an eye because it is very bright with a surrounding halo caused by four rays or "sparks" of light emanating from it at right angles. Fomalhaut was the symbol seen by the three Iranian Magis, as it foretells the coming of winter. Also known as the "Fish's Mouth," Fomalhaut is associated with qualities like spirituality, intuition, creative expression and is often linked with artistic and spiritual pursuits. The star is said to foretell big changes to our life.

Dancers might focus on expressing intuition and creativity, using graceful, flowing motions. Whirling for Formalhaut releases energy for peace, harmony, and freedom. The best time to manifest the energy of Fomalhaut through whirling is at night when the Moon is rising and the stars illuminate the sky. Practice it to release tension, obtain a sense of clarity, and equalize the breath. The four sparks emanating from the star echo the four cardinal directions. The halo surrounding the star conserves and rations the energy released. Fomalhaut is associated with the element of air so its emphasis is on oj or upward, active energy. Whirling to Fomalhaut is strongest when performed only to the sound of the breath, without musical accompaniment. Sometimes it is called the "dance of the breath."

Group choreography involving all the Royal Stars can show them serving as celestial guardians watching over and influencing human destiny. This can be realized through dynamic formations and synchronized movements that represent the interconnectedness between the dancers and the stars.

Shamsa and the Eight-Pointed Star

Stars do not pull each other down to be more visible; they shine brighter. Learn from stars; even in the dark they give off light, not despair.

– Matshona Dhliwayo

Since antiquity, the eight-pointed star has been important to Iranian art, architecture, and philosophy and is ubiquitous in Iranian carpets in the form of a center medallion with eight parts. Referred to as the Star of the Magi, this eight-pointed star is a simple creation made by overlapping two squares rotated 45 degrees from their center. In mysticism, the square is representative of Earth, and the circle represents the celestial world or heaven. A circle in the center, or even on the outside of the square, unites Heaven and Earth together. It portrays mankind in this realm and in the other world as well. The shape is symmetrical to the eye and brings peace and calm. Cultures worldwide have adopted

Figure 16.4: Flag of the Sasanian Empire 224-651 CE.
Wikimedia Commons.

Figure 16.5: Ancient Mesopotamian symbol of sun god Shamash.
Wikimedia Commons.

it as a universal symbol with diverse meanings of balance, harmony, and cosmic order. Found on national flags and religious iconography it carries religious and mystical significance (Figure 16.4). It is symbolic not only of the stars but of humanity's earliest attempts to understand and communicate with the order and unity inherent in Creation and the laws of nature (Norbu 2015).

In astronomy and navigation, the eight-pointed star symbolizes the four compass points plus the points in-between, or sometimes the juncture of the seasons on the calendar, two solstices, two equinoxes, and four cross-quarter days. These extents and phases symmetrically combine the points of the star and suggest the concept of universal completeness, unity, cosmic order, and balance. In some traditions, the motif is considered a protective symbol, believed to bring blessings and ward off negative influences.

In ancient Sumer—the world's oldest civilizations from which Babylonian, Akkadian (Semetic), Elam (proto-Indo-Iranian), Egyptian, Greek, and other civilizations developed—a geometric symbol representing both a star and the Divine was in use long before the rise of Islam. The eight-pointed star represented the goddess Inanna, the Sumerian queen of the heavens, and Ishtar (Astarte), the Babylonian goddess known as "The Lightbringer." The ancient Babylonian star cult was the beginning of astrology. The eight-pointed star enclosed within a circle symbolized the sun god (Figure 16.5). Naturally, the symbol migrated to other cultures and eventually the Yarsan and Zoroastrian traditions and later, Islam and Christianity. In Iranian mysticism, a highly stylized representation of the sun with light beams originating from the center came to be known as Shamsa, the king of stars. While both the Shamsa and the eight-pointed star are geometric designs with spiritual significance, they are distinct symbols in Iranian mysticism. The Shamsa specifically represents the sun radiating light and energy, while the eight-pointed star symbolizes unity, harmony, balance, cosmic order, spiritual ascent, and the interconnectedness of all aspects of existence. In Iranian mysticism, the eight-pointed star is associated with various layers of meaning related to the soul's journey and its connection to the Divine.

All monotheistic religions have accommodated astrology in some way incorporating the ancient symbols into their view of creation. The ancient symbol of the eight-pointed star came to influence art and traditions traveling with the migration of people and ideology. In some traditions, it depicted the cyclical nature of existence, or renewal, rebirth, and the eternal nature of the soul. The points may also symbolize the integration of various aspects of the self, such as mind, body, soul, and emotions, with the lines connecting them symbolizing the path of spiritual realization and union and the sightlines to the center as the view to the Divine. Among the Sufi mystics, the eight-pointed star is regarded as a symbol of spiritual ascent with each point representing a stage of spiritual development, ultimately leading to union with the Divine.

In ancient Iran seven of the points represented the seven archangels, the eighth representing the Divine. It was believed the design brought celestial energy to earth. For this reason, traditional Persian gardens and architecture incorporate the sacred star. When seen from above, the design is apparent in garden plots and water channels. The eight-pointed star began to appear in Islamic art in the Middle Ages, called *khatim* or *khatim-sulayman*, meaning "seal of the prophets." Ibn al-'Arabi, a 12th century Muslim scholar, mystic, poet, and philosopher, was born in Spain about the same time the practice of *zellij* (mosaic design) flourished in Islamic art. Al-Arabi created diagrams with the eight-pointed star and explained that all phenomena are nothing but manifestations of Being, which is one with God. These designs appear in Persian carpets, upon the ceilings of domes (Figure 16.6), or within other kinds of Islamic art. This use of the star may also be related to earlier appearances of the six-pointed star in Judaic designs, referred to as the Seal of Solomon. Muslim legend recounts Solomon using the star to capture *djinns* or genies, the immaterial counterparts to humans.

Figure 16.6: Shamsa within the tomb ceiling of Baba Taher, Hamadan, Iran.
Azarmidoxt, Wikimedia Commons.

The Magis were followers of Zoroastrianism who sought to heal the body and mind through astrology, alchemy, and other forms of spiritual knowledge. An ancient healing practice known as Purification and Unification used the eight-pointed star in healing rituals and whirling, and for balancing negative and positive energies through connection with the Sun and the Moon. The Shamsa was known as a source of understanding and intelligence; becoming one with it indicates reaching the level of a mystic. The inner point means awakening to receive blessings and the outer point means sharing this blessing. In whirling, as one turns in the center of the star, all the elements unify and one becomes purified. When a mystic completes all their studies, they are compared to the Shamsa for their great achievement of wisdom. Once a mystic or a magi passed the seventh level they were seen to actually glow.

The number eight held great importance among mystics, as described in the book *The Number Concept*, by 19th century American mathematician Dr. Levi Conant (Conant 1896). Ian Alexander has also explained the symbolism of the *Nafas al-Rahman* (Breath of the Compassionate), a geometric pattern associated with Ibn al-'Arabi (Figure 16.7):

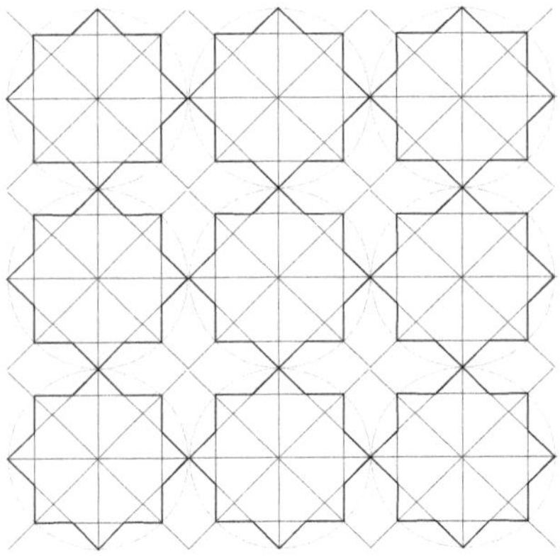

Figure 16.7: Breath of the Compassionate Motif.
Kevin Greek, public domain.

Form is symbolized by the square. Expansion is symbolized by the square with triangles pointing outwards (an eight-pointed star). Contraction is symbolized by the square with triangles pointing inwards (a four-pointed star). The two star-shapes together symbolize the cycle of creation, "the Breath of the Compassionate." (Norbu 2015)

Of the ninety-nine names of God in Islamic tradition, the Compassionate is the highest pronounceable name. More than just an ornamental motif, the Breath of the Compassionate is a cosmological model symbolizing the interplay of polarities that manifest form.

As mentioned, the Shamsa, distinct from the eight-pointed star, is a highly stylized motif for the sun, depicted with numerous rays emanating from the center in a rosette pattern. It, too, carries various meanings across different cultures and contexts and is also frequently seen as an ornamental element in architecture, textiles, ceramics, manuscripts, and other forms of decorative arts. Both symbols are important in Iranian art and mysticism. It is important to note that although the Shamsa motif has roots in pre-Islamic Persia, it was adapted and reinterpreted within the Islamic artistic vocabulary, thereby taking on new layers of meaning within the context of Islamic spirituality and cosmology.

The Shamsa represents happiness, fertility, and masculinity. While it may be depicted in different forms, what is common is the many rays around its center. The rays symbolize every creature in the universe on all different levels, and the center represents the Divine. It also symbolizes unity, an essential concept in mystic and Sufi philosophy. The creatures struggle to reach the center, and when they do, they become one with the Divine. The Shamsa shares both design and significance with the mandala in Hinduism and Buddhism, symbolizing the unity and harmony of the universe.

The Shamsa was applied abundantly during the Safavid dynasty in Iran. The Safavids were one of Iran's most significant ruling dynasties in terms of art, architecture, astrology, philosophy, and theology. An extraordinary example of the Shamsa motif would be the tiling of the ceiling of the Sheik Lotfollah mosque in Isfahan.

After the Islamic conquest of Persia, the ancient forms of astronomy and astrology became absorbed into the science of astronomy of the medieval Islamic world. Medieval scientists studied and compared Ptolemaic concepts (from ancient Greece and Egypt) and adopted a research approach to the field, translating the works of other scientists and integrating already discovered knowledge. This marked the beginning of modern study and calculations in astronomy. The mystical concepts and ideals of ancient Persian cosmology continued to persist, and still inspire spirituality, philosophy, art, and dance today.

The far-away, intangible scope of our universe with its planets and stars, and their celestial inner workings, have been a source of mystery and fascination since earliest times. The Iranians thought of the cosmos as a three-tiered structure consisting of the earth beneath, the atmosphere, and the stone vault of heaven above. Beyond the heavens was the realm of stars, and below the earth was the realm of darkness and chaos. The heavenly bodies were a frequent source of wonder and the subject of great stories by the Persian poets and mystics. Their observable and predictable motion and position in the sky hinted at the divine plan for the universe, from creation to the present.

Little we see in nature is ours.
But nature gives us all the imagination and dreams we possess.

CHAPTER 17

Dance of Divine Nature

Earth and stars, dark and light, wind and waves, fire and ice.
Everything in nature is part of ourselves.
Everything in nature possesses a voice, a soul.
In the grand symphony of existence, everything in nature dances.

Everything in nature is part of ourselves; everything in nature has a voice, a soul. We must try to understand our environment, not just with our minds but also with our hearts. Our souls intertwine with nature. Nature is full of sacredness, secrets, and wisdom! Our path involves seeking balance and harmony within the intricate tapestry known as the Great Circle of Life.

Dance has its roots in nature. Our bodies contain the innate wisdom of the ages, knowledge recorded in our cells and nervous systems, and in each breath we take. The earliest forms of dance movements were based on observation and experience of the natural world, mimicking behaviors and forms of animals, plants, elements, and stars. Natural patterns are perhaps more inborn than we realize. Sacred geometries, such as circles, spirals, and waves are embedded in reality's design. Fire, water, wind, earth, the animals of the land and sea, the planets, the Sun and Moon are all fundamental patterns in what we create. The diverse landscape of deserts, mountains, forests, and coastlines in Iran has deeply influenced poetry, literature, and philosophy. Persian carpets are renowned worldwide for intricate designs and craftsmanship, designs that are largely inspired by natural elements such as flowers, trees, and animals. Dance is a magical movement largely based on nature, and dance restores our relationship with it.

The early Iranians believed nature was inhabited and maintained by spiritual forces: the forests, orchards, fields of grain, and healing springs each had their own intelligent spirit. Persian miniature

Figure 17.1: Invocation of Divine Nature by the author.
Varol Ozkaner.

paintings often portrayed idyllic scenes of landscapes, gardens, rivers, and wildlife with intricate detail. Poets such as Rumi, Hafez, and Saadi drew inspiration from the natural world, using metaphors to convey deeper spiritual and philosophical meanings. Persian philosophers and mystics, like Ibn Sina (Avicenna) frequently incorporated observations of the natural world and references to flowers, plants, trees, and fruit in their philosophical and spiritual writings. They believed connecting with the natural world brought awareness leading to the profound realization of the subtle energy present in plants and the manifestation of a higher spirit. Being in a good relationship with nature meant receiving its blessings and wisdom as necessary for health, prosperity, and spiritual well-being.

Today, our lives can be so complex and full that we rarely find time to appreciate the beauty of nature. Yet we all know connecting with nature makes us healthier physically, mentally, emotionally, and spiritually. This connection helps one see the world and everything in it more clearly. But we must recognize nature not just with our minds but with our hearts; we must understand that everything on Earth is alive with energy, has a purpose, is connected, is to be embraced. When we are filled with nature our dance becomes sacred. Nature is here to teach mankind and has many powerful lessons to give. It reminds us that we are only a small part of creation, that each part of creation has a place, and that each creature has its own skill and wisdom. Man needs to understand himself and his relationship with nature to find peace with the world.

Even within our cities, we find elements that still bear the soul of the earth since they are made from the earth's natural resources. We can find dance in the elements of earth, air, fire, and water, and explore their presence and role in our daily lives (Al-Hakim 2015). Persian culture traditionally placed great importance on the natural world; the classical and sacred dances are primarily devoted to the beauty of flowers and trees in the natural and native Iranian habitat. Dance movements and postures are chosen to imitate natural elements such as flowing water, swaying trees, flowers moving in a gentle breeze, or the flight of birds; even the costumes and accessories incorporate natural motifs.

When in nature, one can connect and find inspiration by activating all the senses, and then cultivate that experience to grow into a movement. Meditation in nature, whether through silent contemplation or structured practices, and observing the beauty of the natural world are ways to find inner peace and spiritual insight. Take some solo time to walk and expose yourself to nature. Even in busy and exhausting times, frequent exposure to nature outside can offer a refreshing boost of energy. Walk barefoot as much as possible, hug a tree, sit with your back to a tree trunk, or visit the beach with its water and wind. Some people find it helpful to be buried in soil or sand for a few hours or overnight; the soil clears negative energy and is very grounding. Visit, stay by, or swim in a lake, river, waterfall, or ocean. Witness the body responding to its innate connection to the natural world. Open the heart and spirit to the nourishment that nature offers. One's impulses and sensory awakenings are a call to remember the natural self. The trickling sound and motion of a stream or the sway of a willow tree in the breeze can inspire the body's capacity to move. Once the power of nature moves, all are invited to become part of nature and to move with it. It is surprisingly easy and immediately gratifying to join nature in movement. Stepping outside, consciously breathing in the fresh morning air, or drinking in a flower's scent and vibrant colors strengthens the relationship and invites the body into movement and meditation.

The pace and way of life in nature is much slower than in urban life. If one compares a city dweller to one that lives close to nature one will notice their rhythm is different. Those who live in the city live at a much faster pace which can cause chronic stress and anxiety. In the village, everything is calmer and people move and talk more slowly. Humanity was created to be in rhythm with nature. Unfortunately, that rhythm has been lost due to technology. As an artist, one should understand the difference in pace and choose whether to follow the rhythm of nature or the modern rhythm of the city. Ecosomatic dance is an emerging interdisciplinary field that connects movement and healing with the natural world. Ecosomatic dancers work to attune to sensations and impulses from both inside and outside their body. They build a kinesthetic understanding of their surroundings by moving in response to environmental stimulation. This often requires the dancer to explore ways to work with or in opposition to features of the landscape, diverse terrain, natural objects, and challenging weather. The creativity of dancing in and with nature exercises us spiritually, awakens us, cleanses the soul, and directs our attention toward healing (Enghauser 2021).

In its essence, Iranian mysticism aligns with eco-spirituality to emphasize the harmony of all living beings and the sanctity of the natural world. The intricate patterns of leaves, flowing rivers, and flowers blooming are seen as signs of the Divine's wisdom and creativity. Mystics thereby advocate for a sense of environmental stewardship and reverence, recognizing that the Earth is our sacred trust from the Divine. As an exercise, go outside and look around; choose a natural element that resonates. Visually notice everything about it: size, texture, patterns, solidness, fragility, and more. Become conscious of the presence of this object and acknowledge it like a dance partner. Feel your energetic relationship with this object. Observe the spirals, circles, triangles, hexagons, rectangles, stars; look for combined patterns, both in planar and spatial structures, within the sacred geometry of plants, sea shells, or snowflakes. In the Iranian mystic tradition, there is a sacred dance involving a tree. We enter the forest and find a tree that we can connect to, talk to the tree, and then begin whirling about the tree as a sama. Try this tree sama yourself and attempt contact with the Beloved that way.

Research exploring the benefits of connectedness to nature has shown that observing and appreciating nature has multiple positive effects on mood, energy levels, concentration, well-being, and ecological consciousness. Through self-training dancers can develop highly attuned, conscious bodies that read, respond to, and acknowledge the interconnections between the body and the natural world (Collard-Stokes 2020). Everyone can learn from the ways dancers come to know and work with nature. Our connection to nature helps ensure consciousness of a world more significant than ourselves.

Dancing in the Mystical Garden

Dance is healing; it is poetry and an intrinsic part of our being. Dance permeates every aspect of life, with movements echoing in everything around us. Nature itself is a dancer, with even the smallest rose petal exhibiting its graceful dance. In the realm of dance, I embody nature, and the essence of nature resides within me.

Flowers are often mentioned in Iranian mystic culture as manifestations of the beauty of divine creation. The ancients talked to the flowers believing they had feelings and would listen. They danced and played music for the flowers and the flowers bloomed. When they cried or spoke of negative thoughts, the flowers would whither of sadness. For them, the Divine itself created certain flowers to represent an angel or deity on Earth and each flower was thought to embody the face of a beautiful angel.

Flowers are sacred because they connect with the human soul. There is a timeless belief that the flower represents the life cycle of a human from birth to death. As it blooms, it shows the progress of human growth, aging, and death. An open flower viewed from a top-down perspective bears a resemblance to the sun, the source of life. A mystic is also compared with the beauty and purity of a flower. There are seven sacred flowers, each with seven mystic qualities associated with angels and deities. They have a fragrance representing their essence, a heart, a soul, a body, and a face for expression and feelings. Flowers are endowed with seven attributes, just as humans are. It is important to understand them because they are just like us.

Flowers are an essential part of the Persian language. Many girls, for example, are named after flowers: Banafsheh (violet), Ra'na (blanket flowers), Yasaman (jasmine), Nilufar (lotus flower), and Laleh (tulip), are some of many. The word *gol* (flower) is also used as a prefix or suffix in several Farsi words. Iran has always been known as the land of flowers and nightingales. In particular, the nightingale and the rose are important in Iranian mysticism. Mystic designs, including calligraphy and miniature paintings, frequently feature flowers. They serve as reminders of the Divine's creative power and the beauty inherent in creation. Numerous Persian proverbs, idioms, and poems lavishly describe the fragrance of flowers. In Iranian culture, the beauty of a flower has been adopted as a standard of merit. *Gol pesar* (literally, flower boy) and *dokhtar-e gol* (flower girl) are used to express the best qualities of young men and women. Lush green Persian gardens famous for their variety of flowers and geometric designs originated perhaps as early as 4,000 BCE (*Tehran Times* 2012). Those gardens undoubtedly supplied the bouquets illustrated in the ancient stone carvings of Persepolis, Iran's most majestic ancient monument. Stone carvings over 2,500 years old include a mural showing Darius I (550 – 486 BCE) holding the scepter of authority in one hand and a lotus flower with two buds in his right hand, the symbol of royalty. Flowers were used for special occasions such as birthdays, religious festivals and rituals, Nowruz, and coronation ceremonies long before Darius I.

The Sacred Dance of Flowers

How did the rose ever open its heart and give to this world all of its beauty? It felt the encouragement of Light against its being.

– Hafez

Iran is home to some of the most beautiful and oldest gardens in the world. Known for their symmetrical layouts, water features, and lush vegetation, Persian gardens are designed to evoke paradise on Earth. They serve as tranquil spaces for reflection, meditation, and leisure. Iranian mystics often sought solitude and retreat in gardens for meditation, contemplation, and spiritual communion. It is worth noting that the word "paradise" originates from a Persian word, *paradisa*, a word used to describe a garden of heavenly beauty. Dances are frequently performed amidst the serene settings of Persian gardens. Dancers may find seasonal inspiration from the colors and fragrances and incorporate flower-like movements and gestures.

Figure 17.2: Tile work illustrating the Divine Rose in Nasir al-Mulk Mosque, Shiraz, Iran. Photo by author.

In Iranian dance, especially the classical and folk forms, dancers often wear costumes and accessories adorned with flower motifs, such as the rose or pomegranate, embroidered on dresses, headpieces, or sashes. Movements and gestures can portray delicate petals or mimic the blooming of a flower, representing the blossoming of the soul. The image of a flower opening and unfolding can be compared to a spiritual awakening or more literally to a darvish spinning. The ephemeral beauty of flowers makes vivid the impermanence of worldly existence. Within mystic culture, flowers are frequently seen as symbols of the Divine's beauty and perfection and are used metaphorically in mystic poetry to represent the Beloved. Several sacred flowers and plants have special meaning in poetry, prayers, and sacred dance including the rose, lotus, saffron, violet, yasmin (jasmine), hyacinth, orchid, narcissus, iris, lavender, lily, and tulip. Especially sacred are the haoma[157] and pomegranate.

The **rose** is the most popular flower worldwide for both its beauty and exceptional fragrance. The legendary Divine Rose of Iran was a figurative marvel in poetry and Sufi culture. It was said to only grow in Iran. In fact, the first roses may have been cultivated in Iran. As the flower of longing and Divine Love, the Divine Rose is also known as the Rose of Daena, the goddess of love. It has a special fragrance and

157 Likely a variant of ephedra.

a color between red and pink; its fragrance is said to please the angels, soothe the stressed psyche, and revive the spirit. The seven layers of petals in the rose symbolize the seven valleys or pathways the darvish must take to reach the Divine and it is associated with St. Davud (David) and Angel Rafael. Known as the queen of flowers, the Divine Rose symbolizes God, giving both fragrance and fruit, and sustaining body, heart, and soul.

I dreamt I came to a magnificent city,
Whose place was the white rose, white rose,
The crown and throne of the great sultan,
His garden and chambers were the white rose, white rose.

– Sinan

The mystics treasure roses, believing they epitomize the enigmatic and beautiful spiritual journey of the Sufis and they are a symbol for the spiritual heart. While the presence of the Divine transcends human description, the scent of the rose closely approximates the feeling of that presence. It is said that the scent of a rose is the closest one can come to experiencing the Beloved on the earthly plane. Mystic poets such as Rumi and Hafez eloquently referred to the rose as the Beloved and the "soul's elixir," for it symbolized divine grace and the manifestation of divinity. They often use the imagery of gardens filled with roses to represent spiritual states and stages of the soul's journey to the Divine. A symbol of the marriage of the spiritual and natural worlds, the rose symbolizes the unfolding self in submission to the Divine; its spiraling petals represent the unfolding of creation (Baker 2018, 79). It is seen as a symbol of the loving embrace the Divine extends to all beings.

In the village of Qasmar, near Kashan, grows a rose that possesses such an exquisite and heavenly perfume that it is nurtured and grown entirely for its nectar. Considered sacred, rose water was used in many ancient rituals and continues to captivate us today. Goddess Daena, born of a rose petal, seduced her lovers by giving them rose water to drink, driving them into ecstasy. Used for hand-washing upon entering a sacred space, rose water is believed to awaken the soul; during zikr, it is splashed into the faces of those who go into ecstasy and fall unconscious;

it is said to be the tears of God. It is believed that splashing one's face with rose water not only revitalizes the individual but also reconnects the soul with the earthly realm.

Figure 17.3: The annual rose water festival, Qamsar Village, Kashan, Iran with author.
Photo by author.

The Persian physician Avicenna used rose water to heal the sick. The rose has found its place in skincare, medicine, and gastronomy even today—rose water and other rose products are an essential ingredient in cuisine, infusing food and drink with their exquisite flavors (Figure 17.3). Shah Jahan, the 17th century Mughal emperor, planned to build the Taj Mahal for his young wife who he adored. When she died prematurely, he completed the building as a mausoleum, and filled the moat surrounding the castle with rose petals and rose water in remembrance of her. When guests were ferried by boat through the rose water in the heat of the Indian sun, the oils rose to the surface of the moat water, filling the air with the colorful fragrance.

For over 5,000 years, Persia has been the habitat of naturally fragrant rose varieties, including those that produce yellow flowers. Yellow roses, symbolizing vibrancy, prosperity, warmth, and happiness are less common than the red rose, which is the most popular flower worldwide and the National Flower of Iran. White roses symbolize innocence, purity, passion, and love while the pink rose is a symbol of strength. In Iran, the velvety texture of the undulating folds of petals varying in shades from white to pink to red is likened to a beautiful lady's rosy-cheeked, blushing complexion. Roses evoke passionate, vibrant living, their thorns the inevitable difficulties one must endure to reach that quality of life.

Dancers use their arms and hands to create shapes reminiscent of blooming roses to express themes of love, beauty, and perfection, especially in romantic or celebratory contexts such as weddings. The symbolism of the rose is also depicted within the sacred ritual of sama. The motion of unfolding the arms out above one's head as one whirls evokes the blooming of a rose as an expression of the soul's unfolding; during whirling, darvishes shed their egos, akin to a rose shedding its petals, drawing nearer to the center and the ultimate truth.

The **pomegranate** fruit is believed to symbolize the essence and vitality of angels and saints. In Yarsan culture, the pomegranate is especially associated with Baba Yadegar, its juice representing the blood of this saint. Legend has it that Ahura Mazda planted the first pomegranate seed and blessed it with abundance. In Zoroastrianism, the pomegranate tree is revered as a perennial and therefore, became a symbol of eternal life. This is why pomegranates are eaten during Yalda, the Winter Solstice—it symbolizes fertility, rebirth, abundance, and eternal life in Iranian culture, making it the best fruit to be eaten on the longest, darkest night of the year. A special pomegranate harvest festival named *Jashn-e Anar* (pomegranate celebration) is held in many cities of Iran with music, dance, special foods, and of course, eating pomegranates (Schuster 2018). The pomegranate is regarded as a magical fruit in Iranian myths: according to the *Shahnameh*, the epic warrior Esfandiyar achieved invincibility after consuming a pomegranate. When Xerxes rode out of Sardis, hoping to complete his father Darius' failed conquest of Greece, one thousand of his finest spearmen bore golden pomegranates on their spear shafts instead of a spike.

In Islamic tradition, the pomegranate is considered heavenly and is mentioned in the Quran as a sacred fruit alongside olives, dates, grapes, and figs. In Zoroastrianism, the pomegranate is the center of every ritual including marriage ceremonies and funerals. Among Sufis, the pomegranate is a symbolic offering and is often included in zikr circles. Its cluster of seeds enclosed within each fruit is considered a symbol of the manifold creation contained within the unity of the Divine. In some interpretations, cutting open a pomegranate to reveal its seeds is likened to the unveiling of spiritual insight and inner wisdom. The pomegranate is sometimes used metaphorically to represent the heart, for just as the pomegranate contains many seeds, the heart is viewed as a vessel for infinite spiritual potential and divine knowledge. In poetry, its richness and complexity serve as metaphors for the depth of spiritual experience, repeatedly mentioned in both classic and contemporary Persian literature such as the *Shahnameh*, Masnavi, Tarikh-e Bayhaqi,[158] and several other books from the pre-Islamic era to the present time. Renowned poets and writers have used its unique features to describe the beauty of the beloved, the heart's sorrows, the taste of life, etc. It is so rooted in Persian culture that there is even a favorite poem for the pomegranate in primary school books. In dance or whirling, embodying the pomegranate through movement invokes healing energies. It has a bright red flower before it becomes a full, round, edible fruit. The flower is connected with transfiguration and prosperity and is considered a symbol of heavenly blessings in Persian culture.

Since the **lotus** grows from a marsh bed, it is the flower of Anahita, the goddess of all waters. In the mystic tradition, it is a flower of unity, creation, and purity. It is a widely recognized symbol of spiritual enlightenment in many cultures and religions, as well as of innocence, insight, wisdom, peace, and serenity. It is a symbol of both light and dark and the veil between them; with its roots in the mud, dark and unseen below the water, it begins to grow when sunlight reaches it down in its bed, and when its flower reaches the surface above it always turns towards the light. This tendency to follow the light symbolizes the loyalty of a devotee. Since the lotus grows in the middle of the marsh, the Zoroastrians believed this an example of how beauty and purity can grow even from within the darkest, most difficult circumstances.

The twelve petals of this flower represent the twelve months of the year and its seasons. It opens with the light, and closes in the darkness, and has the shape of the sun. The blue lotus flower in particular is tied to the elements of wind, water, and earth. Historians have studied the use of the lotus flower in Persian art as a symbol of spiritual growth and transcendence. The lotus is a common embellishment around the

---

158 The *Tarikh-e Bayhaqi* (Bayhaqi's History) is an 11th century CE history book in Farsi of the Ghaznavid Empire written by Abul-Fazl Bayhaqi. Although much of the voluminous book is lost, it remains an important resource of Persian history.

margins of pottery, such as that from Kashan Hill originating more than six thousand years ago. In the Achaemenid period, the flower appeared in official and courtly rituals as a sign of empowerment and was used in decorating buildings. In Persepolis, the lotus is depicted in numerous relief scenes, including soldiers holding it as a symbol of rebirth. It is the official symbol of the city of Kermanshah, where it grows in the headwaters of the Oasis of Nilufar, and is used as a symbol of the Mehr ritual in the motifs of Taq-e Bostan.[159] The lotus was planted on the grounds of innumerable temples and palaces, especially during the Achaemenid Empire. In some places it is shown as a bud in its various stages of opening to illustrate the journey along the seven valleys, ending with it in full bloom, its petals in the shape of the eight-pointed star representing full awakening. At the start of summer when lotuses bloomed, Zoroastrians celebrated the Day of the Lotus (*Jashn-e Nilapur*), honoring goddess Anahita and the Vedic god of wind, Vata, a festival still celebrated today.

As we manifest the lotus in dance or whirling we open to recognize the Divine Light just as the lotus opens to the sun. The whirling motion could be interpreted as symbolizing the cyclical nature of life, growth, and spiritual evolution, much like the lotus emerging from the mud. Dance movements inspired by the lotus may be used to convey themes of enlightenment, purity, and spiritual awakening. Movements that mimic the gentle unfolding and floating of lotus petals capture the essence of its natural grace.

Several plants, including the lotus, **hollyhock**, and **iris**, unite under the theme of rebirth. The hollyhock, another part of the rich tapestry of Persian aesthetics, is a symbol of renewal, radiance, and celebration. Like the pomegranate, the hollyhock is a reminder of Baba Yadegar in the Yarsan culture. The iris flower, too, represents vitality, the spring of life, creativity, fertility, growth, and final unification with Ahura Mazda. The iris is considered a symbol of the heavens and a connection between the earthly and the Divine. In the stone art of ancient Persepolis,

---

159 Taq-e Bostan (Arch of Stone) is the site of large rock reliefs carved around the fourth century CE into a mountainside in Kermanshah, Iran.

the iris is illustrated masterfully and poetically, conveying holiness. The flowers and plants appearing in the stone carvings of Persepolis are symbols of the Amesha Spenta and principles of Zoroaster's faith.

Marking Nowruz, **hyacinth** blooms are another symbol of renewal. Similar to the hollyhock and iris, the hyacinth symbolizes a new beginning. It also represents rejuvenation, new life, and forgiveness. Associated with the Angel Gabriel and St. Benjamin, and dedicated to Aphrodite, the hyacinth is a plant of love and its scent is reputed to relieve grief and keep nightmares at bay. It is also used in healing and love spells (Gallagher 2005). As we manifest the hyacinth in dance or whirling, the Divine Energy of healing is sent through our hands and fingers to cure others. In contemporary Persian dance, especially during Nowruz celebrations, dancers might festively incorporate hyacinth colors, motifs, shapes, or even the flower itself in their costumes or accessories to celebrate a new start and the arrival of spring.

The **orchid** is often associated with femininity, sensuality, and elegance. It is the symbol of beauty and happiness in Iranian mysticism and the symbol of prayer in Sufism, with the white orchid especially favored. An orchid bloom displays exquisite curvature near its opening, reminiscent of an egg's silhouette. Whirling for the orchid is effeminate, soft, and symbolizes the "call to prayer."

Saffron is deeply embedded in Persian culture and is associated with opulence, prosperity, and tradition. Made from the stigmas of the saffron crocus, a small cultivar in the iris family, it is a highly prized spice in Persian cuisine. First cultivated at Derbena, Isfahan, and Khorasan, in the 10th century BCE, Iranians have been using it as a perfume, medicine, and brilliant yellow dye for millennia (Willard 2001). Saffron threads have been found interwoven into ancient royal carpets and funeral shrouds. Saffron and sandalwood were blended in water to make a refreshing body wash. Cyrus the Great sprinkled it in warm baths, believing it healed wounds, and Alexander the Great and his forces enjoyed using saffron during their Asian campaigns mixing it in tea, rice, and baths as well. The amazing saffron flower is subtle and fragrant and tastes slightly sweet; it is said to help evoke the passion a dancer enters when whirling to find the Beloved. Ancient worshipers offered saffron in their rituals to the gods, and in Iranian mysticism, saffron represents concepts like enlightenment, inner transformation, and the seeker's journey toward union with the Divine. A symbol of spiritual insight and growth, saffron's vibrant and radiant color can be seen as a metaphor for spiritual illumination.

Another flower originating in Iran is the **tulip**. It's use spread after the 10th century Turkish invasion and eventually found its way to Europe. A symbol of passion, eternal love, elegance, and dedication, the shape is a motif in many Persian carpets and artifacts. In folklore, the tulip symbolizes those who would die or give their soul for the sake of love, a meaning derived from the Persian tale of Princess Shirin and Farhad, a tragic tale of star-crossed lovers similar to Romeo and Juliet. After being told falsely that Shirin has died, Farhad is overcome by grief and throws himself over a cliff. Legend has it that each drop of Farhad's blood that touched the earth blossomed into a red tulip. This is why when someone dies in Iran, tulips are brought for them to the cemetery, or there's the shape of a tulip on the tombstone for someone lost and dearly loved.

In Iran, the tulip plays a significant role in spring festivities, including a ritual dance around a tree adorned with tulips accompanied by singing and the planting of tulips. The Turkmen festival *Lola Sail* (Tulip-trip), which takes place on the Turkmenistan steppes, is entirely based on the tulip. People enjoy themselves, cooking, eating, singing, dancing, and offering gratitude for the coming of spring, which symbolizes returning life (Sultanova 2014, 193-4). Since spring is a time of renewal after the "death" of winter, its celebration has centered around the tulip which symbolizes martyrdom and resurrection. Stories from pre-Islamic Iran connect martyrdom with the tulip as far back the Parthian passion play *Ayadgar-i Zareran* (Memorial of Zarer) which was sung by minstrels long before it was ever written down, and to the story of Siyavash,[160] which was similarly preserved in oral tradition

160 Siyavash, the son of Kikavous, is a legendary Persian prince of Ferdowsi's epic the *Shahnameh*. A handsome and desirable young man, his name means "the one with black stallions." Siyavash is the symbol of innocence in Persian literature. Before the Islamization of Central Asia, the inhabitants of both

until it was recorded in Ferdowsi's *Shahnameh*. The decorative motif of Martyr's Square in post-revolutionary Tehran features the tulip for this same reason.

In Iranian mysticism, the tulip's elegant and graceful form can be seen as a metaphor for the seeker's inner beauty and ardent love for the Divine. Its dignified, upright growth symbolizes the desire to rise above worldly attachments and limitations on the journey towards spiritual transcendence.

Holy basil, also known as *tulsi* or *ocimum tenuiflorum,* is a medicinal herb believed to have been introduced to Europe by returning crusaders and later by the Moors. It has long been a favorite garden herb in Iran, home of several varieties of basil. A flowering plant of the mint family, it grows throughout Southeast Asia. The herb is widely used in Ayurvedic and folk medicine as an herbal tea or an essential oil with anti-inflammatory, anti-microbial, and stress-relieving properties. Holy basil is classified as an adaptogen, which means it promotes overall well-being. It also has religious significance especially within the Vaishnava tradition of Hinduism. Within the Yarsan tradition, the holy basil flower serves as a remembrance of Angel Hor and St. Khatun-e Ramzbar, the divine virgin mother said to have birthed light and as such it represents fertility and feminine strength.

The Persian genus of **lily** (*fritillaria persica*) is highly significant to the Iranian people. It is a striking flower with a tall, sturdy, unbranched stalk carrying up to thirty bell-like flowers ranging from deep purple to ivory white. For centuries, its captivating beauty has served as inspiration for poets, songwriters, composers, and artists alike. It is often associated with purity, beauty, elegance, transcendence, and spiritual enlightenment. In mythology, its downward-shaped flowers are said to be mourning the death of Siyavash, who was killed unjustly at the hands of the Turanians. According to the story, this flower collapsed, bowing to the ground upon witnessing his death, weeping its colorless

---

Khwarazm and Sogdia performed sacrifices and other rituals dedicated to Siyavash. Siyavash was venerated as the Central Asian god of dying and reviving vegetation.

sap (Fallahi 2020). The beauty of the lily may be linked to the divine beauty that mystics seek to experience and embody in their practice.

Like the lily, **lavender** is a symbol of love and is able to influence love with its beauty. Associated with the element air and the planet Mercury, lavender is used in combination with other flowers in love spells. Lavender is healing and is known for its calming and soothing scent. Lavender's clean and refreshing qualities symbolize the inner purification sought in Iranian mysticism. In a dance performance, the aroma of lavender could potentially contribute to a sensory experience for the audience, enhancing the overall ambiance.

The **yasmin (jasmine)** is the symbol of good thoughts, purity, innocence, beauty, elegance, and love. It is often displayed in wedding ceremonies and celebrations of love and union. Yasmin is the flower for Vohu Manah of the Amesha Spenta who represents the quality of good mind, good thoughts, and righteous thinking. It is associated with women's cycles and sometimes is used in treatments for menstruation or problems with conception. It is used in love spells to attract a true and passionate lover. The beautiful yasmin flower is associated with the Saint Shah Ibrahim and the Angel Aqiq. Jasmine is frequently associated with celebrations and special occasions. In dance, particularly those centered around joyous occasions, the inclusion of jasmine-inspired elements can enhance the overall atmosphere.

The **narcissus**, revered for its ethereal beauty, symbolizes the Divine in all its splendor. The narcissus represents the almighty and helps one see with the spiritual eye. Also closely associated with Nowruz and new beginnings, in poetry the narcissus symbolizes the eyes or an act of prayer or manifestation. The flower and perfume assist in treating headaches and strengthening the mind and vision. In Yarsan culture, the narcissus flower serves as a symbol of remembrance for Sultan Sahak, also known as the creator. In Iranian mysticism, the narcissus symbolizes the process of inner transformation and enlightenment. Just as the narcissus possesses innate beauty, the mystic's journey involves revealing and realizing their inner beauty through spiritual experiences. The blossoming of the narcissus is analogous to the gradual unfolding of the soul in its progression toward spiritual realization. In Sufi poetry and literature, the narcissus has been compared to the seeker's longing for union with the Beloved.

Traditionally, flowers such as the lily, lotus, hollyhock, hyacinth, and lavender have been symbols of vitality and love. On the other hand of the spectrum, the **sul** is a rare green flower of mourning and protection of the soul. The sul flower grows in the dense branches of a species of evergreen tree (platycladus orientalis) and opens up only as it ages. This reflects the belief that wisdom and awakening are born from the trials and hardships experienced throughout life. The sul represents Azrael, the angel of death, and St. Mustafa. Sul flowers are displayed during prayers and remembrances in Yarsan rituals.

Figure 17.4: Zoroastrian Magi carrying baresman, the Oxus Treasure of the Achaemenid Empire, fourth century BCE.

British Museum.

The **banafsheh (violet)** flower is associated with prayers and blessings in the Yarsan tradition, and with Angel Michael and St. Musi. In Iranian culture, the violet flower is associated with modesty, sweetness, and humility. This association can be metaphorically linked to themes of grace, inner beauty, humility, and the expression of gentle virtues. While focusing on these flowers, their qualities, and associated angels or saints, one can bring these healing energies into one's dance and whirling movements, enabling a deeper connection with nature.

Haoma is a sacred plant originally used for healing purposes and later for sacred rituals. Revered for ages across the ancient world, scholars have identified it as the genus ephedra intermedia, a type of shrub native to the arid and semi-arid regions of Central Asia, including parts of Iran, Afghanistan, and nearby. It contains alkaloids, including ephedrine, that can have stimulating effects on the nervous system. In traditional medicine, it may be used to treat respiratory conditions like asthma and bronchitis. In the Persian tradition, haoma was an essential medicinal plant that could be pounded to extract its juice. The strained juice would then be consumed in very small quantities. The potion is a ritual drink important throughout Indo-Iranian culture. Thriving in Iran's climate, haoma continues to be valued for its medicinal properties even today.

In mythology, the source of the earthly haoma plant is a shining white tree that grows on a divine mountain. Sprigs of this white haoma were brought to earth by sacred birds. Haoma is an Avestan term (a more contemporary term is hom) for a genus of plants considered to be divinely created and possessing special holy powers. The word itself is the Avestan form of the Sanskrit *soma*. Once personified as a divinity, haoma bestows essential vital qualities. The source of all healing is said to be contained in the seeds of the plant. According to Zoroastrian belief, the tonic prepared from haoma bestows health, fertility, rejuvenation, virility, strength, and possibly even immortality. It is also a name given to the family of plant-based medicinal and health-promoting extracts made from haoma and other plants.

In Zoroastrian texts, haoma is gathered and carried in a bundle of twigs (known as a *baresman*) from select medicinal plants and trees. Haoma extract is prepared during the Zoroastrian Yasna ceremony. In tradition, two independent preparations are made for the ceremonial offering. Only a few drops of the extract are consumed by the participants of the ceremony or by anyone else. A guiding principle in Zoroastrian practice is to only use enough for mind and body. The Magi frequently carried the baresman with them as medicine, so much so that the baresman became the symbol that identified not just the Magi, but the Zoroastrian faith as well (Figure 17.4). Carrying the baresman bundle was the equivalent of carrying a modern-day physician's medicine bag. Extracts from the different twigs could be combined to create potions to treat many different ailments.

According to legend, haoma traces its origins to the mythical Hom tree, believed to be the Tree of Knowledge created by Ahura Mazda in primordial times. The Hom tree was a symbol of life, vitality, and immortality. It was believed that it grew in the celestial realm, and its branches reached down to the mortal world. The Hom tree was guarded by the divine Simurgh, who prevented any harm from befalling it. One day Ahriman sent his minions to steal branches of the Hom tree. The Simurgh intervened and bravely fought against the forces of darkness but a few branches broke off and fell to earth. Witnessing the falling branches, the Simurgh swiftly caught them, preventing them from reaching the impure earth, then carefully nurtured them ensuring their continued vitality. This legend underscores the significance of the Hom in Zoroastrian worship and the belief in its life-giving and spiritually uplifting properties.

The Sacred Dance of Trees

The tree remains motionless until a breath of wind greets her and sings her leaves to flutter their stillness. I too sit and breathe until… a deeper breath sings me to dance… my fingers flutter and my limbs sway.

– Nina Wyte

Trees have been revered throughout human history for embodying both metaphysical and physical attributes, both mystical and practical uses. Trees offer healing, power, wisdom, and security; they serve as gathering places of love and support. Meetings have been held under the shade of their boughs for centuries. Large fig and banyan trees became natural assembly points for community events and meetings. Since Biblical times, trials and judgments have been held under trees. Even today, no sacred house in Iran nor a Hindu or Buddhist shrine is complete without a tree. The tree is central to the sacred realm; it is a heavenward extension of the revered earth. The venerable tree encompasses an incredible variety of divine meanings.

Various religions, mythologies, philosophies, and traditions portray the tree as a fundamental icon of life and understanding. The Tree of Knowledge, connecting the underworld to heaven, and the Tree of Life, connecting all forms of creation, are common expressions bridging an understanding of both the earth and the cosmos. The growth of a tree, from a small sapling to a towering forest commander, is a metaphor

Figure 17.5: Dakhil draped on trees, Baktar Village, Kermanshah, Iran.
Photo by author.

for the growth of the psyche and the seeker's spiritual journey to wisdom. Because trees are seen as a source of blessing, portions of trees reverently taken serve as tokens, talismans, charms, and medicine. Trees were known to have magical curative powers. In Iran, harmony with the forest and trees was considered essential and trees were likened to angels. Mystics explain that the forest can ground, balance, connect, and stabilize.

Iranians would arrange weddings under a tree to receive blessings from the saint to whom the tree is dedicated. Vows are taken under the shade of a tree just as they are at saints' shrines. These places are channels between the creator and humans where the energy of the saints is felt strongly. Sometimes a green ribbon known as a *dakhil* is tied to a tree when making an oath to God (Figure 17.5) so the oath is evident to all who pass. It also signals the angels to hasten the message to the Divine.

Some traditions considered trees to be the embodiment virtuous people who turned into trees after their death in order to find eternal life. Stones honoring the deceased are placed below a tree upon the death of a loved one. When making a wish to a tree spirit, money may be placed as an offering dedicated to the spirit of the tree, the saint, or a loved one, to be seen by all visitors to the tree.

In the Persian myth of creation, Ahura Mazda created Mashya and Mashyane, two entities that were the ancestors of all living beings. In some versions of the story, Mashya and Mashyane are described as trees. In the Biblical Garden of Eden, God told Adam and Eve they could enjoy everything but forbade them to take from the Tree of Knowledge of good and evil. When they ate from this tree, God expelled them from the Garden of Eden.

While the trees themselves cannot speak, the record they embody has helped modern scientists understand what the world was like in ancient times. Iran's oldest tree is so beloved that it is a national monument. The ancient *Sarv-e Abarkuh*, a Persian cypress tree located in Central Iran in the Yazd Province near the city of Abarkuh, is estimated to be four to five thousand years old. Sprouting about the time that the people of Central Asia were developing wheel with spokes, this giant tree is believed to be the second oldest living thing in Asia and possibly the oldest. Also called Zoroaster's tree, in Persian mythology it was believed Zoroaster planted the tree from seed and promised it would live long. Others believe the son of the prophet Noah planted the sapling after the great world flood. The tree already had global fame by the 14th century, illustrated in stone carvings on monuments, castles, and palaces. It is referenced in Zoroastrian texts, Sufi traditions, and fables. As the national tree of Iran, it appears on carpets, mosques, churches, fire temples, handmade items, and paintings. It has been a symbol of the strength and freedom of the human soul for thousands and thousands of years.

Figure 17.6: Leaves represent the flowing life-force of nature. Valerie Runningwolf.

Zoroastrianism and Yarsanism have always advocated preserving the forest and plants. There are remarkable guidelines in Iranian sacred texts on the importance of preserving nature, purity of water, and forest management. Caretaking of the forest has been a profession since ancient times. A few hundred years before the birth of Christ, when the Jews had rebuilt their temple in Jerusalem, they called upon the Iranians to send caretakers to protect the forests in the land of Lebanon. In the Avesta, Zoroaster commands the Persians to plant and grow trees. For Iranians, planting a tree has been a sacred duty since before Zoroastrianism, an expression of appreciation for the sacrifice trees made and their many important uses. Leaves, bark, and tree sap were used in Persian medicines and scholars and physicians traveled great distances to learn about them. This pharmacological discipline was taught at the Academy of Gondishapur,[161] founded under the rule of Khosrow I[162] during the Sasanian dynasty (Moussavi 2019).

Iranians would devote one day yearly to tree planting and to maintaining forest beauty and productivity. In Iranian culture, the cultivation and care of trees was a measure of affluence and dedication among family and relatives. It was believed the trees carried the souls of the deceased and kept ancestral secrets and memories. Custom forbade cutting down such a tree. In fact, it was forbidden to harm anything in nature because it is the Divine's gift to humanity for survival. Iranians believed that anyone who chops down a tree would lose a loved one that year. Anyone who felled an old tree would suffer an unfortunate life.

Nature, plants, and the elements have played an essential role in Iranian thought and way of life. Protecting nature and taking care of its purity and health was the responsibility of clerics and political leaders. The Sasanian Empire showed great interest in plant and forest management. One day, Khosrow I met an old farmer planting a walnut sapling on a roadside. Knowing the old man would never taste the walnuts from the tree, he asked why he chose to do so. The old man replied: "The others planted in the past so we could eat. Now we plant so others can eat in the future." Pleased with this act, the emperor gave him a bag of gold coins (Moussavi 2019).

Iranians used trees and plants in festivals and celebrations such as Mehregan, Sadeh, and Nowruz, to invoke verdant, abundant growth. Artists and architects adorned houses, halls, and palaces with forests and trees. In the ruins of Persepolis, one can still see palm trees and olive branches among stone relief carvings. Certain trees had magical and spiritual associations. Fruit trees were symbols of life and fertility,

---

161 The Academy of Gondishapur was one of the three Sasanian centers of education and academy of learning in the city of Gundeshapur, Iran, the intellectual center of the Sasanian Empire. It offered education and training in medicine, philosophy, theology, and science in the Persian tradition.

162 22nd Sasanian Emperor of Persia (531-–579 CE).

and long-lived sycamore and cypress were so esteemed that religious ceremonies were held for them.

Many folk traditions about trees and certain types of wood are connected with much older beliefs about tree spirits. Today, the impulse to "touch wood" or "knock on wood" for luck comes from ancient practice of knocking on trees to summon help and support from the angels or tree spirits. Christmas trees and Yuletide logs have their origins in ancient regard for trees as intermediaries with the spirit world. Often what appears to be superstition is actually a remnant of ancestral memory. Trees provide homes, shelter, and shade for insects, animals (including us), and other plant life, and are the lungs of our planet.

Trees provide us with spiritual information. Rooted in the strong foundation of the earth, they grow from soil toward the sky, connecting and belonging to both heaven and earth. The firm roots of the tree anchoring it to the earth are like the mystic's adherence to spiritual principles as the foundation for further growth. Tree roots draw sustenance from the earth as the mystic draws spiritual nourishment from their practices. A tree's leaves and branches reach for sunlight as the seeker's soul reaches for spiritual wisdom and communion with the Divine. Trees respond to the seasons, shedding leaves and sleeping in winter to prepare for rebirth the following spring, a metaphor for inner transformation. The stateliness and serenity that trees embody in nature serve as a metaphor for the inner calm and tranquility sought in mysticism. In mystical poetry, trees symbolize a seeker's inner qualities, spiritual journey, and union with the Divine.

In whirling, our body is like the tree, and as we start to move, extending our limbs, they become like branches reaching toward the sky. As we whirl we feel the wisdom, knowledge, love, and kinship of nature. It's a powerful metaphor for personal growth, development, and transformation. Spirit energy circulates from the roots and around the branches of a tree. A tree is the preferred center for ritual dance, whether ceremonial, celebratory, or meditative. Like the hub of a wheel, the tree stands as the focal point where the energy of the dance can move and circulate most efficiently. A tree offers grounding and strength to a circle of dancers around it. Whirling around a tree is an Iranian ritual that engages healing energy from the tree and forest. This can be good exercise for grounding oneself upon the earth and connecting with the great spirits of the trees.

Dancing Around the Tree of Knowledge

Trees and stones will teach you what you cannot learn from masters.

– Bernard of Clairvaux

Figure 17.7: The tree represents spiritual nourishment, transformation, and liberation.
Valerie Runningwolf.

The concept of a sacred tree as the place of knowledge, the source of life, birth, medicine, magic, or a portal to the spirit world or cosmos is one of the oldest beliefs of man with a deep impact on the religion and customs of the cultures living in the ancient East. The tree connects the four elements of earth, wind, fire, and water and is the link between the three lower worlds and the earth and sky. For the people of the ancient world, the renewal of the tree during spring was an assurance of immortality and protection. They believed that the earth's fertility and the stability of life depended on the greenness and vitality of the sacred life-giving trees, and they wished to become immortal by attaining these qualities. In Iranian mystical culture certain trees are thought to hold the secrets of life and knowledge. These include the three mystical trees—the Tree of Life, the Tree of Knowledge, and the Cosmic Tree—as well as the cedar and cypress.

The mythical **Tree of Life** represents vitality, growth, and rebirth, as well as the ultimate unity and oneness of all creation. Often associated with fruit-bearing, it symbolizes spiritual abundance and the fruits of wisdom. It is the secret of endless fertility, the source of immortality, and the manifestation of absolute truth. This symbol is often seen in Persian carpets and designs. It is known to bring prosperity and luck. The three branches of the tree represent divinity, the human soul, and the spiritual way. Tree roots draw nourishment from the soil, which is composed of what has come before, including our ancestor's remains. The trunk and branches are the Divine, and from them grows our humanity flowering into the mystic arts. This is the mystical truth of life, death, and renewal. Even if a tree dies in its season, it will be reborn again in another.

In Iranian culture, it is believed that trees hold the secrets of ancient wisdom because of their long life. One should not harm trees, but instead talk to them and befriend them. The mythical **Tree of Knowledge**, the *Saena Tree,* is the source of seeds for all plants, all remedies, and wisdom. According to the *Shahnameh*, this tree had fruit that formed the heads of people and animals, and could talk to all living beings. This tree held the nest of the Simurgh. Under the Tree of Knowledge, the great hero Rustam was born, and it is the same tree that talked to Alexander and told him about his day of death.

The **Cosmic Tree** is a universal archetype that appears in the symbolism and mythologies of countless civilizations. It represents the world axis that connects to every aspect of the universe. The Cosmic Tree is at the center of the universe and the source of life for all creatures.

Cedar trees hold a special place in the hearts of Iranians. According to Persian myth, the cedar tree came from paradise. Its durable, aromatic wood has been highly valued for woodworking and construction throughout history. It is also considered the tree of oneness and of angels. The cedar tree has been the focus of poets and authors in many different eras. A tall, slender, beautiful maiden is compared to a cedar tree, which can also refer to the Beloved. The classical Persian paisley motif comes from the image of a cedar tree blowing in the wind, bent over but firm, symbolizing resilience and eternity. The cedar is used in funeral ceremonies for its suggestion of eternal life. Consumption of the cedar's pollen, leaves, and buds was thought to lead to greater longevity. Medicinally, the cedar was believed to help prevent a breakout of fever and infectious diseases. In 445 BCE, King Xerxes of the Achaemenid Empire established the world's first protected forest during a military offensive in which he took his troops to Asia Minor. He delegated a royal guard to protect a cedar forest, going so far as to draw up codified and legally binding laws on the trees' behalf.

Figure 17.8: Relief of cypress tree in Persepolis, Iran.
Photo by author.

The **cypress** tree is another of the most iconic and revered trees in Persian culture, frequently depicted in art, poetry, and architecture. It symbolizes the Tree of Life, serenity, and rebirth. The term *sarv-e kharamān* (strutting cypress) is a metaphor used in poetry to describe the graceful, elegant gait of the Beloved. As an evergreen that can seemingly live forever, it is the symbol of Ameretat, goddess of immortality, and it is the ageless symbol of the persistent triumph of light over the forces of darkness. The cypress is known for longevity, sometimes living for several centuries and even millennia (such as the previously mentioned Sarv-e Abarkuh). It typically grows tall and upright and in any climate, is resistant, strong, and enduring. It stands resolutely as a symbol of freedom, liberty, and justice. It is an upward extension of the earth and symbolizes wholeness and strength because it bends to the wind but doesn't break. Biologically the common cypress has both male and female flowers on one tree (Bakhtiar 1976, 68), adding to its self-sufficiency. Inspired by Saadi of Shiraz, Henry David Thoreau wrote, "… of the many celebrated trees which the Most High God has created lofty and umbrageous, they call none *azad*, or free, excepting the cypress" (Thoreau 1910). It stands as a symbol of great men and for this reason, held a prominent role in ancient texts and all kinds of art as evident from the reliefs of Persepolis to motifs in carpets (Figure 17.8). Its conical shape resembles fire and this makes it a symbol for the sacred fire and transformation. Among Zoroastrians, there is a story that Zoroaster brought this tree from heaven to earth and made it the object of his prayers. Dancers may draw inspiration from the majestic form of the cypress tree with movements and poses that convey a sense of elegance, strength, and endurance.

The animal soul is the connecting link between man and nature.

– Carl Jung

CHAPTER 18

Animals and the Origin of Dance

Only in dance is the mystic bond between man and animals consummated.

– Curt Sachs

One of the central focuses of my research has been exploring the intricate relationship between Iranian dance and the movements of animals. During my training, my masters frequently explained that to deeply understand the sacredness of dance, I needed to observe and study animal behavior, learn their essential movements, and bring them into my dance. They insisted that it was necessary to manifest the animal in spirit, not just mechanically. Venturing into nature, I studied the birds in the trees, swans swimming gracefully in ponds, and peacocks strutting, displaying their plumage in Persian gardens and historic estates. I visited animal sanctuaries. In villages across Iran, I studied how villagers interacted with their animals and what they knew of their character. Returning home, I consulted my elders for their understanding and mystical books for further knowledge.

There is a reason why the Divine put us together with animals on the same planet: animals are here to teach humans many powerful lessons. They remind us that we are only a small part of creation and that every part of creation has a place. Humans were created to be caretakers of the garden of Mother Earth. Our ancestors understood this, and related to the whole of creation as sacred. They knew all things were equal and no animal, including man, held dominion over other parts of creation; they knew that if they attempted to conquer Mother Earth, they would bring great suffering upon themselves. Man knew nature was not "wild" and hostile but a benevolent friend.

In time, mankind came to believe that the animal kingdom was the greatest and most important part of creation, and eventually, modern man has attempted to divorce itself from nature to the detriment of all creation. The Iranians respected the resources of nature and consumed only what they could eat or use entirely. They did not waste life but honored and thanked the spirits for providing life and comfort. Ancient Iranians consulted the animal spirits, requesting guidance and honoring their wisdom with gratitude.

Dancing to evoke an animal—be it a lion, ox, peacock, or horse—is one of the earliest known forms of Iranian dance and the origins of sacred dance. Animals were a symbol of the power and myriad qualities of life and were seen as helpers of or companions to certain deities. Sometimes animals were thought to carry the spirits of the gods or even to be gods themselves. Dancers would act out animal stories using objects such as hides, horns, feathers, and masks. Many stone reliefs illustrate ancient peoples imitating animal movements for healing rituals. This was a time when people saw objects as having souls (animism), when people believed in forbidden, sacred, or imaginary deities (taboo), and related to ancestry through creatures of nature (totem). We have seen evidence that two hundred thousand years ago humans and animals cohabited. Homo sapiens are believed to have emerged around three hundred thousand years ago and prior to that, there were various other hominin species cohabiting with animals. Through storytelling, music, dance, and art, our ancestors collected and transmitted valuable understanding about animal migrations, seasons, edible plants, weather patterns, and more to neighboring tribes. The elaborate cave paintings at sites such as Lascaux and Chauvet, France illustrate the intimate understanding that late ice age humans had of the natural world, especially the animals they hunted for survival (Roos 2021). In Iran, art, coins, and stone reliefs show the persistent connection of ancient humans to animals. The relationship between dance and animals abounds in myths and folktales, stretching back to the beginnings of human existence. Dance rituals for hunting, capturing, planting, reaping, mating, and so on, have sought the aid of deities or spirits to bring fertility, prosperity, and healing through the cycle of seasons.

Iranians recognized their dependency upon animals and admired their superior speed, strength, and other qualities. They believed that animals were capable of predicting the weather, influencing the growth of crops, and had the will of supernaturals. Each type of animal represented a different behavior, strength, or admired quality. Some felt they might acquire animal powers by imitating the animal's gestures in dance, or by applying paints for animal masks and tokens on their faces and bodies.

Figure 18.1: Bull column capital, Persepolis, Iran.
Luis Argerich.

Their practices allowed them to remain connected to the animals in a mutually beneficial relationship. As humans, we too are animals. Like many indigenous peoples, the ancient Iranians viewed all things in creation as having spiritual energy, believed that nonhuman animals possessed souls, and that all beings were connected and worthy of respect and reverence—whether they offered faithful domestic service or were fearful, powerful predators—all had qualities necessary to the whole.

One of the animals considered most sacred across multiple ancient cultures has been the bull with its impressive size, presence, and masculinity. Since prehistoric times, bulls have been admired for their great strength, verility, and ferocity (Clifford 2022). In pre-Roman Mithraism, the bull was elevated to the status of a deity. While Mithra was the Sun or a celestial being, the bull symbolized Earth and mankind (Faraji 2015, 988). The Persians claimed the bull was created by Ahura Mazda and killed by Ahriman. When the bull was killed, his semen was cleansed by the moon and gave rise to a male and a female creature from which 272 kinds of animals were born. The primeval bull's soul was sent to heaven as *Goshurun*, the spirit that cares for domestic animals, and there he sits in the sphere of the sun. The Zoroastrians gave bulls a prominent place in heroic motifs displayed within the palaces and halls of Susa or Persepolis (Figure 18.1).

Figure 18.2: Golpayegan petroglyphs. Teymareh, Isfahan, Iran.
Asef-m-m, Wikimedia Commons.

The cow, too, was admired for her abundant milk, gentleness, and strength, and was representative of nurturing, care, and abundance. One artifact from Iran (2,900 BCE) has been found representing the Mesopotamian mother goddess in a kneeling human form with a cow's head and hoofs. The cow embodied the Great Creatrix and World Mother everywhere in myth and symbolism (Blair 1996, 111). Iranians saw the cow as a divine epiphany of the goddess Mitra. Killing a cow was forbidden and the proper treatment of cattle was an essential measure of human morality; cattle were repeatedly described as a source of human joy (Foltz 2010, 369). The female counterpart of the bull *Goshurun* in the Persian pantheon was the goddess *Drvaspa*, a *yazata*, goddess of fertility, and protector of cattle, children, and friendship.

The **deer** was considered sacred by ancient Iranians and was believed to represent the spirit of the dead or an angel. The Kurdish people also believe the animal embodies a saint or angel, and that if they kill a deer it will bring them bad luck. In Iranian mysticism, poetry, literature, art, and dance, the deer symbolizes calmness, friendship, unity, humbleness, sacrifice, and gentleness. As a prominent motif in Persian art and literature for centuries, the deer is often associated with themes of love, beauty, and the pursuit of spiritual truth. Prehistoric petroglyphs dating to seven thousand years ago portray deer-like forms on rock faces in Teymareh, Isfahan, Iran (Figure 18.2). Among the petroglyphs, the ibex, a type of goat, is the most common image. Human figures are portrayed performing rituals, roping cattle, riding horses, and hunting.

Dancers may emulate the deer to express friendship, gentleness, and humbleness, using gestures that convey its alertness, agility, sensitivity, and awareness of its surroundings. The dance of the deer can also express themes of freedom, purity, and longing. In Iranian mysticism, especially in Sufism, the deer is an important symbol; just as a deer is known for its sensitive nature, the soul is seen as vulnerable and in need of divine protection. Recognition of this vulnerability allows for surrender to the Divine Will, a central aspect of the spiritual journey. The mystic aspires to cultivate the grace, purity, and heightened awareness of the deer. Its elusive and often solitary nature are regarded as a model for the mystic navigating the wild and challenging search for the mysterious Beloved. The profound expression of longing in its dark eyes is often compared to the soul's intense longing for spiritual union with the Divine.

Dogs were seen as essential members of an Iranian family during the pre-Islamic era and were honored in Zoroastrianism for their loyal and protective character. The books of the Avesta divided the dog into two kinds—the "house" dog to protect the owner's home and the "herd" dog, to protect cattle—and adjured man to be grateful to the dog for vigilantly protecting him and his possessions. The dog had a primary role in Zoroastrian funeral customs. They were brought in to inspect a corpse before it was taken to the bier as it was believed they could drive away infesting demons from the dead.

The character of the dog is used metaphorically in Persian mystical poetry and Sufi thought to describe desirable qualities of a practitioner. Particularly in the poetry of Rumi and Attar, the dog is a symbol of the unwavering devotion, persistence, and steadfastness needed on the mystic's path. Its vigilance is a metaphor for spiritual wakefulness and mindfulness. A dog's keen sense of discernment between friend and foe is a metaphor for dividing spiritual truths from illusions. Its tracking ability is sometimes compared to the mystic lover (Sufi seeker) that eagerly seeks the presence of its Beloved. The dancer may incorporate the playful and sprightly nature of the dog in their dance as well as elements related to loyalty, protection, and vigilance.

The **fish** is another sacred animal of Iran that appears ubiquitously in folklore and customs as a symbol of protection, good luck, and prosperity. Iranians always serve fish on auspicious occasions such as

Figure 18.3: Goldfish, the goddesses of water.
Valerie Runningwolf.

the four-day Zoroastrian marriage ritual which begins with the *dahi maachi ni reet*, a dish of raw fish and sweet curd presented to the families. Eating fish during Nowruz symbolizes purity and prosperity for the new year. In the city of Yazd, the Zoroastrian bridal dress (*shalwar kameez*) often has fish embroidered on the legs as a sign of prosperity and good fortune for the new bride. Among the ancient Elamites who dwelled in what is now the Lorestan province, numerous archaeological artifacts, known as A'ah, depict female figurines alongside fish, suggesting a relationship with the goddess Anahita.

In Persian legend, when Ahura Mazda created the Hom tree (the Tree of Knowledge) he placed it in the middle of the ocean. He then created the Kar-fish to swim around and guard it. In the Zoroastrian tradition, the fish was created to protect us against Ahriman and his evil forces. The fish is seen as a symbol of a darvish, known to keep the truth, and appears in many mystic paintings and writings depicting a mystic. Later the fish became a Christian symbol of spiritual awakening. When the feeling of the fish is manifested in sacred dance and whirling, it emphasizes fluidity, grace, and resilience while riding the waves of life, emotions, or spiritual energy. Fish-like movements may depict the element of water in a larger dance narrative. The ability of the fish to live in water but occasionally surface can be interpreted as moving between the physical and spiritual domains. In some interpretations, the fish is seen as a symbol of the heart, the source of spiritual consciousness, and the container of the divine presence.

Since fish reside in the depths of the ocean, they represent a mysterious and hidden existence, just as the Divine Reality is often outside human comprehension. The fish is often used to represent the mystic seeker of truth who longs to return to the deep ocean of Divine Existence, be immersed in the Divine, and dissolve the ego. This immersion represents a state of spiritual annihilation (fanaa) and union (baqaa). When a fish swims against a current or leaps from the water it can symbolize the mystic's efforts to overcome distraction and illusion in order to reach the Divine.

In the Yarsan tradition, the fish represents the soul on its journey and quest for spiritual enlightenment. Water, the fish's habitat, symbolizes the divine essence and the soul's innate connection with it. As creatures of silence, fish offer encouragement to practice silence and contemplation in order to foster a deeper connection to the Divine. Known for their remarkable patience and resilience, they also offer a reminder to navigate life's challenges with determination, faith, patience, and endurance.

In Yarsan culture, fish represent Sultan Sahak, who was said to have emerged from the water; fish therefore symbolize spiritual protection, divine presence, and guidance and may serve as guardians during the soul's journey toward enlightenment. They also represent hidden knowledge, as well as a symbolic bridge between the worlds of water and air. Note that this symbolism can vary among different communities and regions as influenced by individual beliefs and the guidance of local spiritual leaders.

It is believed that a fish promotes water purification which makes it a symbol of cleanliness. In ancient times a goldfish was brought to the home and dropped into the household well, believing it would remove waterborne diseases and clear all negative energy. Even today one might see goldfish placed in small pools or swimming pools to keep the water clean in place of chemical additives. Six thousand year old water pots originating from the Elam province are decorated with drawings of fish, likely to invite positive energies into the water.

Like all fish depicted in Persian dance, goldfish exemplify fluidity, grace, resilience, renewal, and rebirth. Since goldfish are known for their lively nature and vibrant colors, depicting them in dance can convey vitality, energy, and a celebration of life. Goldfish are often kept in ornamental ponds or tanks, requiring care and attention to thrive, so incorporating movements inspired by a goldfish can also symbolize the importance of nurturing and attending to the inner self. The presence

Figure 18.4: Fish stone inlay, Temple of Anahita, Kangavar, Kermanshah, Iran. Photo by author.

of a goldfish in dance might demonstrate spiritual growth, awakening, and a deep connection to the Divine (Figure 18.4).

In ancient Iran, the goddess Melmedas was an angel who descended from heaven to become a mermaid, with the head of a woman and the body of a fish. At first she was a symbol of renewal, but she was tricked by the Lord of Darkness and was banished from light, forced to live in a sea cave. On the island of Hormuz in the Persian Gulf, there were tales of Melmedas enticing men to their deaths (Tschaikner 2021). Legends said she ventured out of her cave on the full moon, swam to shore and sang enchantingly, wearing a skirt covered in gold coins recovered from sunken ships. Sea captains, lured into the sea by her charms would bestow their ship's treasures upon her. She would capture the hearts of wayward men and trap their souls under her golden skirt. When the moon was no longer full she would return to her cave with her catch. This tale was the basis of the mythological Greek sirens.

The **horse** represents physical and spiritual power, strength, and friendship. Since ancient times, horses played a significant role in the lives of the Iranian people, leaving an indelible mark on their culture. Persepolis's walls show the importance of the horse in the Achaemenian Empire, and innumerable artifacts display the skill of a king hunting while riding a horse. All young men learned to ride at an early age, and the Iranians were famous for breeding strong, beautiful horses. A gift of a horse was both a gesture of respect, because of its elegance, and a practical gift as an invaluable means of transportation. In dance, horses symbolize freedom and desire for unbridled expression as well as strength and dignity. Their graceful, powerful movements convey a noble and courageous nature. In sacred dance, incorporating

Figure 18.5: Decorative tile work of lion and sun, Golestan Palace, Tehran, Iran.

Yamaha5, Wikimedia Commons.

horse-like movements pays homage to a rich legacy of bravery, loyalty, and determination.

In Iranian mysticism, particularly within Sufi poetry and teachings, the horse has deep metaphysical meaning. The horse and rider represent the soul journeying to spiritual realization. The elevation of the rider above the ground symbolizes the elevation of consciousness. The harmonious movement, control, mastery, endurance, faith, and trust between the horse and rider are analogous to the inner harmony and discipline of the mystic on their journey toward the Divine, seeking a state of spiritual freedom and transcendence above the material world and ego.

The **lion** had an honored place in the ancient Near East as a symbol of the sun goddess Mitra and an emblem of Iranian royalty; its yellow mane like sunbeams, its ferociousness like the sun's fierce heat. To some mystics, the lion depicts Divine Light in the world or a spiritual elder who shares spiritual learning and mystical experience (Figure 18.5). The lion symbolizes strength, nobility, assertiveness, courage, individual power, and leadership. The lion is suggestive of the directive and creative essence within all things. In Shi'ite circles, Imam Ali is often called the Lion of God, as Rumi describes him in the *Masnavi* (Bakhtiar 1976, 75).

The courage and mastery of the lion evoke the inner strength and fortitude needed on the spiritual path, while its noble demeanor depicts transcendence above the material world, one's base desires, fear, and ego. The lion has a regal presence, symbolizing a commitment to safeguarding and upholding spiritual truth and principles. It guards the doors of the spiritual sanctuary.

The **serpent** was seen as an immoral creature in Iranian culture and represents the darkness and shrewdness of the human ego. The serpent is a symbol of opposites: on the one hand calm, thoughtful, and carefree, but on the other it is very dangerous. In Zoroastrianism, Azhi Dahaka was a serpent demon who slayed the first mortal, Yima.[163] It was the demonic enemy of many legendary battles with classical heroes, including Thraetona, an early cultural hero. The snake was the companion of Ahriman, the god of darkness in Persian mythology. In the Zoroastrian Story of Creation, Ahriman enters the world as a snake and tries to destroy and desecrate the seven creations of Ahura Mazda: the sky, water, earth, plants, animals, man, and fire. The Faravahar sometimes features a serpent curling around its form, but its significance is the opposite of the usual association of serpents with sin and trickery—instead, it forms part of the seraphim, or guardian angel.

For the most part, snakes and serpents are seen as creatures that harm human beings and therefore should be kept at a distance. In fact, the Zoroastrians of Yazd have a specially dedicated day for exterminating reptiles and insects, which threaten the well-being of mankind. The snake commonly represents the contemptible ego. In the *Shahnameh*, the story of Zahak offers a vivid illustration of this. The handsome and clever son of king Merdas, Zahak, was easily swayed by malicious advisors. Ahriman persuaded him to ascend the throne by killing his own father then placed him under a spell making two snakes grow from his shoulders. Thereafter, Zahak became an ugly, dark figure. Tempted and guided by Ahriman, Zahak sowed chaos and disorder in the kingdom, daily feeding the snakes in his shoulders a stew composed of the brains of two executed men.

---

163 In the Avesta, King Jamshid, otherwise known as Yima, was the legendary first human being in the world.

At the same time, the shedding of a snake's skin is often seen as a symbol of renewal and transformation, representing personal and spiritual growth, inner renewal, healing the life force, and shedding layers of ego. Serpents have been associated with knowledge and wisdom and, in some contexts, they are fearless protectors and guardians. To engage the energy of the snake in dance, one may make sinuous, subtle, graceful, and arc-like movements. Serpent-like movements in dance may convey a myriad of meanings, from refinement and poise to spiritual protection and transcendence, to fear, ego, and deception.

The **ram** is a sacred animal of honor and humbleness especially in the Yarsan culture where it represents St. Baba Yadegar, who sacrificed his life to serve the people of God.[164] The ram was a common animal to sacrifice in ancient cultures, including for the Yarsan. The ram exhibits strength, virility, leadership, assertiveness, confidence, endurance, and the protective instincts of safeguarding loved ones and community. Dance movements resembling a ram might symbolize a willingness to make personal and spiritual sacrifices for a greater cause.

Some animals are not considered sacred but serve as examples of various human traits. The **wolf** is one such animal. The wolf takes a single mate for life, is extremely loyal, and has very keen senses. Their independence, endurance, strength, cunning use of strategy, and loyalty as pack protectors mean they can survive long, harsh conditions. Iranian mysticism admires the wolf for its untamed, wild nature, sharp instinct, courage, and resilience. The wolf might represent the seeker's perseverance and intuitive wisdom for navigating the unknown and transcending limitations. Wolf-inspired movements in Iranian dance might illustrate resilience, endurance, and the ability to overcome obstacles.

On the other hand, the wolf can also represent the human ego; therefore "feeding the wolf" means expanding the ego. As a nocturnal predator, the moon is its ally. The lone wolf is sometimes associated with the wayfarer, roaming on the spiritual path through vast realms of realization and spiritual experience. When this lone wolf stalks its prey it could represent the "shadow" of the self, aspects that are often denied

---

164 See page 176.

or hidden. Integration and acceptance of these aspects can lead to a more complete and balanced self. Like the lion, the wolf is sometimes regarded as a guardian of the sacred inner space.

Every culture has produced a rich myriad of animal tales conveying wisdom and inspiring spiritual practice. Real or mythical, animals possess a magic that our earliest ancestors tried to harness by imitating them in dance. In the context of ancient Iranian spiritual practices, Zoroastrianism, and Yarsanism, animals conveyed symbolic significance in mystical poetry, teachings, and rituals. We can access both practical and spiritual wisdom by exploring the movements, qualities, and power of animals as we continue our journey in dance.

Feather of the Beloved.

In the embrace of dawn, with wings of light,
we soar into the horizon of possibility.

CHAPTER 19

Wings of Light

I once asked a bird, "How is it that you fly in this gravity of darkness?" The bird responded, "Love lifts me."

– Hafez

The Huma[165] and the Greedy Man

Exhausted from a long day of looking for work in the market, a peasant man in ragged clothing fell asleep under the shade of a date palm. A Huma bird, gliding high in a gentle wind, saw the poor man below and took pity on him. "I will give him a golden egg so his mind won't be clouded with worry."

When the man awoke, he found the golden egg beside him and was overjoyed. "Now I can feed my family!" he exclaimed. Unsure of the value of the egg, the man returned to the market and asked a merchant for his advice. "How much will you give me for this golden egg?" the peasant asked. "I'll give you a full day's wage for this egg," said the merchant. "That will be enough to feed your family a wholesome dinner, and buy several small gifts to show your love."

But the merchant knew the golden egg's value was much more significant. "Why don't you return where you found this egg, and come back tomorrow with another?" he suggested. "I will pay you twice as much tomorrow." The peasant was lucky as the Huma indeed returned the next day, saw the man in rags sleeping against the palm tree, felt pity, and left yet another golden egg. But now the peasant had become greedy. He pretended to be asleep and kept one eye open, waiting. "If I catch this Huma Bird, perhaps the merchant will pay me triple!" So when the Huma Bird began to fly

[165] A mythical bird said to never land on the ground, instead always flying invisibly in the sky.

off after dropping the golden egg, the peasant suddenly jumped and grabbed her leg. The peasant couldn't have made a bigger mistake. The Huma as if by magic vanished instantly, as well as the golden egg she left for him. In a matter of two days, the peasant had lost two fortunes due to his greed and ignorance, once by selling his treasure and the second by trying to capture the Huma ("The Huma Bird of Iranian Legend" 2020).

A bird traverses both land and air making it a perfect envoy from heaven to earth. Iranians studied the behavior of birds believing they revealed the will and the intent of the angels. They believed birds were guardians of celestial bodies and messengers of light carrying spiritual insights and secrets to seekers below. Magi would watch the birds for signs and advise the king about any messages they might bring. Flying amidst the heavens, a bird portrays the lightness of spirit and the human soul. Throughout the history of religion, the bird has been a symbol of the imprisoned human soul escaping from the body after death to soar to its heavenly reward. In Persian literature and art, birds represent salvation and escape from bondage. In Iranian mysticism, the circular spinning motion of whirling darvishes is seen as a metaphor for the soul's journey toward spiritual union with the Divine. This spinning has often been compared to a bird in flight, soaring towards the heavens.

For ancient man, the wearing of bird masks or a costume of beak and wings was thought to endow the wearer with the bird's powers, and their feathers were thought to especially transmit their wisdom (Johnson 1994, 8). The bird wing was a symbol of "Increasing Glory" and was associated with the glory of Persian kings. It was also said to bring good fortune, prosperity, and spiritual excellence. People have mimicked birds in dance since antiquity for good reason. In nature some birds and insects appear to be born dancers. It is hard to call the dazzling display of a male bird-of-paradise courting a potential mate anything but dance. To make his moves even more visually appealing, the male sometimes tidies the ground of his "performance stage," so that any curious female can see his display in all its beauty. Another example is that of the bee scout who communicates to the other bees using a special dance; a precise number and direction of circles accurately describes the location of the pollen source in relation to the position of the sun. The gatherers receive the directions by encircling the scout who brushes against them while dancing. It is no wonder the bee is considered one of the symbols of wisdom in mystic folklore. Bees, like birds, were thought to carry messages from the Divine.

There are two types of birds considered important in Iranian heritage: royal birds and birds of wisdom. The royal birds convey national power and thus adorned places and objects related to the monarchy or leaders. Birds of wisdom were portrayed in religious places or in mystic art and literature. Sacred or symbolic birds of folklore include the dove, eagle, falcon, hoopoe, hummingbird, owl, peacock, nightingale, rooster, crow, and swan.

Dance of the Sacred Birds

Birds make great sky-circles of their freedom. How do they learn it? They fall and falling, they're given wings.

– Rumi

Figure 19.1: Birds may symbolize freedom, grace, and transcendence.
Valerie Runningwolf.

Like the famous Dying Swan ballet solo or The Firebird ballet by Igor Stravinsky, birds and the mysticism or folklore that surrounds them have captured human imagination across many cultures. From time immemorial, the Persians have incorporated the movements of birds into sacred dance. Elegant, fluid motions represent the fluttering and soaring of birds in flight, with feathered headdresses, swirling capes, undulating skirts, and fans blowing veils into wing shapes enhancing the effect. Group choreography may depict the coordinated movements of a flock of birds. Birds symbolize freedom, grace, transcendence, and the connection between the earthly and spiritual realms. Just as a bird soars in the sky, the soul seeks to transcend the material realm to venture toward spiritual enlightenment and union with the Divine. When whirling, mystic dancers may project the imagery of birds to mimic the graceful and free flight of the bird as they become closer the Beloved. Many such meanings are woven into dance narratives. To emulate a dove, peacock, eagle, or hummingbird, Iranian dancers study the character, habits, and folklore of the bird.

Doves are recognized around the world as a symbol of peace, unity, and gratitude. In Iranian culture, they are also associated with friendship, love, and devotion, and many homes, churches, and mosques attract and care for doves in honor of these qualities. In folklore, the dove carries messages of love, especially between sailors lost at sea and their sweethearts, delivering their final words of love. This may have originated when Greek sailors observed white doves escaping from sinking Persian ships during a naval expedition in the fifth century (Waterfield 2009, 32). The dove is one of the sacred birds associated with the goddess Anahita (the other being the peacock), and is associated with water. In dance this peaceful bird expresses calm, deep affection, spiritual connection, humbleness, reconciliation, harmony, and longing for peace.

Eagles are kings of the sky and protectors of the people. Seeming to fly close to the sun, the eagle abides in lofty, remote, eerie locations, descending to earth to capture prey, ascending once again further than all birds. In folklore, the eagle soars from one world to another to regenerate and guide souls. It embodies the power of swiftness, strength, and fearlessness, as it is said to be unafraid of thunder and lightning. The eagle has a commanding presence, displaying freedom, courage, determination, independence, endurance, control, authority, focus, skill, keen vision, mental acuity, and shrewdness. It is associated with the elements of fire and water. Military officers would often carry spears donned with the head of an eagle and it became a symbol of Persian victory over the Medes when it was seen flying over the battlefield. Sighting an eagle signifies special achievements or remarkable occasions, such as obtaining prosperity or success, recognition for an act of kindness or generosity, or becoming enlightened. In mysticism, the eagle is the metaphor for a spiritual guide or mentor.

Dancers may portray the eagle with a piercing gaze or predatory movements of majesty and grandeur. In Tajikistan, once part of the Iranic land, dancers mimic an eagle beating its wings and "soaring" in the air to portray the ascension of ancestor spirits. The music played for it is meant to create the feeling of an eagle soaring in the sky and the dancers perform with agile and graceful body movements. The men play a flute made of eagle bone, women play frame drums, and the dancers performing with a hammer and tongs. The dance is grounding, invoking strength and power.

Figure 19.2: Tile of the sacred falcon, symbol of the flag of the Achaemenian Empire. National Museum of Iran, Tehran.
Photo by author.

Related to the eagle, the **falcon** or **hawk** in Iranian mysticism portrays spiritual rejuvenation, healing, and wisdom, and serves as a protector of souls. Like all birds, falcons bridge heaven and earth, but they are found only in certain places and are considered to be special messengers of the Divine or the prophets. They were also engaged as messengers and relayed battle plans or notes during war. Mystics would often carry a staff depicting a falcon since it is a bird of wisdom and power. They carry Divine power but also represent the human ego and its mortality. They teach us to be observant, to pay attention to what we may overlook, to courageously face our fears, and fly as high as our heart's joy can take us. In mystical poetry, the falcon may represent the Beloved or the Divine itself. Seen as having protective powers, and as the guardian of royalty, it was portrayed with wings spread over the head of Persian kings. At the same time, it also appears next to those who are humble and pure such as mystics and saints. The *Shahbaz* (meaning royal falcon) is an avian god in Persian mythology described as having a body even larger than an eagle who guided the Faravahar to the Iranian plateau. In Yarsan culture, the falcon represents Sultan Sahak and carries his message. Since antiquity, because of its hunting abilities, and its great strength, agility, and power, the falcon was kept by kings and ordinary people in Iran, leading to theories that the practice of falconry originated in Iran.

The falcon is known to be agile, swift, and precise in hunting. Dancers may incorporate movements that emulate the falcon's swift and precise motions. When a dancer whirls like a falcon with their "wings" extended, and shows comfort turning at a high speed, this indicates their spiritual energy is very potent.

In Iranian spiritual traditions, there is a belief that a **hoopoe** appears to those of pure heart and can speak directly to their soul. It is also thought that wherever a hoopoe lands on the ground is a good site for digging a well. As early as the Middle Ages, this bird with its distinctive crest of feathers was also believed to have magical properties: drops of hoopoe blood would eliminate jinns, eradicate nightmares, and potions made with its heart could cure disease. Unfortunately, these superstitions led to over hunting for sorcery and witchcraft, causing its extinction in some areas of Iran. The hoopoe's magical qualities frequently appear in folk tales and legends. In an old Greek story, when the parents of a hoopoe became old, he plucked their old feathers and licked their bodies until they became young again. In Iranian folklore, there is the story that the hoopoe was a bride who was combing her hair before a mirror when her father-in-law came in and saw her in an uncovered state. Startled and ashamed, she became a bird and flew away with the comb still in her hair. Thus, the bird became known in Farsi as s*hane basar* (scallop-headed).

In Persian mystical poetry, the hoopoe is used metaphorically to represent the seeker on their spiritual journey. The dancer may manifest the hoopoe's graceful, knowledge-seeking, and inquisitive manner. This can include distinctive gestures and tilting of the head. In mystic dance and poetry, express the energy of the hoopoe as a spiritual aspirant in the search of the Divine.

The **hummingbird** symbolizes joy, friendship, giving, and happiness. It is the companion of Ameretat, the Persian goddess of nature. Spreading its message of joy and beauty, it teaches us to appreciate the wonder and magic of everyday existence, and encourages us to protect the environment. Hummingbirds remind us not to lose our balance in life or give our energy away. They can be so friendly it can actually be pestering! A hummingbird can fly in any direction—up, down, backward, and forward—and can hover in one spot as though motionless. They appear to move and act indecisively and are extremely sensitive—quickly flying away from discord or disharmony. Plants and flowers thrive because of hummingbird pollination. It is said that the hummingbird sings a vibration of pure joy, conjures love, and its feathers open the heart. Without an open and loving heart, one cannot taste the nectar and pure bliss of life. The exuberant spirit of the hummingbird represents the seeker's inner joy and delight in spiritual realization. In sacred dance, the energetic movements of the hummingbird are quick and delicate, representing friendliness and the seeker's vibrant yearning for divine communion.

The mysterious **owl** can see, hear, and fly effectively in the dark, inspiring ideas about its magical powers. Symbolic of spiritual communication, it represents wisdom and virtue (in Greece the owl was sacred to Athena, goddess of wisdom and intellect), but is clever to the point of deception, which may explain its association with witchcraft or bad omens, doom and death. In Iranian tradition, however, the owl is seen as a lucky bird that brings good fortune. Its feathers, thought to have protective qualities, were rubbed over the body when leaving on a long journey, or were carried as a talisman; it was believed no enemy could harm a person who carried the feathers of an owl. According to the Behram Yasht,[166] the owl brings victory and glory. Many tribal elders and oral historians call the owl the "night eagle," and farmers favored the owl for its ability to kill rats, vermin, and other creatures that destroy crops. Dancers manifest the owl with gestures and movements that mimic its keen observation, perception, inner wisdom, exceptional insight into the night, contemplation, vigilance, silence, and stillness.

The **crow** symbolizes mysticism, the occult, and transformation in most ancient cultures. Seen as secretive, adaptable, cunning tricksters and masters of illusions, crows are associated with the "other world," and

---

166 Behram Yasht is the Zoroastrian Avestan hymn of invocation. The Yashts are a collection of 21 hymns in the Younger Avestan language.

are believed to represent the souls of our ancestors. The dark plumage of the crow is suggestive of foreboding and in dreams the crow represents an unwanted event. But in mysticism and poetry, the keen intelligence of the crow is linked to persistence, insight, and resourcefulness on the spiritual path. Characteristic of the crow, dancers can incorporate swift and agile movements.

The **swan** symbolizes grace, humility, elegance, purity, serenity, inner beauty, and love. It is the companion of Ufratu, the goddess of rivers and streams. As a swan traverses both water and land, the seeker looks to find balance between the spiritual and material worlds. The graceful motion of the swan upon water is suggestive of the seeker's desire to move harmoniously through life while in union with the Divine. Portrayed as humble and shy, the swan depicts the serenity of a mystic, and teaches us to trust the grace of our own being. In dance or whirling, the humble swan's energy is calming, its smooth and flowing motions evoking a sense of grace, beauty, and poise.

One ancient Iranian story speaks of an angel who bragged about being the best of all angels. When God heard of this egotism he warned him that if this selfishness continued He would remove his power. The narcissism continued until finally God banished the angel to earth transforming him into a peacock. God meant this punishment to serve as an example to the other angels should they ever act selfishly. In consequence, in Iranian culture, the **peacock** became the symbol of ego. Another legend, likely of Sufi origin, suggests that God created a spirit in the form of a peacock. Shown its own divine image in a mirror, the peacock was seized with awe, and drops of sweat fell from it, each droplet creating another being in the world. In another story, the peacock became one of the seven sacred birds seeking the Simurgh to be free of its entrapment in the peacock's body. Folklore surrounding the peacock appears in various religious and spiritual traditions, including Islam, Hinduism, Yazidism,[167] and others. Peacocks appear in the poetry of Persian and Urdu mystics and are used to convey deep spiritual

---

167 The Yazidis are a Kurdish-speaking religious group living in the Kurdish regions of Iraq, Syria, Turkey, and Iran.

Figure 19.3: The peacock motif symbolizes immortality and divine protection and is associated with paradise, Golestan Palace, Tehran, Iran.

Photo by author.

and metaphysical concepts. The peacock came to be associated with the concept that true beauty lies within, and that the soul reflects inner spiritual radiance and the recognition of the Divine's beauty.

In Persepolis, peacock images have been found dating to the Achaemenid dynasty. It was a symbol of immortality as the ancients believed its flesh did not decay after death. Since the peacock replaces its feathers every year, it also came to be a symbol of renewal and resurrection. For entertainment, dancers of the royal court would often wear peacock feathers and enact the movement of a peacock. This practice was also done for ritual purposes inside the Temple of Anahita. Today, for ceremonial purposes, many dancers from Iran, Central Asia, and East Asia imitate the peacock by wearing peacock costumes and dancing with delicate arm and head movements.

The story of the peacock was presented in ancient Iranian temples and the royal courts through a dance known as *Raghs-e Tawus* (Dance of the Peacock). Still performed for cultural events and celebrations, the dance involves a series of graceful, flowing movements that seek to emulate the elegance and beauty associated with peacocks. Dancers stand tall and proud, mimicking the peacock's splendorous display of its feathers, then glancing down to symbolize repentance and letting go of our ego. Eventually, the peacock would come to be associated with Anahita, the goddess of water.

The peacock has played an important role in mystic poetry and iconography (Figure 19.3). Its tail may be compared to a beacon of light spreading the infinite richness of divine beauty. It symbolizes the soul of the mystic when it reaches the Presence of Light or the Intellect, and moves from contraction to expansion, radiating from the center in all directions in order to present itself to all realities (Bakhtiar 1976, 74-75). Its display can also be seen as a metaphor for the unfolding of spiritual qualities within the seeker. While the Yazidis consider the peacock angel (Malek Tawus) to be an incarnation of God who has power on the earth, in the sky, in the sea, on the mountains, and in all parts of nature, whether celestial or terrestrial, with the decline of Zoroastrianism and the introduction of Christianity and Islam in Iran, the peacock came to symbolize darkness and ego.

The **nightingale,** though small and plain, is the bird of longing and love. It is a fixture in Persian mystical poetry, representing the impassioned human lover pining for the unattainable beauty of the Divine Rose, a metaphor for our yearning for spiritual transcendence. The nightingale's persistence and devotion to the rose is akin to the seeker's dedication to the Divine. Its song is considered an expression of Divine Love. Some maqams for the tanbur as well as Iranian chanting are patterned after the song of the nightingale. In Sufi poetry, the nightingale's passionate and plaintive melody is seen as an allegory for the soul's fervent desire for the Beloved. That it sings in the dark of night is also seen as a metaphor for spiritual illumination and seeking the Divine Light. The nightingale or sparrow movement in Iranian sacred dance or whirling is full of spirals, representing love, longing, and a dedication to be unified with the Beloved.

The **rooster** symbolizes honesty, physical fortitude, moral strength, protection, vigilance, fidelity, luck, and authority. It also symbolizes spirituality and the awakening of new ideas. The rooster's crow at dawn can be interpreted as a metaphor for the seeker's call to spiritual devotion and connection with the Divine. As the bird that welcomes the sun, it wakes us up and heralds the creator of light. According to legend, when the dark lord Ahriman was about to attack, the rooster crowed to warn and awaken the people. The dog is a co-worker of the rooster and they both help *Sraosha* (also known as *Sorush*), a Yazata guardian, the angel of conscience, to protect the world from evil influences. Sraosha is associated with the concept of Asha (righteousness and divine order). The rooster is often said to carry the spirit of saints and has a special role in Iranian mysticism as it was created by Ahura Mazda to fight demons. The white rooster is said to be the companion of the Yazata, the guardian angels.

The rooster's crowing mirrors a form of zikr, a repetition of a sacred word, so it is believed to be calling the name of the Divine for us. When he calls us to wake up, it symbolizes a new beginning and gives us hope and enthusiasm for a new day. It could also be metaphorically compared to the seeker's spiritual awakening or realization of higher truths. The rooster represents gratitude, one of the seven traits of Sufism. Mystics view the rooster as the harmonizer of light and darkness, integrating all aspects of being, including our shadows, on the journey to spiritual realization. Since the rooster is known for its spirited, lively nature, dancers can incorporate this energy in dynamic movements to herald hope, rejuvenation, and a fresh start. Roosters are known for their alertness and vigilance as guardians of the flock, therefore dancers can represent the seeker's need for vigilance on their spiritual journey.

The **moth** is always searching for the light and has an intense desire to be unified with it. Here, the light serves as a Sufi metaphor for the Beloved, and the moth's tendency to plunge into it illustrates the Sufi concept of fanaa, the annihilation of ego. Dancers can evoke the moth with soft, gentle wing movements mimicking its curiosity, or by circling and spiraling like the moth in pursuit of the flame. Other movements may show the moth's intense desire for the candle, its yearning, or its state of spiritual ecstasy as it achieves union with the Divine.

Figure 19.4: The butterfly is a symbol of hope, transformation, and faith.
Valerie Runningwolf

The caterpillar's transformation into a **butterfly** is a perennial symbol of renewal and rebirth. Its flight from flower to flower represents the soul's journey in search of spiritual nourishment and enlightenment, and the graceful and delicate nature of the butterfly is associated with the tenderness of Divine Love. Butterflies are often associated with beauty and freedom, inspiring dancers to mirror these qualities in their movements. Their vibrant patterned and colorful wings can symbolize the many-colored aspects of the self. Dance movements may convey the idea of shedding old limitations and embracing new forms. Dancers may convey a process of spiritual transcendence similar to when the caterpillar lifts into the air as a butterfly.

Birds in Iranian Mythology

Among lovers, only those with wings
flee this worldly cage before death comes.
The condition of these lovers is hard to recount,
for such souls speak a different tongue.
The one who learns and speaks their language
will hold the elixir of happiness at Simurgh's court.

– Attar

Figure 19.5: Winged bulls at the Gate of All Nations, Persepolis, Iran.
Carole Raddato (left) and Sima Farshid (right), Wikimedia Commons.

In Persian literature and art, mythical creatures amalgamate the finest attributes of various animals and birds. Sometimes the combinations symbolize three or four natural elements or domains. For example, in the ruins of the ancient city of Persepolis, there are enormous and magnificent winged bull statues that are said to be the guardians of the Gates of Heaven, built by Xerxes (486-465 BCE) (Figure 19.5). Known also as a **Lamassu**, their wings represent the spiritual world, the human head represents the psychological world, and the bull body represents the physical world. Thus the winged bull is the guardian of the three worlds. The **sphinx** is another composite, in this instance of four creatures, that appears in many ancient Persian carvings, as well as in Greco-Roman mythology and later in the Bible. The body and tail of the sphinx is a lion, it has wings like an eagle, the head is a man, and the head has horns and ears like a bull. These four parts also signify the four sacred directions of the universe and the four sacred elements of life: earth, wind, fire, and water.

Figure 19.6: Huma column capital figure, Persepolis, Iran.
Photo by author.

The **Huma** is a legendary mythical bird within Iranian mythology and Sufi fables. It is said to live its entire life flying invisibly over the earth, so high it is impossible to spot. Also referred to as the bird of fortune or paradise, the Huma bird is a compassionate creature with a majestic presence that brings good fortune, happiness, and prosperity (Figure 19.6). The Huma is said to have both the male and female natures in one body, each type commanding one wing and one leg. Its presence brings blessings to those it encounters—according to some, if one catches even a glimpse of its shadow, happiness will ensue for the remainder of one's life. If a Huma bird flies over or alights on a person's head or shoulder it is said to bestow kingship. It is also said that the Huma cannot be caught alive, and if a person kills a Huma they are cursed. The name Huma means "spirit face" where the word "hu" means spirit and "mah" means "face." In Farsi it means "fabulous bird," and to Sufis, it is the "auspicious bird." It can represent the liberated soul flying free, able to view the whole universe. Its ability to soar to great heights is seen as an allegory for the soul's climb towards the Divine. The Huma is sometimes confused with the self-immolating and reborn Phoenix. In *The Conference of the Birds*, the Huma bird refused to undertake the journey because it would compromise the privilege of bestowing kingship on those whom it flew over.

The **Simurgh** was another mysterious composite creature of Persian folklore, one of the most famous and beautiful. It took the shape of a bird—gigantic enough to carry off an elephant or a whale—with the body of a peacock, the head of a human, the claws of a lion, and wings made from thousands of birds representing each species in the world. The Simurgh was revered as an immortal, benevolent guardian entity endowed with protective and healing abilities. Representing the union between the Earth and the sky, it served as a mediator and messenger between the two. According to Persian legend, the Simurgh possessed the knowledge of all ages and had witnessed the world's destruction threefold. The Simurgh purified the waters and land and bestowed fertility. Making an appearance in numerous ancient creation tales, the Simurgh became a frequent metaphor for the Divine in Persian literature and Sufi mysticism.

The idea of a bird reborn from its own ashes has been a compelling metaphor across cultures. Before the Greeks had the Phoenix and the Egyptians had the Bennu, the Iranians had the Simurgh. Approaching the end of one life cycle around 1700 years, the Simurgh transforms into a red and gold bird of fire, bursting into flames only to reincarnate from the ashes. This regenesis is sometimes used as a symbol of spiritual transformation and rebirth in the poetry of Persian mysticism. The Simurgh is indeed a firebird, unspeakably beautiful, old, and wise, but differs slightly from other similar creatures. In *The Conference of the Birds*, it embodies itself in the guise of a flock of birds who journey against all odds over seven mountains, through seven valleys, and across seas in a quest to ultimately find itself whole once again.

The phenomenon of birds in flight and their beautiful song has served as inspiration for our ancestors, artists, and mystics, just as they do today. They portray for us a range of concepts, traits, and powers including fertility, generosity, joy, authority, wisdom, kingship, spiritual longing, freedom, love, and healing. The most sacred and popular birds of Iranian culture appear frequently in folklore, myths, and art. Imaginative dance movements accompany poetry and narrative to help tell a story of birds in Iranian culture. Befriend the birds, become aware of their energies and feelings, let them inspire sacred movement, music, and healing.

It is through geometry that one purifies the eye of the soul.

– Plato

CHAPTER 20

From Sacred Art to Sacred Dance

When the artist loses himself in his art, then the art comes to life.

– Hazrat Inayat Khan

Since the Achaemenid Empire,[168] Iranians have enjoyed expressing themselves in elaborate, innovative, and evolving art (Figure 20.1). The Safavids[169] decorated their mosques and palaces with gold and precious jewels and enjoyed a vivid culture of art, music, and dance. About this time, the art of miniature painting began to emerge. Poetry of love flourished, and the Persian carpet was at its finest, becoming a major export. Calligraphy rose as an art form as the Persians enhanced and developed it into Kufic[170] writing. Royal court dancers brought to life the art of miniature paintings and the words of classical poetry. In Persian paintings, a European influence became evident as Flemish and Florentine elements appeared.

Figure 20.1: Stained glass window in Nasir al-Mulk Mosque, Shiraz, Iran.

Photo by author.

Everything we see in sacred Iranian and Persian art is based on observation of natural patterns considered to be expressions of a Divine order, or the "architecture of the universe." This idea, common to many

168 550-330 BCE.

169 1501-1736 CE.

170 Highly geometrical script developed for its beauty and used ornamentally in Persian art.

ancient cultures, attributes spiritual significance to specific geometric shapes and proportions. Sometimes referred to as "sacred geometry," it simultaneously satisfies the left brain's desire for the logical, sequential, and objective, and the right brain's desire for the beautiful, intuitive, and subjective.

We enjoy seeing symmetrical forms because our brains like to hunt for patterns. We like regular geometric shapes for the same reason. Structures of geometric patterns form the building blocks of matter, such as the distribution of atomic bonds in molecules, the helical structure of DNA, the patterns of snowflakes, and the lattice pattern of crystalline structures. On the mystic path, the aesthetics of the world and its perception are experienced rapturously, the overpowering beauty of the world filling the heart with love as the mind opens to cosmic revelations.

The history of humanity's engagement with sacred geometry dates back millennia. The Egyptian and Babylonian sciences from which the Pythagorean theorem is derived, and Persian mathematics, are based on an assumption of the sacredness of numbers and their symbolism. In Iranian culture, geometry was inseparable from the other sciences, music, and astronomy. Geometric forms such as the spiral, circle, triangle, square, and various regular polygons, were studied, described, and reproduced mathematically (Hejazi 2005). Recurring in nature, these primary geometric forms were seen as deeply meaningful and worthy of application in architecture, paintings, tile work, monuments, textiles, and pottery.

In ancient Greece, Aristotle divided philosophy into three parts—physics, mathematics, and theology—physics to address the natural or material world, theology to address the spiritual world, and mathematics (and the associated sciences of geometry and music) to address our realm in between. Plato described beauty as the splendor of truth, and thought the inability to discern between beauty and ugliness was equivalent to the inability to discern between true and false. This notion of the inseparability of the arts and sciences was later seen in the medieval Christian idea of *ars sine scientia nihil est* (art without science is nothing) (Ogunnaike 2017). For the ancients, beauty was a timeless reflection of the unseen, leading to tranquility and remembrance of the Divine.

Figure 20.2: Honeycomb dome in Sheikh Lotfollah Mosque, Isfahan, Iran.
Wikimedia Commons.

The ritualistic origins of sacred geometry extend back many millennia, to man's first attempts to imitate nature on cave walls, and later in architecture and designs. Ancient civilizations regarded architecture as a means by which the heavens could be manifested. Certain specific ratios found in the design of all lifeforms were reflected in the structures and embellishments of buildings. Persian architects ventured to make beauty from geometric order. Star-shaped and polygonal motifs, honeycomb structures, and other geometric patterns of varying scale were used to create mesmerizing compositions in temples, churches, and mosques. The purpose of such intricate beauty was to ensure that those who entered would be enveloped by the impressions and fall into a trance-like state of awe. Sacred geometry encourages contemplation on a deep, somatic level, facilitating a receptivity to its meanings and connection to the Divine. In contrast, modern buildings are devoid of representation of the Divine. The ancient architects knew their task was to show the majesty of the Divine. It is said that sacred animals and birds would gather outside a mosque or temple because of its mystic innocence.

The honeycomb shape inside historic mosques or other sacred places is a powerful example of sacred geometry. The spirit of the Divine is invited inside just like a honeycomb invites bees inside to create their honey. The honeycomb structure pays homage to the profound intelligence and industry of bees in nature and the divine order and intelligent design guiding the universe. In Iranian mysticism, it symbolizes inner wisdom, sweetness, and spiritual sustenance. Ascending layers of the structure may be interpreted as a metaphor for the soul's journey toward spiritual enlightenment. The individual cells of the honeycomb seamlessly fit together, representing the interrelation of all existence and, in mysticism, the ultimate unity between the Divine and the soul (Figure 20.2).

Many sacred buildings in Iran feature another architectural feature dedicated to honoring the Divine—an intentionally low entry. Whether it is a mosque, khanqah, jamkhaneh, or church, the main entrance doors are purposely low so one must bow to enter. Unlike the churches of the Western world with their oversized and tall doors, the entrance doors to sacred buildings in Iran are so small that one has to bow one's head or even crawl in to show humility before the Divine. A couple of years ago I visited an old church in Iran with such a small, low entrance one had to crawl in. I asked the priest why this was. He replied that because you were born of the land and soil, you should show respect by kissing the earth before raising your head to the Divine. This same form of respect is shown when bowing during a sacred dance.

A critical concept of sacred art is that the symmetry appears to continue infinitely. Patterns progressively reduce in size until they become a point and are no longer visible to an observer. The patterns will also appear to continue backward in reflection, and embedded geometric shapes, circles, and lines seemingly never end. As the eye follows these patterns, it observes apparent motion within the design.

When entering a sacred building in Iran one sees a multitude of sacred symbols—the shamsa (eight-pointed star), flowers, elemental symbols, sacred colors, and spiritually significant patterns—integrated into the building's art, architecture, and lighting. Elements like flowers, leaves, and vines entwined with geometric designs reflect a reverence for the natural world and its connection to the Divine. This symbology is also seen in paintings, tile work, textiles, carpets, pottery, gardens and landscaping, and urban design.

Every design leads to or surrounds a point at the center of a pattern, which may represent the individual or the Divine, but always suggesting oneness and unity. Central medallions, featuring complex geometric arrangements, are a common feature in Persian carpets and textiles. They serve as focal points, representing unity and wholeness, the principle and origin of all numbers. Within that framework, patterns of three, four, seven, fifteen, fifty, seventy, and one thousand are most common, as these numbers are considered magical.

The motion created by sacred geometry is found throughout the entire universe and can be seen everywhere in the natural world. Dancers naturally use symmetry and geometry in their movements which illustrate the basic underlying forms that are found in nature. This is exemplified by the circle and spiral. As circular motion in nature progresses inward or outward in spirals through space and time, a dancer's movements grow and expand, radiating from the center out, or spiral in to a central, still point. Many forms of city order, architectural geometry, and patterns of movement, including the basic rhythms of music and the representation of space in miniature art, comply with such an understanding of space and time.

Sacred art, textile motifs, and planetary energies have always been an inspiration for mystical rituals and dance. Iranian dance embodies sacred geometry, mystical symbolism, symmetry, and universal patterns. In sacred dance, we map ourselves to a point but we are also always in motion. If the motion stops, we cease to exist along the sacred geometric dance plane. The world is always turning; therefore art should always be moving. Whirling dance is in complete harmony with cosmic movement and this deep understanding of the sacred nature of art (Erzen 2008).

Geometry in Motion

God is an infinite circle whose center is everywhere and whose circumference is nowhere.

\- Nicholas of Cusa (1401-1464)

All the known phenomena of this universe, regardless of size, have a specific geometric structure. The proportions of the human body, the structure of crystals, the spots on a leopard, musical scales, etc. Everything in the universe unfolds in geometric patterns of fractals over and over again. Within this are endless possibilities of movement, light, color, shape, and sound that can be represented when we are whirling. When we are whirling we are intertwined with creative spirals and shapes aligned with the Golden Ratio, the "divine proportion," that occurs throughout the natural world. This ratio describes the balance, harmony, and proportionality that naturally arises when aligned with the spiritual and artistic ideals that permeate Iranian mysticism.

Geometric analysis of many ancient Persian and Greek buildings has proven that the Golden Ratio was widely used in architecture for its ideal structural stability as well as beauty, and was the basis of Persian aesthetics. Geometric analysis has shown that the Golden Ratio was applied in the plans of the ancient city, Persepolis (518-330 BCE). Closely related to the Golden Ratio is the Fibonacci sequence, first described by mathematicians in India around 700 CE, then introduced to the West by Leonardo of Pisa, also known as Fibonacci.

The easiest place to find this sequence in nature is in plants. This spiraling pattern is found in the spacing of branches in trees, the spirals in flowers, and the unfurling of ferns. It governs the spacing of leaves around a stem, ensuring that each leaf has maximum access to rain and sunlight. The crisscrossing spirals of seeds that radiate from the center of a sunflower also follow the Fibonacci sequence. Your own fingers have segments that are related according to the Golden Ratio, the cochlea of the inner ear spirals in the ratio of the Fibonacci sequence, in fact our whole bodies are formed this way. You can see this pattern in sunflowers, pine cones, galaxies, whirlpools, the coiling of snakes, an elephant's trunk, even in the chronology of rabbit populations. The Fibonacci sequence reveals how things grow, building and multiplying from what is already there. These sacred ratios connect all living things in the universe, describing an order that exists in and unifies all of creation.

The spiral has introverted and extroverted movements; it is both concentric and eccentric. It represents both the inner and the outer world and signifies the variation or transition between them (Al-Hakim 2015). Learning and bringing these spirals and circles into dance improves awareness, communication with one's surroundings, and confidence.

Circling the Divine

Look at the Perfect One
At the Circle's Center:
He Spins and Whirls like a Golden Compass,
Beyond all that is Rational,
To show this dear world that Everything,
Everything in Existence
Does point to God.

– Hafez

Figure 20.3: Large bowl with sacred circle of human figures. Iranian, Chalcolithic, 5250- 3000 BCE. MFA Boston.

Photo by author.

The circle is perhaps the most ancient of mystical symbols and most universal of all dance formations. In dance, the circle represents community and equality; each member has an equal view of the other, an equal part to play; everyone shares responsibility for maintaining the circle's integrity and ensuring its continuity. The dance circle can turn only when all members participate and only as fast as its slowest member. The center of the circle provides a focus—a tree, a candle, a fire, an altar, or a person to receive the energy—or it can be empty, allowing the dancers to feel the stillness of the unmoved center. The circle and anything within, conceptual or concrete, is charmed by the music and coordinated movement, enlivened by the concentrated attention of the group. Dancing as one, the energy in response, ever-flowing and ever-changing, radiates equally among all, tapping into the rhythm and cycle of nature. A circle leads back into itself and symbolizes unity and perfection. Every time we step into the circle, we are developing our sacred potential in the company of the Divine.

Evidence shows that the circle dance was practiced as far back as the Upper Paleolithic era and was used in some form by all civilizations to strengthen community, celebrate, pray, support one another, and heal. In Iran, archaeological evidence shows that circle dances were practiced

Figure 20.4: Tree of Life (a), Seed of Life (b), and Flower of Life (c) sacred geometries.
Wikimedia Commons.

as far back as the Elamite dynasty (3200-539 BCE). *Lak Sari, Cheke,* and *Sangin Sama* are among the various forms of circle dance found in Iranian culture. The Tibetans also created a circle dance for the New Year, centering around a wise elder in the middle.

Circles are employed in Persian art to compose intricate mystical designs, similar to mandalas in India and Tibet—tools for meditation and contemplation, leading the seeker towards higher states of consciousness. Three basic geometric forms and principles are important to remember for studies in the sacred geometry of Iran: the Seed of Life, the Flower of Life, and the Tree of Life (Figure 20.4). Many additional geometric patterns developed from these simple components.

The Seed of Life is a universal symbol representing the sacred number seven. It is found in all major religions and can be seen in churches, mosques, ancient temples, scripture and prayer books. The symbol is comprised of seven overlapping circles creating a hexagonal pattern (Figure 20.4b). It illustrates the process of creation and transformation. For centuries, it has served as a symbol of blessing and protection, revered for its spiritual significance. In dance, movements that reflect expansion, growth, and the unfolding of creative energy help convey the concept of the Seed of Life.

The Flower of Life (Figure 20.4c), similar to the Seed of Life, contains nineteen overlapping circles, creating a flower-like pattern. This universal geometric form which has been found in ancient depictions worldwide is said to be the actual blueprint of the universe, describing the underlying structure of material life. Thus it represents the unity in diversity of all creation. Historically, the Flower of Life and its associated knowledge were kept secret, preventing widespread dissemination. Now, quantum physics is confirming the cosmic significance of these ancient geometric forms. In dance, movements that emphasize the interplay and harmony between different elements can symbolize the Flower of Life.

The Tree of Life (Figure 20.4a) represents everything to do with nature. With roots grounded in the earth and branches stretching towards the heavens, it describes the connection between realms. There are ten special points in the diagram, called *sephiroth* in the Jewish Kabbalah. These represent different qualities of the Soul, with cosmic consciousness at the top, the material world at the base. In sacred dance, a dancer's torso is the trunk, their legs are the roots, and their arms are the branches of the Tree of Life. Movements that manifest grounding, reaching upward, and connecting with the Divine can symbolize the concept of the Tree of Life. The Flowers of Life are found upon the leaves of the Tree of Life, and these can be seen in the little details that appear in dance such as the movements of the head, hands, and a bit of shoulder or hip.

Symmetry is a primary aesthetic principle in Persian dance, contributing to appeal and expression. Choosing a central axis as the point of reference for a dance helps maintain symmetry and build dancer awareness in position and relative distance. Choreographers create lines and angles with symmetry and asymmetry to make their dances more appealing. Symmetrical arrangements with two or more dancers create a sense of harmony and order. Dancers may mirror each other or dance aligned to the central axis.

In terms of both movement and symbolism, circles, spirals, and arcs play a significant role in Iranian dance and whirling. They are fundamental elements that add beauty, depth, and meaning to the dance. Without beginning or end, the circle embodies unity, indivisibility, infinity, and the eternal and boundless nature of the Divine. The circle demonstrates the cycle of life, endless potential, and boundless creativity. Circular group formations express cohesion of the community. Circular shapes created with the arms can emulate breeze-like motions, trace the outline of flower shapes, or evoke the circular patterns in Persian art and design. Spinning in place or traversing the floor in an arc invokes dynamism and grace; an arc is symbolic of ascent, decline, evolution, or transformation.

Figure 20.5: Spiraling.
Valerie Runningwolf.

Spirals are frequently associated with growth, transformation, and evolution; they can represent the continuous process of spiritual development and the quest for higher states of consciousness. They embody the natural flow of energy, both within the dancer's body and in the universe. Spirals in Iranian mysticism convey profound spiritual truths and serve as a means to contemplate the mysteries of existence. For some, the spiral describes successive cycles of incarnation, each turn representing a new phase in the soul's journey. The unwinding spiral can symbolize the process of the Divine revealing itself to the seeker. Executing spirals requires precise control and balance, requiring skill and artistry. Spiraling movements are believed to activate and balance the body's energy centers, contributing to a sense of vitality and spiritual awakening.

Iranian dance delineates various types of spirals and circles that can be used, such as *riz,* which means tiny and refers to movements suggesting particles, molecules, atoms, and cells. Other examples are *sho'levar,* meaning big flames, and *shenavar,* meaning a steady ocean wave. *Maidan* is the large circle that encloses the dancer (the center); it is frequently encountered in Sufi poetry and represents a gathering of lovers or a circle of unity; any large circle created within the bounds of the dance space is considered a maidan.

Motifs in Iranian Art and Dance

I wish my life were a Persian carpet—full of colors, full of spirals, full of life.

- Rumer Godden, Author, Historian

Distinctive motifs appear in ancient Iranian art—in textiles, carpets, tile work, dance, and more—which derive their meaning from their ancient origins. The symbolism of these motifs can be divided into three main groups: fertility, vitality, and protection. Fertility expresses the need for sustenance—ancient tribes depended on the abundance of crops and Mother Earth's fertility for survival. Vitality describes the health and potency of love, marriage, childbirth, and procreation. Protection is about preserving the fragile balance of life for which man can do nothing but pray, especially protection against ill fate or destructive spirits. An example of a motif is the depiction of male and female by animals in light and dark colors. Another is the *boteh* (paisley), variously interpreted as a leaf, flame, bending tree, pear, almond, or pine cone, which can represent fertility or vitality. A larger boteh encapsulating a smaller one represents a mother and child.

Persian carpets have always been inspiration for sacred dancers. A Persian carpet might exhibit several beautiful motifs in its design, informed by the unique weaver's tradition and cultural context. Woven within a carpet is the story of a particular region and its people. Three classifications of carpet designs have inspired dance: primitive, nomadic, and classical. The primitive two-toned design was first developed in the Achaemenid Empire, primarily depicting scenes of hunting or warfare. These motifs feature strict and rigid figures like crosses, double lines, or animals such as deer and bears. These ancient motifs influenced ancient hunting or battle dances and became the foundation of sacred dance movements today, highlighting the importance of the human-animal relationship in their development. Nomadic carpets are characterized by deep, dark, earthy colors, reflecting the feelings, thoughts, customs, and stories of nomadic tribes. The classical genre was introduced when a new awareness of art, geometry, and symmetry emerged during the Golden Age of Persia. Everything in carpet art became more poetic and romantic during this period. A prominent motif of this classical style was the eight-pointed star. Many of the movements of Persian classical dance came to be influenced by this pattern.

The beauty of Persian art springs from its sacred geometric patterns and tessellations incorporating a wide variety of polygons, stars, squares, circles, arcs, shapes from nature, and motifs in multitudinous colors and shades. This art is both ancient and timeless. The human eye enjoys finding and following these patterns in art, whatever its age. In addition, this art—whether in the form of architecture, painting, sculpture, music, poetry, or story—conveys a spiritual philosophy offering wisdom about nature, the Divine, and humanity.

Spiritual Philosophies Interwoven in Art

The artist must have something to say, for mastery over form is not his goal but rather the adapting of form to its inner meaning.

– Wassily Kandinsky

The philosophy of Persian art is based on six aesthetic ideas: *noghteh*, *naff*, *eghna*, *gharineh*, *tekrar*, and *vahdat*. Both noghteh and naff refer to the outstanding feature, sometimes arbitrary, that draws the observer's focus into a piece of art, something that makes it unique and describable. This focus is known as its noghteh[171] when it creates a positive perception, and as naff when it creates a negative perception. The noghteh and naff are considered opposites and form a duality together. For example, visualize the Great Sphinx of Giza. The most remarkable feature of the sphinx is its face. To admire the face for its unique construction and beauty would be to focus on its noghteh. To zero in on the deeply eroded space of the missing nose would be to focus on its naff. Art illustrates the duality of our world, the good and the bad, in a simple fashion.

Eghna is a spiritual belief or sense of something as "true" even if common sense tells us otherwise. Eghna comes from the heart and, as a mystic, one should always pay attention to this aspect. Scholars may point out a noghteh or naff within a piece of art, while others may focus on eghna. For

---

171 In Farsi, *noghteh* means dot, point, or place depending on the context.

Figure 20.6: Mosaic tile work arranged for gharineh. Golestan Palace, Tehran.
pxhere.com

example, some feel the Great Sphinx is the spiritual guardian of the Great Pyramid—this view represents its eghna. Metaphorically, eghna is the point between two or more connections, a joint. The path of eghna enriches our understanding of the deep spiritual root of art and dance.

Gharineh refers to the mirrored image of a pattern or shape. Gharineh represents reflection, where left is right and right is left, and the duality of opposites (Figure 20.6). We need to observe both sides of things to understand ourselves and the universe better. A copy of a pattern or shape is its tekrar. Tekrar means repeated. Persian or Islamic tile patterns are tekrar when the patterns appear repeated in a grid. This is evocative of karmic law—whatever we do returns to us. In dance, the tekrar is a repeated sequence, mirrored or not, and the multiple turns in whirling are also tekrar. Tekrar may also refer to repetitive practices such as chanting, reciting prayers, or zikr.

The vahdat is the center that unifies us, such as in whirling—it is the point of singularity if we become whole with the Divine. Vahdat is a profound concept that highlights the interconnectedness and unity that underlies all existence.

These concepts are well-demonstrated in Persian miniature art, *neghar ghari,* meaning "to look upon the Divine." When one looks deeply at this art, all is seen as an expression of God. When the spiritual artist draws or paints, it is an attempt to portray heaven, a paradise given by God. The beauty of Persian miniature art is that every artist depicts what they imagine heaven looks like. Pictured within may be idyllic landscapes, sacred birds, animals, plants, the elements, and human figures, as well as spirals, circles, and other geometric designs indicating the divine order of nature. It may also include signs of the seven sacred souls or angels. Each time one looks at this art a new metaphor for the sacred will be revealed.

Persian art serves as inspiration for dance, with both forms deeply rooted in mysticism. One needs to understand the principles of art to understand dance. Art in Iran has always been grounded in spiritual symbolism, no matter the artist, architect, background, politics of the day, or dynasty. Since ancient times, artists, architects, physicians, astrologers, and mathematicians studied mysticism or were mystics themselves. Of course, architects would study geometry and mathematics to perform successfully in their profession, but they knew whatever they built had to represent the Divine. Physicians knew the reason they healed others was due to the energy of the Divine. The Magi of ancient Persia were mystics first, who underwent deep training and developed spiritual understanding before they became engineers or physicians. This is why one must understand the underlying spiritual philosophies of Iran to appreciate its art.

Illumination

You are the light of the universe; never dim your shine.

– Rumi

Light and color are fundamental principles within Iranian art. White light denotes the sun and the Divine itself, while the seven colors of the rainbow signify the seven archangels that watch over us. Upon entering a sacred building in Iran, one encounters white light and the seven colors. The golden halo surrounding the heads of saints, messengers, and prophets represents the essence of the Sun, the Divine. This nimbus of light indicates they have reached enlightenment and have become God's messenger; it is a metaphor for the inner radiance that comes from spiritual practice, producing a deep connection with divine presence and grace; it signifies spiritual enlightenment, wisdom, purity of heart and soul. This Divine Light is a guiding force that leads seekers on the spiritual path, a force that purifies and cleanses the inner self from negative qualities and attachments, allowing one to approach union with the Divine.

As previously mentioned, colors have special meanings in Iranian mysticism. White is the color of light and virtue, the garment color of

Zoroastrian priests, Sufi mystics, and many other religious orders. Its opposite, black, is considered a worldly color, the color of the lower self, the *nafs* (the ego). Black is also the color of misfortune in Iranian folklore and often the color of mourning. Zoroastrians, however, dislike darkness and the color black so much that even in mourning ceremonies they avoid it. In ancient Iran, red was the color of power, fire, passion, and blood, and symbolized the power of the Iranian people and the military. Green symbolizes spiritual flourishing, vitality of soul, life, growth, and renewal; for the ancients, it was the color of Ameretat, the goddess of the earth, and the symbol of the Persian nobility and kings. It is associated with the mystic path and is the color of aristocracy as well.

Iran has been an important source of the mineral turquoise ("blue gold") for at least two thousand years, so the coloring often appears in Iranian sacred art of any age, adorning sacred sites, mosques, churches, synagogues, and mystic lodgings. It was used to cover domes of palaces and mosques because its intense blue color symbolized heaven on earth, and it is often used to represent the elements of air and water together. Considered a sacred stone, turquoise is believed to have protective and healing qualities, to guard against negative energies, providing spiritual and physical protection to the wearer. It is believed to align the chakras and promote balance and harmony within the body, mind, and spirit. Calming and soothing, it provides a sense of tranquility and relaxation, spiritual renewal, and is associated with love, faith, courage, and strength.

Knowledge and spiritual elevation are expressed by yellow, gold, blue, and purple. Yellow is linked to wisdom and spiritual insight, symbolizing the inner guiding light of awareness. If yellow is the path upward, then gold is the pinnacle, indicating spiritual wealth, divine wisdom, and the highest states of consciousness. Blue represents the depth of the soul, the infinite realms of the spiritual world, transcendence, and inner peace. If blue indicates one's current position then purple is the accelerator. Purple is linked to spiritual elevation, refinement of soul, and signifies pursuit of higher states of consciousness and divine knowledge. The color silver represents spiritual clarity and purity of intention, untarnished devotion and sincerity.

Music alleviates pain to the extent that it dissolves the concept of time.

– Abu Naşr Farabi

CHAPTER 21

Harmony Divine: Spirituality in Iranian Music

Music and rhythm find their way into the secret places of the soul.

– Plato

Iranian music has been so finely perfected over the ages by great masters that it has changed very little today. In Iranian music, feeling is considered more important than technique, despite the amazing and intricate techniques that have arisen in Eastern art. These skills have always taken a back seat to the passion of the performer whose duty is to convey moods from a higher realm to the audience. Dancers should be trained to recognize whether music serves mystical or classical purposes, adjusting style and expression according to the genre. To understand which movements should accompany the music, the dancer must be able to classify the poetry and music presented. A dancer should become acquainted with basic music history, modes, and styling to interpret and present dance appropriately. Iranian music and dance reflect central concepts in cultural themes and heritage, particularly mysticism.

The creative and advanced society of ancient Iran developed an intricate musical system that inspired the Indians, Chinese, Turks, the Arab world, and eventually Western music as well. While Rome and Greece are most often cited as the origins of civilization, both were heavily influenced by the culture of ancient Iran—including its architecture, philosophy, forms of governance, science, art, and music—all of which spread along trade routes throughout the ancient world. Written historical records, etchings on silver dishes, sculpture and painting from pre-Islamic to the Islamic period, indicate that Iranian music has roots in ancient history and further evolved during Persia's Islamic age. This long history of Iranian music falls into six periods: mythological, Median-Achaemenian, Seleucid, Parthian, Sasanian, early Islamic, and the modern age. From the earliest period music played an essential role in the development of numerous magical, metaphysical, and mystical traditions (Miller 1977b, 51). Music appeared in religious hymns such as the *Gathas* of the Zoroastrian Avesta. During that era, according to Ferdowsi in his *Shahnameh*, King Bahram Gur commissioned ten thousand musicians from India to perform for ordinary Iranians. As a result, Indian music influenced Iranian classical music to some extent. During the Sasanian era, Persia invited instrumentalists from India. Later, the Perso-Afghan master Amir Khosrau,[172] brought Iranian musical concepts such as the *setar*[173] to India. During the Sasanian dynasty, from the third to seventh century CE, music became a central aspect of the culture of the empire, which served as a benevolent patron for the arts. Music was a rich and vital force in the lives of the people. For instance, in one Mazdak faith community,[174] one of the four statues representing major spiritual powers was a musician (Miller 1999, 139).

The Sasanian kings valued their court musicians so much they were treated as though they were aristocrats. One celebrated Persian court musician, Barbad (late sixth to early seventh century CE), performed and composed an impressive body of music. Many music theorists in Iran attribute to him the invention of the Persian system of modes (sets of musical scales and performance guidelines) that are still followed by contemporary masters and students. The music of the Sasanian period became the foundation for the systems of much of the Islamic world today.

When the Arabs came to Persia and encountered a superior musical culture, they also quickly absorbed and adopted what they had discovered. Arab artists traveled to Persia to study, and after returning to

---

172 Abu'l Hasan Yamīn ud-Dīn Khusrau (1253-1325), better known as Amīr Khusrau, was an Indo-Persian Sufi singer, musician, poet, and scholar who lived during the period of the Delhi Sultanate.

173 A type of lute.

174 Mazdakism was an egalitarian religious and philosophical movement founded by a Zoroastrian priest Mazdak the Younger (died c. 524 or 528). It caused revolutionary social upheavals in Iran until suppressed at the close of the reign of King Kavad (488-531).

Figure 21.1: Music Hall of Aali Qapu Imperial Palace, Isfahan, Iran.
Photo by author.

their home cities began teaching. Iranian musicians propagated their art in Arab capitals where they were welcomed by people eager for refinement. The arrival of Islam resulted in limiting the use of music in public to only special events such as weddings and family gatherings. However, music was quietly practiced and taught, passing down the ancient traditions over the ages. The advent of Islam increased the popularity of the Persian musical system throughout the Islamic world and spanning the Silk Road from China to Spain, allowing the exchange of musical styles and systems. Of the twelve modes named by early Arab musicologists, seven are of Persian origin.

Musicians of Iranian origin enjoyed wide popularity in the Abbassid dynasty (750-1258 CE) in Baghdad, Iraq as well as the Umayyad court in Cordoba, Spain. Persian music first arrived in Spain when Ziryab[175] and his daughters left Baghdad in 801 CE to establish a school of music and dance in Cordoba. Their instrumental, vocal, and dance techniques strongly influenced the local culture. Two schools of music developed from these cultural exchanges: the school of Baghdad and the school of Cordoba, which later became the North African and Flamenco systems respectively.

Along with the spread of Persian musical influence to the West and East, was the Persian lute formerly known as the *barbat*, and later called the *oud* or *al'oud* by the Arabs. This instrument was adopted in Europe

175 Abu al-Hasan 'Ali Ibn Nafi', better known as Ziryab, Zeryab, or Zaryab (789-857 CE) was a singer, oud, and lute player, composer, poet, and teacher who lived and worked in Iraq, Northern Africa, and Andalusia during the medieval Islamic period.

where its name was pronounced *lute*, and, on the other front, was carried by the Mongols to China where its name barbat was pronounced *pipa* by the Chinese and *biwa* by the Japanese.

Seven Modes, Seven Expressions of Dance

In the house of lovers, the music never stops. The walls are made of songs and the floor dances.

– Rumi

A basic understanding of Persian music and poetry is needed to understand its dance. The present system of Persian music emerged from the maqal system played during the Safavid dynasty. This evolved into the *radif*, which was further restructured during the Qajar dynasty (late 18th century) by two brothers, Mirza Abdollah and Agha Hosseingholi, who organized and systematized these melodies into what is known as the *dastgah* system: twelve groups of melodies arranged in a traditional order. This became what is known today as the Persian classical system. Persian dastgah music draws from many sources, including regional music styles, religious genres of melody, chants, and popular songs that have been reworked by master musicians and their students. These melodies serve as the basis for a performer's extemporized pieces, similar to the use of melodies in jazz improvisation in the West.

In Iran, modes or notes were associated with certain colors, elements, times of day, and emotions. Even though in modern Iran this knowledge has been lost, such information might be reconstructed through mysticism and meditation (Miller 1977b, 65). Dr. Dariush Safvat,[176] after many years of close study in music and mysticism, has compiled a hypothesis of modes and their connotations (Figure 21.2). In contrast to Western musical compositions that are created solely by one composer, the Persian *radif* embodies the work of a multitude of

176 Dr. Dariush Safvat (1928-2013) was a master Persian traditional musician, instructor, and ethnomusicologist. He was the founding director of the Center for the Preservation and Research of Music in Tehran. Many credit him for saving traditional music from extinction in the 1970s.

composers and musicians, inspired by Iran's diverse musical traditions (Miller 1977b, 65).

The term *gah* comes from the Zoroastrian word *gatha*, meaning song, chant, or prayer—the name for the prayers in the Avesta. In Pahlavi (Middle Persian) it means both "prayer" and also "time" or "place." Each dastgah consists of seven basic notes plus several variable notes used for ornamentation and modulation. Each has come to identify a mood, color, movement, or style, and a recognizable beauty in classical Persian dance.

The dastgah in turn is composed of numerous unique component melodies known as *gushehs* which musicians come to know through experience. The seven notes of a dastgah and their composition are by nature sacred, and great masters believe each one of the seven modes should be played on a certain day of the week and/or at a certain time of day. For example, on Saturday they play *Shur* and on Sunday *Segah*. These dastgahs are more spiritually aligned when played at that particular time, and a dancer receives the Divine Energy of that time or day. Musicians and dancers should be respectful of sacred traditions passed down over the millennia. Tampering in any way with the sacred music of the twelve traditional dastgahs and their gushehs is discouraged.

The role of music in Islam originates from pre-Islamic forms of prayer. The call to prayer or *azan* is said to have been adopted from the Zoroastrian practice of chanting a prayer while walking on the housetop, and is sung in the traditional manner passed down over the centuries. Before the Muslim conquest, melodies used for recitals from the Avesta were set to seven specific modes, namely, *Yekgah, Dogah, Segah, Chahargah, Panjgah, Sheshgah,* and *Haftgah*. When translated, they mean respectively, first place, second place, third place, fourth place, etc. It is believed that gah, or "place," in the context of medieval music, referred to the position of the respective finalis (concluding note or tonic) of these modes as played on the fingerboard of lute-type instruments (Kitarist 2020).

Most of these modes, except probably for Sheshgah and Haftgah still exist in the system today. However, it is virtually impossible to know how the music sounded during that era. During the Islamic occupation,

<table>
<tr><th>Mode</th><th>Time</th><th>Element</th><th>Spiritual Connotation</th><th>Characteristic or Mood</th><th>Spiritual Connotation</th></tr>
<tr><td>Shur</td><td>Late morning 10-12</td><td>Fire red</td><td>Fire</td><td>Meditation or longing</td><td>Tariqat to Marafat</td></tr>
<tr><td>Mahur</td><td>After sunset</td><td>Sky blue</td><td>Wind</td><td>Happy, easy going</td><td>Shariat</td></tr>
<tr><td>Homayun</td><td>From sunset to dark</td><td>Dark green</td><td>Flame</td><td>Attraction</td><td>Haqiqat</td></tr>
<tr><td>Nava</td><td>Bedtime</td><td>Transparent</td><td>Combination wind and fire</td><td>Advice</td><td>Maratat</td></tr>
<tr><td>Segah</td><td>From 4 until before sunset</td><td>Deep blue</td><td>Water</td><td>Pain or sorrow culminating in hope</td><td>Tariqat</td></tr>
<tr><td>Chahargah</td><td>Early morning 6-8</td><td>White or yellow</td><td>Steam (water)</td><td>Excitement</td><td>Tariqat</td></tr>
<tr><td>Rast Panjgah</td><td>Morning 8-10</td><td>Tan</td><td>Earth</td><td>Concentration and intellect</td><td>Shariat</td></tr>
<tr><td>Isfahan</td><td>Dawn</td><td>Light green</td><td>Light of fire</td><td>Spiritual love</td><td>Haqiqat</td></tr>
<tr><td>Abu-Ata</td><td rowspan="5">Afternoon 12-4</td><td>Bright brown</td><td rowspan="5">Earth</td><td>Melancholic and moving</td><td rowspan="5">Shariat to Tariqat</td></tr>
<tr><td>Dashti</td><td>Brown</td><td>Harrowing and plaintive</td></tr>
<tr><td>Afshari</td><td>Burnt brown</td><td>Full of sadness</td></tr>
<tr><td>Bayat-e Kord</td><td>Dark gray</td><td>Like Shur, sweet and clear</td></tr>
<tr><td>Bayat-e Tork</td><td>Smoke black</td><td>Nostalgic, meditative, and spiritual</td></tr>
</table>

Figure 21.2: Modal Systems, Characteristics, and Connotations (Miller 1977b; "Persian Classical Music: System of Modes" n.d.).

it is suggested that the five prayers are in the modes of *Yekgah, Dogah, Segah, Chahargah,* and *Panjgah* (Miller 1999, 17). The five daily prayer times correspond to the time the mode is performed and are, respectively, dawn, noon, afternoon, evening, and night.

Only seven of fifty extant dastgahs are in use today. Each may be compared with one of the Seven Valleys of Sufism. These are *Shur, Mahur, Homayun, Nava, Sehgah, Chahargah,* and *Rast Panjgah* (Figure 21.2). The five *avazes* (secondary modes) are: *Bayat-e Kord, Bayat-e Tork, Abu-Ata, Dashti,* and *Afshari*. Each dastgah contains a specific set of modes or avazes, which contain melodic motifs and patterns, and each is associated with specific emotional and aesthetic qualities. For example, some dastgahs are considered better suited for expressing joy, while others may be more appropriate for contemplative or melancholy moods. As a dancer, it is important to take these elements into consideration, to understand the themes to be played, to listen deeply to the music, and respect its rules.

Persian classical music, rooted in Sufi philosophy, strives to facilitate a spiritual journey. The dastgah system, characterized by its emotional associations and intricate melodic structures, is considered a means to transcend worldly concerns and connect with the Divine. The specific character of each dastgah should be applied by both the musician and dancer. Dance is a prayer and music is the path to that world. Masters can study music for twenty or thirty years, listening to and practicing these Persian dastgahs day in and day out, and still not fully fathom the depths of them.

Figure 21.3: Qajar Dynasty Musicians. Music Museum, Tehran, Iran.
Photo by author of exhibit.

The mode of **Shur** has an ancient origin and serves as the basis for many folk songs and tribal music. It is characterized by burning passion and longing, portraying the emotional intensity of separation from the beloved. The word shur itself means "passion," its element is fire, the color is red, and it should be performed from morning until noon. Its mystic connotation is tariqat (which means "path" or "way"), which is connecting one to that longing for God. Considered the "mother of modes," it possesses a very intense, fiery quality, yet it can also evoke tranquility, since it is in our longing that we find God. Dance with the Shur dastgah expresses the burning sorrow of separation most often descriptive of man's separation from the Divine. It should reflect the burning and intensity of unrequited love, which is vulnerable to destruction once attained. This should be combined with the beautiful feelings of faith and a symmetry in movement. Shur manifests the spiritual essence.

The mode of **Mahur** is happy, cheerful, dreamy, majestic, and noble. Its color is sky blue and its element is wind or breeze. Blue represents healing, harmony, love, emotions, psychic abilities, dreams, and intuition. It should be performed after sunset and its mystic connotation is shariat, which connects us to the dignity of the path, which makes us feel happy. A dance to Mahur suggests light, airy movements of the wind, and can be enhanced by a light sky-blue costume. Any dance to Mahur should interpret the joyful, dignified spirit of this dastgah. The dancer's expression throughout should remain relaxed and pleasant rather than appearing distraught, pained, or dreamy as in some other modes.

The mode of **Homayun** is stately, dignified, mobile, ecstatic, and both joyous and melancholic as if reunited with one long lost. Its color is dark green and its element is fire. Green symbolizes fertility and the earth. It should be performed in the early morning hours before sunrise and its mystic connotation is haqiqat, which indicates you have arrived at your purpose, which is divine beauty. Homayun creates a royal atmosphere and expresses both the sorrow of life and the greatness of love in its higher form. The description of the beloved reaches the Divine in Homayun. A dance to Homayun follows the rhythmic sections and passages of the music in a purposeful and stately manner, careful not to bounce or frolic along with the rhythm. The sense of royal dignity should be maintained throughout and the melancholy or ecstasy expressed should be subtle and not overt.

The mode of **Isfahan** is a derivative of Homayun and is often considered synonymous with Homayun. Its state is mystical, metaphysical, spiritual, profound, wise, reflective, nostalgic, and meditative. Compared to Homayun, its color is a lighter green or turquoise green and its element is the light of fire as opposed to being the fire itself. It should be performed at dawn, before sunrise, and its mystic connotation is haqiqat. Isfahan expresses spiritual love, the sorrow of love, and longing for past love. The dance to Isfahan can begin with a rhythm-free interpretive solo followed by a *chahar mezrab,*[177] a rhythmic sequence before the main degree of the mode shifts to the second note of the scale for another free-rhythm melodic sequence.

The mode of **Nava** is peaceful, serene, sacred, and admonitive. The color is transparent but might also be a pastel derived from red. Nava combines the power of fire and wind to evoke its unique essence. It

---

177 A *chahar mezrab* is a genre of traditional Persian instrumental music.

should be performed for the late evening and its mystic connotation is marifat, meaning deep integration of the spiritual teachings. Nava expresses distant memories of past love, a love so complete nothing else matters, a childish puppy love when the world seems so beautiful. It may also represent an individual experiencing sorrow, or longing nostalgically. Poetry recited in Nava is philosophical. It expresses calmness and peace and is recommended for a tranquil period of prayers such as from midnight until 5:00 am. Although rarely performed, Nava holds an eminent position in Persian classical music.

The mode of **Segah** expresses pain, chagrin, and sorrow, culminating in hope. Visualize a deep mountain lake, with the color of dark lapis blue and the element of water. Blue represents harmony, love, emotions, psychic abilities, dreams, and intuition. It should be performed from late afternoon to sunset and its mystic connotation is tariqat. Segah expresses the past and the successes and sorrows of love, culminating in hope. Segah means "three steps" or "three paths," and in mysticism, itcan represent the third valley, the Valley of Understanding. When one starts to understand things, that is when reality may set in. Often the truth hurts, so the feeling of Segah is one of pain and sorrow. But with understanding comes growth and learning, and ultimately hope. Dance in Segah can portray various aspects of water, either turbulent, placid, or tossing waves. Segah creates an atmosphere of melancholy followed by a more intense positive emotional outburst at the end of the mode.

The mode of **Chahargah** is powerful, heroic, festive, exciting, wise, philosophical, profoundly moving, and patriotic. Its color is yellow, gold, or white and its element is steam or water. Yellow represents intellect, communication, learning, movement, and beginnings. Gold represents happiness, fulfillment, and success, and white represents purity and light. Chahargah is best performed in the morning from 6 to 8 am and its mystic connotation is tariqat. Chahargah accompanies the recitation of the *Shahnameh*. It features nuanced changes in rhythm and tone and expresses the past, the joy of love, and boasts of love's success. All the melodies of Chahargah can also be played in Segah.

At times Chahargah reminds one of flamenco guitar and the spirit of *duende,*[178] passionate ecstasy and possession, a likely product of the confluence of the Persian and Spanish influences through Iranian music master Ziryab and his daughters in Cordoba, Spain. Another mixing agent came from nomadic Romani musicians and dancers born in India, who brought an Indo-Iranian influence to Spain and countries under Spanish influence as they migrated from India. Although the full flare and fire of flamenco or Indian Khatak or the related styles of Central Asia can be an inspiration for dance to Chahargah, the emphasis should be on the mood of epic power of the ancient Persian Empire of the Achaemenians, and the accompanying Persian motifs. During the Achaemenian period and since, the Iranian influence that stretched from the walls of China to Egypt resulted in pronounced cultural crossover in modern-day Uzbekistan, Tajikistan, and Sin Jiang province of western China, as well as other nations that were formerly part of the Iranian realm. Thus, some dance concepts that have remained in those areas might be tapped for ideas in dancing to Chahargah. One of the gusheh in Chahargah is called *Lazgi* which is the name of the standard dance melody of the Khwarazm province of Uzbekistan, which was formerly a Northeastern Iranian province (St. John and Miller 1987, 72).

The mode of **Rast Panjgah** resembles Mahur, setting a mood conducive to thinking, concentration, and enlightenment. It is an intellectual mode, easily associated with logical reasoning. Rast Panjgah expresses a color of light tan and its element is powdered earth cast by wind or dust. It is most effectively performed in the late morning hours, from about 8:00 to 10:00 am, and its mystic connotation is shariat. Rast Panjgah encompasses the emotions of the other modal systems and denotes mixture and expansion. Mahur and Rast Panjgah express a definite joyful, light, and lilting feeling.

---

[178] A Spanish term referring to highly evocative artistic expression, emotionally or spiritually powerful and charged.

Avaz: Chanting of the Sacred

We have fallen into a place where everything is music...
Open the window in the center of your chest, and let the
spirits fly in and out.

– Rumi

Before the invention of what we call music, people danced, prayed to, and mimicked the sounds of nature. According to Iranian legend, the first melody originated from nature, in the voice of the nightingale. Researchers suggest specialized Persian vocal melodies called avaz originated from the sound of this small songbird, inspiring the Gathas, the prayer chants of the Zoroastrian priest, which later became the avaz of today. An avaz is an unmetered portion of a Persian mode, typical of vocal chants. Avaz also refers to the character or manner in which a singer delivers a melody by the interpretation, ornamentation, and expression they bring to the music.

Figure 21.4: Musicians and dancers of the Safavid court, Shiraz (c. 1600). Probably from a Diwan of Yazdi.
Wikimedia Commons

Iran is undisputedly one of the most important countries in the Middle East in the realm of music. One could say the art of instrumental and vocal technique was carried to a point of perfection and refinement unequaled elsewhere. This level of refinement is the foundation of the avaz chanted today. All avazes are recommended for performance during the afternoon, from noon to 4 pm (see Figure 21.2). Their mystic connotation ranges from shariat to tariqat (Miller 1977b, 69). Avazes *Abu Ata*, *Afshari*, *Dashti*, and *Bayat-e Tork* are all considered derivatives of Dastgah Shur. The characteristic element shared by all these avazes is the Earth. Not all sacred music is accompanied by dance. If movement is appropriate to accompany the music it is simple and repetitive, completely unattached to the material plane.

Abu 'Ata, melancholic and moving, recalls the experience of past love in a wise, idealistic manner, and is similar to Shur but less intense. The dance to Abu 'Ata should recall the sorrow and longing of separation. Its color is purple, representing wisdom and tranquility, or a bright coffee color representing earth. The traditional costume color is purple in varying shades.

Dashti is harrowing and plaintive, expressing the unique love of youth, the complaint, whining, and pining of the lovelorn. Its element is earth and its color is brown, representing grounding and friendship. Many of the folk songs of northern Iran, in particular those along the Caspian coast, are in Dashti.

Afshari brings to mind sorrow, separation, and metaphysical depth, expressing love, regret, the fear of loss, and metaphysical love. The dance invokes a feeling of spirituality and metaphysical searching, but with hope despite an atmosphere of melancholy. The theme of unrequited love is less burning than Shur and less harrowing than Dashti. Its color is burnt brown matching its element of earth.

Bayat-e Kord is a component of Shur, though it has a personality of its own and is sometimes performed independently or even as a part of Dashti. Its color could be described as pink, and the mood it conveys is considered similar to that of Shur with sweetness and clarity. The name Kord refers to its possible origin in Kurdish folklore.

Bayat-e Tork is nostalgic, meditative, contemplative, and spiritual. Its sound is like the reed flute[179] whose sorrowful song tells of man's longing to be reunited with the Divine. It expresses only Divine Love and the love of nature (St. John and Miller 1987, 43). The first three gushehs carefully and respectfully divulge various metaphysical symbols

---

179 Especially as in the story (*Ney Nameh* or "Reed Story") told by Rumi in the opening lines of his great work, the *Masnavi*, in which he speaks in the voice of a reed cut from its bed to be made into a flute, its voice full of longing to be reunited with its Source.

of Sufism. Certain gushehs of Tork are used for Islamic religious chants such as the azan, the Islamic call to prayer. Since Tork is often used for Islamic liturgical chant and is associated with religion, care should be taken to use appropriate spiritual movements. Tork lies between the joyfulness of Mahur and the intensity of the other modes. Its color is black representing protection and stability like its element earth. Dancing to Bayat-e Tork should be sincere with a piercing stare but without flirtatious smiles or drawing attention to oneself. Occasional slow turns and head sways from side to side are appropriate if not overly used.

The Sacred Sounds

Please God, offer honey to musicians
Who bring us such joy!
Give them strong and untiring hands
To keep playing their music.

Give them vision so, like birds in love,
They can bring Your message to our ears.
Let them drink plenty from Your river and
Grace them with Your strength
So their music becomes the pillar of Your glory.

– Rumi

The most common instruments used for traditional Iranian sacred music are the dutar, tanbur, daf, and ney. These are considered so venerated the musician often kisses them before and after use. While other instruments (*tombak*, *tar*, *setar*, and *santur*)[180] may also be used for Persian classical performances, the dutar, tanbur, daf, and ney are the primary ones suitable to the sacred genre. The following is a brief description of these instruments, where they originated, how they are

---

180 The *tombak* is a single-headed Persian goblet drum; the *tar* is a long-necked instrument of the lute family with a "waisted" bowl; the Persian *setar* resembles the tanbur but with a smaller bowl; the *santur* is a hammered dulcimer originating from Iran. All these instruments have been in use for several centuries with regional variations.

constructed, what music is played on them, and their symbolism and healing properties.

As mentioned previously, the **tanbur** is a long-necked, three-stringed instrument sacred to the Yarsanis and Iranian mystics. The Yarsanis regard the tanbur as a living entity that has the power to change human emotions and induce healing. In its construction, it symbolizes the human body, angels, and the voice of the Divine. Measuring between seventy and eighty cm in length, it has a pear-shaped resonating bowl and fourteen frets made of gut or metal strings wound around the neck several times. When playing, musicians occasionally tap the instrument, creating a drum-like effect to add percussion to their piece. The heavenly sound of the tanbur can take complete control of the soul, inducing incredible calmness and peace of mind, or inspiring ecstasy.

The **dutar** is the two-stringed ancient cousin of the tanbur. It is traditionally played in Greater Khorasan as well as in many regions of Afghanistan, especially the Herat and Farah provinces, and is an integral part of the cultural heritage of these regions. It has a pear-shaped soundbox chiseled out of mulberry wood with a long neck. It is similar to but a bit larger than the traditional Persian setar and has movable frets wound around a neck made of jujube, walnut, or apricot wood. The old dutar was strummed skillfully with the bare fingers but later the *nakhonak* (metal plectrum) came to be used. Renowned for its "feminine" shape, it has a light, elegant body, with a slim, long neck and round belly. In ancient Khorasan, the dutar was connected with women's domestic music, performance, poets, and dance, as well as poetic images of femininity. The dutar's tender sounds are associated with the sounds of a cooing, flying flock of birds (Sultanova 2014, 109); its silk strings and soft whispering tone correspond with idealized feminine affectations. In contrast, the tanbur has a lower, louder, brighter sound evocative of rougher, more vigorous masculine energy.

The **ney**, or reed flute, holds a special place in Persian culture and spirituality. This simple wind instrument has been in use for almost five thousand years, making it one of the oldest musical instruments still in use. It is made from a long piece of giant reed or hollow cane into which seven finger holes have been burned—six on the front and one in back for the thumb. These holes are said to represent human nature and correspond with the main sensory openings of the human body (two eyes, two nostrils, two ears, and the mouth). The ney is also a symbol of the inner world. The enchanting sound of the ney, especially when played in an expansive acoustic environment, evokes a transcendental dimension. It is said to represent the breath of mankind and recite "poetry" as it plays.

The tempo and manner in which the ney is played can present a mood and even identify the classic poet associated with the mood. For example, the ney played for Hafez tends to be more joyful or brisk than others. The ney also provides cues for dancers. A pause in breathing or special note may indicate a stop or alteration, while a change in pitch and tone between rests can identify call and response. If the ney alternately plays at a high pitch, stops, and then plays at a lower pitch, this can depict the call of the nightingale (high) answered by the rose (low). When dancing to ney an expression of longing is the main feature.

The drum is a force in its own right, its mesmerizing pulse enlivening both body and psyche. Rhythm is energy, so it is not surprising that when we move to the rhythm of the drum we feel as though it carries us along. It seems to lift us out of the ordinary realm, and transmute time into timelessness. Rhythm is essential to transcendence. Joy and fear are energy-based and easily become rhythmically expressed; energy-depleted moods, such as grief and depression, can shift with the drum. Drum-inspired dance has the potential to restore our sense of balance, change our focus, and soothe the nervous system.

Drums have been used in various cultures since the beginning of human history, whether for healing, celebrations, festivals, rituals, or dancing. The first drums likely were simple objects that resonated when hit by a stick, however artifacts from the Neolithic period in China (5500 BCE) reveal drums made from alligator hide and hollowed out logs (Liu 2007). Traditionally, drumming has been used for invoking an element, a deity, or specific forms of energy. Used for healing in all traditional Iranian cultures, certain drum rhythms became associated with specific spirits or saints. Healing rhythms are multidimensional, like the pulse, and act on the heartbeat; if we allow ourselves to enter the drumbeat, in some circumstances our pulse alters to match it. In ancient Iran, drums came to represent the rhythm and passion of the human heartbeat and the celestial universe.

The **daf** (originally known as dap), one of the most ancient frame drums in Asia and North Africa, consists of animal hide or synthetic skin stretched over a wooden frame, with chains or rings around the inside of the rim. Ancient stone reliefs at the Bisotun and Taq-e Bostan archaeological sites near Kermanshah city, dating to the Sasanian period (224-651 CE), show priests making offerings to deities while musicians play daf and harp. Played since ancient times during sacred rituals in the khanqah, the daf is considered the primary percussion instrument for sama or zikr. The daf's vibrant and lively rhythms infuse energy into dance, and when played in complex and intense rhythms can induce trance or an ecstatic state. Many present-day Sufi orders consider one or more dafs or large frame drums indispensable for singing, sacred dance, and zikr. The circular shape of the daf evokes the image of the Sun, Moon, and planets, and symbolizes the cyclical nature of life that connects us with the infinite universe. In traditional mystic music, the rhythm of the daf symbolizes the heartbeat, and its element is fire—we are connected through the fire of our heart to the Divine. It is said that when a daf is torn, someone close by will be hurt or pass on, or your heart will break.

Though difficult to trace historically, many of today's daf rhythms likely came from western Kurdish areas of Iran, dating back thousands of years. Three popular rhythms used in the Sufi tradition today are *Hey Allah* (4/4), *haddadi* (4/4), and *daem* (2/4). The Hey Allah rhythm is a call to God that starts at a slow pace and then increases in speed. Characterized by a meditative pattern, it serves as a foundation for spiritual gatherings and is typically used to introduce a sama or zikr. Once started, the haddadi rhythm may be introduced, which raises the tempo to a moderate pace, then finally daem is played during the climax of the sama or zikr. Daem in Farsi means "to repeat" and this rhythm is used to accompany the repetitive motions of sama and zikr. Another frequently used rhythm, *hal ghertan*, means "turning" or "circles" and is likened to the cycle of life.

The daf has become so popular (second only to the *tonbak*) that its use has expanded into popular music, world music, and percussion bands, including the use of traditional Sufi rhythms such as daem and Hey Allah. True to its origins, however, classical Persian music still functions more as a spiritual tool than for entertainment. Students who learn the dastgah system in close association with a master are cautioned against change. Without the shepherding of this tradition by the masters, the thread of Persian music, art, dance, and culture could be lost. Music is a vital component of Iranian spiritual traditions. It guides attention from the realm of intellect to the realm of the heart, bringing our awareness out of the future or past to be fully in the present; it helps awaken the soul, and provides a source of healing and inspiration.

The dance is a poem of which movement is a word.

– Mata Hari

CHAPTER 22

Poetry in Motion

Dance is poetry; it narrates a tale, expressing the profound connection to beauty, love, and divinity. The delicate gestures of the fingers, the nuanced facial expressions, and the mystical turns inherent in Persian dance serve as a dialogue between body and soul. As an audience, you are invited to immerse yourself in the narrative, just like a reader falling into a captivating book.

Poetry is ubiquitous in Iran: it was a vital part of its history and remains an important part of its everyday popular culture. Almost all Iranian customs and traditions include poetry in one way or another, and nowhere in the world is poetry more highly treasured than in Iran. Iranians of all classes and education levels can recite their favorite Persian verses from memory, not only as an enjoyable pastime, but as a means to learn essential life principles. At times, a Persian poet captivates the entire nation of readers, keeping them in suspense with their verses. An interpretation of a poem can become the subject of a heated debate among Iranian literary critics, sometimes requiring a judge to arbitrate matters.

Persian poetry was born in the centuries following the arrival of Islam in the Iranian plateau, but Persian speakers generally consider its pinnacle to be the 13th and 14th centuries. Sufi thought was expressed primarily by poetry or prose works by the 13th century in Persia, and the romantic era of Persian poetry brought images of beauty, harmony, and a utopian world. The passion the poets evoke with their words is the reason Iranians often refer to their poetry books more than some religious books—many will turn to poetry when they are in despair or need help from the Divine. Hafez's poetry in particular is as significant as sacred text, its poetic passages considered messages from the Divine. When some people have a difficult decision to make or are uncertain about something, they open a book of Hafez to a random page and ask for guidance.

Persian (Farsi) itself is considered one of the world's most poetic languages. Over the centuries, from Ferdowsi in the ninth century CE until the present, Persians have crafted and exchanged poetry, packing meaning into every word, every line. Additionally, Persian poetry is closely affiliated with music, often recited with musical accompaniment and providing the lyrics for music. Each mode of expression empowers the other. The 10th century Central Asian scholar al-Farabi said, "The most perfect is a melody united with verse. This is what can move a man and change his morals" (Sultanova 2014, 201).

Mystical poetry is the universal language of the human soul, "a harmony of religion, philosophy, and art, constituting the deepest and finest expression of the mystic spirit… a synthesis of thought, feeling, and imagination which recalls and awakens the inner senses" (Bakhtiar 1976, 112). Poetry embodies a spontaneous expression of human emotions, intense passion that connects us to the heart, and the heart connects us to the Divine. We then move, dance, whirl, and express ourselves through this Divine Force. Persian poetry is highly rhythmic and most sacred and classical dance and music owes its existence to mystical poetry. There is a powerful creative interplay between poetry and the visual and performing arts; when we understand, feel, and appreciate poetry, we can create beautiful art and dance. The works of revered poets were transcribed into manuscripts artistically illustrated with exquisite calligraphy and illustrations. The beauty of the poetry inspired paintings, ceramics, and embellished metal engravings. When this poetry influences painters, musicians, and dancers, their art becomes a pathway to the Divine. As dancers, we bring these masterpieces to life.

Persian literature, poetry, art, music, and dance have cross-pollinated for generations in the garden of expression and imagination. Poetry has inspired art, art has inspired dance, dance has inspired feeling, and feeling has inspired poetry, creating a continuous chain of creative expression. Poetry has fostered a sophisticated artistic culture within which the great Persian poets extolled the virtues of dance and music.

When Movement Becomes Devotion

Everything in dance is poetry. Every movement describes a story, a feeling. The dancer takes the audience into a world of fairy tales.

Figure 22.1: Poetry in motion exemplified by the author.

Photo and retouchment by Varol Ozkaner.

There is language and story in dance, with a beginning, a middle, and an end. A dancer tells the story through gesture and movement, interacting with the audience with coquettish glances or a variety of expressions: reluctance, joy, sensuality, pride, laughter, and even sadness. Dance is poetry in motion, each movement a word; what dance expresses cannot be put into words yet refuses to remain silent. It takes years of training to understand the relationship between Persian music, dance, and poetry and the many forms of each. Poetry provides the narrative framework for many dances, while dancers help bring to life the drama and emotions underlying the poetry. The beauty of Persian poetry is that it is so universally understood. However, to capture the true meaning of some of the mystical connotations, an understanding of some of the attributes of Persian poetry can be of great help.

When creating a dance based on poetry, it is essential to understand the poet. Most revered Persian poets can be identified by a particular poetic style, theme, and meter. Knowing this helps the dancer to interpret the feeling, gestures, and rhythm correctly. The dancer must understand and honor the words and meaning of the poetry. Do the research. Practice listening to the poetry for tempo and inflection to prepare movements for the dance. Capture the feeling whether you are a native speaker of the language or not. Feel the energy of the poetry and put it into motion.

Reading and comparing the works of poets like Omar Khayyam, Hafez, Rumi, Ferdowsi, or Saadi reveals the distinctive ways in which they express emotions and rhythm. Each has a way of putting the reader into another state, and each has their own rhythm. Omar Khayyam expressed that everything is of Divine creation, criticized religious orthodoxy, and exhorted his readers to seek transcendence by seeing and accepting the truth of the present moment. Shiraz, the city of poets, was the birthplace of the lyrical, mystical style of poetry used by poets like Hafez and Saadi. Rumi's work is well known worldwide and his message has spread the ideas of Sufism among multitudes. From the East, too, many significant poetic works have stood the test of time. The work of Attar, Ibn' Arabi, and Nizami Ganjavi stand out as classics in both their own languages and in English.

The oldest form of poetry in Iran was the pre-Islamic verse of the court minstrel poets, which lost favor after the Islamic conquest. There is little left of this form today to analyze since many books written prior to Islam were lost or destroyed following the Arab invasion. Yet a form of meter known as *dobeti* survives in the Zoroastrian Yashts and Gathas. Dobeti is two couplets or four lines of verse (a quatrain). A common folk form, it often appears in fables and songs or poems of traveling, loneliness, rejection, discomfort, and other misfortunes. The poetry of Rumi or Baba Taher[181] is written in dobeti.

Another common form of verse is the *rubai*, an arrangement of four lines (quatrain) with a rhyming pattern of A-A-B-A or A-A-A-A. This may also be called *rubaiyat*, as in the literary work of poet Omar Khayyam. The *charbaiti* is similar to the rubai, although its rhyming patterns are less strict. The rhythmic structure of much of Rumi's poetry has been identified as charbaiti. Over the centuries, in Greater Iran, charbaiti poetry was sung by people inspired by nature as they worked in the fields, while they traveled through the countryside, or rested between their labors. In Western Afghanistan, it appears in short poems

---

[181] Baba Taher-e Oryan of Hamadan, Iran was an 11th century darvish poet.

on the subject of love which are sung one after another, often inspiring new compositions (Sakata 2012, 19).

In each region, several melodies are usually in vogue for singing charbaiti verses and what is popular changes yearly. One can generally distinguish between Tajik melodies and the more plaintive Khorasani songs (Miller and St. John 2011a, 222). The writers of charbaiti verses are almost always unknown; an interesting verse is remembered by whoever hears it, and it is passed on orally in slight variations from region to region. Charbaiti was initially used in the *qawali*, the Islamic Sufi devotional songs traditional in Pakistan and parts of India, although the Arabic *ghazal* has since replaced it. The ghazal is a set of between five to fifteen couplets with the same meter and length, and a repeating rhyme and word or phrase ending each couplet.

The *masnavi* is a series of couplets in rhyming pairs (aa bb cc), with a restricted number of meters (which would be different according to the subject), and a limited number of syllables (usually eleven per line). Masnavis were primarily used for collections of mystical poetry and stories. Poets such as Shams, Rumi, and Attar have written masnavis based on themes of mystery and longing. In a masnavi, the reader falls into the story, whereas in dobeti or charbaiti the reader follows someone else in. When a masnavi expresses a deep yearning for the Beloved, the lover seeks to transcend the limitations of the self and attain a state of spiritual ecstasy and union with the Divine. A masnavi of Rumi is usually sung in traditional Persian dastgah; his verses are strongly defined and follow a steady rhythm like a drum beat conducive to dance and zikr.

Practice integrating the themes and philosophy of the poet, style, and their characteristic meter into a dance. A dancer might choose short passages of the epic poems of Attar or Ferdowsi to weave into an interpretive dance performance. This might include heroic battle scenes using Persian martial arts movements to evoke the spirit of Ferdowsi's *Shahnameh*. Full of rich symbolism and vivid imagery, dancers may select certain verses, metaphors, symbolism, and concepts that resonate with them. To further integrate the poet's work into the performance, an interactive reading might help create a visual connection to the poetry. The costumes and set design for the performance might be inspired by the cultural context of the poet's era or the symbolism of the characters in the narrative. The choice of music for the dance performance might be selected from traditional Persian melodies or compositions that evoke the spirit and era of the poetry.

It is challenging to choreograph multiple dancers to Persian poetry, as each dancer brings their own feelings to the dance. Persian dance is very much an individual improvisational art. Even if one reads the same poem each day it can communicate a different message based on your current experience. Because of the personal, expressive nature of such poetry, a presentation by each dancer is likely to differ, and it's important to let the poetry take control and improvise with it. A dancer may master the technique of Persian dance and whirling, but in the end, it is what the poetry inspires and conjures in the dancer that brings it alive. Understanding the nuances of the poetry makes it more expressive, and allows more feelings to be captured in your dance.

Poetic Metaphors

Poetry is an echo, asking a shadow to dance.

– Carl Sandburg

Poetry has been one of the most common vehicles for expressing wisdom and cultural knowledge throughout human history. When a burdensome message is carried aloft upon the gentle zephyr of a poem it is easy to recall, less forbidding, and a delight to hear. The enchantment and beauty of metaphor, figurative language, allegory, and allusion in a poem are generative. Their use is not rigid, but open to interpretation, and can have many meanings depending on the poem and the poet. Mystical poetry is filled with references to wine and its cup, the goblet, the cupbearer, the tavern, the rose, the butterfly, and madness as metaphors for love and longing or the intoxication one feels when approaching the Divine. Pre-Islamic poetry was usually passionately amorous. The most powerful human emotion is love, after all, both in its personal, material form and its impersonal, spiritual form. When the poets wrote of the Beloved, they often visualized the form of an ideal woman, representing the Divine essence, a concept inherent to ancient pre-Islamic Persia.

Wine, also called *mey* in Old Persian, has deep significance in Persian mythology, poetry, and miniature art, with symbolic, metaphorical, and literal meanings. Just as grapes undergo the process of fermentation to become wine, the soul undergoes a spiritual transformation and purification to reach union with the Divine. Wine metaphorically refers to the potion or spell that causes a spiritual transformation, a state of ecstasy, or a total abandonment of ordinary life as a result of God's love. Over many centuries, wine and the wine bearer or cupbearer, the *saghi,* became essential elements in most Persian miniature paintings (Sorkhabi 2010).

In Persian poetry, the saghi (or *saqi*) is one of the most popular, enchanting figures. In Hafez's poetry the saghi is the woman or being that is idolized for her beauty, but can never be possessed. His detailed description of what the saghi wore became the model for the classical Persian dancer. Yet the saghi defies what is tangible or conventionally enchanting and beautiful. Additionally, the poet's use of the word and its meaning depends on the context. The saghi is also the wine bearer, one who brings the wine of spiritual intoxication. The saghi can represent God, a dancer, a love, a spiritual guide to lead the seeker to union with the Divine, or it can represent longing. It is used in mystic poetry to convey the intense longing for spiritual union and the ecstatic state that arises from the presence of the Divine. Sometimes referred to as the cupbearer, the saghi may be a lovely maiden or a *mogh bathe*, a young boy or youth. It all depends on the poetic image. We must immerse ourselves deep inside the poetry, understand who the poet was, and who the saghi was to them, because saghi is the personification of the Divine. To the poet, drunk with the wine of the Beloved, the cupbearer appears in different forms.

Classical Persian poems not only speak of the saghi and mey, but also *masti* (drunkenness). However, spiritual masti refers to being taken over by the power of the Divine, not to alcoholic inebriation. It is the ecstasy of love's intoxication, of communion with the Beloved, of truth, grace, or knowledge. The tavern (khanqah), likewise, represents the house of the beloved, or a secret house (dargah), a place of seclusion or spiritual awakening. The consumption of wine, in the mystic sense, symbolizes fanaa, the dissolution of the ego, and the merging of the soul with the Divine. A cup or bowl carries the wine to those who thirst for spiritual joy and the intoxication of Divine Love.

Depending on the poet, using the word *raz* may signify a secret, secretiveness, or an aesthetic form. If it is Rumi speaking of raz then it is an aesthetic state. If it is Hafez, it refers to his secrets. The word *niyaz* can also have different meanings based on the context: it may mean longing, or that one is in need, or that one is passionate for something. *Khoon-e del* (blood of the heart) is a more literal expression that signifies extreme sadness and longing.

In Persian dance, the theme of love is a central and cherished motif, drawing inspiration from the rich tradition of Persian poetry and Sufi mysticism. Love in this context often encompasses various dimensions, including romantic love, Divine Love, and spiritual yearning. The word *eshgh* usually means love, but depending on the context it may also mean fire. If Rumi uses the word then we know that he is talking about the fire of the Divine, the fire of God, as if "the love of God has put me on fire." If it is Saadi then he is referring to a real fire as in, "the house is on fire." Ferdowsi would use eshgh as if he is referring to the heart's passion.

Majnun usually refers to the lover. Again, it depends on who the poet is and how they are using the word. Hafez often uses the word Majnun to describe himself as one who fell in love. Rumi writes about love itself as a form of God. *Sheyda* is a state of madness in love. Although there is no exact word to translate it, it can be described as a state of manic passion driving one to abandon everything for the Beloved. In dancing, we are to leave behind our sense of self and become one with the music and with the soul. Once you lose yourself, you yourself are found.

In Persian poetry, the wind represents a message or a forthcoming announcement. On the other hand, a breeze indicates that a message from the Beloved is coming. The sun is a metaphor for the source of Divine Light, enlightenment, and spiritual illumination. It represents the ultimate truth and source of all existence. One can discover hidden messages by understanding the key words and images used in the poetry one is choosing. If you are not a Farsi speaker then create a dictionary for the poetic meanings of these words and the story behind them. To simplify, focus on the meanings you understand and not all the words at first.

The great Persian poets chose many visually and emotionally evocative metaphors, inspiring sensuous miniature artwork, rapturous music, ancient and devotional rituals, and prayers, all of which have informed Persian dance. Delicate, refined, and full of meaning, its spirit is derived from the spiritual treasures conveyed by mystical poetry and thought.

The Art of Improvisation

Dancing faces you toward heaven whichever direction you turn.

– Unknown

Historically, the purpose and meaning of Iranian dance have been quite different from that of Western dance. Iranian dance is primarily a form of worship and spiritual practice rather than entertainment; it was sacred and formed a gateway to spiritual transformation. In many Eastern cultures, the human body was an instrument of the spirit in relationship with the Divine. In contrast, the ancient Greeks, who idealized man, considered the human body a tool of individual action. Thus, dance in the West became an expression of action, synonymous with entertainment in the social arena. Since Western dance is predominantly for entertainment, it is also highly choreographed. Eastern dance, more focused on contemplation and expression from the heart, is not as focused on choreography or audience appeal, but rather, on holding space for improvisation, to free the mind and soul from the restrictions of ordinary life. In sacred or ritual dance, the "choreography" is so ingrained that dancers need not break their meditation. Furthermore, they are often led by a master or elder so that the dancers are free of the responsibility to remember or decide what comes next.

Improvisation gives personal expression to word and prayer. When we surrender ourselves to a dance that unfolds from within, the mind becomes focused upon the dance of the heart. We enter a deep level of joy, bliss, and a feeling of union with the all-pervading spirit. In offering ourselves fully to the present moment in sacred dance, the spirit enters, transforms, and moves us. It awakens our soul's passion and enlivens every cell of our body. In sacred dance, technique is only useful if it is accompanied by inspiration from the celestial realms. We become the essence of spirit in motion, one with the cosmic dancer. Sacred dance can enable us to cross from one world to another, from one state of mind to another, from contraction and fear to expansion and love (Stewart 2013, 134).

When dancers engage in interpretive Persian dance, they use movement to express the meaning and emotions of a narrative or poetry. This allows for a deeper connection between the dance and the poetic meaning. Improvised dance is spontaneous, using familiar patterns in unique ways or entirely original movements without pre-planned choreography. A vital element in Persian dance, improvisation allows for creative expression and an interactive connection to the musicians, audience, and feeling of the moment. Improvisation has long been a part of dances throughout Iran, whether in formal or informal situations. It enables dancers to convey a wide emotional spectrum, from joy and celebration to introspection and contemplation. They can adapt their movements to match the emotional content of the music.

Improvised dance often utilizes delicate, graceful movements and expressions. Seamless transitions between movements create a natural and flowing performance enhancing its visual appeal. Improvisation requires a keen sense of spatial awareness and adjustment of movements in real time to navigate the performance space. The choice of costuming, props, and accessories during the improvisation enhances the visual impact. For sacred dance, improvisation can be a means of expressing spiritual concepts and experiences for a deeply personal connection to the dance.

Traditionally, Iranian dance and music were not written down or codified. The melodies, oral traditions, and folk stories, some of which are up to five thousand years old, have been handed down person to person. In improvisational dance, the dancer, whether part of a group or dancing alone, creates a free-style dance by selecting movements from a well-defined and established vocabulary from the Persian dance genre. Traditional Persian dances also have a call-and-response dynamic between the musicians and the dancers. For example, a daf player's rhythms could prompt specific movements or gestures from the dancers. Due to the complexity of the art, improvisation is to be used by artists and musicians who have completely grasped the tradition.

The Art of Expression

The most beautiful women in Persia are devoted to the profession of dancing; the transparency of their shift, the exquisite symmetry of their forms, their apparent agitation, and the licentiousness of their verses are so many incentives to a passion, which requires more philosophy than the Persians possess to restrain.

– Edward Scott Waring, 1807

Figure 22.2: Poetic gestures exemplified by the author.
Lynne Fried

The Golden Age of Persia was a time of significant poetic, scientific, architectural, and medical innovation. The great mystical poets of the age such as Hafez, Omar Khayyam, and Rumi created beautiful poetry with evocative symbolism which inspired paintings and manuscript illumination, which in turn developed a language of gestures to depict emotion in elegant, stylized figures. As these artistic expressions became readily recognized, they naturally were incorporated into dance, where the graceful words of Persian poetry and gestures of miniature paintings could come to life. In fact, within the royal court during the Sasanian dynasty, hand gestures were a common means of communication as a way of showing respect. During the Elamite empire, one could not speak in the royal court at all except by hand—it is said the king was germophobic and preferred no one open their mouth unless necessary. Of course, the art of expressive hand gestures became an essential part of dance and theater where dancers and artists used their hands and fingers to tell a story and show emotions.

Because the emphasis is on expressiveness, Persian dance is said to be best suited for intimate settings as subtle movements are more visible to a small, close audience than in larger venues. Dancers use their eyes, brows, mouth, and overall facial expressions to communicate a wide range of emotions and intentions, from joy and longing to contemplation and determination. Hand gestures, body language, and facial countenance all work together for the deeply artistic and multifaceted transmission of emotions, cultural themes, and character interpretations in a dance narrative. Each body part becomes a symbol, each movement displays a feeling (Figure 22.2). Overall, the dancer must allow narrative and verse to command the mind and feeling. Persian dance is not just about technique, it is about passion.

A gesture is a movement of the face, body, or limbs to express an emotion, idea, purpose, or feeling. In contrast, expression is a particular *way* of phrasing an idea. In dance, the gesture is the position or movement, and expression is the emotion or story it conveys. In terms of Labanotation (a means of writing down dance and movement), a gesture is the movement of any part of the body that is not weight-bearing. In actuality, a dancer can and does gesture with any part of the body, weight-bearing or not (Lille 2002). While these gestures hint at various familiar symbols in the cultural heritage of Iran, a system of specific hand symbols and positions is not highly codified, such as those that exist in India and Indo-China.

When dancers are not physically linked by holding hands, their hands are free to move in various ways, oftentimes using objects such as sticks and scarves. When the hands and fingers are free they have a refined symbolism that may suggest these objects or have other meaning. In Iranian culture, especially in folklore, hand movements that are used in dance are distinct and clear. One must know when and how to use hands with the style of dance one is performing. It is also important that the unused hand should be under control at all times during the dance. Most dancers forget that if one hand is included in the dance expression, then the other also has a role. It is essential to be conscious of the whole body and what the passive hand is doing.

More complicated combinations of gestures and movements symbolizing specialized sacred or classical emotive narratives can only be described by example. More recently, scholars have collected a glossary of these (Miller 1999, 293-7). For example, to depict receiving a special or secret message, the dancer covers her eyes with her hands peeking through the slits between fingers and from the corner of her eyes, all the while her eyebrows alternately dance. This expression is known as *payam*, the "message" (St. John and Miller 1987, 26). In another expression depicting a spiritually inebriated state of semi-trance accompanied by distraught inner turmoil, the dancer dishevels her tresses with the fingers of her hand while moving her head and turning. This expression is called *parishan*, the "disheveled."

Persian dance movements are very lyrical, poetic, defined, and distinct. As previously discussed, they manifest the energies and expressions of nature, animals, birds, flowers, and the five elements. Some propose the hand represents the five elements, with the thumb representing the element of ether (Williams 2014). All fingers might move or shake to represent fire. Another representation of fire is an open palm.

Figure 22.3: Gestures and props in Persian classical art. Fresco of a beautiful lady, Safavid dynasty, Chehel Sotoun Palace, Isfahan, Iran.

Photo by author of exhibit.

Gestures in sacred dance may express inward confinement and contemplation or outward praise to show devotion. The two middle fingers closed together represent humbleness. Sacred gestures include the finger on the mouth, the hand on the face or heart, and arms that open to the sky to refer to the heavens, fate, or rejoicing. Pointing demurely with the index finger is a sign of longing. Mystical symbolism such as this may have influenced classical Greek or European artists enough to include such gestures in their work (such as the ceiling of the Sistine Chapel).

Props in dance rituals carry a mystical significance and add a layer of expression and meaning to the performance. When a dancer physically holds a prop it is a symbol of a sacred entity. For example, when we hold a wine jug, cup, or bowl, it may be a representation of the saghi, the wine bearer, or may symbolize the ecstasy in the Divine, or an offering to the Beloved. Holding a drum may be symbolic of the sun or the moon. Illustrations in manuscripts or miniature art paintings of the Qajar period show dancers playing a pair of tiny finger cymbals, castanets, or spoons, holding a tambourine, or a small frame drum in one hand or both. Pantomime is also used—holding a pot on the shoulder, applying facial makeup with a brush, holding a basket.

The eyes tell magical stories from the heart in the form of silent communication. Cultural limitations on self-expression through body movement and verbal limitations have made Persian women particularly creative using their eyes for expression. Persian literature and poetry vouch for this. In the *Loghat-nama*, an Iranian encyclopedia, there are many terms regarding the eyes. Specific eye movements have culturally symbolic significance in Persian dance. The eyes are doors to one's inner self and windows to the outer world (Shahshahani 2008, 73).

> *But when it comes to eyes, eyelashes, and eyebrows, there are few women in the world who can compete with the Persians. There is exuberant fire and expression in the Persian feminine organs of vision, large and almond-shaped, well-cut, and softened by eyelashes of abnormal length, both on the upper and lower lid... The women seem to have wonderful control over the muscles of the eyelids and brows, which render the eyes dangerously expressive.* (Landor 1902, 204, 206)

The eyes play a crucial role in conveying emotions, intentions, portraying specific characters, and establishing relationships with other actors in the narrative. They can be used to direct attention to specific body parts, props, or other areas. They can signal the start or end of a particular sequence in a dance. The eyes are a powerful means for expressing a wide range of emotions, and even subtle changes in gaze, intensity, or expression can effectively shift the mood of the performance or reveal inner thoughts, feelings, and the internal dialogue of their character. Confidence, vulnerability, determination, or playfulness can be portrayed. Overall, when a skilled dancer makes dramatic use of the eyes it enhances the performance, adding depth and nuance. I always tell my dancers if you have the right expression and make people follow your eyes, they will never see the mistakes in your technique because they're so fascinated by your gaze. Have your audience look at your face rather than your body. Make eye contact with the audience to establish a connection and draw them into the performance. Expression with the eyes takes a bit of practice. The best practice is using a mirror—I would ask somebody to read a story or poetry as I portrayed feelings with my own eyes. When not conveying something else, the classical and sacred dancer's gaze is demure and downcast symbolizing humility; it is not direct.

The composition of the body is also important in Iranian dance. In epic or warrior dances, the body becomes rigid and straight, with a military-style appearance, the arms usually straight up or down, almost like semaphores. Folk dances, such as Kurdish line dances and Circassian dances, often use this style. Folk dances that symbolize non-military functions (i.e., farmers, shepherds, and tradespeople) are more relaxed with bent knees and elbows. The stance of the feet represents initiative as demonstrated in many historical paintings and statues; a right foot forward represents a leader, whereas a left foot forward represents a follower.

Dance performed with mastery of traditional movements enhances a performance's authenticity and expression. Audiences recognize the interplay of a dancer's movements with music. When music and dance are presented together on stage, the audience understands the narrative better. There is no codified system of expressions in Persian dance, but there are common gestures and poses from paintings, art, and poetry, which should be studied, as well as practicing hand, arm, and facial expressions with a dance mentor. Remember that the emphasis in Persian dance is on passion, so when we dance our hand and body expressions naturally tell a story with eloquence and persuasion.

To touch, to move, to inspire. This is the true gift of dance.

– Aubrey Lynch

CHAPTER 23

Connecting with Sacred Dance

Connect, Channel, and Transform

I see dance being used as communication between body and soul to express what is too deep to find words.

– Ruth St. Denis

Dancing is an elemental, eternal form of human expression. At its simplest, it is the body expressing itself rhythmically. Dance helps us communicate from our innermost soul in ways that cannot be expressed through words. In its sacred form, dance is a language that unites body, soul, and mind. Sacred dance allows dancers to both find and lose themselves. One can pick up a book and judge it by size, volume, and cover but one needs to open and read the book to understand it. Anyone can speak about dance, but it is hard to fully appreciate it without doing it.

Whether your dance is for an audience or not, follow the best practices and rules proposed for effectively creating a dance to reach the Divine. Sacred dance connects the soul of a dancer to the deities and spirits, to mythical and religious beliefs, and to poetic meditation. It blends movement, poetry, and passion with fluidity and grace. It elicits a unique balance of the left and right hemispheres of the brain combining art, science, creativity, and spirit. It engages our emotions,

Figure 23.1: Sacred dance unites body, soul, and mind, exemplified by the author.

Photo by author.

creativity, and desire for relationship, directing them toward the sacred, emphasizing feeling more than technique. A dancer becomes spiritually elevated and invites others to join in that experience. Sacred dance was, at one time, a method of healing and attaining spiritual elevation, the mind connecting with the body so both become more receptive to the universe.

If you seek to practice sacred dance then you first need to prepare and clarify your purpose. Study the previous chapters of this book for details on the history, traditions, rituals, and practices of Iranian sacred and traditional dance. Immerse yourself in the rich universe of mystic music, art, and poetry. This will deepen your understanding of the spiritual themes and emotions often expressed through dance. Incorporate mindfulness and meditation into your routine. These practices can help you cultivate a deeper connection to your inner self and facilitate a more profound experience. Endeavor to investigate and study additional books, literature, or online sources to help supplement your study. Look for and attend workshops, classes, or retreats focused on sacred dance. These gatherings can offer immersive experiences and opportunities to learn from seasoned instructors. Seek out teachers or practitioners who have expertise in the field who can provide you with valuable guidance, techniques, and insights. As you study, embrace the sacred symbolism and themes like longing, surrender, and union with the Divine.

It is ideal to establish a dedicated space where you can practice. This could be a room in your home or a tranquil outdoor setting where you feel a spiritual connection. When you perform sacred ritual dance for others, it is equally important to choose and create a sacred space. Define boundaries that are large enough for you to move freely without disturbance. Quiet, peaceful spaces are preferred. Choose a clean area or clean it if needed, and clear any negative energy by smudging. Use incense such as frankincense or myrrh to evoke a spiritual connection. If possible, invite elders to guide and bless the space. Pay attention to the light and define the space with the use of candles if appropriate. Sacred space can be created indoors or outdoors—nature has always been a sacred sanctuary for mystics, where it is believed angelic forces are more present.

Consider why you are doing this ritual. What does it mean to you? Will you need props or musical instruments? Who are the participants? Will there be observers or is it personal? Be aware that observers can be led to a state of ecstasy. The goal is unification, becoming one with the dance, the observers, the surroundings, and the Divine. Create an intention for the ceremony. Determine the energies you are summoning into your sacred space, such as angels, saints, or spirits. Remember the energy of sacred dance originates from the elements, animals, plants, and the universe.

If outside, become aware of the sounds of nature. Start by being fully aware and feeling relaxed in your own body, then gradually become connected to and present with the surrounding conditions. Less movement in sacred dance fosters a deeper meditative and reflective state. Carefully attend to each movement, allowing yourself and those watching to meditate on the presence. For beginners, moves should be simple, slow, and steady. As observers, allow the spiritual energy to flow uninterrupted, and refrain from unnecessary distractions or conversations. Allow silence and stillness to penetrate the dance. A silent pause is part of the experience after the sound, music, and movement stop. In this silence, one can absorb and assimilate the qualities evoked during the dance. Allow time for silent prayer and meditation. A quiet respect enhances the overall experience for everyone.

Let go of expectations and self-consciousness. Sacred dance is not an athletic competition or a formal presentation. It is an opportunity for expression and interaction. It takes a while for the mind to recognize how to yield control—don't let it discourage you. Bypass negative thoughts, overthinking, and ego. Allow the heart to open up to the Divine; that is where improvisation begins. Be kind to yourself. Your dance is unique, unlike any other artist. There is no judgment, everything is a prayer.

Technique is only a means by which to create a mood. To be able to create mood, the performer has to have discipline and self-honesty. They need to see their shortcomings and constantly practice correcting them. That is why a dishonest artist will never advance spiritually. The four virtues necessary to be capable of conveying a mood without ego are: purity, honesty, humility, and love of others (Miller 1999, 99). When a dance represents a traditional people's culture and beliefs, choose appropriate traditional instruments, music, and garments to be respectful of that tradition. Cultural traditions naturally evolve over time, but when presenting traditions of cultures not your own, resist the temptation to alter them. The study of cultural music, symbolism, and movements is essential to access the inner meaning and metaphysical wisdom.

Traditional sacred garments can enhance the experience and lift a dancer out of their ordinary, everyday identity. Appearing in a sacred costume during the ritual marks the boundary between the realm of the personal and the archetypal, the Divine. As the dancer, permit yourself to feel deeply. Allow the dance to refine and purify your emotional state. Ritual movement can lead to states of calm, tears, or joy. Practice mindfulness of the surroundings. As an observer, practice mindful observation. Allow yourself to be completely present in the moment, to appreciate the beauty of the dance without distraction. Remember this dance is not merely a performance but a spiritual journey, and one's respectful attention adds to its significance.

Visualization is an important component of sacred dance. We create what we want by visualizing and seeing things in front of us. We can use our minds to imagine something, visualize it, see it through dreams, ask questions, and communicate through intuition. Permit yourself to repeat moves. Ritual dance is usually a simple formula repeated again and again. In sama or zikr, repetition takes one beyond the realms of everyday life; the simplicity activates the message, passed down for generations, that reaches us through the body. Concentration on a sacred phrase or symbol and the movement of everyone together moves our deepest being. It is very important to integrate passion and understanding into a performance, whether it is dance or music. Knowing what one is doing and what it represents in tradition is essential. Commit yourself and your passion to the dance. I've seen dancers who have excellent technique but their faces show no feeling so they don't connect with the audience. Feelings, understanding, and technique are all meant to work together.

Time, Space, and People

Dance is a transformation of space, of time, of people, who are in constant danger of becoming all brain, will, or feeling. Dancing demands a whole person, one who is firmly anchored in the center of his life, who is not obsessed by lust for people and things and the demon of isolation in his own ego. Dancing demands a freed person, one who vibrates with the equipoise of all his powers.

– Unknown

When doing any kind of sacred dance or ritual, a few key factors determine how one connects with the Divine Energy. These are: the *zaman* (time), the *makan* (place), and the *yaran* (companions). Whenever music is played or dance is presented, the results are influenced by these three variables which can subtly (or not so subtly) affect the feelings, energy, and mood of the performers, audience, or space, creating distraction or increased focus. Light and dark, sun and the moon, day and night, seasons, weather, temperature, and the energy of those present all contribute to the quality of the gathering. Oftentimes those with too much ego or negative energy are not allowed in a sacred space because their activity can inhibit the Divine Energy from revealing itself. On the other hand, those entering the circle who have a pure heart and soul, who respect the space and others in it, lift the energy level and help create a safe and attractive environment for the Divine Energy to enter. When a ritual includes the right energy, music, people, and ceremony, one can experience the magic of a beautiful sacred gathering. No one is a stranger any longer when the community participates in mutual regard. We become companions on the same journey.

Dancing with Reverence

Do everything with gentleness, with kindness, with reverence. That is how Grace moves; that is how Love dances.

– Heather K. O'Hara

Important distinctions need to be made between non-mystic and mystic dancing. I have traveled the world connecting with people who continue to practice sacred mystic dancing; I have immersed myself in their communities, rituals, dances, and prayers. These traditions have been challenging to access whether due to political climate, societal changes, lack of access to information, or prohibitions against sharing customs. To learn or teach many sacred and traditional dances, one must obtain permission from spiritual elders. Traditionally, music and dance could only be passed along through personal instruction. In contrast, accessing dance from the internet is easy but provides very little real education and experience. Even worse, some modern resources explain sacred dances misleadingly or incorrectly. If the dance is not shared accurately, if the sacred details are not known or respected, then our elders would question why we would share it. Sacred dance is a treasured legacy and we need to honor this connection.

A non-mystic may be quite skilled, learning by the book, and using sophisticated technique. A mystic does not go by the book but by the heart. The inner practices that free one of ego allow the true artist to develop. If a dancer does not follow the inner path of mysticism, if they do not give themselves to the universe and let the Divine lead the dance, they are not a genuine mystic or Sufi dancer. An ordinary dancer performs to impress, to entertain, to enhance their own ego. Mystic dancers are engaging in deep worship and surrender to the Divine, inviting observers in the room to join them in this state of spiritual communion. Sacred dance and whirling were given to us from a divine source, and we must protect it. We must honor the sacred traditions, lineages, and protocols. Participants wear appropriate clothing, arrive in a state of cleanliness, pray, use proper musical instruments, and engage a master to guide the proper rituals. The gathering is for devotion, not entertainment.

Those who falsely call themselves mystics or darvishes do a great disservice to the traditions and mislead others. The problem with modern forms of "Sufism" or new-age spirituality is that they are disconnected from the traditions and the Divine Source so the real essence is lost—they are providing nothing more than a sensationalized and popular entertainment business, with few who care to truly study and discipline themselves. Entertainers need to respect the tradition of sacred dance, and if they are depicting a sacred dance, proper ritual garments should be worn, and the rituals must be acceptable to mystics. One should respect the master, the ground they dance on, and the mysticism itself.

As a sacred dancer, the space and body become your temple and spiritual ground, therefore be careful about what you study and with whom. Verify that the dances are authentic and the teacher is well aware of what they're teaching. Be sure the sacred tradition is carefully represented. When manifesting sacred dance movements, the dancer should be humble and demure. Be careful how and with whom your sacred dance is shared. Be respectful when sharing an esoteric ritual. Understand the purpose and intention of a sacred dance and its culture and people. Also, realize that regardless of whether a sacred ritual is for performance or prayer, it is imbued with power. Its energy will be present no matter what.

You can expect your life to transform through sacred dance. You will discover new means and best practices to reach the Divine from personal experience and interactions with participants and the environment. Approach sacred dance with a sense of reverence, humility, and sincerity. Allow yourself to be open to the spiritual experiences that may arise. With practice in breathing and meditation, and in humble reverence, you will find your dance improving. Be patient with yourself, and allow the practice to unfold naturally. As you delve deeper into this sacred art, you may find it becomes a profound means of spiritual expression and a source of deep inner fulfillment. Dedicate regular time to your practice. Consistent practice will help you deepen your connection and proficiency in this art form. Seek out like-minded individuals who share an interest in sacred dance. Engaging with a community can provide support, encouragement, and opportunities for group sama, practice, or performance.

There are two types of master artists: those who are naturally gifted, and those who have studied, developed understanding, and are spiritually connected. Those who don't have the gift of mastery can still learn to bring that gift into their life. The craft of sacred dance requires training in body and mind, in technique and philosophy, a process that is never quite complete. Each mystic or sacred dancer should seek training not only in whirling and dance but also in spirituality and music, and one should always follow the rules of purity, truth, selflessness, and service. With training, knowledge, understanding, the ability to bring meditation and concentration into movement, and denial of self, one can become a better dancer or musician; dance becomes a gateway for growth and spiritual transformation. In this transformation, the promptings of the Inner Divine are found, and loving kindness and compassion flow naturally into our daily lives.

The mission to preserve Iranian dance and rituals requires an understanding of their history and the spiritual philosophies behind them. Dance and music have always been an everyday part of Iranian culture, not just as a part of life, but as a lifestyle. Even within the last century, elders taught their children the traditional family dances to be carried on as a legacy. Nuances of style became the signature of a family or the village where they originated. Dance and music have served as a means of expressing and transmitting the culture, civilization, language, and history of a nation or tribe. Maintaining and developing traditional arts is one of the best paths to honor and preserve cultural identity. These ancient traditions, passed down for thousands of years, are priceless treasures that need to be preserved for the future. Whether uncovering historical dances from thousands of years past, or promoting cultural dances and historic rituals within our communities, sharing them with our children, or simply practicing them with integrity ourselves and with others, we can contribute to the continuation of these traditions. Because my mother passed along these dance traditions to me exactly the way it was passed along to her, I am able to share these traditions with my students.

We must allow the spirit to live and show itself in our work. This is what makes teaching and performance powerful. When I teach or perform, my soul guides me. I open up to the universe and allow my ancestors and spirit to take control. Dance and mysticism have generated profound changes in me, both internal and external, and connected me with a community of people who live in harmony with each other and nature. It is lovely to witness how much sacred dance changes lives and creates love and unity. This sense of connection is possible because people can be seen, heard, and felt. Once divested of the worries of the past and concerns for the future, a sacred artist can ascend to a sphere of beauty in the present where spirituality and serenity reign. It is in this domain that the creative artist and mystic emerge as messengers of the Divine, to heal, empower, and uplift when needed. The unification promoted by dance is a vital resource for our modern world. Dance is a powerful pathway to spiritual enlightenment and brings us closer to the Divine.

When we look deep inside our dance
we come to realize as human beings how we are all connected.
Dance creates peace, love, harmony, and understanding among all people.

Selected Bibliography

Akman, M. Kubilay and Donna M. Brown. "Ahmad Al-Buni and His Esoteric Model." *The Esoteric Quarterly,* Spring 2018.

Alavijeh, Ali Zamani. "A Comparison between the significance of Number 7 in Persian Context and Number 9 in Chinese Context." *ISS & MLB,* (September 24-26).

Alexander, Kathy and Kevin Kaiser. "Native American Totem Animals & Their Meanings: Legends of America." *Legends of America.* Accessed December 27, 2022. www.legendsofamerica.com/na-totems/.

Al-Hakim, Aya. "Sufism: How Creativity Can Reconnect Us With Nature." *The Huffington Post,* (Dec 29). 2015. www.huffpost.com/archive/ca/entry/sufism-how-creativity-can-reconnect-us-with-nature_b_8887686.

Allan, Tony, et al. *Wise Lord of the Sky: Persian Myth.* Time-Life, 1999.

Amirullah, Seyed and Shah Ebrahimi. *Divan-e Hazrat Shaiky Amir.* Sahnah Publishing (Farsi), 1995.

And, Metin. *Pictorial History of Turkish Dancing.* Dost Yayinlari, 1976.

Arberry, Arthur John. *Fifty Poems of Hāfiz: Texts and Translations.* Cambridge University Press, 1970.

Arberry, Arthur John. *The Legacy of Persia.* Clarendon Press, 1963.

"Arpana 7: The Influence of Sufism on Hindustani Music." Uploaded by Nitya Nritya Foundation, July 29, 2022. youtu.be/2-Y5f1dNmXI.

Arshi, Z. and N. Kasraian. *Nomads of Iran.* Translated by Minoo Alian. Seké Press, 1994.

Asiabani, Ali. "Saving Iran's Own Music." *The Tehran Journal,* January 12.

Attar, Farid al-Din. *The Conference Of The Birds.* Translated by Afkham Darbandi and Dick Davis. Penguin Books, 1984.

Avicenna. *A Treatise on the Canon of Medicine of Avicenna, Incorporating a Translation of the First Book.* London: Luzac & Co., 1930.

Azabdartari, Behrooz, trans. *The Glass on the Shoulder and The Pelting of Rocks.* Samir Publications, 2013.

Bābānāvis and Allāh Dakkah'ī Sayyid Fazla. Dīvān-I Ḥaẕrat bābānāvis = Baba Naousi. S̱ālis̱ (Farsi), 2015. ISBN 9789643809584.'Bahar-Naz, Mohammadreza. *Nomads of Iran: Photographs of Iranian Tribes.* Farhang-Sara Publications, 1994.

Baker, Miriam. *Sacred Voices: Stories From the Caravan of Women.* Secret One Publishing, 2018.

Bakhtiar, Leleh. *Sufi Expressions of the Mystic Quest.* Avon Books, 1976.

Balkhi, Mawlana Jalaleddin Mohammad. *Mathnavi Ma'navi, Matn-e Kamel Hamrah ba Kashful Abyat va Vajehnameh.* Tehran Publications (Farsi), 2010. ISBN 9789642911226.

Bashiri, Iraj. "From the Hymns of Zarathustra to the Songs of Borbad." *Historical Site of Mirhadi Hosseini.* 2003. m-hosseini.ir/zar/articles-1/21.htm.

"Beauty unbound: Flowers in Iranian culture." 2012. *Tehran Times,* January 15, 2012. www.tehrantimes.com/news/395819/Beauty-unbound-Flowers-in-Iranian-culture.

Behrends, Andrea, Sybille Müller, and Isabel Dziobek. "Moving in and out of synchrony: A concept for a new intervention fostering empathy through interactional movement and dance." *The Arts in Psychotherapy*, vol. 39, no. 2 (2012). doi.org/10.1016/j.aip.2012.02.003.

Berenji, Farima. "'Parsi' A Brief Look into the History and Changes of the Persian Language." Language and Culture 3800, California State University, East Bay, student paper, n.d..

Berenji, Farima. *"Seeds of Change," Prospects for a Better Cross-Cultural Education Path in Iran.* Masters' Thesis, California State University, East Bay. August, 2006.

Berenji, Farima. *Dance of the Soul.* Msc.D. Thesis, University of Sedona, September, 2023.

Berenji, Farima. *Parallels of Traditional Iranian Sufi and Eastern Meditation Practices.* M. Msc. Thesis, University of Sedona, August 2023.

Blair, Nancy. *Amulets of the Goddess.* Wingbow Press, 1996.

"Bowl." n.d. *The British Museum.* Accessed Oct. 3, 2023. www.britishmuseum.org/collection/object/W_1936-0613-2.

Boyce, Mary. "Bībī Shahrbānū and the Lady of Pārs." *Bulletin of the School of Oriental and African Studies,* London: University of London, 30 (1): 30-–44. 1967. www.jstor.org/stable/611813.

"Breath meditation: A great way to relieve stress." 2014. *Harvard Health Publishing,* April 15, 2014. www.health.harvard.edu/mind-and-mood/breath-meditation-a-great-way-to-relieve-stress.

Briant, Pierre. *From Cyrus to Alexander: A History of the Persian Empire.* Eisenbrauns, 2002.

Brosius, Maria. *Women in Ancient Persia*, Mahomoud Toloui, trans. Intishārāt-i Tihrān, 2010.

Būrahkah'ī Ṣiddīq Ṣafi'zādah. *Farhang-I Būrahkahyī: Kurdī-Fārsī.* Pilīkān (Farsi), 2001. ISBN 9649137874.

Chehabi, Houchang E. "Zurkhana." *Encyclopedia Iranica*, August 15, 2006. 2006. www.iranicaonline.org/articles/zur-kana.

Chishti, Hafizullah et al. T*raining in Breath for Sufi Order Leaders vol. 1.5* (AKA "The Breath Module"). Inayati Order Training Notes, 2015.

Chishti, Shaykh. *Book Of Sufi Healing*, Inner Traditions, 1985.

Clifford, Garth. "Bull Symbolism & Meaning (+Totem, Spirit & Omens)." *World Birds*, August 8, 2022. worldbirds.com/bull-symbolism/.

Collard-Stokes, Gemma. "What can dance teach us about our relationship with nature?" *University of Derby*, June 9, 2020. www.derby.ac.uk/blog/what-can-dance-teach-us-about-our-relationship-with-nature/.

Collins, Billie Jean, editor. *A History of the Animal World in the Ancient Near East.* Brill, 2022.

Conant, Levi Leonard, Ph.D. *The Number Concept: Its Origin and Concept.* Macmillan and Co., (1896) 1931.

Culican, William. *The Medes and Persians.* Thames & Hudson, 1965.

Darvishi, Mohamad Reza. *Encyclopaedia of the musical instruments of Iran – vol. 1,* 4th edition. Mahoor, 2011.

Das, Hirok. "7 Major Stages Of Spiritual Awakening According To Sufism." *Realized by Grace,* Apr 19, 2019. www.realizedbygrace.org/post/7-major-stages-of-spiritual-awakening-according-to-sufism.

Dayton, Tian, PhD. *The Quiet Voice of Soul: How to Find Meaning in Ordinary Life.* Health Communications, Inc. 1995.

De Warren, Robert and Peter Williams. "Discovery in Persia." *Dance and Dancers,* January, 1973.

Deagon, Andrea. "Dancing at the Edge of the World: Ritual, Community, and the Middle Eastern Dancer." *Arabesque*, September/October 1994.

Dell, Catherine. *Ballet Dancing.* Hamlyn Publishing Group, Ltd., 1979.

Dinavari, Hirad. "A Thousand Years of the Persian Book: A Curator's Tour." *Library of Congress*, March 2014. 2014. www.loc.gov/item/2021689519/.

"DNA: Cracking the Ancestor Code." California State University East Bay, Research, 2007.

Döşer, Öner. "Hermetism: Sufism and Islamic Cosmology." *Constellation News,* May 22, 2021.

Douglas-Klotz, Neil. *The Sufi Book of Life: 99 Pathways of the Heart for the Modern Dervish.* Penguin Books, 2005.

Ducharme, Jayme. "Dance Like Your Doctor is Watching." *Time Magazine,* December 20, 2018.

Duncan, Isadora. *The Art of the Dance.* Edited by Sheldon Cheney. Theatre Arts Books, 1970.

During, Jean. *Music and Mysticism.* Tehran: Porsesh, 1999.

Dyr, Wayne W. *You'll See It When You Believe It.* Enteshar (Farsi), 2020.

Ebrahimi, Amr Allah Shah. *Pardivar 1.* Des Eilya Tahamtani (Farsi), 2010.

Eduljee, K. E. *Mithra, Mithraism, Christmas Day & Yalda.* Zoroastrian Heritage Monographs, November, 2016.

Ekins, Carrie. "Dancing and the Brain: The Neurological Effects of Dance." *NFO News,* January, 2019.

Emerick, Yahiya. *The Complete Idiot's Guide to Rumi Meditations.* Alpha Books, 2008.

Enghauser, Rebecca. "The Quest for an Ecosomatic Approach to Dance Pedagogy." *The Journal of Dance Education.* 2021. doi.org/10.1080/15290824.2007.10387342.

Ernst, Carl W. "7. A Fourteenth-Century Persian Account of Breath Control and Meditation." *Yoga in Practice*, edited by David Gordon White, Princeton: Princeton University Press. 2012. doi.org/10.1515/9781400839933-012.

Erzen, Jale. "The Dervishes Dance – The Sacred Ritual of Love." *Contemporary Aesthetics,* Volume 6. 2008. hdl.handle.net/2027/spo.7523862.0006.007.

Fadiman, James and Robert Frager, ed. *Essential Sufism.* Harper, 1997.

Fairservis, Walter A, Jr. *Costumes of the East.* Chantam Press, 1971.

Fakhri, Kamran Pashayi, Rogayye Mahmoodivand Bakhtiari, and Parvaneh Adelzadeh. "Hoopoe in Persian Literature and Myths." *International Archive of Applied Sciences and Technology*, vol. 5, June 2014.

Fallahi, Ghazale. "Persian Flowers from ancient Persia to Iranian culture." *EasyGoIRAN,* October 8, 2020. goirantours.com/persian-flowers-from-ancient-persia-to-iranian-culture/.

Faraji, Nader. "A glance at Mythology of Sacred Bovine in the Indo-Iranian Ancient Beliefs." *Scholars Journal of Arts, Humanities and Social Sciences.*3 (5A). 2015. saspublishers.com/media/articles/SJAHSS_35A986-989.pdf.

Ferdowsi, Abul-Qâsem. trans. Ahmad Sadri. *Shahnameh, The Epic of the Persian Kings.* Quantuck Lane Press, 2013.

Flowers, Stephen E., PhD. *Original Magic: The Rituals and Initiations of the Persian Magi.* Inner Traditions, 2017.

Foltz, Richard. 2010. "Zoroastrian Attitudes toward Animals." *Society and Animals*, vol. 18, www.animalsandsociety.org/wp-content/uploads/2016/04/foltz.pdf.

Friend, Robyn C. "The Exquisite Art of Persian Classical Dance." *Habibi*, Spring 1996.

Frye, Richard N. *The Heritage of Persia.* Mazda Publishers, 1993.

Frye, Richard N. *The Golden Age of Persia: The Arabs in the East.* Phoenix Press, 2000.

Frye, Richard N. *Greater Iran: A 20th-century Odyssey.* Mazda Publishers, 2005.

Gallagher, Anne-Marie. *The Wicca Bible.* Sterling Press, 2005.

Garfinkel Y. "Dancing and the Beginning of Art Scenes in the Early Village Communities of the Near East and Southeast Europe." *Cambridge Archaeological Journal.* 1998;8(2), 207-237. 1998. doi:10.1017/S0959774300001840.

Gaviri, Susan. *Anahita in Iranian Mythology, (Anahita dar usturah ha-yi Irani).* Intisharat-i Jamal al Haqq, 1993.

Ghani, Kashshaf. *Sufi Rituals and Practices: Experiences from South Asia, 1200-1450.* Oxford University Press, March 29, 2024.

Gholami, Saloumeh. *Dance in Iran: Past and Present.* Dr Ludwig Reichert, 2016.

Gowin, Philip. *Practical Sufism.* Quest Books, 2010.

Grey, Laurel Victoria. *Women's Dance Traditions of Uzbekistan*. Bloomsbury, 2024.

Grimal, Pierre, editor. *Larouse World Mythology*. Gallery Books, 1965.

Gündüzöz, Güldane. "Some Symbolic Elements In The Mawlawi Order." *The Journal of Kırıkkale Islamic Sciences Faculty*. 2018. www.academia.edu/36551348/.

Halman, T. S. and Metin A. *Mevlana Celaleddin Rumi and The Whirling Dervishes*. Dost Publications, 1983.

Halprin, Anna. *Returning to Health with Dance, Movement, and Imagery*. LifeRhythm, 2002.

Hathaway, Genevieve. "Turning Point: Istanbul's Female Dervishes." *G Adventures*, June 10, 2015. www.gadventures.com/blog/turning-point-istanbuls-female-dervishes/.

Hejazi, Mehrdad. "Geometry in nature and Persian architecture." *Building and Environment*, January 22, 2005. doi.org/10.1016/j.buildenv.2004.11.007.

Hendren, Trista. et. al. *Jesus, Muhammad and the Goddess*. CreateSpace Independent Publishing, 2016.

Henkesh, Yasmin. *Trance Dancing with the Jinn*. Llewellyn Publications, 2016.

Henry, Richard. "Pattern, Cognition and Contemplation: Exploring the Geometric Art of Iran." *Journal of the Iran Society*, September 2007.

Hojjati, Mahsa. "Sistani Dances as Connective Paths to Group Identity: The Dances of Migrant Sistani Communities in Golestan Province." *Dance in the Persianate World*, edited by Antony Shay, Mazda Publishers, 2023.

Hosseini, Seyedehbehnaz. "Life after Death in Manichaeism and Yārsān." *Bulletin of Kurdish Studies*, Institute Of Oriental Studies, June/September 2016. Jagiellonian University, Kraków.

Houseal, Joseph. "Dance at Dunhuang: Part Three – The Sogdian Whirl." *Buddhistdoor Global (BDG)*, January 8, 2016. www.buddhistdoor.net/features/dance-at-dunhuang-part-three-the-sogdian-whirl/.

Ḥusaynī, Muḥammad. *Dīvān-I Gawrah*. Bāgh-i Nay (Farsi), 2003.

Inayat Khan, Hazrat. *The Mysticism of Sound*. Ekstasis Editions, 2002.

Ivanow, W. *The Truth Worshippers of Kurdistan*. E. J. Brill, 1953.

Jafari, Rayhaneh. *History of the Iranian Kings from Media until Pahlavi*. Khashayav (Farsi), 2003.

Johnson, Buffie. *Lady of the Beasts: The Goddess and her Sacred Animals*. Inner Traditions, 1994.

Kaboli, Marzbani and Mehravar Soroush. *The Gathas Revisited A Re-appraisal of Zarathushtra's Vision*. Ph.D. Thesis, University of Sydney, December 2005.

Kasraian, N. and Z. Arshi. *Nomads of Iran*. Seké Press, 1994.

Kakavandi, Ramtin. *72 Maqams of Tanbour*, Aref Music Publishing (Farsi), 2017.

Kanga, Kavasji. *Khordeh Avesta*. Lulu.com; Bilingual edition, September 30, 2014.

Keshaviah, Prakash. *Practices of the Himalayan Tradition as taught by Swami Rama*. Himalayan Institute Hospital Trust, 2013.

Khan, Korosh Ali. "Saving Iran's Traditional Music." *Iran Tribune*, August, 1972.

Khan, Sufi Inayat. *Indian Music.* The Sufi Publishing Company, 1971.

Kheradmand, Amir. "Why don't figure skaters get dizzy when they spin?" *Scientific American*, November 1, 2016. www.scientificamerican.com/article/why-don-t-figure-skaters-get-dizzy-when-they-spin/.

Kiann, Nima. "Persian Dance and its forgotten history." *Iran Chamber Society*, November 10, 2014. www.iranchamber.com/cinema/articles/persian_dance_history01.php.

Kitarist. "RE: Looking for good book on music theorie." *Foro Flamenco* Online Forum, Oct. 17 2020 0:10:57. www.foroflamenco.com/printable.asp?m=328785&mpage=4.

Kjellen, Tore. n.d. "Ahl-e Haqq." *Looklex Encyclopedia.* Accessed 4 June 2022. archive.ph/7DcAu.

Knapp, Bettina L. "Dance Encyclopedia: Iranian Dance–The Spectrum Magic." *Arabesque*. 1979.

Kreyenbroek, Philip G. and Ulrich Marzolph, editors. *Oral Literature of Iranian Languages: Kurdish, Pashto, Balochi, Ossetic, Persian and Tajik.* I.B. Tauris, 2010.

Landor, Arnold Henry Savage. *Across Coveted Lands or a Journey from Flushing (Holland) to Calcutta Overland.* Macmillan and Co. 1902. www.gutenberg.org/files/22117/22117-h/22117-h.htm, www.google.com/books/edition/Across_Coveted_Lands/TgcpAAAAYAAJ.

Lewis, C. S. *The Four Loves*. Geoffrey Bles, 1960.

Lewisohn, Leonard and David Morgan, eds. *The Heritage of Sufism, Vol I.* One World Publications, 1999.

Lewisohn, Leonard and David Morgan, eds. *The Heritage of Sufism, Vol II.* One World Publications, 1999.

Lewisohn, Leonard and David Morgan, eds. *The Heritage of Sufism, Vol III.* One World Publications, 1999.

Lewisohn, Leonard, editor. *Hafiz And The Religion Of Love In Classical Persian Poetry.* I.B. Tauris, 2010.

Lille, Dawn. "Gesture as a Human Indicator." *Art Times.* December 2002. www.arttimesjournal.com/dance/J_F_04_Dawn_Lille/Gesture.htm.

Liu, Li. *The Chinese Neolithic: Trajectories to Early States.* Cambridge University Press, 2007.

Lonsdale, Steven. *Animals and the Origin of Dance.* Thames & Hudson, 1981.

Mackrell. Judith R. et. al. "The aesthetics of dance." *Encyclopedia Brittanica,* Nov 19, 2020. www.britannica.com/art/dance/The-aesthetics-of-dance.

Mandavi, Messam Meldin. *Festivals and Rituals of Iran.* Avazeh Abrisham (Farsi), 2018.

Marzolph, Ulrich. "Persian Popular Literature in the Qajar Period." *Asian Folklore Studies*, vol. 60, 2001.

McClure, Hannah. "Dervish Dance: A Path of Love." *Critical Muslim.* 2018. www.academia.edu/38112246.

"Mevlevi Sema Ceremony." *UNESCO Intangible Cultural Heritage.* 2022. ich.unesco.org/en/RL/mevlevi-sema-ceremony-00100.

Miller, Lloyd. *Music 327: Music of the East*. University of Utah, 1977a.

Miller, Lloyd. *The Center for Preservation and Propagation of Iranian Music*, The Center for Preservation and Propagation of Iranian Music, 1977b.

Miller, Lloyd. *The Ostad.* The Society for Islamic and Eastern Mysticism, 1977c.

Miller, Lloyd, editor. *Sufi Sects, Saints, and Shrines*. The Society for Islamic and Eastern Mysticism, 1978.

Miller, Lloyd. "A light snack and a few currents for dessert," *The Middle East,* November, 1979.

Miller, Lloyd Clifton. *Persian Music.* Eastern Arts, 1991.

Miller, Lloyd Clifton. *Music and Song in Persia: The Art of Avaz*. University of Utah Press, 1999.

Miller, Lloyd Clifton. *Sufi, Saint And Swinger.* Lloyd Clifton Miller, 2007.

Miller, Lloyd Clifton. *Rumi & Sufi Poets: Origins of Meter & Rhyme and Influence in Europe*. University of Utah Press, September, 2013.

Miller, Lloyd. "Impact Of Persian Poetry From India To Iceland," Eastern Arts, November, 2023.

Miller, Lloyd Clifton and Katherine St. John. *Afghan Music and Dance.* Eastern Arts, 2011a.

Miller, Lloyd Clifton and Katherine St. John. *Persian (Iranian) Dance & Music.* Eastern Arts, 2011b.

Miller, Lloyd Clifton and Katherine St. John. *Persian and Silk Road Dance.* Online Lecture, November 24, 2020.

Miller, Lloyd Clifton and Katherine St. John. *Traditional Persian Music: The Seven Dastgahs.* Online Lecture, October, 2021.

Miraftab, Mohsen. *Garden of Paradise.* Mohagehgh Publishing (Farsi), 2023.

Mohajer, Reza. *Social Movements in Iran and the Trends of Political Expressionism,* Ph.D. Thesis, University of Hawai'i at Mānoa, May, 2018.

Motahedi, Mohammad. *History of Bastam.* Asr-e Javan (Farsi), 2014. ISBN 9789648806809.

Moussavi, Kazem. "Love of nature in ancient Iranian culture." *Green Party of Iran*, June 6, 2019. www.iran-e-sabz.org/english/love-of-nature-in-ancient-iranian-culture-on-the-occasion-of-world-environment-day/.

Mürer, George. "Chubbazi ("Stick-Dancing") in Khorasaniajn Kurdish and TransEurasian Perspective." *Dance in the Persianate World*, edited by Antony Shay. Mazda Publishers, 2023.

Mystic Iran: The Unseen World. DVD. Directed by Atyana Farsha. Shohreh Aghdashloo, narrator. Chicago, IL: Questar. 2008.

Nicholson, Reynold. editor. Tadhkiratu 'L-Awliya. "Memoirs of the Saints." by Farid al-Din Attar, Vol. 1, Luzac & Co. 1905. archive.org/details/tadhkiratulawliy01atta.

Nikoghosyan, Ruben. "What is the difference between Persian and Farsi?" *Aspirantum*, Jan 16, 2020. aspirantum.com/blog/difference-between-farsi-and-persian-language.

Nizami. *Haft Paykar: A Medieval Persian Romance.* Translated by Julie Scott Meisami. Hackett Publishing, 2015.

Norbu, Dorje. "Origins and Meanings of the Eight-Point Star." *Somathread*, June 2, 2015. somathread.ning.com/groups/sufi/forum/origins-and-meanings-of-the-eight-point-star.

Noroozy, Heidi. "Anahita–The Water Goddess." *Novel Adventurers*, April 22, 2013. noveladventurers.blogspot.com/2013/04/anahitathe-water-goddess.html.

Nyberg, Henrik Samuel. *Irans forntida religioner.* Daneshgahe Shahid Bahonare Kerman (Farsi), 2005. ISBN 964-6336-53-x.

Ogunnaike, Oludamini. "The Silent Theology of Islamic Art." *Renovatio*, December 5, 2017. renovatio.zaytuna.edu/article/the-silent-theology-of-islamic-art.

Olmstead, A.T. *History of the Persian Empire.* University of Chicago Press, 1959.

Pahlavān Kayvān. *Mūsīqī Va Ẕikr Dar Tamaddun-i īrān-I zamīn.* Nashr-i 'Ilm (Farsi), 2014. ISBN 9789642246359.

Panaino, Antonio. "PLANETS." *Encyclopædia Iranica*, online edition. Accessed 20 Sept. 2020. www.iranicaonline.org/articles/planets.

"Persian Classical Music: System of Modes." *Foundation for Iranian Studies.* Accessed 18 Aug. 2023. fis-iran.org/ebook/persian-system-of-modes/.

Pirnia, Hasan Mushir Al-Dula. *Tarikh Iran Bastan (History of Ancient Persia).* Peyman, 2009.

Poikonen, Hanna. *University of Helsinki.* "A dancer's brain develops in a unique way." August 30, 2017. www.helsinki.fi/en/news/healthier-world/dancers-brain-develops-unique-way.

Pourjavady, Amir Hosein. "Professional Dancers in Iran: A Historical Survey." *Dance in the Persianate World*, edited by Antony Shay, Mazda Publishers.

Prasad, Sahil. "My Zoroastrianism Adventure." *Skipping Stones,* January-March 2020.

Quli´zādah Khusraw.*Farhang-I asāṭīr-i īrānī: Bar pāyah-I mutūn-I pahlavī.* Shirkat-i Mūṭāla'āt-i Nashr-i Kitāb-i Pārsah (Farsi). ISBN 978-600-5026-0. (Farsi). 2009.

Radner, Karen, Nadine Moeller, and D. T. Potts, eds. *The Oxford History of the Ancient Near East: Volume I: From the Beginnings to Old Kingdom Egypt and the Dynasty of Akkad, Vol. 1.* Oxford University Press, August 4, 2020.

Raftis, Alkis. *Dance in Classical Greece. A Handbook.* Dora Stratou Dance Theater, 2019.

Rajabzadeh, Hashem. "The Five Elements In The Literary Heritage Of Iran And Japan: A Comparative Study." *Orient*. 1987. www.jstage.jst.go.jp/article/orient1960/23/0/23_0_77/_pdf/-char/en.

Rama, Swami. *Path of Fire and Light: Advanced Practices of Yoga.* Himalayan Institute, 1996.

Reinhertz, Shakina. *Women Called to the Path of Rumi.* Holm Press, 2001.

Rezaeian, Farzin. *Persepolis Recreated.* Sunrise Visual Innovations Ltd., 2004.

Rezaeian, Farzin. *Iran: Seven Faces of a Civilization.* Sunrise Visual Innovations, 2007.

Rezvani, Medjid. *Le théâtre et la danse en Iran*. Maisonneuve at Larose, Paris, 1962.

Rezvani, Yadullah. "Ahriman in Iranian Mythology." Unpublished work, Tehran (Farsi), 2013.

Rezvani, Yadullah. "Fish and Norouz in Iranian Culture." Unpublished work, Tehran (Farsi), 2014.

Roos, Dave. "How Early Humans Survived the Ice Age," *History*, July 15, 2021. www.history.com/news/ice-age-human-survival.

Rumi (Jalal ad-Din Muhammad ar-Rumi). *Mystical Poems of Rumi.* University of Chicago Press, 1968.

Rumi (Jalal ad-Din Muhammad ar-Rumi). *The Soul of Rumi: A New Collection of Ecstatic Poems.* Translated and edited by Colman Barks, Harper, 2001.

Sachs, Curt. *World History of the Dance,* W. W. Norton & Company, 1963.

Safvat, Dariush. *Eight Lectures in Regard to Philosophy of Music vol. 3*. Nashr Aras (Farsi), 2014.

Safvat, Daryush. *Improvisation in "Radif" Traditional Persian Music: Shur & Segah—Setar.* The Center for Traditional and Spiritual Music of the East, New York, 1985.

Sakata, Hiromi Lorraine. "Music in Afghanistan," *Education about ASIA.* Vol. 17, Number 2. Fall 2012. www.asianstudies.org/publications/eaa/archives/music-in-afghanistan/.

Sanjabi, Jonas. "Yarsan and their beliefs, learn more about Yarsan in Iran." *Yarsan Democratic Organization,* November 12, 2016. www.yarsanmedia.org/ku/.

Schimmel, Annemarie. *Mystical Dimensions of Islam*. The University of North Carolina Press, 1975.

Seidel, Kathleen. n.d. *Serving the Guest: A Sufi Cookbook.* Accessed 1 Sept. 2022. www.superluminal.com/cookbook/.

Selected Works of Mahmoud Farshchian 1975-2000. Yasavoli, 2009.

Shahshahani, Soheila. "Body as a means of non-verbal communication in Iran." *International Journal of Modern Anthropology,* vol. 1 (2008): 1-121.

Shakiba, Fahimeh. "The Social Life of Zoroastrians in the Safavid Era 1501-1722." *Journal of History Culture and Art*, June 2019.

Shay, Anthony. *Choreophobia: Solo Improvised Dance in the Iranian World.* Mazda Publishers, 1999.

Shinn, Florence Scovel. *The Wisdom of Florence Scovel Shinn.* Simon & Shuster, 1989.

Schuster, Ruth. "Before Judaism: The 8,000-year-old History of Pomegranate Reverence." *Haaretz*, September 9, 2018. www.haaretz.com/archaeology/.premium.MAGAZINE-before-judaism-the-8-000-year-old-history-of-pomegranate-reverence-1.6461970.

Silverman, David P. *Ancient Egypt.* Oxford University Press, 2003.

Sipper, Joshua. "Funerary Beliefs, Practices & Tombs in Ancient Persia." *Study.com*, study.com/academy/lesson/funerary-beliefs-practices-tombs-in-ancient-persia.html.

Smith, Huston, ed. (forward). *The Illustrated Rumi.* Translated by Philip Dunn, Manuela Dunn Mascetti, and R. A. Nicholson. Harper, 2000.

Solukian, Saba and Fatemeh Modaresi. "Metamorphosis Of Water Of Life Myth In Mystic, Lyrical And Contemporary Persian Literature." *Proceedings of Academics World 78th International Conference*, Los Angeles, September 2017: 55-58.

Song of God. A film by Aref Mohammadi. New Wave Production, Inc. 2018. https://www.imdb.com/title/tt8296242/.

Sorkhabi, Rasoul. "Garden of Secrets: The Real Rumi." *Quest,* Summer 2010.

Soudavar, Abolala. *Mithraic Societies From Brotherhood Ideal To Religion's Adversary. academia.edu.*, 2014. Revised September 2016. ISBN 978-1-312-10598-0.

St. John, Katherine and Lloyd Miller. *Radif-E Raqs.* Eastern Dance Sequence. Eastern Arts, 1987.

St. John, Katherine. *Dance and Music of the Islamic World.* Eastern Arts, 2010.

St. John, Katherine. *Traditional Afghan Dance and Culture.* March 28, 2021, Online Lecture.

Stewart, Iris. *Sacred Women Sacred Dance.* Inner Traditions, 2013.

Stone, Merlin. *When God was a Woman.* Barnes and Noble, 1976.

Sumit, Paul. "Empathy, the essence of Persian mysticism." *SpeakingTree.in*, Apr 28, 2019.

Sultanova, Razia. *From Shamanism to Sufism: Women, Islam, and Culture in Central Asia,* I. B. Tauris, 2014.

Swami Rama Himalayan Institute. *Path of Fire and Light, Vol. 1: Advanced Practices of Yoga.* Himalayan Institute Press, 1986.

Tapper, Richard and Jon Thompson, ed. *The Nomadic Peoples of Iran.* Azimuth, 2002.

"The Huma Bird of Iranian Legend." 2020. *The Cultured Chef*, June 15, 2020. www.culturedchef.com/the-huma-bird-of-iranian-legend/.

"The Musical Legacy of Ostad Elahi." 2019. *The Met.* Accessed 14 June 2020. www.metmuseum.org/perspectives/ostad-elahi-concert

"The Royal Stars of Ancient Persia." n.d. *Stellar Codes*. Accessed 10 August 2022. stellarcodes.com/content/royal-stars/.

Thoreau, Henry David. *Walden*. Thomas Y. Crowell & Co., 1910.

Tschaikner, Bianca. "Melmedas – a story from Hormuz Island in the Persian Gulf," December 12, 2021. biancatschaikner.com/stories/2021/12/17/melmedas-a-story-from-hormuz-island-in-the-persian-gulf.

Vatanpour, Azadeh. *The Healing Power of Music and Chants Amongst The Ahl-E Haqq People*. Masters' Thesis, Western Kentucky University, Spring 2017. digitalcommons.wku.edu/theses/2014.

Vibert, Milesent. "16th Century Persian Dance." Middle Kingdom A&S Competition, May 2006.

Walter, Carla Stalling. *Sacred Dance Meditations*. North Atlantic Books, 2020.

Waterfield, Robin. *Xenophon's Retreat: Greece, Persia, and the End of the Golden Age*. Belknap Press, 2009.

Waterman, David. n.d. "Whirling darvishes – Altered State Of Consciousness." *Sleep and Health Journal*. Accessed 27 Dec. 2022. www.sleepandhealth.com/whirling-darvishes-altered-state-consciousness/.

Willard, Pat. *Secrets of Saffron: The Vagabond Life of the World's Most Seductive Spice*. Beacon Press, 2001.

Williams, Jenn. "The elements at your fingertips." *Fire up Water down*, July 24, 2014. fireupwaterdown.com/2014/07/24/the-elements-at-your-fingertips/.

Xenophon. *The Persian Expedition*. SMK Books, 2018.

Yatsenko, Sergey. "Shamans of Ancient Iranian Nomads: Artifacts and Iconography." *Archaeological Approaches to Shamanism. Mind-Body, Nature, and Culture*. Edited by D. Gheorghiu, E. Pásztor, H. Bender, G. Nash. Cambridge Scholars Publishing, 2017.

Zarrinkoob, Abdolhossein. n.d. *Step by step to meet God*. Translated from Farsi, with permission from author.

Zavieh, Seyedeh Sara Seyedahmady, Mohammad-Reza Darvishi, and Azadeh Mehrpouyan. 2015. "Tanbur As Stringed Music Instrument: Role, Qualities, Influences On Yarsanism." *Abstracts of ADVED15- International Conference on Advances in Education and Social Sciences*, 12-14 October 2015 - Istanbul, Turkey. www.ocerint.org/adved15_epublication/papers/187.pdf.

Zehr, Leslie. *The Alchemy of Dance*. iUniverse Books, 2008.

"Zoroaster and the Zend-Avesta." *The Atlantic,* August 1869. www.theatlantic.com/magazine/archive/1869/08/zoroaster-and-the-zend-avesta/630001/.

Glossary

adab – the practice of doing the right thing, at the right time, in the best way possible. Adab is common sense with respect. It is the way of harmony, acting with deference to the scheme of the whole. The expression of adab is shown in courtesy, politeness, and a pleasant social demeanor. The aim of adab is to act and speak in a way that pleases the Divine and the people around you. In Farsi, adab means etiquette, manners, morals, and respect. The word adab comes from an Old Iranian/Persian word *aadaab* which means proper conduct and etiquette.

Al-Fatiha – see Sura Al-Fatiha.

alif – the standing position of a samazan with feet together, arms crossed on the chest, and hands clasped to the shoulders. The crossed arms attest to the unity of God.

Amesha Spenta – in Zoroastrianism, a class of seven archangels or divine entities created by Ahura Mazda to assist him in representing truth, power, immortality, devotion, wholeness, and other qualities. The Amesha Spenta are Vohu Manah (Good Mind), Asha Vahistah (Truth), Khshatra Vairya (Good Dominion), Spenta Armaiti (Devotion), Haurvatat (Wholeness and Health), Ameretat (Immortality). and Spenta Mainyu (Holy Creative Spirit).

atash – fire, the fire of the Divine.

avaz – an unmetered or rhythm-free portion of a Persian mode typical of vocal chants.

Avesta – the sacred book of the Zoroastrians.

baqaa – the state in which you become a permanent part of God.

chakra – a focal energy point in the human body referenced by numerous ancient meditation traditions. *Chakra* (*cakra* in Sanskrit) means "wheel" as they are thought to be spinning disks of energy corresponding to bundles of nerves, major organs, and areas of the body that affect emotional and physical well-being.

charbaiti – an arrangement of four lines of verse (quatrain) with matching rhyme and meter, of which the first, second, and fourth lines must rhyme as in the pattern A-A-B-A.

chobazi – a type of stick dance.

daf – a large wood frame drum with a hide or synthetic skin head and metal rings or chains arranged around the inner edge.

dargah – shrine of a Sufi saint. In South Asia, the words *khanqah* and *dargah* are used interchangeably to refer to Sufi shrines.

darvish (Farsi), **dervish** (Turkish) – a mystic with an open heart who has studied the mystic world and who is granted that title by a master of the path.

dastgah – the standard Persian musical systemc, standardized in the 19th century. A dastgah consists of a collection of musical melodies known as gushehs.

del – Farsi word for center; the heart; the abdomen; the soul. In the Iranian tradition, the word del means the mystic center. Del is also the abdomen, the body's life center, and may also represent the heart as the mystic center. Ancient physicians once believed that the abdomen functioned as the heart to provide life, blood, and energy, so they called it del.

destegul – a short white jacket with long sleeves worn by a samazan with the *tennure, elifinemed,* and *sikke.*

dobeti – a poetic form written in two couplets, or four lines of verse (a quatrain). The poetry of Rumi is written in dobeti.

doon – a lifetime or reincarnation.

elifinemed (*alif–i namad*) – (*kamarband* in Farsi) is a traditional belt of cloth about four fingers wide and two and one-half feet long that is wrapped about the waist of the samazan. Traditionally black, the elifinemed represents the conscious separation of the higher chakras from the lower, the divine self from the human. The word itself contains the first letter of the Arabic alphabet, *alif,* representing those who are spiritually free and in true union with the Divine. Once a Mevlevi samazan completes his training he receives and wears the elifinemed to signify his status.

eghna – Eghna is a spiritual belief or sense of something as "true" even if common sense tells us otherwise.

eshqh (Farsi), ishq (Arabic) – "love" or "passion." The term *eshqh (ishq)* is used extensively in Sufi poetry and literature to describe a selfless and burning love for the Divine. It is often conceived in an ascending hierarchical order: natural love, intellectual love, and Divine Love.

fanaa – *fanaa* is the annihilation or "passing away" of the self. It is generally interpreted as the abandonment of the consciousness of self and replacing this with contemplation of God alone or becoming united with the One Truth.

faroud – in mystic music or dance, a stage marking descent and completion.

fravarti, fravaşi – in Iranian folklore, the holy guardian angels of human beings. *Fravarti* is Old Persian, whereas the Avestan language form is *fravaşi.*

Faravahar – the ancient Zoroastrian symbol for the guardian spirit of light, knowledge, law, and order; the essence of God.

gusheh – a collection of Persian melodies that compose a *dastgah.*

Ha – One of five different spiritual names of God spoken with the breath (e.g., during zikr): *Hu, Hai, Haqq, Ha,* and *Hey.*

haft – seven.

Haft Tan, Haftan – the "Seven Souls." The seven spirits of the Yarsan belief that combined represent God.

hal – an inspiring, impermanent spiritual state that enters the heart through pure love from the Divine without the initiation of the seeker; ecstasy. *Hal* is an intense state of the soul, the feeling toward the Divine.

haqiqat – the mystical truth.

Haqq – "the truth." One of five different spiritual names of God spoken with the breath (e.g., during zikr): *Hu, Hai, Haqq, Ha*, and *Hey*.

Hey – Exclamation used when asking the supreme being to listen. One of five different spiritual names of God spoken with the breath (e.g., during zikr): *Hu, Hai, Haqq, Ha*, and *Hey*.

Hai – One of five different spiritual names of God spoken with the breath (e.g., during zikr): *Hu, Hai, Haqq, Ha*, and *Hey*.

Hirke, Hurke – (Kesve, in Farsi) a long black ceremonial cloak that represents the tomb. It often symbolizes the hypocrisy of a religious pretender. A blue cloak worn by some Sufis to exhibit celestial aspirations can represent hypocrisy, deceit, and false humility, and is also sometimes found in exoteric religions. In Persian, the term is *kherqe-ye sālus,* or the hypocrite's robe. When a samazan first receives a black robe it is a mark of honor and respect like a graduation ceremony. During the Mevlevi sama ceremony, the hirke is worn over the tenure before and after whirling. Before whirling the Mevlevis remove their hirke, kiss it, and lower it to the floor nicely with three folds. On arising to whirl in a Mevlevi sama ritual, the samazan casts off the blackness of the grave (hirke) and appears radiant in the white shroud of resurrection (*tenure*).

Hu – in Sufism, Hu is the ancient name for God or "breath of God." In Arabic, Allah means God and with Hu attached as in "Allah Hu" means "God himself." *Hu* is the name for God that is sung or chanted for prayers and spiritual upliftment. One of five different spiritual names of God spoken with the breath (e.g., during zikr): *Hu, Hai, Haqq, Ha*, and *Hey*.

hukhta – good words.

humata – good thoughts.

huvarshta – good deeds.

Iran – home to one of the world's oldest civilizations, Iran is a country in West Asia. The name Iran originates from Middle Persian referring to the land of the Aryans (Iranians).

Irfan – (Erfan) mysticism. A spiritual and philosophical tradition deeply rooted in Persian culture and history.

ishq – "love" or "passion." See *Eshqh*.

jam – (1) a service or sacred gathering or (2) the .

jamkhaneh – "house of unity"; a place of worship wherein sacred gatherings take place.

Kalam, Kalam-e Saranjām – Yarsan sacred text collection which is believed to originate from the period of founder Sultan Sahak.

kamarband – Farsi word for *elifinemed*.

kesve – Farsi word for *hirke*.

Khandan – a Yarsan holy family, and one of the 11 spiritual dynasties: Shah Ibrahimi, Yadegari, Khamoushi, Qalandari, Mirsuri, Mostafayi, Hajji Babu Isa, Zolnuri, Atash Beygi, Baba Heidari, and Shah Hayasi.

khanqah, khangah – Farsi word meaning a house of abode of Sufis and darvishes. This building is designed specifically for gatherings of a Sufi brotherhood, a place for spiritual retreat and character reformation; a tekke.

kolah – Farsi term for *sikke*.

Magi – Persian Zoroastrian priests. The Magi were mystics highly trained in fields such as science, medicine, history, philosophy, and astronomy.

maidan – circle of encompassment.

makan – a place, one of the three variables (time, place, and people) that influence the effectiveness of a performance.

maqam – a system of music or melodies that contain healing power and are connected with human experiences.

marifat – the mystical knowledge.

Masnavi, Mathnawi – a collection of rhymed verses or couplets. Typical *masnavi* poems consist of an indefinite number of couplets, with the rhyme scheme AA-BB-CC. The poetic form is closely tied to mysticism, philosophy, and legends. The *Masnavi* written by Jalal al-Din Muhammad Balkhi (Rumi) is an extensive poem written in Farsi and is considered to be the greatest mystical poem in world literature.

mast, mastan – a drunken or the drunken one; a whirler in ecstasy. Drunk in the context of the Divine. There is a lot of Persian poetry that uses the word *mast—mastan*, the drunkens. It means being in a trance.

Mawlana – Persian mystical poet, Sufi mystic, and Islamic philosopher Jalal al-Din Muḥammad Balkhi (1207-1273 CE), otherwise known as Rumi.

moj – low level, near the earth or sea, connecting with our roots. In music, a slow tempo or low pitch or energy. Descending.

mukhannath - literally, "dancing boys." During the Safavid period, adult male cross-dressers and passive homosexuals engaged in the business of entertainment by dance, music, or acrobatics in public places.

murid – a Sufi initiate or student (Islamic). *Murīd* means "committed one" and refers to a person who is committed to a spiritual guide (*murshid*) committed to a spiritual path.

Murshid – a spiritual guide.

mystic – a person who seeks to use contemplation and self–surrender to obtain unity with the absolute. A mystic is someone who believes in the spiritual apprehension of truths that are beyond the intellect.

nafs – ego, a vice.

nisti – inexistence, nothingness.

Nowruz – Iranian New Year, the festival that celebrates the beginning of a new year on the Persian calendar and starts on the spring equinox. Also spelled Nawrouz, Novruz, Nowrouz, Nowrouz, Nawrouz, Nauryz, Nooruz, Navruz, Nevruz, Norouz, and Navruz. The Kurdish celebration is spelled Newroz or Nawroz.

oj – high level, sky, the heavens. In music, a lively, fast tempo or high pitch. Ascending. Oj can be interpreted as "force" or "intensity" in Farsi.

Ostad, Ustad – master, in Farsi. Ostad is often used to denote a person's expertise in the field of arts and higher education.

pākī – purity, both internally and externally.

pahlevan – wrestler or athlete trained in the practice of the *zurkhaneh*, the house of strength. *Pahlevan* is derived from the Farsi word meaning noble, wrestler, hero, or champion.

paibazi – a style of dance focusing on feet.

paikobi – a stamp or stomping dance style.

Persia – the land of the Pars, the Farsi-speaking people.

Persianate – A Persianate society is a society that is based on or strongly influenced by the Persian language, culture, literature, art, and identity.

pir – spiritual guide of the path who leads the masters, community, and order. Pirs have the authority to set guidelines for the path and members.

Pishdadian – the mythical first Iranian dynasty, pre-dating written history and the Achaemenids. The existence of the Pishdadian dynasty has no historical basis.

post – a red sheepskin that is the ceremonial spiritual post, representing the sheikh, the spiritual leader Mawlana Jelaluddin Rumi. It is the archetypal symbol of love, blood, life, self-sacrifice, and the sunset at Rumi's passing. In the Mevlevi tradition, it is the place where the *postneshin* stands or sits during the *Sheb-i Arus* ceremony.

postneshin – for the Mevlevi sama, the master darvish who directs the ceremony. Translated as "he who sits on the sheepskin." The *postneshin* is initiated as a living representative of the lineage of Mawlana for the Mevlevi sama, at least once yearly for *Sheb-i Arus* which marks the passing of Jelaluddin Rumi on December 17.

qalb – the spiritual heart, the center of personality, or the center of gnosis and deep spiritual knowledge.

rada – self-sacrifice to provide services to help human beings, service.

rasti – righteousness or truth. Abstinence from falsehood and sin.

riz – tiny, as in movements that suggest particles, molecules, atoms, and cells.

ruh – arwah (pl): Soul.

Rumi – Mawlana or Jalal al-Din Muḥammad Balkhi (1207-1273 CE), a Persian mystical poet, Sufi mystic, and Islamic philosopher.

saghi – a woman or being who is poetically idolized for her beauty, and can never be possessed.

samacheh – in Farsi, masked or masks.

sama, sema – a ritual dance. Iranian folk dances may carry the word "sama" in their name to indicate it originated as a ritual dance (e.g., Cheka Sama or Lak Sari Sama). In its sacred form, it is a whirling and prayer ritual for mystics (Farsi: sama, Turkish: sema).

samazan, semazen – one who has undergone formal training in the Sufi turning practice. The word is derived from sama (Arabic, meaning listening), and zan (Farsi, meaning doer) (Farsi: samazan, Turkish: semazen).

samakhaneh, semakhaneh – Sufi ritual hall for Sama ceremonies, including Sufi whirling, zikr, and *sohbet.*

samazanbashi, semazenbashi – the lead samazan(s) who assists the *postneshin* in conducting the Mevlevi sama ceremony (Farsi: *samazanbashi*, Turkish: *semazenbashi*).

sepehr – sky, heaven.

Seyed – the spiritual leader of a *khandan*, a Yarsan spiritual house or family. Sadat is the plural form of Seyed.

shah – king.

shariat – the fundamental defining laws of a spiritual belief.

Sheb-i Arus – a left-turning sama ceremony honoring the passing of Mawlana Jelaluddin Rumi upon December 17 or any similar sama to honor a passing.

shenavar – steady, literally, a "steady ocean wave."

Shiraz – the capital of Fars province in southwestern Iran.

sho'levar – large, literally "big flames."

sikke – (Kolah in Farsi) the samazan's camel hair hat represents the tombstone of the ego. The sikke is never removed while observing the traditional Mevlevi sama. The ceremonial *postneshin* or shiekh of the order wears a green scarf wound around the base of his sikke.

sohbet – a spiritual talk or lecture.

souri – a traditional war dance that is often performed with swords, meaning "to battle against darkness."

Sufi – a mystic. Practitioners of Sufism are referred to as Sufis. The ultimate aim of Sufis is to seek communion with the Divine through spiritual realization.

Sultan Sahak – a religious leader considered the founder of modern Yarsanism and who is also known among his followers as a messenger of God. Also known as Sultan Izhak.

Sura Al-Fatiha – the first passage of the Quran, the most recited prayer in the Muslim tradition.

taksim – a solo musical improvisation, a term commonly applied to Balkan or Middle Eastern music.

tanbur, tambur – an ancient long-necked stringed instrument originating in Mesopotamia, Southern or Central Asia (Farsi: tanbur, Turkish: tambur). The instrument is sacred to the Yarsanis of Iran. Variations of the instrument are used in the traditional music of Iran, India, Kurdistan, Armenia, Afghanistan, Azerbaijan, Pakistan, Turkey, Tajikistan, Kazakhstan, and Uzbekistan.

tariqat – the mystical path.

tekke – a khanqah. In Mevlevi tradition, the Sufi lodge for communal life that includes a kitchen, sleeping quarters, study, meditation, and samakhaneh (ritual hall). In Turkey, Iran, and formerly Ottoman areas like Albania and Bosnia and Herzegovina, tekke is the preferred use; in the East, khanqah is in more common use.

tennure (ten'-yur-ay) – a whirling dress with a wide skirt worn by samazans; a sleeveless frock. It ceremonially represents the shroud of the ego, the grave clothes. The tennure is traditionally white, the symbol of purity, although they appear in other colors. Tennure, literally translated, means "skin of light."

wheel of Mitra – the ancient Persian symbol of the mother goddess Mitra. Resembling a cross, it represents the four directions or the four elements. It is the ancient Iranian astrological symbol for the passing through the equinox and solstice by the relative position of Ursa Major to the north star.

yar – Farsi word meaning friend.

yaran – people or literally "companions about you." One of the three variables (time, place, and people) that influence the effectiveness of a performance or sacred gathering.

yazata – In Zoroastrianism, a yazata refers to a divine being considered worthy of worship. They are essentially good powers under the supreme deity, Ahura Mazda, and are often described as angels or spirits.

zaman – time, one of the three variables (time, place, and people) that influence the effectiveness of a performance or sacred gathering.

zikr – a practice of remembering and evoking the presence of God. Zikr is an essential form of prayer that includes ritualistic and rhythmic focused recitations, movement, and breath control.

zurkhaneh – a traditional regimen of martial arts, calisthenics, and strength training, accompanied and inspired by epic poetry and traditional music. Zurkhaneh is also the name of the traditional Iranian gymnasium for this practice, meaning "house of strength." The spiritual practice is derived from elements of Zoroastrianism, Mithraism, and Gnosticism with the spirituality of Shia Islam and Sufism.

Index

ABOUT THE AUTHOR

Farima Berenji

Farima Berenji is a distinguished scholar with an MA in Anthropology, and Archaeology, and an additional MA in Iranian Ethnochoreology, both earned at Cal State Hayward. Her academic journey is marked by the achievement of an M. Msc. and a PhD in Metaphysics specializing in Iranian mysticism and rituals. She is also an integrated healing practitioner and an initiated master in the Iranian Sufi and mystic order. She brings a unique blend of academic rigor and spiritual depth to her work, performances, and teachings.

As an award-winning and internationally acclaimed performing artist and choreographer, Farima has been recognized as one of the foremost global scholars in ancient and mystical Iranian ethnochoreology. Notably, she is honored as the first Iranian woman to direct a Persian dance company, showcasing performances for notable figures such as President Obama, President Biden, the EU, the UN, and other international dignitaries.

Farima is the Founder and Artistic Director of the Simorgh Dance Collective as well as the Assistant Director and Program Coordinator of Eastern Arts. Additionally, she is the founder of Dance of the Soul™ and serves as an Advisory Council Member of Mosaic America, as a member of the International Dance Council (CID-UNESCO), and as a member of the National Folk Organization. Distinctively, Farima Berenji is recognized as the first Iranian-American woman TEDx lecturer and performer in the field of performance art and spirituality.

As an artist, scholar, and spiritual guide, Farima's contributions span the globe, encompassing research, lectures, performances, and education. Her mission is to inspire the cultivation of dynamic creativity and rejuvenation through the transformative power of dance, movement, and music. Explore her profound insights and connect with her online at *farimadance.com* to experience the richness of her work.

ABOUT THE ARTIST

Valerie Runningwolf

My education and background have always centered around art. I graduated from San Jose State University with a BA in Art and graduate studies in Art and Education. However, the most valued art education I have received has been from working with children who have taught me to be honest, brave, and bold and to be able to express myself through art without fear or judgment.

It is my belief that the process of art is an opening and vital expression of the deepest part of ourselves. It is also an enjoyable undertaking with remarkable and amazing outcomes. It is through this process that I found spiritual healing within my art. I share a reverence for the life force which connects all beings.

My most recent art has been creating mandalas. This art reflects interpretations from motifs and images of cultures that honor the earth, awaken the spirit, and offer a sense of inner peace.

ABOUT HOHM PRESS

Founded in 1976, Hohm Press is committed to publishing books that promote self-awareness, the recognition of interdependence, and compassion.

We publish an eclectic range of books across spiritual traditions, with a focus on the work of contemporary spiritual teachers, such as Lee Lozowick, Arnaud Desjardins, J. Krishnamurti, Taisen Deshimaru, and Richard Collins.

In addition to spiritual teachings, our subject areas include biography and autobiography, hatha yoga and tantric studies, transformational psychology, poetry, and poetry translations.

Learn more at hohmpress.com